genealogies
for the present

in cultural anthropology

genealogies
for the present

in **cultural anthropology**

routledge
new york and london

Published in 1996 by
Routledge
29 West 35th Street
New York, NY 10001

Published in Great Britain in 1996 by
Routledge
11 New Fetter Lane
London EC4P 4EE
Copyright © 1996 by Routledge

Printed in the United States of America
Design and typography: Jack Donner

Permission to use material from previously published articles is gratefully acknowledged from *Ethos* for "Foucault Meets South New Guinea" (22:391–438, 1994); from *Critique of Anthropology* for "Pushing Anthropology Past the Posts" (14:117–52, 1994); and from *Oceania* for "Like Money You See in a Dream," (64:187–90, 1993).

Library of Congress Cataloging-in-Publication Data

Knauft, Bruce M.
    Genealogies for the present in cultural anthropology : a critical humanist perspective / Bruce M. Knauft
        p.   cm.
    Includes bibliographical references and index.
    ISBN 0–415–91263–6 (hardcover) —   ISBN 0–415–91264–4 (pbk.)
    1. Ethnology—Philosophy.   I. Title.
GN345.K593   1996
306'.01—dc20   96–28099
                                                                                    CIP

contents

preface

Taking stock of recent developments in cultural anthropology—even selected ones—is both a humbling task and an exciting one. I hope this project can be of use to students now grappling with cultural anthropology's complexity as well as to scholars engaging the field's larger direction. This includes rather than omits those worried that the field has been disappearing over postmodern cliffs. But rather than attempting to review seasoned approaches in cultural anthropology, my goal is to evaluate some of its sharp and current cutting edges. As will quickly become evident, I am at once enthusiastic about and critical of these developments. My larger purpose is to configure a perspective that retains the best of anthropology's received past without dismissing the crucial contributions of its present and the potentials of its future.

It may be stressed from the outset that critically humanist sensibilities emphasize critique at least as much as they do humanism. In contrast to the totalizing strains normally associated with humanism, the perspectives herein developed are positional, reflexive, and tactical; they are intrinsically self-challenging and directed in significant ways against their own competing moments of representation. A critically inflected view of humanism hybridizes modern and postmodern sensibilities; it takes positionality seriously even as it also refuses to give up on the importance of objectification and the potentials of intersubjective understanding.

My theoretical arguments are complemented by ethnographic illustrations. This reflects my belief that theory must be empirically responsive and not just abstract; it becomes tangible through detailed ethnography. Many of my examples are from Melanesia, which is the region I know best, but they could be extended readily by analyses drawn from other world regions and areas closer to home. I remain optimistic that cultural anthropology has a future and that its future lies in rigorous ethnography and theoretical innovation. If current discourses in cultural anthropology sometimes deemphasize the value of either ethnography or theory, it can be fruitful to work across their grain.

This book owes much to my Gebusi friends, who taught me practically about the potentials and limitations of crossing the intersubjective divide. It also owes much to students now embarking on anthropology's ethnographic and theoretical minefields. I have had the particular good fortune to have helped orchestrate a vigorous and well-supported graduate program in anthropology. Besides keeping me on my toes, Emory's graduate students have inspired me with a fresh generation of voices and field research concerns and have increased my commitment to combining ethnographic issues with theoretical ones.

I am also indebted to my family and colleagues. My wife, Eileen, and my son, Eric, have not just accommodated but supported my schedule of work, even as it has been sandwiched between bureaucratic and teaching commitments. The Center for Advanced Study in the Behavioral Sciences at Stanford, California, afforded me a splendid fellowship year in 1991–92, supported by NSF grant BNS–8700864 and by Emory University. It was during this year that the seeds of the present work were sown. Since then, my colleagues at Emory and elsewhere have refreshed my perspective and given me a sense of humor about trying to bring so many strands together in one project. Special thanks for feedback and commentary go to Laura Ahearn, Eytan Bercovitch, Aletta Biersack, Robert Borofsky, Jacqueline Brown, Donald Donham, Thomas Ernst, Carla Freeman, Lawrence Hammar, Gilbert Herdt, Ivan Karp, Kathryn Kozaitis, Corinne Kratz, Wynne Maggi, Sherry Ortner, Randall Packard, Renato Rosaldo, Edward Schieffelin, Debra Spitulnik, and James Weiner. The editors at Routledge have been wonderfully supportive, and I thank the Emory Graduate School of Arts and Sciences for support to help defray processing and production costs. I thank you all but the blame is mine.

Note: References include context-salient listings for most authors mentioned without citation in the text.

a p e r t u r e

Has cultural anthropology progressed in recent years, or is it self-destructing? Is ethnography being rejuvenated or destroyed? Given recent expansions in cultural theory and ethnographic writing, it seems as important as it is difficult to step back and view the positions that inform these questions. The task itself is undercut by self-doubt. What view can authenticate and justify such stock-taking—as if the author pretends to climb higher than others or to look down omnisciently on the landscape?

Justifications are never really prior; they are ultimately pragmatic. In the present case, I have poignantly felt the tension between what seemed to be a "knowable" range of sociocultural theory as a graduate student of anthropology in the 1970s and the plethora of theoretical tracks across and beyond anthropology that are so daunting and enriching today. My desire to penetrate and figure some of this contemporary scene is fueled as I see anthropology students searching for guideposts, sometimes in vain. In an intellectual world that sees itself losing coordinates and coordination, it goes against the tide to wish for lost confidence. But in my teaching as well as my writing, I retain the hope that a larger compass of understanding about these developments is possible. Perhaps it is my modernist training refusing to die a postmodern death. But then, I don't find recent developments in cultural anthropology to be nearly as dismal or disintegrating—to either fieldwork, theory, or the field of anthropology itself—as more pessimistic views might have it. This book is written in large part to assert and defend this perspective.

The turnover in cultural theory and ethnography is amazingly quick these days. It is almost as if anthropologists need new graduate training every few years to keep up with fresh influences. The downside of this is top-forty anthropology; today's new fad is tomorrow's rubbish. But the bright side is the holistic openness to world conditions and emerging paradigms that has been one of anthropology's enduring strengths. If a larger view is taken, a tour through recent provocations can be quite productive. Most intellectual waves generate a good bit of dross at first, especially when done badly. But most also house core insights with potential for growth. To retain scholarship and discern these strengths amid complex surroundings, it helps to see current directions in the context of anthropology's received past, its burgeoning present, and its hoped-for future.

Recent developments in cultural and social theory can be seen through many alternative lenses. It has long been suggested that American anthropology "owed the greater part of its theoretical armament to importations from across the Atlantic" (Wolf 1964:6). And the last fifteen years have been no exception. But in recent years, anthropology has grown and changed to reflect a wider diversity of perspectives and voices. Cultural anthropology is now more interdisciplinary than ever. A field with fuzzy edges, it feels both the stimulation and the threat of this diversity. Competing trends heighten the importance of intellectual influences from other humanities fields and subaltern authorships that engage literature, critical theory, historiography, philosophy, media studies, cultural studies, queer theory, and a range of other perspectives. These come to American anthropology in diverse colors and locations, and not just as enlightenment from across the Atlantic. New venues of thought cannot be ignored; they are vital if anthropology is to seriously confront a contemporary world and engage its knowledge in reflexive as well as topical terms. But the highest standards of scholarship must be maintained. And just as innovations enter anthropology with increasing speed, there are fewer vantage points from which one might coherently view these developments or put them in meaningful context. The half-life of innovation gets shorter; an ever-accelerating turnover of ideas itself becomes normal as an aspect of late modernity. In such circumstances, it can be useful to put developments in perspective and identify larger trends that are common and useful for analytic and pedagogical purposes.

Criticisms of cultural anthropology now come from within the heart of the discipline as well as from divergent views across the campus and across the world. The task, accordingly, is to maintain a productive tension between the strengths of anthropology's past and the new innovations that both enliven it and threaten to overwhelm it. Producing smoke as well as light, this combustible diversity fuels intellectual debate that is highly stimulating at the same time that it can be deeply deconstructive of competing points of view. The balancing act is thus to maintain the benefit of diverse innovations, plow them into substantive work, and avoid the threat that they will polarize the field, narrow it, and become mutually exclusive with anthropology's past contributions. If we need to open up our genealogies of anthropology's ancestry to new sets of voices, we also need to preserve traditional strengths and avoid present excesses.

One of my primary goals in this book is to encourage articulations across several major and overlapping divides—between modernist and postmodern anthropology, objectivity and reflexivity, theory and ethnography, and ethical engagement versus academic distance. To this end, I often mediate perspectives, serving as a kind of interlocutor or juxtaposing them in a dialogue of reciprocating critique. The notion of complementarity runs through many of my discussions; a number of theoretical and conceptual stances in anthropology can be viewed effectively as complements to one another. Some of these oppositions can be productively mediated or balanced against each other's intellectual or historical context. This entails articulation between different analytic moments.

I also pursue complementarity as a reflexive and textual strategy. Thus, for instance, I sometimes raise objections to my own preceding analysis or intrude an alternative point of view that forces a more balanced assessment. In some respects, later chapters that consider some of the newer alternative voices in cultural anthropology serve as a complement to earlier chapters, which consider more widely known approaches or figures. My larger hope is that importantly opposed points of view can facilitate a deepening of critical thought that is neither dismissive nor too easily satisfied with its own resolutions. The same hope applies to the complementary audiences this book is addressed to—those who see themselves at the cutting edge of a new anthropology, and those who want to preserve the field's long-standing strengths. In both cases, it is important to be self-challenging in ways that engage rather than give up on intellectual commitment.

IN FORMAT, MY TREATMENT COMBINES DESCRIPTIVE EVALUATIONS OF major theoretical approaches, selected reviews of individual figures, and a range of ethnographic engagements. Anthropology's genealogy can now include a number of recent perspectives, including strands of postmodernism, cultural studies, practice theories, post-Marxism, postmodern feminism, and multicultural concerns. I do not propose a recipe for evaluating these emergent trends, much less a rigid standard or method to police the field. But I do try to discern general themes to think with, point out general excesses to avoid in contemporary work, and illustrate these through theoretical and ethnographic applications.

My vantage point for this review and assessment is a critically humanist perspective on cultural anthropology. As discussed in chapter 2, Western humanism carries both historical strengths and troubling biases. Against this background, a *critically* humanist perspective adopts alternative or *competing* humanist values that question and challenge each other, both as strategies of representation and as theoretical viewpoints. In the process, they undercut the universalism that has been one of humanism's biggest problems.

In the context of received wisdoms and current developments, two complementary strands of humanism seem particularly important for late-twentieth-century cultural anthropology. One is the appreciative understanding and portrayal of cultural and subjective diversity; another is the exposure and critique of inequality. Taken individually, each of these strains harbors difficulties, including an uncritical cultural relativism, on the one hand, and absolutist assumptions about power and domination, on the other. And neither of these goals is ultimately consistent with the other; the drive to critique inequality or hegemony can short-circuit the valorization of cultural or subjective diversity, and vice versa. In the final analysis, these strands of contemporary anthropology compete with each other. Yet as yoked complements, the appreciation of diversity and the critique of inequality do work productively. In pragmatic terms, they challenge each other's excesses and provide an open framework for both representational critique and outward-directed analysis. These complementary emphases reflect some of the most prominent and productively competing strains in cultural anthropology. They also provide breadth for considering and evaluating recent trends. Valorizations of diversity and critiques of inequality are both "models of" and "models for" an expanding anthropology (cf. Geertz 1973:93–94). They bridge anthropology's

historical legacy, its present trends, and its future possibilities, thus allow-
ing us to draw strength from older genealogies even as we construct new
ones.

In the present perspective, cultural contestation emerges through
assertions of subjective diversity in the context of inequality or domination. This assessment draws upon many current views and seems valuable
for considering the circumstances that cultural anthropology engages in
a late modern world. Taken reflexively, this means that cultural anthropology—and critically humanist sensibilities within it—are appropriately
subject to negotiation and contestation between differing points of
subjective view.

As part of this process, a critical appraisal of anthropology's ethics
comes to center stage. Though ethical considerations have often been
viewed as a methodological issue, they are now increasingly—and appropriately—relevant to anthropological theory. For critically humanist
sensibilities, ethical concerns provide the basis for theory as well as the
reverse. Since no ethical stance is itself unpositioned, this entails a consideration of cultural, pedagogical, and other motivations.

I claim no originality for any of these formulations, which are spelled
out in due course. They are a synthesis and framing of trends well known
and in some ways eminent in contemporary writing. But if contestation
is an ethos as well as a topic in cultural anthropology, it is also important
to recognize objectives and themes that provide a rough sense of shared
direction. Given the increasing competition between academic disciplines
for limited economic and symbolic capital—for money and prestige—it
is important for strategic reasons that cultural anthropology have images
of its coherence, its concreteness, and its contribution to the university
and to the larger public. In academic practice, this is relevant for teaching and for placing cultural anthropology in the university curriculum.
The goal is not just to attract a new generation of students but to communicate clearly and effectively the missions and, yes, the passion for cultural
anthropology that most of us faculty still feel beneath our crusts of cynicism. For me, this means grounding cultural anthropology in scholarship
that encourages appreciation of cultural diversity and the exposure and
critique of conditions of inequality.

The present volume opens with a sketch of competing stories about
anthropology's history, including the contested legacy of figures such as
Karl Marx, Max Weber, and Emile Durkheim. Recent criticisms of these

theoretical ancestries now posit a very different kind of anthropology, but it remains uncertain what grounding such a renewed anthropology has. In confronting this problem, I distill traditional humanist strengths from anthropology's received legacy but open them up to a dialogue of criticism, both by each other and by alternative voices. Chapter 2 suggests a productive response by delineating parameters, strengths, and implications of critically humanist sensibilities in cultural anthropology.

The remainder of the book analyzes recent theoretical developments that are particularly relevant for the valorization of diversity and the exposure and critique of inequality and domination. In the process, the divide is articulated between modern and postmodern sensibilities and also between Western and non-Western ones. The former interface is approached in chapter 3 through a critical reappraisal of postmodernism that considers the relationship between humanist and antihumanist legacies. In the course of this discussion, substantive consideration of several authors, including Nietzsche, Heidegger, and Baudrillard, exposes philosophical and ethical problems that the postmodern impetus has been heir to. This criticism forms the basis for complementary insights in later chapters that invigorate rather than overdetermine moments of reflexivity and representational creativity.

The book's middle chapters use critically humanist perspectives to engage a range of recent approaches that intersect issues of culture, power, and representation in cultural anthropology. These include a variety of post-Marxist, epistemic, and reflexively oriented theorists, including Pierre Bourdieu, Michel Foucault, Antonio Gramsci, and Mikhail Bakhtin. The purpose here is to illustrate and critically evaluate a few recent important theorists rather than pretend a coverage of all possibilities. One goal is to encourage a more detailed and penetrating engagement with important authors than cultural anthropology's invocation of them now commonly provokes.

In the course of these analyses, I characterize, evaluate, and historicize larger intellectual and philosophical contexts now relevant for cultural anthropology. These, in turn, provide a vantage point from which to assess the European male ancestries that some newer as well as older perspectives in anthropology often tacitly assume. A sharper critique of these ancestries is undertaken in the book's later chapters, first from the vantage points of gendered anthropology, feminism, and queer theory, and then from the perspective of multicultural agendas and concerns.

These perspectives challenge and recontextualize the critical humanism developed in previous chapters. The final chapter provides summary evaluations of major approaches considered and offers concluding assessments from a critically humanist standpoint. It then finishes on a note of critical reopening by means of an autocritique.

Being limited by time and stamina, my treatment of different perspectives is neither equal nor equally tempered. Depending on one's point of view, a given approach may be accorded too much attention (or criticism), or not enough. The same may be said for various intellectual figures. Many of the more established topical areas within cultural anthropology rest in the background. I also admit a lack of emphasis on approaches that stress individual subjectivity via specifics of language or emotion. With respect to interdisciplinary connections, I give more attention to international cultural studies, postmodern feminism, and black cultural criticism than to a fuller range of media and literary studies or specific subaltern currents from Indian, African, Latin American, Native American, or other areal venues. Given this bias, my treatment of multicultural concerns and feminist issues may appear too selective for some and too cursory for others. I accept this criticism in advance but would have felt worse for having neglected such crucial developments altogether.

The book's chapters engage theory with ethnography through a number of different styles. This variability is intentional; my goal is to explore alternative ways that substantive ethnography can both illustrate and challenge recent profusions in cultural theories. My own view is that concrete and rigorous ethnography remains indispensable to cultural anthropology. In the present context, this can include using ethnography as a counterpoint against theoretical abstraction (chapters 3 and 4); engaging ethnographic specifics in a reciprocating dialogue with theoretical suppositions (chapter 5); considering indigenous voicing as its own voice of theory (chapter 6); reviewing monograph clusters that organically instantiate new theoretical directions rather than rendering them programmatic (chapter 7); and pursuing a reflexive critique of our own academic practice (chapter 8). The larger point is that vigorous ethnography remains crucial and creative for the theoretical future of cultural anthropology. This necessity is not undercut but underscored as anthropology explores multi-sited research and other creative forms of ethnography that penetrate the complexity and connectivity of a late modern world (Marcus 1995). In newer as well as older guises—and as supplemented by texts from history, mass media, fiction, and other forms of representation—ethnographic documentation based on participant observation can endure as the field's methodological cornerstone.

As part of its stock-taking and its argument for renewed commitments in cultural anthropology, this volume has two larger purposes. The first is to stimulate a broader and more productive discussion about the trajectory of late modern anthropology and the principles that may give it meaning, ethics, and theoretical direction. The second is to show how this discussion engages ethnographic scholarship and a commitment to intersubjective understanding.

chapter 1

stories, histories, and theories

Agendas in Cultural Anthropology

Recent initiatives in cultural anthropology are importantly inflected by—and often opposed to—preceding theoretical legacies. To provide some context for these complexities, selected stories about anthropology's theoretical past provide a convenient point of departure.[1] These stories are not neutral or balanced in coverage. They compress and telescope, emphasizing the well-known, on the one hand, and the strains most relevant for current sensibilities, on the other. Somewhere between fact and myth, variants of these stories are often told by anthropologists about themselves; they encode basic perceptions that can be useful for pedagogical purposes and initial awareness. Unavoidably broad, they use basic themes to sweep across territory that is more complicated on a closer view. The same is true of individual authors; their reification as icons of particular approaches belies the nuances that should lead one back to the specifics and diversity of their works. It is important for students to realize that all of the authors considered below need to be read and considered more deeply. As Jack Goody (1995:208) reminds us, "lumping together anthropologists and ideas in single categories makes it difficult to understand their work." Even as the following stories reveal themselves to be inadequate, their shortcomings provide a context for considering current views, which is the larger purpose of this book. As will become evident, the status of "stories" versus "histories" is itself a subject of much debate in recent attempts to theorize culture and representation. For simplicity, we can start with high modernist strains of cultural anthropology and then consider them against trajectories that are more recent and those that are more historically distant.

Story #1
Levels and Objects: The Apogee of Modernity in Cultural Anthropology

Once upon a time, in a story of high modernism, anthropology's world was simple, objective, and divided into three levels: the symbolic, the social, and the material. Competing approaches to culture emphasized the priority of one or another of these levels. One approach was symbols-and-meaning anthropology, which proposed that culture was a symbolic system. The system of symbols in each culture was said to be public, real, and recordable through ethnographic verve and nuance. Profoundly compelling and highly different in different cultures, symbolic systems entailed distinctive world views, psychologies, and social institutions. Relative and irreducible, cultures could not be understood through a priori explanatory principles; they had to be uncovered inductively and interpreted in each case. At the same time, cultural interpretations were held to be verifiable; symbolic anthropology was in principle scientific. During its heyday of the late 1960s and 1970s, symbols-and-meaning anthropology was epitomized by figures such as Clifford Geertz, David Schneider, and the midcareer Marshall Sahlins and was associated iconically with anthropology at the University of Chicago.

Materialist anthropology, in contrast, saw culture as the rational process of adapting to ecological and economic constraints. In this view, anthropology was the explanatory science of deciphering how humans used the material world to satisfy practical needs. Materialist perspectives charted the growth of subsistence practices and technology over the course of human evolutionary history and explained recent cultural practices on the basis of their infrastructural rationality. During the 1950s and 1960s, materialist approaches to culture were strongly associated with anthropology at schools such as the University of Michigan; during the 1970s, they were perhaps most strongly associated with Marvin Harris and anthropology at Columbia University.

British social anthropology, so the story goes, was primarily concerned with how tribal societies were structured and organized. In this view, the norms, roles, and institutions of decentralized societies could be analyzed according to a small number of kinship and descent principles. The resulting structural types revealed the limited number of ways in which societies satisfied their functional demand for social integration. This perspective, which was most prominent from the mid–1930s to the early 1960s, was inflected by Malinowski but associated especially with A. R. Radcliffe-Brown and his students-cum-colleagues E. E. Evans-Pritchard and Meyer Fortes in England.

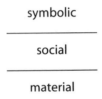

These three strands could be associated with what sociologist Talcott Parsons (and anthropologist Alfred Kroeber) distinguished as distinct levels of social life. The symbolic level revealed how human groups represented the world; it included a collective or "cultural" dimension as well as an individual or "psychological" dimension. The social level, by contrast, concerned what people actually did and how they were socially organized—their system of social action. Finally, the material dimension concerned the constraints of the physical and bodily world and how human groups functioned to meet or overcome these constraints, for instance, through subsistence production and economic relations. If, as Arjun Appadurai (1988) has suggested, modernist anthropology has often associated certain concepts or labels metonymically with certain ethnographic regions, the same point could be made concerning the conceptual space of anthropology's high modernist past.[2]

The story continues that these three perspectives on sociocultural life could not be content with their respective places; each tried to argue that its own level of sociocultural life was primary and the others were secondary or derivative. They were never able to agree, and their debate continued over time until their perspectives lost value when considered independently of one another. The levels of reality they had assumed to be discrete became too blurred and blended to be theoretically separated.

IN FACT, MODERNIST ANTHROPOLOGY OF THE POST–WORLD WAR II era was never so simple; even a sketch of exceptions sounds thin or banal. For one thing, the symbolic level had important individual as well as collective dimensions. If personality was to the individual what culture was to society, many anthropologists were concerned with the relationship between individual and collective processes. In addition, linguistic anthropology, psychological anthropology, physical anthropology, and archeology all explored the diverse connections between mental life, on the one hand, and material or social life, on the other. In the study of signification, Lévi-Strauss and French structuralism loomed large; the tendency of the mind to classify through diametric opposition was seen to play itself out in the classificatory structure of kinship, myths, totems, and other features of simpler human societies. In this view, the structure of society was analytically tied, if not fused, to the structure of mind. The totalizing strains of French anthropology did not accept the divisions among mental, social, and material aspects of life the way that American anthropology often did.

Other border crossings were also prominent in anthropology during the decades following World War II. In the United States, George Peter Murdock looked through an inductive rather than a deductive lens to correlate social structure to a global array of material, geographic, and economic variables. Developing from the late 1950s through the 1970s, British-turned-American anthropologist Victor Turner ultimately suggested that social organization was a field of drama and metaphor. Robert Murphy connected the cultural to the material and the psychological in a dialectics of social life. The ecology of mind was connected to material ecology by the great iconoclast Gregory Bateson. Ethnoscientists at Yale attempted to link the structure of cultural classifications to individual cognition. Many other strains from the 1950s through the 1970s could also be mentioned. In short, avenues across the symbolic, the social, and the material provided some of cultural anthropology's most important modern developments.

But for a graduate student of my own generation, the 1970s, there was solidity if not comfort in a tripartite ideology of discrete levels: the material world, the social world, and the symbolic world. Like a triumvirate, the principal perspectives that championed these levels agreed about their relative positions even as they tried to dominate each other and assume primacy in anthropological theory. Across the middle of this debate was the long-standing axis of antagonism between interpretive understandings, on the one hand, and explanatory and presumably scientific ones, on the other. Particularly in the United States, symbolic perspectives tended to see cultures as relative, based in subjectivity, and demanding of interpretation. Materialist and many structural approaches, on the other hand, stressed anthropology as an objective science that could explain culture by reducing its diversity to a small number of explanatory principles.

Story #2
The Marxist Intellectual Revolution

A second story is that Marx's ghost erupted into anthropology during the 1970s and put a critical wrench to the differentiated study of sociocultural life. By this time, intellectual life in the United States had been rocked by the civil rights movement, feminism, urban riots, and protests against the war in Vietnam. In Europe, social unrest flared as student uprisings over social injustice and the legacy of European colonialism. On both sides of the Atlantic, interest in anthropology grew along with an increased concern with critical theory.

In academic circles, so the story goes, Marx's critique of social inequality became the epitome of intellectual revolution; all three levels of sociocultural reality were now recast from this levering point. Culture as a symbolic system was now seen as an opiate of the masses—the ultimate ideology that masked social inequality most deeply. The organization and structure of social action were no longer seen as functional ways of maintaining society, as in British structural-functionalism. Instead, organizational structure became an oppressive means of perpetuating divisions of wealth and power between the haves and the have-nots. Finally, at base, the ostensibly "rational" appropriation of the physical world, which materialists had emphasized, was now seen to mask unequal wealth and labor among men versus women, elders versus juniors, elites versus commoners, and those of different classes, nationalities, and ethnic or racial groups.

In the same way that Marxist critiques crosscut symbolic, social, and material dimensions of reality, so too the level at which "inequality" was most fundamental was increasingly thrown into question. One of Marx's strengths had been to assign a dynamic and ultimately dialectical quality to the relationship among material, social, and symbolic factors; none of these could be easily reduced to the others.

The critical theory of the late 1960s drew largely on Marx's later work, such as *Capital* and corroborative work written up and published by Engels as *The Origin of the Family, Private Property, and the State* (e.g., Althusser and Balibar 1970; Althusser 1969; Engels 1972). The initial impression was that Marx's dialectic was highly determined by its more materialist side (the infrastructure or "base") and that its more symbolic and ideological dimensions (the superstructure) formed a secondary category. However, with growing interest in Marx's earlier and more philosophical work, it was increasingly argued during the late 1970s and 1980s that revolutions of the mind and of consciousness were extremely important in determining resistance (or capitulation) to economic and political domination. Further, Marx's early emphasis on "species being" and relations of production suggested that material forces engaged key features of *social* relationship and affiliation.

The question then became: What was the relationship between different dimensions of inequality? Was inequality at one level of human reality any less pernicious, motivating, or important than inequality at another level? What was the relationship between inequity of material possession, discrimination at the level of social action, and the moral inequality of prestige or stigma? These questions grew as Marx's theory was applied to concrete ethnographic situations. In the course of these applications and debates, the divisions among symbolic, material, and social—which had never been rigid for Marx himself—were increasingly questioned. Besieged from various quarters, the separation between these levels began to crumble in anthropology's story about itself as well.

Notions of stability and coherence in high modernist anthropology— that societies and cultures were persistent if not synchronic systems— were also undercut by Marxist emphasis on history, change, and transformation. What anthropologists had been seeing was not the whole picture of culture. Rather it was a narrow slice of reality framed by the short time and limited space of fieldwork. Further, this fieldwork had often been conducted under a mantle of Western colonial or neocolonial influence (Asad 1973). Anthropologists had neglected and thus accepted as unproblematic the broad historical and geographic patterns of Western domination and inequality within which their ethnographies had been situated. In the wave of such criticism, it was sometimes forgotten that many anthropologists had fought vigorously to assert indigenous rights or to valorize indigenous peoples' customs.

As part of these lasting criticisms, the ghost of Marx itself did not remain intact. The high-water mark of Marxism in anthropology came in the wake of the 1960s and 1970s protest movements, during which it almost seemed possible that a social if not political revolution might be on the horizon from the political left. It is hard to accurately convey to a newer generation the then-present feeling that structural change through collective action might really be possible. Droves of students entered left-of-center fields such as anthropology.

But with the subsequent waning of this protest and the fizzling of the May 1968 revolution in France, leftist thinkers took a more critical look at Marx. Despite the domestic and global crisis of postcolonial capitalism, the Western revolution had not occurred. What had gone wrong? By the early 1970s, French critics such as Baudrillard, Foucault, and Bourdieu were actively critiquing and reshaping the Marxist yardsticks by which the critique of social science could be recast. English Marxists such as E. P. Thompson and Raymond Williams suggested that subjectivity and consciousness were particularly important in class struggle. Maybe historical materialism had it backward. As Lukács and Gramsci had earlier foreshadowed, maybe it was actually the cultural or symbolic dimensions of power that ultimately underpinned social and material inequality. Maybe one had to cultivate and hope for a deeper change in public consciousness before a political and economic revolution could take place.

As the basis for human inequality was itself debated and deconstructed, the framework for an encompassing Marxism became shifting and unstable. Even apart from ultimate causes, it was unclear what kind(s) of inequality a rejuvenated Marxism should be most dedicated to redressing. Marx had focused on class. But how was resistance against gendered, sexual, racial, and national inequality to be brought under the umbrella of Marxist thought and action?

Following its eminence in European philosophy, sociology, and history, interest in Marxism trickled and then flowed into French, British, and American anthropology during the 1970s. But even as its coherence as an anthropological paradigm faded again during the 1980s, the larger Marxian mission was secured as an enduring anthropological legacy: the explicit critique of inequality across a full range of cultural, sociohistorical, and material dimensions.

Story #3
The Postmodern Ideology of Anti-paradigms

As doctrinaire versions of Marxist analysis were left aside as too rigid, their thrust melded with an alternative approach that ultimately burgeoned as its own intellectual wave: postmodernism. That modern knowledge—including Western arts and sciences—provided a limited if not myopic view of progress was not a new idea. Fragmentation, pastiche, and the juxtaposition of images and genres had been used to make this point at least as early as Nietzsche's writings of the 1860s through the 1880s. In art, this trend was foreshadowed by French impressionism and then made explicit in cubist and surreal art during the early twentieth century. The use of the foreign to point out the limitations of our own values and assumptions had also been important in asserting the value of cultural anthropology to Western audiences, as illustrated in the classic works of Margaret Mead and Ruth Benedict.

But these themes took a distinctive and more reflexive twist during the late 1970s and 1980s. In contrast to the social activism of the sixties and seventies, this was a period of retrenchment and doubt among Western intellectuals. Politics had turned to the right: Reaganomics dominated in the United States, Thatcherism reigned in England, and neo-Gaullism refused to die in France. The Western empires struck back overseas as well, fueling the arms race against the Soviet Union, brokering wars in Third World countries, and conducting safer mini-wars of their own.[3] Conservative politics at home and abroad contributed to the declining influence of organized labor and socialism. Progressive Western leaders had to compromise if they wished to keep influence or power; they ended up in the political center if not on the right. The Communist alternatives provided by the Soviet Union and China seemed little better, and leftist revolutions in the Third World often seemed as bad if not worse than the colonial regimes they supplanted. Overall, the seeming failure of the left or even of the progressive center provoked a growing political disillusionment and apathy among many academics as well as among the disaffected ranks of the more truly disempowered.

The response of the intellectual avant-garde was increasingly to refuse the contest or to capitulate and find solace in cynicism, comic detachment, and irony. Mainstream protest gave way to questioning the terms of the debate. Representational order was intrinsically doubted. Across a wide range of humanities fields, the decentering of Western knowledge intensified during the late 1970s and early 1980s. Socially and politically, academics were losing faith in the Western paradigm of progress, growth, and development that had long sustained them. The destruction of World War II—ranging from the Holocaust to atomic bombing by the United States—had been followed by the futile attempts of Western powers to suppress the political independence of their colonies, the neocolonialism of multinational corporations, and the Vietnam war. By the late 1970s, it was hard for intellectuals to believe that Western ideas and institutions provided a guiding light for the world. Progressive intentions had produced sour consequences: The war on poverty at home had backfired; attempts to modernize the world had resulted in peasantization, ecological degradation, and neocolonialism; Marxist dictatorships abroad had become a parody of themselves. Even successful attempts to reduce world mortality produced devastating population growth and increased misery as more Third World people competed for fewer resources.

Skepticism about Western progress had been an important intellectual strain at least since European Romanticism of the late eighteenth and early nineteenth century, and it had taken a more poignant turn in the twentieth century after each world war. But following upon Heidegger's later philosophy, this disaffection received a new intellectual twist from French deconstruction, spearheaded by Jacques Derrida. In the late 1970s, deconstructionism and poststructuralism spread widely in the humanities fields of philosophy, literature, and art. It was not just that representations had to be unraveled to expose their underlying assumptions; the drive to reestablish order was itself suspect as a dominating or reactionary strategy. To fight this trend, self-conscious and meticulous dis-ordering of Western ways of seeing, speaking, and writing were called for.

Because such criticisms were easily cast against the stable order and faith of Western intellectual progress, they were ultimately seen as auguring the end of liberal modernism and portending the postmodern. Beginning in the early 1970s in architecture, and developing by the late

1970s in philosophy and literature, postmodern trends were intrinsically pluralizing; they were against master narratives, against coherence, and against programmatic themes. Fragmentation and pastiche were used to question the assumptions of representation that underpinned the ostensible order of the modernist agenda. Class and taste were turned upside down. Las Vegas rivaled the Louvre as a site of art and representation. At extremes, everything became blurred, and politics lost meaning.

In due course, these trends found resonance and then active influence in cultural anthropology. Presaged by work in linguistic and hermeneutic anthropology in the 1970s and in further essays by Clifford Geertz in the early 1980s, cultural anthropology witnessed a growing interest in blurred genres. This was followed in the mid-1980s by a burst of postmodern sensibilities. Championed by figures such as George Marcus, James Clifford, and Paul Rabinow, postmodern interests drew upon anthropology's cultural relativism but went beyond it.[4] The objectivist assertion that each culture should be considered on its own terms was replaced by doubt that such things as "cultures" could ever be said to exist. This was not just cultural relativism, but relativism of our basic concepts, of our perception and motivation, and of our cultural and class and racial and gendered position as ethnographers and writers. It was relativism raised to a higher power—reflexive relativism, hyperrelativism. In the process, perspectives that resisted or chose not to foreground an experimental approach to representation were devalued or considered passé.

Thus the 1980s, so the narrative goes, moved from a trickle of postmodern influences toward a sea change of cultural theory. At least this was the converts' hope. A Pandora's box of reflexivity was opened. In anthropology, this engaged a particular concern with what ethnographers wrote and how and why they wrote it. No longer could we assume a firm or authoritative stance as authors, as if representing other peoples objectively. Our lens of perception was not a transparent window but a filter characterized by the inequities of scholarly power. Proponents heralded a ground-breaking advance of experimental ethnography. Detractors called it the navel-gazing of New Age ethnographers absorbed in their own abstruse writing.

Since modernist ethnographers were largely white, Western, and middle- or upper-class, their biases were ripe for the criticism that they perpetrated power and domination in their very assumptions about knowledge—at the epistemic level. Modernist anthropology, like other branches of academic study, was seen as complicitous with the epistemic as well as the political and economic imperialism of the West. Notwithstanding many ethnographers' personal convictions and commitment to the people they studied, anthropology was perceived as the handmaiden of colonialism. Anthropologists, in this view, had unwittingly both imposed Western categories of knowledge upon the "natives" and supplied details about their social lives to the ultimate benefit of colonial officials. It was no accident that modernist anthropology had been particularly strong in the European colonies of Africa, Oceania, and Asia. Nor was it an accident that British, French, American, Dutch, Belgian, German, Australian, and South African anthropologists had a special focus on their own nations' colonies and indigenous populations.

Against this hegemony, breaking out of anthropology's dominating box required experimentation with new forms of writing and knowledge. It required listening to other voices. And it criticized deep Western notions: that knowledge exists in stable, objective, and factual categories; that these categories can be used to encode a single verifiable reality; and that the accurate depiction of this reality results in knowledge that is universally "true." This truth was now exposed as only a Western white reality. Given the effect on perception and authorship of being empowered or being disempowered, there could be no such thing as objective cultural traits subject to "truthful" description, much less comparison or explanation.

Despite these new criticisms and disenchantments, "normal" cultural anthropology—now expanded to engage critical theory and history—continued to form the bulk of the discipline through at least the end of the 1980s. Many older anthropologists were incensed, including those who had maintained long-standing commitments to and advocacy for disempowered peoples. Leftist anthropologists had themselves been subject to discrimination and professional cost in the conservative climate of earlier decades. But postmodern renegades had the symbolic capital of the avant-garde; they came on as lefter-than-thou. As influential as they were resisted, they provoked remarkable controversy in anthropology during the mid- and late 1980s, particularly given their relatively small number of core adherents. Regardless of its excesses, the postmodern critique had certainly hit a raw nerve. And it had the appearance of riding a new and potentially massive wave of transdisciplinary change.

Confronted by experimental forms of writing and representation, the postmodern reader encountered a pastiche of fragments, genres, and voices. Odd texts, including drawings and photos, were taken out of context and juxtaposed to provide newly ironic or subversive meanings. Temporal and geographic contexts were disrupted. History was not a fact but a Western story that now appeared strange. We had to defamiliarize this story by going back to it, jerkily, and holding "scare quotes" around our unseemly past.

Story #4
Getting Hit by the Canon: The Ancestry of Modernist Anthropology

From a postmodern perspective, the notion that anthropology had a distinct and valuable intellectual history was a story, a myth. Part of this myth had been the high modernist creation of great European thinkers— theorists such as Marx, Durkheim, and Weber. Anthropology had not always recognized this ancestry. Indeed, many would say that these ancestral invocations were not completely hitched to anthropology until the 1960s at schools such as the University of Chicago (Geertz 1991:607; cf. Stocking 1979). Before this time, figures such as Franz Boas and E. B. Tylor—who had inaugurated anthropology's place in the university in the late nineteenth-century—had been credited with much of anthropology's theoretical direction. Such figures had been foregrounded in influential earlier works such as Lowie's *History of Ethnological Theory* (1937).[5]

As chance would have it, a wider cast of European social theorists was also introduced to American social scientists in 1937 by the soon-to-be-famous sociologist Talcott Parsons in his voluminous *Structure of Social Action*. But the idea that nonanthropologists such as Max Weber—much less Marx—should be taken as seminal to anthropology's interests did not take hold until more than two decades later. By the leftist heyday of the late 1960s and 1970s, however, the canonical works of Weber, Durkheim, and Marx were increasingly read by the droves of graduate students attracted to anthropology, especially in the United States. To simplify the story into levels, Weber resonated through Parsons and Geertz as the intellectual precursor of interpretive or symbolic anthropology; Durkheim was seen through Radcliffe-Brown as the grounding point for social and structural anthropology; and Marx was recast against figures such as Lewis Henry Morgan as a critical giant for materialist explanations of history. But how was it that figures such as Marx, Durkheim, and

Weber (none of whom were anthropologists, much less Americans) became seminal figures for high modernist cultural anthropology by the 1970s, particularly in the United States?

From a genealogical point of view, it is important to retrace and expose this history. Of course, many other figures besides Weber, Marx, and Durkheim have been relevant to anthropology's deeper ancestry—and have been perceived as such.[6] But this trio was particularly important for high modernism in cultural anthropology. Their influences—and the perception of their influences—were mutually reinforcing during an era of late master narratives.

Weber and American Symbolic Anthropology

Before the late 1960s and 1970s, cultural relativism in American anthropology was considered primarily through the intellectual lens of Franz Boas (1858–1942) and his students. Coming to America from Germany, Boas was highly influential in the institutional founding of professional anthropology in the United States. Grounded by his extensive field research among Arctic and Northwest Coast Native Americans, Boas had a fervent and meticulous zeal for documenting indigenous customs, beliefs, languages, artifacts, and art. As retrospected by Stocking (1968), Boas was credited with having originated the modern anthropological concept of culture—notwithstanding contrary views by some of his own students (Kroeber and Kluckhohn 1952). In contrast to the Victorian notion that "Culture" was a single evolving form—a prototype for the advancements of "Civilization"—Boas was seen to have pluralized and decentralized cultures, to have made them as valid as they were diverse. However, even apart from Johann Herder's stress on *Kultur* diversity in the late eighteenth century,[7] Raymond Williams (1958:ch. 3) had documented a highly relativized and appreciative sense of "culture" in English at least since the 1830s.[8] But cultural diversity was foregrounded in Boas's detailed ethnography and in his relentless attacks against evolutionism, which extended from the late 1800s to the early 1940s. Even if it was not explicitly theorized, Boas's antievolutionism had a strongly antiracist cast; Boas fought against the disparagement of primitive peoples, of ethnic immigrants, and of blacks in the United States by valorizing their customs and showing these to be at least as sophisticated and intricate as our own. Boas's commitments had a formative influence on his large number of students, many of whom helped disseminate anthropology as an academic discipline in the United States: Alfred Kroeber, Robert Lowie, Edward Sapir, Margaret Mead, Ruth Benedict, Melville Herskovits, Gladys Reichard, Leslie Spier, Walter Goldschmidt, Frank Speck, Paul Radin, and Alex Goldenweiser, among others. If Boas's influence was great, part of this story was the indelible respect and value he placed on cultural diversity in American anthropology.

By the late 1950s, however, Boas's legacy seemed old and tired. In academic and scholarly portrayals, Boasian cultures were turgidly particularistic rather than sweeping or galvanizing. Kept alive in the 1930s, 1940s, and 1950s by Kroeber's "culture climaxes," Benedict's "patterns of culture," and various permutations on "culture and personality," the tradition of relativizing cultures ultimately ran short on theoretical steam. Stuck in the deep recesses of descriptive scholarship, Boas's dry documentation had pulled its punches when it came to exciting an analysis of cultural alternatives.

At this juncture, the story continues, an important infusion occurred. In the 1950s the influence of sociologist Talcott Parsons was at its peak in the American social sciences. Parsons had introduced important European social theorists to America. These included Max Weber (1864–1920), the monumental German sociologist and historian. Weber's work combined immense world-historical knowledge with brilliant analytic syntheses. Working on a breathtaking scale that combined knowledge of China and India with that of Eurasia, America, and the full depth of Western history, Weber had developed ideal type portraits of subjective motivation and linked these to different kinds of social or bureaucratic institutions. Deeply appreciative of zeitgeist—the subjective spirit of particular peoples during different historical periods—Weber strove for an interpretive and yet objective understanding of large-scale cultural differences and similarities.

In retrospect, Weber appeared as the complement to the roughly contemporary Boas; the two shared strong intellectual roots in nineteenth-century German social thought, including the legacy of Wilhelm Dilthey's interpretive sciences and Herder's earlier appreciation of *Kultur* diversity. (These earlier orientations are central to a deeper history of cultural anthropology.)[9] Where Boas's relativism had lacked analytic and theoretical power, Weber supplied exactly these strengths. However, the sweep of Weber's analytic characterizations came at the expense of the detailed ethnography in non-Western contexts, which was Boas's strongest contribution. Posthumously married in the wake of Boas's own legacy, the interpretive power of Max Weber's sociology was combined with the Boasian tradition of relativism in American cultural anthropology. The prime synthesizer was Clifford Geertz, beginning in the late 1950s.

One of the features this Weberian infusion omitted from the Boasian tradition was the investigation of material culture, diffusion, and prehistory, all of which had formed an important part of the anthropological paradigm both prior to Boas and through many of his students.[10] On the other hand, notwithstanding the prior importance of Sapir and others, linguistics became less important than literary interpretation. Against these, the cultural anthropology of high modernism became both more interpretive and more autonomous from material concerns than it had been before. Energized in the flowing prose of Geertz's thick descriptions, this newer cultural relativism developed via a host of Chicago, Berkeley, and Harvard influences into the now-classic perspective of American symbolic anthropology. In the process, Weber became a theoretical progenitor, with particular stress on his analyses of collective subjectivity.

Durkheim and Social Structural Anthropology

A complementary perspective was seen to begin with the French thinker Emile Durkheim (1858–1917), also late in the nineteenth century. Though the influence of earlier French scholars such as Auguste Comte was recognized, Durkheim was credited with establishing sociology on positivist grounds—the study of social life as an objective science. Durkheim stressed that beliefs and values were social facts that should be subject to dispassionate examination; the goal was to reveal their contribution to the organization, solidarity, and integration of society. Focusing on norms and the constraints posed by social rules, Durkheim emphasized that social facts should be considered as things-in-themselves with their own properties and significance, even when these might seem on the surface to be idiosyncratic or irrational. Durkheim's interests ranged from statistical and historical features of European societal development to the ethnography of religion and morality. Though an armchair scholar, he was very broad in geographic and intellectual sweep.

Durkheim's French sociology included strong academic institutionalization and detailed field research by his students. This development was brutally compromised, however, by the death of most of his students as soldiers during World War I. But, the story goes, Durkheim's link between social function and social structure had already been concretized and narrowed for anthropology in the early 1910s by the British anthropologist A. R. Radcliffe-Brown. An early convert to Durkheimian principles, Radcliffe-Brown focused Durkheim's interests and applied them to the study of social organization in tribal societies. He concentrated on kinship and descent structures, foregrounding their functional relationship to the successful operation and maintenance of pre-state social groups. In this view, social structure was as real and as rule-governed as physical or skeletal anatomy; comparative sociology was the societal analogue of comparative natural history.

Consistent and single-minded in his approach, Radcliffe-Brown traveled widely and had a strong influence on the development of British social anthropology in Australia and South Africa as well as in England. Though Radcliffe-Brown's strength was not in field research or nuanced ethnography, his students melded his interests with a dedication to rich participatory fieldwork as promulgated by the Polish-turned-British anthropologist Bronislaw Malinowski. Radcliffe-Brown's focus on sociological theory and Malinowski's emphasis on field research came together in British structural-functionalism. During its heyday from the 1930s to the 1950s, this perspective foregrounded the study of social and political organization in the colonial ethnography of Oceania, South Asia, and especially Africa.[11] According to Radcliffe-Brown and many others, Durkheim was the key theoretical ancestor for British social anthropology.

Durkheim's thought also exerted a profound influence on his prescient nephew, Marcel Mauss, and via him to the French paragon Claude Lévi-Strauss during this same period. Whereas Durkheim had stressed the connection between structures of thought and institutional structures, Lévi-Strauss extended this connection through theoretical perspectives from structural linguistics, drawing upon the insights of Saussure and Jakobson. Expanding the deductivist side of Durkheim, Lévi-Strauss stressed the logical structure of mental operation over the manifest meaning of symbols, the organizational dynamics of society, or the external constraints of material life.

Lévi-Strauss's increasing emphasis on mental structure came to be at odds with British anthropology's focus on social structure and political organization. Whereas British structural-functionalism held social structures to be manifestly evident in social life, Lévi-Strauss's structuralism held that surface events belied deeper structural relationships—in the same way that spoken language presumes grammatical rules that are highly regular even though they are largely unconscious to speakers. Despite disagreement between British and French views of structure, Durkheim's perspective spanned their gap. Indeed, he provided the intellectual terrain that made their debate possible. American anthropology, for its part, absorbed Durkheim in part through the structural concerns of British and French anthropologists. Radcliffe-Brown taught from 1931 to 1937 at Chicago (where he influenced Fred Eggan, among others), and Lévi-Strauss taught in the early 1940s at the New School in New York.[12] Both of these Durkheim-presuming influences were reinforced by Talcott Parsons's introduction of Durkheim along with Weber as a major social theorist in the United States. By the late 1950s, Durkheim was widely read by American as well as French and British anthropologists, and his legacy was alternately embraced and criticized (e.g., Eggan 1968; Geertz 1973:ch. 6, 1991:607).

Marx and Materialist Anthropology

Material evolution has long been integral to anthropology's ancestry,[13] and it continues today to provide an armature for many of the discipline's undergraduate textbooks. Formal features of social evolution are often traced to the early work of Herbert Spencer (1820–1903) (e.g., Bohannan and Glazer 1988:ch. 1), but these features also have a much longer intellectual history. Well prior to modernism, their strains resonated with the brilliant and underappreciated *Muqaddimah* [*An Introduction to History*] by the fourteenth-century Arab scholar Ibn Khaldūn (1332–1406), if not with the work of ancient Greek materialists.

Prior to Marx's eminence in anthropology during the late 1960s, the study of material evolution, particularly in the United States, was often traced back to the American Lewis Henry Morgan (1818–1881). This placement was selective, since the bulk of Morgan's work on kinship and social organization allies him at least as much to British and French structural concerns as to American materialism, and a number of nineteenth-century scholars from different parts of Europe had already attempted detailed scenarios of human social and material evolution. Underlying these attempts, the Western interest in evolution had historical roots in sixteenth- and seventeenth-century anthropology, which drew upon Christian notions of enlightenment (Hodgen 1964; Stocking 1987). This divine progress along the Great Chain of Being was believed to push upward from savage roots and culminate in European civilization. At the very end of *Ancient Society*, Morgan (1877) himself found recourse in God as the ultimate shaper of human evolution, that is, "the plan of the Supreme Intelligence to develop a barbarian out of a savage, and a civilized man out of this barbarian."

In hindsight, however, Morgan's distinctive contribution was to have linked stages of human development to specific material accomplishments. Cultural evolution, in this view, dovetailed with the discovery of technological innovations such as fire, pottery, metalworking, and the alphabet. These advancements and their institutional concomitants allowed man to "win his way to civilization." Morgan's emphasis, as such, was entrepreneurial, inventive, and quite American. At least in the United States, Morgan's materialist legacy has been highly influential, and his own most famous invention, *Ancient Society*, has never been out of print since its first publication in 1877.

During the first half of the twentieth century, the material dimensions of culture were also important to Boas and his students, who often considered archeology and physical anthropology among their concerns. But Boas had been a staunch antievolutionist. And when American cultural anthropology refashioned its own genealogy to become more interpretive and symbolic during the 1960s, American materialists increasingly diverged and channeled their theoretical roots in more materialist directions. This process was galvanized by Marvin Harris's influential *The Rise of Anthropological Theory* (1968). In this updated and more theoretical paradigm of American materialism, the study of culture was seen to have been energized by Morgan and kept alive during the period from the 1930s to the 1950s by the evolutionary syntheses of anthropologists such as Leslie White and Julian Steward. This impetus was expanded during the 1960s by Harris and cultural materialists such as Andrew Vayda, Roy Rappaport, Eric Wolf, Elman Service, and the early work of Marshall Sahlins.

Cultural materialism emphasized that humans were everywhere subject to limitations of environment and energy; culture was a process of adapting to these constraints. The goal of the anthropologist was to explain individual features of culture by their specific adaptive function and to explain commonalities across societies on the basis of their shared environment or shared level of technical and cultural development (e.g., White 1949; Steward 1955; Sahlins 1960; Rappaport 1968; Harris 1979). One of the most influential moves was to replace Morgan's dated developmental sequence of savagery → barbarism → civilization with one that emphasized the evolution of subsistence intensification and political centralization: bands → tribes → chiefdoms → states.[14]

Consistent with its faith in technological advance, the materialist paradigm saw itself at the forefront of anthropology's attempt to gather data, test hypotheses, and establish itself as a real science. At least until the mid-twentieth century (and the wake of the atomic bomb), materialist anthropologists tended to agree that cultural adaptation and technological progress should go hand in hand. That they did not always do so, however, brought forth the ghost of Marx—that is, the notion that material advancement would ultimately lead to a better world even if more conservative and anachronistic institutions had to be swept aside in the process.

Many materialist scholars had socialist leanings, and some, such as Leslie White, were members of the Communist Party. Given the public stigmatization of leftist theory between the 1930s and the 1950s, however, Marx was seldom mentioned, much less explored, in the publications of Western anthropologists, especially in the United States. Even White's magnum opus, *The Science of Culture* (1949), mentions Marx only once—and then in a footnote (p. 186). Concerning the cultural evolutionists he knew during the 1940s and 1950s, Eric Wolf notes, "All of us were some variant of red. Some of us had actively been members of 'the Party' at some point. Others were Fourth Internationalist, or Three and Three-quarterth Internationalist. I think that was one of the strong bonds among us. . . . A Marxian stew but not necessarily with any commitment to a particular party line" (quoted in Friedman 1987:109). And yet Marx was avoided as an explicitly anthropological theorist through most of the 1950s. This was the era of McCarthyist Red-baiting, including in academia. Maurice Bloch notes that

> during the Second World War Leslie White was seen by many American anthropologists as a dangerous subversive because of his earlier contact with Soviet anthropologists. . . . White's enemies used this link with Soviet ideas to try to undermine his reputation. M. Opler wrote of his work: "It is curious that our neo-evolutionists constantly acknowledge

their debt to Darwin, Tylor, and Morgan and never have a word to say about the relation of their ideas to those of Marx, Engels, Bukharin, Plekhanov, Labriola, Suvorov, Lenin, Stalin, *et al.*" He finishes darkly, "anthropologists might well take a closer look at recent intellectual history and at some recent trends." (Bloch 1983:129)

A less-than-explicit exploration of Marx is more than understandable in this context. Even for Wolf, "It wasn't until the early- or mid-fifties that I began to read Marx firsthand, seriously. I still don't command that corpus the way I would like to" (quoted in Ghani 1987:356). The situation was slightly better in Britain, where a leftist tradition of critical theory was developed in history and sociology by Eric Hobsbawm, E. P. Thompson, Raymond Williams, and others. Max Gluckman developed a significant if still implicit use of Marx in the study of conflict in the Manchester School of British social anthropology during the 1950s. Despite this and the leftist commitments of individual figures, however, explicit use of Marx in British anthropology remained slight during this period. It is indicative that the British Marxist Peter Worsley was for political reasons denied permission to conduct fieldwork in Melanesia during the 1950s; his landmark study of Melanesian cargo cults as incipient movements of anticolonial resistance, first published in 1957, had to be written entirely from secondary sources (Worsley 1968). Marx continued to be a liability if not a professional stigma for anthropologists.

Marx's theory had unmasked nineteenth-century social science, which had often excused class oppression as a rational if not adaptive aspect of economic development. Instead, Marx pursued a critical analysis of economic and material conditions—and conditions of consciousness—that maintained this oppression. In Marx's view, capitalism was based on the exploitation of wage labor through unequal ownership of the means of production. The internal contradictions of capitalism—its relentless pursuit of wealth through profit-squeezing, labor exploitation, and free-market competition—would lead it to the brink of collapse. As the crisis deepened, Marx argued, relations of wage labor in industrial production provided workers a growing potential to collectivize and seize control of the productive process. As such, a class revolution could take place and pave the way for a more equal and communal society. As a method, Marx maintained his commitment to objectivist scholarship (as in *Capital*). However, he gave up the pretense that objectivism was unmotivated or dispassionate. Critical theory demanded its due on behalf of the downtrodden; like material relations themselves, it was ultimately revolutionary.

Though *The Communist Manifesto* was written on the cusp of the 1848 revolutions that shook and threatened to transform Europe, Marxist theory was unquestionably "wrong" in the narrow sense that capitalism was much more resistant to collapse than Marx first envisaged. Marx himself became increasingly aware of capitalism's long-term accommodations. (In his "Eighteenth Brumaire," he sardonically analyzed the reactionary backlash that subverted revolutionary upheaval and co-opted its impetus in order to restore autocracy.) But as a theoretician, Marx's strength was less in his predictions than in his mandate for a broad genre of critical thinking about the material and ideological basis of exploitation. Moreover, his last unfinished work—on primitive and Asiatic modes of production, the family, and stages of non-Western development—was pregnant with ethnological potential (Marx 1965; Engels 1972; Krader 1972; see Bloch 1975, 1983). Throughout this work, critical analysis of social development exposed the material bases of inequality and the cultural ideologies that legitimated domination.

Viewed from the Marxist renaissance of the late 1960s and 1970s, the critical spirit of Marxist analysis had been twisted and almost lost. According to this view, the late nineteenth century had seen Marx's work cast into a rigid materialism by Marx's supporter Frederick Engels and then used in increasingly dubious ways by the Communist Party, particularly in the Soviet Union (see Bloch 1983:ch. 4; McLellan 1975). Some of Marx's earlier works had remained untranslated and unpublished well into the twentieth century. During this period, most Western academics, including Talcott Parsons, had downplayed Marx. But the true Marxist flame, so the story went, had been kept alive in the West by a dedicated core of leftist scholars, renegades, and refugees.

During the social upheavals and protests of the late 1960s, a resuscitated Marx erupted into the academy. From sources as unlikely as the Chinese Maoist press, *The Communist Manifesto* was making its way to students of anthropology. Among their anthropological colleagues, many cultural materialists were outspoken activists who protested the U. S. war in Vietnam.[15] Materialists in British and French anthropology were also strongly leftist. Presaged in the 1950s, there were varieties of cultural and economic Marxism in Britain.[16] A tide of structuralist Marxism emerged from France in the late 1960s and 1970s.[17] Turning Lévi-Straussian structuralism on its theoretical head, structural Marxism held that the material mode of production determined the structural principles of social and mental organization, rather than the reverse. In the United States, the relationship between Marxism and culture became hotly and creatively debated at prestigious schools such as Chicago, Berkeley, Columbia, and Michigan.

In American anthropology, the 1970s relationship between Marxism and cultural materialism was itself contentious; the new generation of Marxists was highly critical of older positions, including materialist ones. Though the ills of the modern world seemed obvious, cultural materialists had continued to focus on adaptive rationalities and homeostasis; they only occasionally allowed for "maladaptation" or social transformation (cf. Rappaport 1977). Where cultural materialists saw functional beliefs and practices across disparate cultures, Marxists saw conservative ideologies that perpetuated widespread domination on the basis of age, sex, rank, or class. Cast as positivist or "vulgar" materialism, the theories of cultural adaptation advocated by Vayda, Harris, and Rappaport were deemed by Marxists to be uncritical at best and an incarnation of nineteenth-century social Darwinism at worst (see Friedman 1974).

As the debate between cultural materialists and structural Marxists eventually lost energy, the strands of both camps were increasingly picked up by figures such as Eric Wolf.[18] Wolf emphasized the world-historical interface between political power, economic development, and modes of production. In the process, what had been economic anthropology and political anthropology were increasingly recast as "political economy," which connected rather than separated global and local patterns of commerce and power. Though cultural and symbolic orientations were relatively neglected, this growing field linked itself with larger trends in structural history to analyze the development of economic influence and political domination over the large-scale canvas of world history as well as in the specific trenches of fieldwork.[19] Even the field of ecological anthropology eventually melded with these critical perspectives, for instance, as "political ecology."

Since its explicit entree during the late 1960s, the Marxist focus on inequality and domination has remained central to anthropology, not just for materialism but as a critical lens for diverse topics and articulations. Wolf (1982) developed a permutation of Marxist modes of production as the linchpin of his wide-ranging synthesis of global political economy and modern world history. Even Marvin Harris (1968) claimed that Marx could be a true ancestor of materialist theory—so long as one discarded his dialectic and enshrined him as a positivist. Critical theories of sexual, gendered, racial, and ethnic or national inequality developed as complements to analyses that foregrounded economic and political subordination. In the process, Marx was welcomed as a key intellectual ancestor for cultural anthropology. More specifically, his work gave contemporary and critical grounding for the historical materialism that had been traced back to Morgan.

Consolidation and Contention

To generalize as if it were a simple story, then, by the 1970s, material, social, and cultural emphases in anthropology were each supplied, retrospectively, with a late-nineteenth-century founding father, especially in the United States. Marx became the icon for material determinism (at least in the final instance), Durkheim grounded the study of social structure, and Max Weber bequeathed the interpretive analysis of cultural subjectivity and action (alongside his other sociological insights and categories). It is important to note that the work of each founding figure was in fact *not* limited or restricted to a stratified view of the symbolic, the social, and the material. Rather, each used a complementary set of analytic priorities to move across these boundaries. Each was more complex and important than these metonymic associations suggest. For a mid-twentieth century anthropology that had largely given up dialectical traditions and found itself ensconced in topical boxes and levels, however, these older European invocations were particularly innovative and stimulating. Moreover, each founder was a renowned social theorist, a genius, with the kind of world recognition and symbolic capital that ancestral *anthropologists* had typically lacked. None had himself done fieldwork or participated directly in the founding of anthropology as an academic discipline; indeed, part of the greatness of each was their exploration of universal themes that could be used to gain insight in all societies and cultures. At least indirectly, moreover, each figure could be seen in retrospect to have left a key intellectual legacy to early anthropologists: Marx to Morgan and White in the study of material life,[20] Durkheim to Radcliffe-Brown and Lévi-Strauss in the study of social and mental structure, and Weber to Geertz in the study of cultural and subjective orientations. This telescoping of theoretical ancestry was significant for a discipline that had been developing for the better part of a century and was simplifying and repositioning its stories for a new period of unprecedented academic and pedagogical growth.[21]

By the late 1970s, graduate theory courses in anthropology tended to embrace the work of these founding European thinkers. Permutations and additions emerged, of course, depending on the institution and the department. And the legacies of all major paradigms continued to be at odds with each other. At least in the United States, however, a theoretically current graduate student was supposed to know the background and current legacy of the Marxist, Durkheimian, and Weberian strains in materialist, structural, and symbolic anthropology. In the same way that Talcott Parsons had brought Durkheim and Weber to the mainstream of empirical social science in the 1940s and 1950s, so Anthony Giddens (1971) trenchantly summarized the thought of Marx, Durkheim, and Weber for a new generation of graduate students in American anthropology and European social sciences.[22] The master trope continued to be one of intellectual progress: the carrying of ancestral legacies to new heights through personal commitment and dedicated scholarship.

In opposition to these canonical goals, however, postmodern perspectives saw a fabricated genealogy rather than a substantive ancestry. A genealogy, in Michel Foucault's terms, has little to do with the linear connection through descent that was important to modernist knowledge. It is not a path of historical realization and progress, either temporally or intellectually; it is not a story of who bequeathed what to whom in a line of florescence. Rather, following Nietzsche, a genealogy is a trail of human concepts as a kind of idiosyncratic linguistic history—not a tracing of ideas or people, but of the images, categories, and words used to convey them. According to the early Foucault, these tracings tend to be relatively static or even random over relatively long periods of time, such as the period of Western modernism. In the social or human sciences, argued Foucault, this history of intellectual influence was not a path of discovery in which true insights about our relationship to the world were progressively realized. Rather, it was a path of superficial invention—the production of terms and ideas that were accepted (or discarded) not because they were in any meaningful sense true, but because they were consistent with the overarching structure of Western knowledge as a kind of epistemic power. Grand theory, like other kinds of grand narrative, was seen to be a relic of modernist pretense. Postmodern sensitivities could be appropriately ironic, absurd, or playful in their unseating of received wisdom. But postmodern practitioners had to be indirect even in this regard. Our declarative hegemonies could not be given in to. It was best to write with bracketed sensibilities.

Bringing Stories Up to Date

It is difficult to continue these stories in anthropology during the late 1980s and early 1990s—even as a superficial genealogy. There is certainly no unpositioned position from which to view the present. Among other things, my own graduate training in anthropology at the University of Michigan in the late 1970s influences my assessment of what directions have been important or unimportant. It is hard not to be either sympathetic to (or overly critical of) approaches one was strongly exposed to in graduate school. In my own case, I had a relatively balanced exposure to materialist, social structural, and symbolic perspectives.[23] This likely reflects and reinforces my sense that these paradigms were complementary, both among themselves and with then-current critical theory. On the other hand, my exposure to reflexive, post-Marxist, and a range of cultural studies perspectives only after completing graduate school probably reinforces my sense of divide between preceding modernist perspectives and those influenced by postmodern sensibilities.

Though recent developments always look more complex and prolific than those of the past, it is especially hard to trace or justify narrative coordinates when the very notion of paradigms is being undercut and questioned. In these circumstances, I think, it is important to review legacies from the past and critically evaluate their relevance for the future. The present story charts surface features of recent developments; the following chapter suggests ethical and philosophical grounding. The point is not to summarize all views but to see cultural anthropology through some of its emergent edges.

The 1980s saw a range of approaches proliferate and crosscut one another in cultural anthropology. Chicago-style symbolic anthropology was increasingly expanded and questioned, both through poetic and reflexive engagements and by issues of power and history. Marxism and materialism inflected social history and developed as political economy. And the post-Marxist view of culture as hegemony began to consider cultural resistance as well as cultural domination.

One attempt to cohere and maintain a notion of structure within this fluid theoretical mix emerged in theories of practice. Prominent during the late 1970s and 1980s, theories of practice brought the individual actor back to center stage and emphasized individual agency as the fulcrum around which sociocultural life was structured. Practice theories have placed particular emphasis on how relations of domination are ensconced in actors' strategies and taken-for-granted habits. They have been associated especially with the work of Pierre Bourdieu in France and Anthony Giddens in England, and have been significantly encouraged in the United States by Sherry Ortner, among others (see chapter 4). In several respects, practice theories provide a highly innovative expression of high modernism in cultural anthropology—a creative attempt to synthesize the strengths of Weberian, Marxist, and Durkheimian perspectives into an integrated strategy for social research and theoretical analysis.

By the late 1980s, however, theories of practice, like those of political economy, were swept over—some would say sideswiped—by the postmodern influence that had finally burst into anthropology. As described above, these new approaches have combined experimentalism with critical reflexivity about ethnographic writing. What they have portended is an antiparadigm shift, and it is clear that they have been highly influential in cultural anthropology even as their excesses have attracted sustained criticism.[24]

During the 1980s, older ancestors were increasingly challenged in the light of newly discovered authors. Figures such as Antonio Gramsci, Mikhail Bakhtin, Michel Foucault, and others intruded upon Marx, Weber, and Durkheim—not to speak of Tylor, Morgan, and Boas—as paragons of ancestral allegiance in cultural anthropology (see chapters 5 and 6). Like the old ancestors, many of these new ones were European and male, and few if any of them were anthropologists. But they also have reflected an opening to alternative views and experiences of disempowerment. In the 1990s these alternative colors of perspective are increasingly read across the grain of classical Western authorship to decenter its claim on social and cultural theory.

As opposed to integrated systems or coherent units of culture or society, recent approaches emphasize culture as a site of contested representation and resistance within an inescapable field of power. Under the initial label of British cultural studies, post-Marxist themes have proliferated in American anthropology and linked up with interdisciplinary modes of inquiry such as postcolonial studies, the study of public culture, the study of diasporas, black studies, postmodern feminism, queer theory, literary criticism, media studies, and many other intellectual developments that have drawn on postmodernism but moved past it to more topically substantial or politically committed agendas.

In my own opinion, these recent developments carry special potentials and also special difficulties. One the one hand, they invigorate anthropology by casting a large and creative net of cross-disciplinary developments that are important, stimulating, and far-reaching. Cultural anthropology is being strongly and effectively moved to consider the discordant representations, displaced imaginaries, and cultural contestations of a late modern world. These are increasingly considered closer to home, in complex societies, and in public culture, as well as in arenas distant or remote on the world stage. What emerge are not just new theories and new sites of study but new genres of perspective and orientation. We see through a rainbow of perspectives, as opposed to black and shades of gray as defined through white. Anthropology is enriched by these diverse racial, ethnic, sexual, and gendered positionings.

At the same time, it is important that an emphasis on positioning not take the place of scholarly or ethnographic content. And it is important to recognize that identity on one axis of disempowerment, such as ethnicity or race, can be compromised by differences in personal experience along others, including class background. Many new orientations are inflected through humanities fields of literature, art interpretation, and philosophy, which place little emphasis on ethnographic rigor. Their primary research experience is with texts rather than emerging from fieldwork with living people. Though they are strong on interpretive nuance, creative hybridity, and aesthetic critique, many of these newer perspectives are very weak when it comes to sociopolitical, economic, or even symbolic documentation. They can be ironically distant from the lives of everyday people, even as they creatively mine sites such as the media, the museum, and the history of literature.

In cultural anthropology, the flesh-and-blood experience of participant observation—the "living with" that provides the information for "writing up"—has been central. Presently, however, interdisciplinary forces can converge to discourage rigorous field research. Heightened concern with authorial position and experimentalism undercut the importance of careful or systematic description. Documentation may indeed be dismissed as a totalizing or master narrative. And the disappearing line between research abroad and research at home can encourage a cavalier attitude about "research" at all in favor of superficial musings or light reflections. Of course, matters of textuality and representation are integral to ethnographic field research as well as to the humanities. And it remains crucial to problematize this fact. But we still need detailed accounts of people's lives; their discourses, beliefs, and aspirations; their spirituality, world views, and ethos; the details of their struggles, their interpersonal organization, their patterns of labor, possession, and consumption; the particulars of their political subordination or domination; and the individual and collective histories of their disputes and social or mythic affiliations.

Given the difficulties of empiricism in late modernity, there is little wonder that the notion of ethnographic field research is being questioned (and in some cases dispensed with) by graduate students of anthropology, particularly in the United States. In some programs, the privileged venues of field research threaten to become the library, the personal diary, and the popular media—without adequate appreciation that these important sites themselves require detailed empirical treatment. The interpretative cast on these and other textual sources is increasingly evident in journals that are highly important to cultural anthropologists from both inside and outside the discipline.[25] It does not minimize the value of these discursive sites to emphasize that rigorous ethnography remains crucial. We must continue to vigorously document and deeply analyze alternative ways of life.

In the reaction against ethnographic neglect, there now lurks the contrary danger of a retreat into neoempiricism. This danger comes equally from the experience-far descriptivism of political economy, on the one hand, and the experience-near immersion in the pain of disempowerment, on the other. Particularism has long presented difficulties as well as potentials to anthropology—dating back at least to the concern with minutiae by Boas and Tylor. Indeed, the tendency to take reactionary refuge by simply presenting more and more specifics—as if their significance were self-evident and precluded larger analysis—may be particularly great in times of theoretical turmoil. But either as an escape into history, ethnographic minutiae, aesthetics, or personal voicing, the failure of neoempiricism to provide a comprehensible theoretical context makes it ironically uncritical of its own assumptions. One can perhaps take a warning from the descriptive but ultimately meek and theoretically at-sea kind of empiricism that now lurches between macrohistory and microaccount in the once-proud Annales School of French structural history (e.g., Nora 1984–92).[26]

In my own view, detailed ethnography can productively enlarge to engage new theoretical directions in cultural anthropology. And those who too radically question or reject fieldwork will have special difficulty getting jobs, particularly within anthropology departments: Fieldwork that is superficial will exert a diminishing impact within cultural anthropology over time. The field will favor those who bring intensive ethnographic experience and detailed documentation together with new developments in representational and critical theory.

In the context of apparent fragmentation, a more general view of cultural anthropology's direction is perhaps excusable. Viewed in a larger perspective, the tension between new theory and ethnographic trench work can be seen as a continuing part of anthropology's past. In cycles of the long term, theoretical innovations have often been upbraided for neglecting the details of sociocultural life. Victorian evolutionism was so criticized by Boas; structural-functionalism was assailed by Geertz; ethnographic engagement was the hard stone against which Marxism, materialism, Lévi-Straussian structuralism, and ethnoscience were sharpened. The theoretical push that is strong and abstract at the beginning gets powerfully refined through ethnographic specifics in subsequent years. I hope and forecast the same for post-Marxist and cultural studies legacies in anthropology, along with other approaches that move beyond strictures of modernism.

In the face of present complexities, influential figures such as Clifford Geertz, Marshall Sahlins, and Eric Wolf are critical of tendencies in cultural anthropology and sometimes skeptical of its future as an academic discipline.[27] Notwithstanding the misgivings of such elders, however, the university demand for anthropology's perspectives should continue to grow. The world is getting smaller, and the purview of the humanities and social sciences is getting correspondingly larger and more international. Anthropologists' ability to engage theories of culture and action with a world of diverse lives should prove increasingly important. Anthropology is certain to expand its voices and its concept of ethnography. The most important advances are likely to come from the interface between theory, antitheory, and ethnography as seen through freshly positioned eyes. And though the university itself has been greatly

criticized, it will continue to provide an important space for critical and
sometimes creative thought and analysis—as our colleagues out of academia and from other, less wealthy countries remind us. Anthropology's
place within the university is likely to grow rather than diminish, and the
university itself is likely to remain a valuable site for producing and
contesting knowledge.

Does the future of cultural anthropology lie in new master narratives,
or is it destined to burst apart? As we confront the contested space
between modern and postmodern sentiments, it is tempting to feel we
must choose between these alternatives. But such a choice may be premature. Without prejudging whether a given theoretical line is masterful or
only pretentious, there will always be an ebb and flow between more
centripetal moments, which strive for relatively greater coherence, and
more centrifugal ones, which expand our horizons in a more diffuse and
fragmentary way. The relationship between these alternatives may not be
either/or so much as one of complementary, hermeneutic, or even dialectical moments. Whatever words are used to describe these moments of
larger and lesser coherence, neither is likely to disappear in anthropology's future. To mediate modern and postmodern sensibilities implies
both deconstruction and reconstruction. The strengths of older
approaches should not be forgotten even as our changing sensibilities
and the objectively changing conditions of a late modern world force us
to explore theoretical and ethnographic horizons that are new and important. To describe these alternatives as mutually exclusive may itself
become, in hindsight, an anachronism.

What is lacking in the present story, as in the others, is a justification
for anthropology's purpose and mission. As it engages its second professional century, anthropology is nagged by fin-de-millénaire confusion
and can appear to lack purpose. In my view, however, cultural anthropology does have greater direction. It is important to analyze larger directions and make them more explicit through frontal consideration of the
field's received suppositions, its present priorities, and its future goals.
Stories of anthropology's past provide a context for this discussion. In the
present account, an all-too-selective view of these stories is left somewhere between history and genealogy. This can be irritating; the particular strain of thought that each of us holds most dear becomes
compromised in telescopic collapse, in underattention, and in the space
between fact and interpretation. Such irritation may be intrinsic to larger

intellectual assessment in an era of late modernity. But this instigation can brighten rather than dim our appreciation of past and present orientations, including some that are regretfully underplayed here. Past paragons are worthy of reading and rereading, and the present account cannot replace this deeper engagement. Ancestors that include but are not limited to Marx, Weber, and Durkheim remain highly important; personally, I find it indispensable to teach a large corpus of their work and other classics in my courses on anthropological theory. If we do not benefit from our intellectual past—even as we criticize it and recognize it as a changing construction—it is difficult to confront our present or chart our future.

critically humanist
sensibilities

What is the goal of ethnography, and of cultural anthropology more generally? What are its justification and purpose? As anthropologists, we are all too cognizant that we cannot predict the future accurately or exert much impact on its general course of development. Our potential as activists aside, we serve primarily to detail and analyze variation among cultures in the present and the past. This role demands rather than precludes careful documentation, on the one hand, and theorization, on the other. But this also implies a wide notion of understanding—more akin to the broad German notion of systematic knowledge, of *Wissenschaft*. The type and end of knowledge, its human and pragmatic justification, are important. What is the larger purpose of the knowledge we seek?

In an era of late modernity, objectivism is best considered as a means of understanding rather than as its final end. It remains important to be as objectively accurate as possible in our portrayals, even as we realize the ultimate impossibility of this attempt. But in the realm of human experience, we cannot assume that competing perceptions and values will ultimately reconcile—that different accounts will ultimately agree on "truth" if only they are objective enough. Objectivism in the human sciences is a tool that can be used in the service of different values and different goals of understanding that do not converge, even when targeted on a common phenomenon.

The ends of objectivism cannot themselves be legitimated objectively. Indeed, it is arguably just when objectivism is assumed to be a neutral or transparent path to ultimate truth that its larger values go most unquestioned. This puts the human sciences in danger of being fulfilled as tautologies. Analysis can have the guise of an unbiased search for knowledge while in fact perpetuating unexamined cultural biases that are legitimated through the symbolic capital of Western scholarly discourse.[1] To minimize such pitfalls, the detailed empiricism and objectivist scholarship that academic discourse encourages—and demands—need to be used in relation to larger goals. These goals cannot be justified by objectivism alone.

Our mission as anthropologists is arguably to use the tools of social science to further humanistic knowledge as much as the other way around. But humanism is itself problematic in anthropology, as reflected in Clifford's (1988) castigation of it. It is no longer possible to pretend that we can approximate truths that will transform social orders through the force of our understanding. The constraints of the larger world and the unintended consequences of our actions are simply too powerful. Negative if not pernicious effects can emerge.

> If anthropologists are committed to a kind of humanism, they will not necessarily endorse it by focusing their descriptive efforts on it—the problem is that it is also the route to racism, terrorism, and ethnic violence, to purifying populations into great and lesser examples of it, to including some and excluding others. (M. Strathern 1995:170)

Even classic anthropologists such as Kroeber and Kluckhohn (1952:32) explicitly distinguished cultural relativism from the humanist notion that culture was "absolutistic" and striving toward perfection.[2]

Nonetheless, selected humanist values are often tacitly adopted by anthropologists, and for good reason, despite the rejection of any canon. The pursuit of "criticism," "scholarship," "knowledge," "understanding," "compassion," "fortitude," "judgment," "eloquence," and "activism" may sound like a crude Boy Scout credo. But who has not had a version of some of these words echo inside after reading a particularly powerful ethnography, critique, or theoretical analysis? Such tenets of humanism still tacitly inform a large part of what is good in cultural anthropology. The question is how to selectively draw on this tradition even as we move critically beyond it.

Cradled as we are in the late twentieth century, it is easy to forget that the fourteenth- and fifteenth-century humanists were vigorously resisting the conservative traditions of European feudalism and Christianity. Focusing on the abovementioned goals, they emphasized argument, correspondence, writing in vernaculars, textual criticism, the possibility of self-definition, and finding value in alternative voices—such as those of Roman and Greek antiquity—that were debunked by existing religious and political institutions. That the goals of the early humanists were later rigidified and cast as hegemonic need not undermine either an understanding or an appreciation of the way these values were originally used.

The same is true of the modern notion of culture, to pick a more current example. The notion of *Kultur* arose in the late eighteenth century in celebration of local folk traditions in regions of what is now Germany. The term was in part an expression of Germanic social and intellectual resistance against the trumpeted "civilization" of centralized nation-states such as England and France.[3] That the relativist connotations of culture later became the more rigid notion of Culture as a synonym for Civilization in Victorian anthropology does not preclude either its earlier meaning or the continuing importance of alternative understandings. From early in the twentieth century, Germanic influences made the former sense of culture widespread in American anthropology, both in intellectual content and personal style (Wolf 1964:15–19; Stocking 1968). By contrast, a less personal and more structured notion of "society" has had greater salience in modern British and French anthropologies.

As this case illustrates, the intellectual and strategic value of a term or concept is not absolute; it depends on use and historical position. The spin-offs of *Kultur* in the Germanic tradition also included Bismarckian totalism (*Kulturkampf* as the "fight for culture") and the distinction between those people who had "culture" and those who had "nature" (*Kulturvölker* versus *Naturvölker*). The tension posed by these alternative meanings was actively wrestled with by early German anthropologists such as Boas (Stocking 1968:201).[4] In England, on the other hand, the Germano-Coleridgian emphasis on a more relativized notion of "culture"—for instance, in the early work of John Stuart Mill—led nonetheless to a singular notion of cultural progress in Mill's later and much more influential work, as well as in Victorian anthropology.[5]

In the high modernism of the mid-twentieth century, with its faith in democracy and liberalism, "culture" came to mean a publicly shared symbolic system. Particularly among American anthropologists, cultures were taken to be as valid and internally coherent as they were distinctive. But this concept of culture has itself become ill-at-ease with time. Amid changing world conditions and intellectual outlooks, we can no longer justify a stationary notion of culture as a fixed entity or stable system. In late modernity, culture betokens the politics of representation in the local-cum-global marketplace. People and ideas move with increasing speed; information circuits the globe as a ubiquitous commodity; the world shrinks while its inequalities widen. In the process, the ability to assert, define, and represent human identity is increasingly negotiated and valuable—and is increasingly recognized as such. *Culture is now best seen not as an integrated entity, tied to a fixed group of people, but as a shifting and contested process of constructing collective identity.* In a contemporary world, this is as true in New Guinea as it is in New York.

This evolution of "culture" is both reflected and reinforced by the social realities of academic theorizing. Academic discourse, including that in anthropology, engages a much wider and more diverse group of speakers and listeners than it did just twenty years ago. There is a greater profusion of national, class, ethnic, racial, gendered, and sexual perspectives. Conversations and debates abound in print and other media, not to mention E-mail and the World Wide Web. The sheer number of anthropologists has grown enormously. Changing realities of political economy are also relevant. The United States no longer has the economic hegemony on a world stage that it enjoyed following World War II. As part of this shift, it has less of a lock on global symbolic or intellectual capital; alternative perspectives increasingly compete. Domestic constituencies also change. Over the past thirty years, feminism, civil rights, gay and lesbian liberation, and other activisms have actively questioned apolitical views of culture and representation. The percentage of anthropologists who are women has risen dramatically in recent decades. Demographic trends in society are also relevant; between immigration and differential rates of increase, the United States will have a population that is largely nonwhite within a few decades. It is highly important that fields such as anthropology both absorb and reflect this change. Given all these factors, it is no wonder that "culture" is so vigorously contested within anthropology as well as in the larger world.

In this contemporary context, humanism cannot simply continue its received historical perspective.[6] It is too much *hubris* to assume some objective standard of human virtue (much less "man") as the center of our universe. Information and objectivism do not guarantee progress. The humanist tradition has been particularly uncritical of Western bias in its quest for truth. As a result, humanism has easily exported and imposed Western standards in the guise of Enlightenment, upon non-Western peoples. Practically speaking, the humanist drive for assertion and control has easily reflected and reinforced domination over others.

Antihumanism, however, has its own difficulties. Its shifting perspective is initially valuable as a point of criticism, but it quickly wears thin and begs for substance. Intrinsically subject to self-deconstruction, it is ethically ungroundable. At its extremes, antihumanism may be less a war of progressive position than an ineffectual or even regressive war in which positions are only virtual. The result can be arbitrary and idiosyncratic justifications exercised through the symbolic capital of academic advancement or identity politics. It would be unfortunate to accept Heidegger's (1977a:75) antihumanist notion, following Nietzsche, that "values are the condition of itself posited by the will to power."

A more positive alternative may be found in Abu-Lughod's statement when she responds to charges that in privileging the integrity and dignity of the human subject, humanism tends to essentialize humanity and fails to comprehend cultural difference and inequality.

> Why invoke humanism when it has been so discredited in poststructural and postmodernist circles? There are certainly good reasons to be wary of this philosophy that has masked the persistence of systematic social differences by appealing to an allegedly universal individual hero and autonomous subject.... Yet because humanism continues to be in the West the language of human equality with the greatest moral force, I do not think we can abandon it. In advocating new forms of writing (pastiche, dialogue, collage, and so forth) that break up narrative and

subject identities and interfere with identification, posthumanists ask
their readers to adopt sophisticated reading strategies along with social
critique. . . . If experimental ethnographies are criticized for being solip-
sistic or hard to read, how can their theoretical, political, or human
messages get through? (Abu-Lughod 1993:28)

I recognize humanism as a local and historically specific language of the
post-Enlightenment West. Yet it is a useful language because from our
positions as anthropologists we work as Westerners (however tenuous our
identification) and we contribute to a Western discourse. Positionality
cannot be escaped. . . . That does not mean that the goals are not provi-
sionally worth pursuing or that working within Western discourse is not
crucial. (Abu-Lughod 1993:36)

Abu-Lughod pursues a "tactical humanism" that aims to be politically
useful even as it recognizes the limitations of anthropology as a discourse
located "on the side of power in a world organized unequally along lines
of cultural difference" (1993:29). She uses this perspective to introduce
powerfully nuanced stories of women's worlds in Bedouin western Egypt
(see chapter 7). How this agenda is to be pursued and justified more
generally, however, remains an open question.

Considered as a broad impetus for understanding, tactical humanism
can have alternative dimensions. One is a reflexive critique that examines
the history, politics, and strategic voicing of authorship and the voices
and texts we rely on. It now seems crucial if not axiomatic that ethnography must be critically aware of its own relationship to power and representation. If reflexive concerns take over the entire project, however, we
are left spinning our wheels; we shed the light of analysis almost exclu-
sively on texts and on ourselves rather than on the people we study with.
This is a trap Abu-Lughod herself avoids. Epistemological relativism
(which is often commendable) should not devolve into ontological relativism, in which existence itself becomes relative and attempts at systemic
analysis become meaningless. Granting a relativity of perspective should
not deter us from trying to understand the external world as clearly as we
can. To do otherwise, to paraphrase Bateson (1972:455), is not only to
mistake the map for the territory but to preclude the possibility of
mapmaking altogether.

While ultimate knowledge of others' experience or actions (or even their existence) is impossible, greater or lesser approximations of this otherness *are* possible; indeed, they provide the basis of all social living. Absolute impossibilities should not blind us to pragmatic possibilities for comprehension, translation, and representation across the intersubjective divide.

One of anthropology's key strengths is the ethnographic experience of learning about people's experiences. The possibilities for intersubjective understanding and communication are pragmatic; they continue to exist in the face of our difficulties in explaining them. In contrast to the agenda of Habermas (1981, 1984, 1987), we do not need to devise a universal paradigm for social communication and understanding; we are not seeking the philosopher's stone or attempting to be Heideggers of the ethnological world. But equally, the fact that we can't step totally inside someone else's skin should not result in paralysis of social effort. We need to reach out and understand as fully as possible across social divides. A position of partial outsidedness is valuable and even vital to communication and understanding in a dialogic world, as Bakhtin effectively emphasized.[7]

That significant communication and understanding occur has important implications. Among other things, it empowers us to temporarily bracket questions of reflexivity, to stop spinning our analytic wheels, and to take the "as if" leap of faith that presumes subjects and meanings outside ourselves. It is this latter move that makes possible substantive documentation and rigorous analysis. On the other hand, the appreciative portrayal of others' lives (not to mention others' texts) can be productively complemented by examining our own discursive assumptions. The will to truth is neither given up nor given in to, but pursued as one vital voice in a critically complemented dialogue. Such an internal dialogue is necessary because neither objectivism nor critical reflexivity is adequate by itself. The objectivism that most assumes itself to be neutral poses the ever-present danger of unselfcritical scientism. But hyperrelativism easily results in parlor games of in-house textuality—a competition for avant-garde status or symbolic capital at the expense of meaningful content. *Taken together, however, these perspectives encourage a spiraling challenge between moments that assume objectivity and those that stress perspectival relativity.* That each must be "bracketed" for the other to work is more of a logical problem than a pragmatic one. Neither is adequate without the other as complement; both sides are needed for the wheel to roll.

Critically Humanist Sensibilities
Ethics and Theoretical Grounding

Critical humanism is the self-conscious application of alternative or competing humanist perspectives to keep their respective excesses in check. A humanism that is "critical" retains the concept of humanism in a postmodern or posthumanist era by employing the term against itself. It does this by embracing competing goals that act as a check and balance against each other in alternating moments of analysis. As a result, analysis retains a progressive spirit without indulging in progressive hubris or grandiosity.

As method, critically humanist perspectives weave together the competing goals of objectivism and critical reflexivity. However, they also require deeper ethical grounding; their object and purpose need larger justification. Given our Western vantage point, what is deemed particularly valuable as anthropological knowledge, both proximately and ultimately, does not rest solely on judgments of fact, much less on unexamined assumptions. It entails judgments of cultural value concerning the ultimate goal and purpose of knowledge. Addressing this issue presumes—and reveals—one's underlying ethics.

It is increasingly evident that ethics are not just a procedural issue; they come to center stage for anthropology in matters of theory as well as method. We need to be clear that anthropology assumes an ethics. But what ethical goals can provide a check and balance for critical humanism in late modern anthropology? The legacy of antihumanism has effectively exposed our fragmentation of value, but it neither extracts a direction from this plethora nor gives us guideposts that point very far beyond a weak and compromised identity. Science or scientism, on the other hand, is posited on untenable assumptions of value-neutrality. Certainly there are no simple answers. However, some crude assertions can provide grist for debate.

My own view is that cultural anthropology should pursue two ethical purposes that have long and positive legacies in our field. One of these is **to document and valorize the richness and diversity of human ways of life.** This entails a sympathetic investigation of peoples' experiences, expressions, and actions across the intersubjective divide. Such an emphasis relates to the general value of social understanding by attempting to see the world through the lens of people different from oneself. It is reflected in observations and reports from diverse cultural backgrounds and is evident in the Western intellectual tradition at least as far back as *The Histories* of Herodotus. In the German interpretive legacy, this goal arises from a hermeneutic concern with actors' subjectivity that can be traced at least from Vico, Herder, and Dilthey to both Weber and Boas. Despite the vagaries of historical abuse,[8] documentary valorization of social and cultural diversity has been a strong and important theme in anthropology, particularly against available alternatives. It is simple but still important to assert the passion and rigor of anthropology's desire to understand and appreciate alternative ways of thinking and acting. Recent approaches that emphasize reflexivity ultimately do not depart from this tradition. Rather, they self-direct it.

The relativist side of a critically inflected humanism considers others not just in abstraction or in histories, but as living peoples whose knowledge, imagery, and experience enrich and question our own. Here again, it is self-evident that ethnography is crucial. Ethnography has long had— and should continue to have, in my opinion—a strong side of sympathetic understanding. This no longer implies an Enlightenment desire to expose a single path through human diversity to moral or technical improvement, but rather the late modern or Foucauldian desire to illuminate a diversity of potential alternatives to choose from. This is not the essentializing of foreignness as a static "thing out there"—a token of our own search for definition against dark or radical Otherness. It is rather a desire to promote rich understanding of differences across intersubjective borders. Reflexively speaking, this means facilitating diverse voices and perspectives within anthropology itself, including those of different class, racial, national, gendered, religious, and sexual backgrounds.

Documentary appreciation of cultural diversity is configured against an implicit assumption: that fundamental features of humanity are shared and can be understood. This theme also has a deep and important resonance in anthropology's history and its precursors. The presumption that human diversity can be appreciated and valued gains force from the notion that some degree of identification and understanding are possible across the full range of human differences. Though it is highly questionable whether all humans are completely equal, and though it is doubtful whether interpersonal understanding could ever approach completeness, it is important to the appreciative comprehension of cultural diversity that we are all equally human. There is no assumption here about universal meanings or shared motivations. Taking cultural diversity seriously means embracing rather than suppressing a diversity of understandings, voices, and assumptions. Conversely, the goal is not a "butterfly collecting" style of gathering information from different cultures but the discernment of patterns and themes that make this diversity meaningful.

A second, complementary goal is to **expose, analyze, and critique human inequality and domination.** Interest in this issue is undoubtedly as old as patterns of unequal power and privilege in human relationships. In contemporary academic terms, this means being rigorous in investigating and exposing how subordination and disempowerment are perpetrated by means of sex and gender, age, race, ethnicity, nationality, religion, socioeconomic class or caste, and other recognized and as yet unrecognized features. This endeavor requires attention to the epistemic as well as the social and material dimensions of inequality—how power is instantiated and perpetuated by different forms of knowledge, discourse, and representation. Reciprocally, it entails documenting and analyzing the paths of subversion that counter or resist inequality.

The exposure and analysis of inequality require an honest and sometimes painful analysis of how dimensions of resistance impede as well as facilitate each other. Particularly in a postcolonial world, it is myopic to assume that axes of resistance, much less those of power, naturally line up. It is in just this respect, again, that concrete and empirically dedicated ethnography remains important. Under exactly what conditions do given dimensions of inequality resonate with or counteract one another? Under what circumstances does resistance counter some forms of inequality only to reinforce others? How are these patterns reproduced and how do they change? An emerging generation of newly dedicated field research is key to addressing these questions in late modern contexts.

It is important that the critique of inequality not be limited to some version of identity politics, even as this development has been highly important in its own right, as implied earlier and as discussed at length in chapter 8. Amid the legitimate and, indeed, crucial concern to explore diverse forms of inequality, we should not make essentializing assumptions about an author's or speaker's identity. In the context of current post-Marxist sensibilities, it is especially easy to underplay the differences of class and wealth that continue to inflect inequality within as well as between racial or subaltern ethnic groups, genders, and those of alternative sexual orientations. Encouraging a diversity of voices is crucial but does not *by itself* ensure a diversity of trenchant scholarship concerning inequality.

At various stages of anthropology's history, it has been tempting to use different theoretical models for different forms of inequality—class inequality, gendered inequality, racial inequality, nationalist inequality, epistemic inequality, and so on. But it is now almost a truism that inequalities intertwine theoretically as well as on the ground. A conceptual emphasis on one dimension of inequity—previously social but now epistemic, previously class but now race, sex, or gender—does not imply that the others are less important. In the symbolic capital of the academic marketplace, "inequality" is not a limited good to be fought over by competing intellectual interests or alternative brands of personal affiliation. In the realm of inequality, as in the realm of culture, there are plenty of places available. It is time to document the empirical relationship between these places with greater scholarship and passion, and with greater nuance for their interconnection. Scrutinizing these relationships empirically, rather than a priori, serves as check against too rigid a definition of inequality at the outset—or too romantic a definition of resistance. If basic ideas help make sense of tangible circumstances, they can have pragmatic utility even as a conceptual fuzzy set.[9]

Complementary Moments

These twin objectives—to document and valorize cultural diversity, and to expose and critique inequality—are among anthropology's strongest assets. Both endure in much current ethnography and theory. But they are also opposed to each other. Are cultural formulations "genuine," rich, and deserving of empathic analysis from the inside? Or are they ideological masks that justify inequalities—inequalities that can never be adequately exposed from within the logic of indigenous cultural reasoning?

In epistemic critique, human diversity and human inequality are two sides of the same coin: our Western projection of differences onto others. But it is a mistake to think that these differences emanate only from ourselves or that the attempt to understand them must be fruitless. In a critically humanist perspective, this attempt entails outward-looking as well as inward-looking moments. It also entails complementary valuation of different kinds of difference. Cultural diversity in general should be valorized; it implies equivalence across divergence in social and representational space. Those differences grounded in inequality, however, should be critiqued as disempowering; they connote domination by hierarchy, rank, or power. A critically humanist perspective places positive value on cultural diversity in general while placing negative value by way of critique on differences most grounded in inequality and domination.

On the empirical ground, these moments of valorization and critique have opposite excesses. Overfocusing on cultural diversity leads to endless relativity; cultural relativism can lead to an infinite regress of differences, each of which is only considered in and of itself. The same difficulty applies reflexively. The goal of including a limitless number of voices in our discourse produces cacophony rather than conversation. It can also lead to blind empathy or uncritical sympathy, particularly when romanticism makes us excuse forms of domination in other societies or in other speakers that we would vehemently oppose among ourselves. Against this, exposing inequalities of gender, race, ethnicity, and socioeconomic status in other social groups can sensitize us to analogous or alternative patterns of inequality closer to home; it defamiliarizes and deromanticizes that which is taken for granted.

Critiques of inequality, on the other hand, have their own excesses. They universalize notions of domination and resistance and assume the will to power as a constant across cases. They can also be restrictive in privileging discourses based on disempowerment and omitting those based on other kinds of argument or conversation. It seems inadequate to read culture relentlessly as a mask of deception over a core of inequality. This reduces culture to mere ideology and dehumanizes our subjects of study, as well as ourselves. And it makes the assessment and manipulation of power relations the only concern in our own practice of academic politics. While power and domination are important causes of action, they are not its only cause. To assume otherwise is to impose a single standard and universal motive. Domination and inequality demand consideration because they are common and socially important, not because they always determine thought or action in the final analysis. We cannot assume that our own positioned understandings of power or interest, however sophisticated they may be, are universal prime movers.

In practical terms, then, the delineation of human diversity and the exposure of inequality work at cross-purposes. Much ink at the heart of contemporary anthropology has been spent in the failure to admit this intractable opposition. If cultural relativism and the critique of inequality are good bedfellows in cultural anthropology—as I think they are—it is because they are complements and not because they are consistent; they form the necessary "outsidedness" for each other (cf. Bakhtin 1986b:110). This antinomy is often blurred by our own need to create consistency. But lack of consistency is a problem only if one takes a rationalist position. From a more hermeneutic perspective, appreciations of cultural diversity and critiques of inequality provide checks and balances on each other in alternative moments of research and analysis. As reciprocating dimensions, they invigorate and challenge each other.

It would be presumptuous if not fruitless to specify exactly how and when one of these moments should articulate with the other. The larger point is that there is tremendous value in maintaining them in reciprocal tension. They point to the strengths of cultural relativism and to the critique of disempowerment. When analysis becomes too relative or too absolutely critical, a complementary emphasis can provide balance without sacrificing larger direction or continuity. Amid winds of change, one continues to move ahead by tacking strategically from one edge of productive movement to another.

As against grand narratives, critically humanist sensibilities are not intended as a recipe or a means of policing approaches. They supply complementary poles of orientation and guidance that are useful to think with, especially when one becomes empirically entangled or theoretically uncertain. As noted above, uncertainty has become an increasing problem in anthropology in recent years. In this context, larger goals can provide general grounding and orientation even though their application is pragmatic depending on the case at hand and on analytic and personal circumstances. The goal is to stimulate productive possibilities rather than mandate specifics. Given the large issues raised by critically humanist sensibilities—including the relationship between ethics and objectivism in fields such as anthropology—it would be shortsighted to forward an easy path or precise procedures. But it does seem time to reassert basic and important values. The remainder of this book engages these complementary values with prominent trends in contemporary cultural anthropology.

The appreciation of human diversity and the critique of inequality are prior evaluations of what is important in cultural anthropology. As Weber would put it, they are judgments of value. They stem from our own Western assessment of differences across a shared humanity. And they place special value on diversity and special stigma upon inequality. As such, critically humanist perspectives in anthropology are subject to criticism as a Western or neo-Western enterprise. Their goal is to use the language and the more progressive edges of this tradition to push against the envelope of its own excesses and constraints (cf. Todorov 1993). In so doing, fields such as cultural anthropology can continue to draw deeply upon as well as to criticize Western intellectual traditions.

By contrast, other anthropologies drawing on other cultural or historical legacies could have other moral orientations or make alternative point-of-departure assumptions. It may be queried from many alternative cultural traditions whether inequality in general deserves to be critiqued. Within anthropology itself, there has arguably been more acceptance of inequality in the classic traditions of British and French anthropology than in the more democratic (if not anarchistic) sentiments prevalent in American cultural anthropology. Certain forms of inequality and asymmetric influence, such as that exerted by parents on children, seem to be indispensable (even as they can have their own excesses). Conversely, whether cultural diversity should be valued—as opposed to being criticized for fragmenting national or other identities—remains a hotly contested issue. Even within anthropology, goals that amplify or redirect those suggested above could be posited: the search for explanatory truth (objectivist anthropology), the alleviation of physical suffering (medical anthropology), or the solution of human problems (applied anthropology).[10]

Evaluating these alternative goals is certainly an important field of exploration. Indeed, my own formulation is made explicit in part as a critical target—to facilitate debate and discussion over the underlying values that should inform our theoretical suppositions in the future of anthropology.

It is from the vantage point of cultural anthropology in late modernity— at the crossroads between its modernist legacy and its newer possibilities—that I find the twin goals of engaging human diversity and exposing human inequality particularly important. I fully admit that these values house an Americanist bias, as does the focus on "cultural" as opposed to "social" or other forms of anthropology. To me, however, the valorization of human diversity and the critique of inequality are defensible on moral grounds as well as being prominent in the largest and fastest-growing branches of the field. They challenge each other productively to achieve new levels of insight. Simultaneously, they provide a control on each other that helps forestall tunnel vision, myopia, or monologue. Intellectually, each has a rich and valuable tradition that extends in and out of anthropology and through different genres of ethnographic experience and writing. As such, valorization of human diversity and critique of inequality afford wellsprings of information and historical inspiration and are particularly relevant to our contemporary world; they provide an initial and basic justification for cultural anthropology in late modernity.

Critically humanist sensibilities dispense with the illusion of objective truth value while retaining a continued direction for cultural anthropology that includes rigorous empiricism and a commitment to objectivism as a tool of analysis. They do not give up on the reality and the knowability of an external world even as they recognize that the lens of perception and even the definition of what constitutes an objective entity is culturally and historically mediated; these are highly variable across time and space. The tension between subjectivism and objectivism is neither transcended nor given up but admitted and continually wrestled with.

Given this perspective, however, a prominent traditional goal of anthropology—the objectivist "explanation" of sociocultural forms—needs to be contextualized. Though the attempt to explain or account for ethnographic data by using higher-order generalizations remains absolutely indispensable, it does not float in a valueless vacuum. Without some guidance with respect to larger values or some other pragmatic groundings, authors are licensed to spin rarefied personal aesthetics, on the one hand, or to proliferate "facts" and "hypotheses" that perpetuate unexamined biases, on the other. By themselves, objectivism or aestheticism can weave their own justification as tokens of scholarly capital in academic discourse—to what larger end? Critically humanist sensibilities derive impetus from their ethics as well as from their objectivism.

A comparison between critical humanism and received grand theories, including those bequeathed from Marx, Durkheim, and Weber, is appropriate here. All of these authors had a strong commitment to analyzing the consequences of modernity. And part of this commitment included an exposé of modernity's ills—for instance, the social anomie identified by Durkheim, the iron cage of capitalist bureaucracy considered by Weber, and the alienation and impoverishment of wage workers considered by Marx. Each also cultivated a significant interest in diverse societies, including Durkheim's studies of non-Western classification systems, and especially those of Australian Aboriginal religion (Durkheim and Mauss 1963; Durkheim 1965); Weber's studies of the sociology and subjectivity of major world religions (1978a); and Marx's researches into the diversity and precapitalist progression of economic formations (Marx 1965; Engels 1972; Krader 1972). Each took a different stance toward the critique of inequality and the significance of cultural diversity—and they disagreed with each other implicitly if not explicitly.[11] But part of their continuing importance in anthropology is the way that concerns about human diversity and inequality articulate with the immense erudition, scholarship, and analytic acumen of each of these thinkers.

Of course, Weber and Durkheim in particular attempted to ground their theories in assumptions of valueless objectivism. This seems less defensible in the present era, in which objectivity and humanism are intrinsically problematic. As cultural anthropology confronts the contestations of a late modern world, the exploration of diversity and the critique of inequality reflect contemporary dynamics and provide purpose for understanding them.

Particularly in late modernity, shared assumptions about the appropriate goals of research are more contested and more difficult to sort out than ever. In this context, some acknowledgment of larger purpose, even if diffuse, may be appropriate. Goals that are broad rather than restrictive can encourage discussion across an array of alternative perspectives. Of course, terms such as "inequality" or "cultural diversity" can be easily deconstructed, if not destroyed. The same is true of the proposed virtues that have underlain humanism. But in our present cultural context, we make practical choices about what values to draw upon. If these remain implicit and unexamined, they are much more difficult to question or transform. Just as criticism is indispensable, so too it is important to be explicit and pragmatic about the values of our anthropological past that we like in our present and want to expand in our future.

Appreciative understanding of cultural diversity widens our horizons and awareness of humanity, questions the limitations of received experience, and illustrates the viability of alternative possibilities. Our fascination and wonder at the range of human variety are encouraged. Understanding this diversity remains a key means of combating ethnocentrism. In the process, the taken-for-granted assumptions of our own social and cultural traditions can be productively challenged.

The exposure and analysis of inequality, on the other hand, gain purchase on subordinations that have benefited a few but increased the level of human misery, pain, and suffering for many others. This opens for critique the success story of our own cultural history, including patterns of colonization and ostensible modernization. It illustrates how human freedoms are compromised by coercion, constraint, and various forms of domination. It opens a consideration of how and through what means inequalities are combated, and it illustrates the complexities and legacies of resistance.

These are well-trodden ideas. Indeed, it may seem almost an embarrassment to state them so starkly in a scholarly forum; they are more comfortably enunciated as basic fodder for students. Yet why this uneasiness over the assumptions that inform our own habits? Why can't openness about core beliefs be a more frequent aspect or tactic in anthropology? Theory and method can be linked to ethics rather than divorced from them. Despite the criticisms and limitations that academics are heir to, I believe it is still important to cultivate the role of the engaged intellectual, both as scholar and as teacher. This entails judgment and honesty about values that need not be less important for being basic.

Double Sides of Method

> It is a peculiar sensation, this double-consciousness, this sense of always looking at one's self through the eyes of others, of measuring one's soul by the tape of a world that looks on in amused contempt and pity. (DuBois 1993:179)

W. E. B. DuBois's early and brilliant understanding of double consciousness poses special demands and possibilities for critically humanist sensibilities. As method, double consciousness provides an important link between the valorization of cultural diversity and the critique of inequality. As Gilroy (1993) has richly emphasized in the context of the African diaspora, double consciousness confronts the relationship between the social inside and outside through the lens of disempowerment. In the process, it provides special awareness and creativity for countervoicing. The cultivation of double consciousness is a productive way to combine a rich appreciation of subjective diversity with a powerful critique of social inequality.

At least on the surface, such awareness poses a special challenge for cultural anthropology, given its encapsulation "on the side of power in a world organized unequally" (Abu-Lughod 1993:29). But cultural anthropologists have long moved inside, outside, and between cultural identities, at least on a temporary basis. While double consciousness may be difficult to develop from a position of relative power, this is by no means impossible. On a gut level, many fieldworkers have felt the pity or condescension of others as they enter the field—and then again as they return to the strangeness that is supposed to be their own society. Indeed, the reflexive cultivation of consciousness from alternative sides of a cultural divide is all the *more* important when one begins the intersubjective journey from the privileged side of the looking glass.

The resulting connection among theory, method, and ethics can be illustrated in permutations on the ethnographic ebb and flow between "living with" and "writing up." In cultural anthropology, the ethnographer has often striven for social immersion through the participant observation of fieldwork.[12] Empathic understanding typically develops as one lives with others during extended field research, even if this is often difficult and stressful. Appreciating alternative ways of life through shared experience has been one of cultural anthropology's great strengths and enduring contributions. In a late modern era, this intercultural immersion remains as important as it is demanding. By contrast, it is most difficult to constitute the richness of other peoples' lives from a textual distance. This problem of determining from afar intensifies as the analysis assumes universal motives of epistemic hegemony, political-economic inequality, or material determinism.

On the other hand, the emotional distance of leaving the field, if only temporarily, is also important; it provides the impetus for broader and more critical understanding. Though this detachment compromises or effaces the social immersion of the field situation, it also provides an important lengthening of focal distance. This reflective interval encourages analytic comprehension. The strangeness and liminality of reentering one's own culture can increase the drive to comprehend and translate experiences that one has left behind. The professional demands on fieldworkers to write up and publish dovetail with this impetus. This broadening of perspective can also facilitate greater understanding of power inequalities that may have been felt or recorded but not so trenchantly analyzed in the field. These include not just gross forms of inequality that are easy to spot and criticize, but the more nuanced and often crosscutting and conflicting inequalities that one comes to accept in the field once the initial period of newness has worn off. These include larger power relations that provide the taken-for-granted context of fieldwork but which may not be easy to study directly in the field—for instance, the structural inequalities bequeathed by states, classes, ethnic groups, or anthropology itself. These can be analyzed outside the field setting even as they may remain refractory in the daily consciousness of the people one has been living with. As Bourgois notes in his ethnography of crack dealers in Spanish Harlem,

> Engulfed in an overwhelming whirlpool of personal suffering, it is often difficult for ethnographers to see the larger relationships structuring the jumble of human interaction around them. Structures of power and history cannot be touched or talked to. Empirically this makes it difficult to identify the urgent political economy relationships shaping everyday survival. (Bourgois 1995a:140; cf. 1995b)

As Bourgois and many others have emphasized, the analytic distance of a larger perspective on power and history is particularly important in this regard.

As they interact over time, moments of cultural appreciation and those that critique inequality challenge each other to deeper levels of understanding. This occurs progressively as ethnography is lived, written up, and reengaged in new projects.

IF THE PRESENT ACCOUNT HAS SKETCHED ONE SCENARIO OF RATHER traditional fieldwork, it is all the more important to mention other possibilities closer to DuBois's original insight. We need not presume an "outside" researcher who cultivates double consciousness by climbing partway inside a foreign way of life only to climb out again. Such an exclusive focus closes off indigenous voices who increasingly author their own accounts. *From a critically humanist perspective, insider authorship is neither a threat nor a replacement for "traditional" ethnography; rather, it is an extremely important complement.* The productive tension between immersion and detachment, as between experience and analysis, is not thrown aside. It becomes relevant in a newly important key.

If the challenge for the "outsider" anthropologist is often to gain experience-near understanding, the challenge for the "insider" anthropologist is often to complement the power of lived understanding with the analytic strength of experience-far comprehension. For those steeped in subaltern experience, analytic and scholarly distance can provide an invaluable context for broader understanding. This easily includes both the comparative study of inequality and the appreciative understanding of cultural diversity outside one's primary affiliation. These broader understandings promote deeper awareness of how culture and inequity are inflected by different histories and different identities.

Diverse cultural voices should be encouraged to speak for themselves, academically as well as otherwise. But it is equally obvious that experience unmitigated in its intensity or its pain can be blinding. Analytic distance provides balance to social immersion; reflection and analysis gain purchase on experience. As the Chicago Cultural Studies Group (1992) reminds us, the university remains an important space for this reflection.

Experience-near and experience-far moments are integral to critically humanist sensibilities in anthropology, including across the artificial boundary that need not divide insider from outsider ethnographers. Indeed, the distinction between insiders and outsiders can productively crack if not crumble as field research develops into long-term commitment or resonates with earlier cross-cultural experiences. The kind of "halfie" anthropology described by Abu-Lughod (1991) and the associated "enactment of hybridity" suggested by Narayan (1993) point beyond divisive or exclusionary oppositions in anthropological fieldwork. As opposed to this separation, ethnography grows through bicultural learning and socialization. These possibilities underscore the value and benefit of multiple awarenesses in intercultural understanding. Given the acceleration of demographic and intellectual crosscurrents on a shrinking globe, these trends should exert increasing force as well as welcome effects in fields such as cultural anthropology. Anthropology's method and theory should broaden to foster these trends at the heart of the discipline, even as they do not thereby soften the expectation of scholarly empiricism or sophisticated theory.

Broadly cast, critically humanist sensibilities grapple with long-standing dualities in the social sciences and humanities—between subjectivity and objectivity, diversity and similarity, insider and outsider, and experience and theory. As opposed to rigid or restrictive methods, they emphasize pragmatic engagement with these issues—a struggle of complementary position rather than a Hegelian drive to divide problems only to conquer them through synthesis and resolution. In both outsider and insider ethnography, culture and life can provide a double consciousness informed by complementary goals that have ethical as well as intellectual value: the appreciation of human diversity and the critique of inequality. By means of these values, a critically humanist perspective struggles to maintain objectivism as a rigorous and progressive tool rather than being subsumed into its rational hegemony. The remainder of this book uses this perspective to engage a range of recent theoretical perspectives and associated ethnographic concerns.

pushing anthropology past the posts

Critical Notes on Cultural Anthropology and Cultural Studies as Influenced by Postmodernism and Existentialism

From a critically humanist perspective, the potentials of postmodernism must be considered in light of the ethical and political problems they pose for fields such as cultural anthropology. Though they place great value on relativity and a diversity of perspectives, postmodern sensibilities provide little real basis for the exposure and critique of inequality. Nor do they encourage the moments of objectivity that are crucial to penetrate discursive inequities, much less social and material ones.

Certainly, the representational crisis in anthropology has had many salutary results.[1] It is important to open new spaces for creative representation and practice, to question received objectivities, and to empower voices from the margins of discourse. Having been brought to light, the relationship between representation and discursive power informs many important developments. Even if one wanted to, these developments could not be put back into Pandora's box. Their critique revaluates myopically progressivist Western agendas. Though long questioned by

Nietzsche and others, these agendas have been ensconced in Western intellectual traditions since at least the onset of modernism, if not since the Enlightenment. Epistemic ruptures may not be as neat as the early Foucault would have it, but the approaching millennium clearly finds us in a critique of modernity that cannot be ignored.

In this climate, however, newer experimental strategies now carry their own risks. An ironically uncritical habitus informs many of the otherwise interesting developments in reflexive and experimental anthropology. These problems are illustrated in many of the contributions published in the journal *Cultural Anthropology* from its inception in 1986 until the early 1990s. The rules of this unspoken game have been infused with textualism—a privileging of literary self-consciousness and tropistic creativity over sustained analysis. Concern with representation and self-representation, though important, is not frequently enough complemented by a detailed portrayal of social action. One also finds a surprising ahistoricism. Instead, pastiche and juxtaposition imply that history and scholarship can be neglected in favor of ironic flair. It is perhaps for this reason that the new habitus shies away from authorial declaration, explicit program, or systemic exposition in favor of veiled authorship, indirection, and irony.

These tendencies have been absorbed from larger trends in postmodern thought. The exact nature of these connections, however, is often refractory to awareness: indirection, textualism, and fragmentation protect themselves against explicit awareness of their own intellectual history. Most anthropologists who were influenced by postmodernism now see themselves as having expanded beyond it, and few are concerned with the strains of existential philosophy that predisposed it. Histories of postmodernism are being published.[2] The question, as Michael Rosenthal put it in *The Socialist Review*, is now "What *Was* Postmodernism?" (Rosenthal 1992). Yet ethnographic indirection, disclaimers, and shiftiness reflect philosophical and ethical problems that are more persistent for not having been more directly confronted.[3]

These problems are thrown into relief by the many positive developments in cultural anthropology that selectively combine the insights of postmodernism and literary criticism with sustained social, historical, and symbolic analysis. The legacies of 1970s interests in political economy, feminist theory, history, and symbolic anthropology now meld creatively with awareness of Gramscian hegemonies, Bourdieuian practices, Foucauldian genealogies, and Bakhtinian dialogics. Received categories of social and cultural study have been effectively transformed by awareness of strategic fields, wars of position, and discursive resistances. Ethnographies have been energized by these interconnecting strands.[4] Postmodern insights have been productively appropriated in this mix, as illustrated, for instance, in the reflexive exposition of gender and power so impressively crafted by authors such as Lavie (1990), Abu-Lughod (1986, 1990b), Tsing (1993), and others.

The point is that many other potentials waiting at the gate in cultural anthropology—concerning discourse, memory, affect, economism, labor, governmentality, colonialism/postcolonialism, and so on—are kept from moving further and faster "past the post" by lingering shackles of textualism and excessive reflexivity bequeathed from postmodernism and existentialism. The empirical strengths of anthropology are yet to be fully engaged. Having blown holes in old approaches and opened up new spaces, many of those most instrumental in initiating the reflexive turn in cultural anthropology seem preoccupied with surfaces, veneers, and adjudicating innovations in textual form.

Postmodernity

For the comparative study of political economy and culture, it is important to distinguish postmodern*ism* as a genre of refractory expression from postmodern*ity* as a socioeconomic and cultural trend. Postmodernity in the latter sense is linked to the time-space compression of late capitalism that informs large-scale changes in Western societies and cultures (Harvey 1990, cf. 1982; Jameson 1991; Berman 1982; Lash and Urry 1987; Mandel 1975; Bell 1978). These include:

- the enormous growth of service industries; the relative decline of factory industrialism; the relative shift from an industrial economy to an economy based on electronic and mass media
- the increase of information, information flow, and the speed of communication and movement across social and geographic boundaries
- the relative shift from the production of commodities to the production of signs—from the production of "use value" to the production of consumption

- time-space compression; heightened experiential dislocation
- the organizational shift from Fordist centralization to flexible accumulation
- the collapse of large-scale Communist and socialist regimes; an
  increasing disillusionment with grand visions of modern Western
  liberal democracy; the decentralization of political capital

The growth of mass mediated consumerism and the shrinking of the
global marketplace are social and economic trends of late capitalism.
These resonate with an increasing pastiche of identity in both popular
culture and the halls of academic theory and writing (Bauman 1988).

As an intellectual fact, postmodernism caught on; for several years,
new books on the subject were entering university libraries on an almost
weekly basis. However, the concrete ethnography of postmodernity
remains in its infancy (e.g., Rouse 1991; Gupta and Ferguson 1992;
Fischer and Abedi 1990). This ethnography is particularly important since
the global influence of Western postmodernity is certainly as variable and
uneven as it is diffuse. The degree and type of engagement with late
modern developments are as diverse across the world as they were when
regions were first responding to capitalist expansion. One contemporary
reflection of this diversity is the creative proliferation of public cultures
and national mass medias (Appadurai 1990; Spitulnik 1993; Foster 1991).

Ironically, the influence of postmodernism as a disjointed, reflexive
genre of writing hurts as much as helps our ethnographic understanding
of these changes. It is here, by contrast, that political economy and careful documentation of experience in the lived present become particularly
important. While the postmodern author dissolves in semiotic apotheosis, the social and political dimensions of late capitalism continue (Dirlik
1994). People continue to create meaning in their lives, even in the most
postindustrial contexts (Gilroy 1987; Willis 1977; Hebdige 1988). As the
reflexive turn has emphasized, this process engages disempowered voices,
whose partiality and disorder have long decentered discursive hegemonies. But this pattern underscores rather than diminishes the need for
human substance (see Chakrabarty 1992). How do people assert meaning? When and how does resistance occur, not just discursively but
socially and institutionally? What larger patterns emerge from postcolonial conditions—not just ours but theirs? A critically humanist perspective on postmodernity is aptly positioned to engage these questions.

"Postmodernism"

The postmodern impetus as refracted to ethnographic writing from literary criticism, philosophy, and other humanities fields was diffuse and influential during the late 1980s. Major exemplars in cultural anthropology include work by Clifford and Marcus (1986), Clifford (1988), Marcus and Fischer (1986), Taussig (1987, 1992, 1993), Boon (1990), Strathern (1988, 1991, 1992), Tyler (1990), and Steedly (1993); cf. Coombe (1991). Now in the mid–1990s, postmodern influence has diffused and is far from dead. It has been selectively drawn upon to inform post-Marxist, post-cultural, and postmodern feminist developments. As well as relating complexly to a number of other "posts" (poststructural, posthistorical, posttheoretical, and so on), this transdisciplinary groundswell has influenced the work of many anthropologists who initially opposed it. Postmodern inflections have exerted major influence on the proliferation of cultural studies, postcolonial studies, critical pedagogy, and multiculturalism (see Grossberg et al. 1992; During 1993; Ashcroft et al. 1995; Williams and Chrisman 1994; Chambers and Curti 1996; Shohat and Stam 1994; Giroux 1992; Kanpol and McLaren 1995; Trend 1996). All these developments underscore rather than undercut the dispersing legacy that postmodernism has had in the humanities, arts, and some of the social sciences. They also indicate the importance of considering its larger historical and intellectual context.

Despite much discussion, the philosophical underpinnings and critical implications of postmodernism have been only lightly touched upon by most anthropologists (contrast Habermas 1981; Huyssen 1986; cf. Rorty 1980). Since those most sympathetic to the postmodern impetus have been openly suspicious of voices that are declarative, much less programmatic, it is unsurprising that they themselves have not been trenchant in specifying postmodern suppositions. They *do* it rather than describe it. By contrast, postmodern trends have been more effectively characterized by secondary commentators, especially those more strongly influenced by Marxist traditions, such as David Harvey (1990), Fredric Jameson (1991), Mark Poster (1990), Linda Hutcheon (1989), Mike Featherstone (1991), and the early rather than the later Lyotard (1984; cf. 1988). The same tendency is found in anthropology, as illuminated obliquely by Pool (1991). It is therefore to be expected that few of the anthropologists who have pursued threads of postmodernism explicitly delineate its influence in their work. This indirection combines with an increasing sense that the postmodern as an "ism" is passé and has declining symbolic capital in the academic marketplace (e.g., Fox 1991). In the process, however, the continuing legacy of postmodern diffusions is underacknowledged and underanalyzed.

Postmodern perspectives have been valuable in forcing us to grapple with a jarring juxtaposition of genres, voices, and identities (see fig. 1).

Figure 1

POSTMODERNISM	is to AS:	MODERNISM
pastiche, codes	are to	coherence, style
subjectivities	are to	authority
fragment, appearance	is to	monad, essence
reflexivity/signifier	is to	referentiality/signified
change, contingency	is to	progress, determinacy
space/simultaneity/flatness	is to	time/historicity/depth
defamiliarized, unmoved	is to	familiar, romantic
voices	are to	narratives
polytropes		master tropes
posttheory	is to	grand theory
mimesis, simulacrity	is to	originality, authenticity
evocation, intertextuality	is to	representation, interpretation
dialogue, polyvocality	is to	monologue, monovocality
ellipsis, duplicity	is to	assertion, declaration
indirection, dissensus	is to	direction, consensus
detachment, facelessness	is to	passion, "face"
panic/schizophrenia	is to	angst/alienation
information, bytes	is to	wisdom, knowledge
nihilism, cynicism	is to	liberalism, faith
mass communication	is to	intelligentsia
pop culture		high culture
Las Vegas		the Louvre
postcolonialism, diaspora	is to	colonialism, nationalism
postindustrial capitalism	is to	industrial capitalism
electronic media		factories
consumption		production

The ironies of intertextual pastiche expose the crisis of objective representation by highlighting the relativity of perspectives, the impossibility of grand theory, and the absurdity of searching for ultimate meanings, explanations, or master narratives. These patterns are illuminated by the contrastive and intrinsically relational status that postmodernism has to modernism.[5] Against the modernist notion that human development and academic study march toward greater wisdom, objective knowledge, and progress, the postmodern impetus relativizes knowledge as information and mocks the attempt of high culture or grand theory to imbue experience with transpersonal meaning or historical depth. In significant respects, postmodern voices have not provided documentation or analysis of the postmodern condition so much as providing a reflection of it. Postmodernism has been more a *symptom* of postmodernity than a way of comprehending or analyzing it.

In the 1990s, with the passing of postmodernism per se, there is growing interest in its phenomenological, hermeneutic, and existentialist antecedents. As presaged by the genealogical work of Foucault (e.g., 1984), there has for several years been great interest in Nietzsche, who anticipated the end of modernism over a century ago. There is also renewed scholarly interest in the work of Martin Heidegger. The critique of Heidegger's work by Derrida formed an important basis for the deconstruction that subsequently energized the postmodern turn. In addition, the later Heidegger's (1977a) critique of modernist technology and its relationship to Being articulates with anthropologists' interest in the changing nature of human "existence" across more and less capitalized contexts. The recent work of Gregory Smith (1996), among others, reflects an increasing sense that "Nietzsche and Heidegger are the primary philosophical progenitors of contemporary postmodernism" (1996:281). In fact, however, Nietzsche, Heidegger, Foucault, and other authors currently of major interest, such as Walter Benjamin, tend now to be engaged not so much as an intellectual field of Western influence but rather (and rather ironically) as individual geniuses who transcend time and space.

To take this trend on its own terms, a few well-known authors can be taken as figureheads to reveal common underlying difficulties in their starkest form. They can then be viewed together as a larger intellectual field. Ideal types acknowledged, I make no assumption that Baudrillard stands metonymically for the many different stands of postmodernism, that Heidegger could stand for the various antihumanist, much less the

humanist, varieties of existentialism, or that Nietzsche was the ultimate
master who encompassed the link between postmodernism and existentialism. The intent, rather, is that a bright critical light reflected off a few
important sources will illuminate a larger historical trend. Certainly there
are different and less critical ways of reading these authors than those I
present below, including readings that unearth more socially progressive
tracks. What informs my critique, however, is the way these authors are
now typically invoked and used in contemporary academic argument, as
if their ethical baggage can be forgotten amid their big-man brilliance. A
counterbalance is appropriate against recent trends that are less critical of
our intellectual heritage than they purport to be.

I admit and indeed emphasize that the reflexive side of cultural
anthropology and cultural studies is less directly implicated by this
critique. These fields do not manifest postmodern and existentialist difficulties so directly, even though they are secondarily affected by indirect
writing, antitheory, and excessive irony. This is symptomatic of ethical
problems that are ostensibly being exposed but which are in significant
ways being reinstated.

Postmodernism and Existentialism

Great differences separate postmodernism and its preceding existential
orientations. Trajectories of intellectual influence that cross this divide,
such as Heidegger-Derrida-Lyotard, entail opposition and rejection as
much as adoption. And yet such linkages share common assumptions
about social life and agency that are difficult for cultural anthropology.

Postmodernism and existentialism have both questioned the ultimate
meaning of existence and our ability as thinkers and writers to comprehend ourselves, much less others. In both these perspectives, being
human is an ambivalent state, one fraught with doubt and panic. In the
modernist tradition (e.g., for existentialism), this despair is the angst and
depression of facing our own isolation, finitude, and death. In postmodernity, the problem of meaningful being becomes the panic and
schizophrenia at being swallowed up by a promiscuity of sign images and
simulations. These define our existence as devoid of purpose: a shadow
with no substance, a reflection with no authenticity.

Second, existentialism and postmodernism have both tended to be
ahistorical if not antihistorical. Living proceeds in the moment, not as the

realization of the past but as a series of fragments willed in the present. Both have emphasized choice—either the modernist existential choice of facing the fact of one's death and nonexistence or the postmodern choice of being self-conscious about the competing tropes, simulations, and signifiers that come together in a haphazard moment of postmodern identity. Both deny a developing movement through which the present might be the progressive realization from the past.

Third, existentialism and postmodernism have both expressed themselves through interiority, reflexivity, and incongruity. The text is cut through with involution, contradiction, or aphorism. Kierkegaard wrote under numerous pseudonyms, so that his works would not be subject to expectations of authorial integrity. Nietzsche reveled in disparity and aphoristic inconsistency. Heidegger's later work, increasingly informed by Nietzsche, juxtaposed Greek and German philology in a jarring and idiosyncratic manner. Postmodernism pushed Derrida's deconstruction to extremes—traces of textual snippets, repositioned in irony.

In cultural anthropology, the postmodern impetus fractures the description of other peoples against the relationship of the text to other works, the writer's history, and the political circumstances of text production. Fragments, voices, and aphorisms are positioned to show the ironies of hybrid identity, the meaninglessness of objectivity, and the absurdity of modernist enterprise.

Fourth (and perhaps most poignant for critically humanist sensibilities), existentialism and postmodernism—at least in their purer forms— have been basically asocial; they have been highly dubious of our ability to assert or analyze intersubjective meaning. Existentialism enshrined the monad of Being, which echoes the Western cult of the (typically male) individual. This individual must face the fact of his death and bathe himself in this dread to make personal choices and assertions in his fragments of personal time. The existential world is depressingly atomized, cut off from social worth, and despairing of human connection. As is amply evident in the regressive social attitudes of Nietzsche, Heidegger, and now Paul de Man and Derrida, this gap between the individual and the Other easily pits the individual's drive for assertion against the masses, blacks, women, non-Germans, unenlightened, unartistic, unreflective, ungifted, and so on. The writer writes for the choice of his personal Being. The ultimate audience, what Bakhtin has called the superaddressee, becomes the God that doesn't exist. Under these circumstances, the author easily becomes his or her own audience; communication becomes autoreference.

Analogous prospects have loomed for postmodernism, though with no redemption through pure authorial Being. In radical postmodernism, social life is likewise dead—a disembodied relic of modernism. Meaning becomes impossible; it founders on signs that shift wildly as new needs, wants, and identities emerge in the postmodern hash. There is no possibility of establishing or analyzing understanding between people; we chart the play and play with the chart of signs as they ricochet ironically in a world of random semiosis. It makes little difference if our audience is restricted, a few intellectuals whose sign-machines can share the twisted smile and the reflective nuance of postmodernism's perverse ironies. Indeed, the fewer who can understand, the better. Writing becomes indulgent, cursory, self-referential—the pure will to discursive power. But eventually the author disappears, leaving a shadow of shifting signifiers that may signify nothing.

Certainly it can be argued that existentialism and even postmodernism were progressive in their own time and place. Viewed in their intellectual context, they pushed against formalism and forced an admission and confrontation with ethical, moral, and representational dilemmas that academic scholarship had often neglected in favor of naïve faith in wisdom and the progress of knowledge. But in a contemporary climate, such countermoves of refusal seem shopworn; their edge seems dull when weighed against the baggage they carry.

Baudrillard and the Legacy of Postmodernism

The political relationship between postmodernism and existentialism can be traced by considering the work of Jean Baudrillard. A quintessentially French critical theorist, Baudrillard presaged much of the anthropological decentering of signification. He is an extreme and perhaps terminal extension of French thinkers such as Lévi-Strauss, Bourdieu, and Foucault, who have provided a provocative and invigorating influence for English and American anthropologists.

Baudrillard's brilliant *Notes for a Critique of the Political Economy of the Sign* (1981) infused critical theory into semiotics and critical semiotics into Marxism. The political economy of semiotic exchange was taken by Baudrillard as the basis for commodity production. Baudrillard argued that late capitalism has exploded with a fetishism of signifiers. Increasingly, signification creates needs and consumption; consumption is itself a semiotic product. This is reflected in electronic communication and mass marketing; needs and consumption are themselves produced by the production of signs.

In a sense, Baudrillard stands the received Marxist model of infrastructure and superstructure on its head. The signs that used to be considered as the superstructure now provide the engine of production: They became tantamount to the infrastructure. In the mid-1970s, Baudrillard's *Mirror of Production* launched a devastating critique of Marx and showed how Marxist concepts of "labor," "value," and "commodity" uncritically presume an ability to signify substantial referents. He argued that the integrity of such entities in the external world was not a given but rather a product of the concepts used to identify and designate them. In essence, Baudrillard deconstructed the signification process through which labor values and commodities were conceptually constituted. Beneath this, "the strategy of the capitalist system is to generate this abstract structure of signification of which the commodity is merely one example" (Poster 1975:7). As is increasingly evident in postmodernity, the underlying secret of the commodity lies not in physical production but in signification—semiotic alienation of the material object in favor of its image.

Arguing that the relationship of the signifier to the signified is analogous to that between exchange value and use value, Baudrillard showed "how the logic, free play and circulation of signifiers is organized like the logic of the exchange value system" (1981:63). Thus, in the same way that Marx critiqued the operation of commodity fetishism by critically exposing the exploitation that is smuggled in when exchange value is taken for use value, Baudrillard showed that an analogous but more general process occurs in the promiscuous and manipulative substitution of signifiers for the thing signified—as in contemporary media and advertising. Seeing the political importance of this semiotic exchange in modern consumer society, Baudrillard pointed to the need for a radical critique of signifier fetishism—of the increasing substitution of the simulated for the real.

Through his trenchant studies of consumer society, mass media, advertising, and popular culture in the 1970s and 1980s, Baudrillard provided innovative critical analyses of semiotic traffic—the plastic mass

culture that blurs propaganda, politics, and advertising, trivializes meaning, and can turn the silent majority into a passive and politically apathetic
mass (e.g., 1968, 1970, 1975, 1981, 1983a, 1983b, 1987, 1990b). In pursuing this line of critique, Baudrillard became a leading and influential
exponent of postmodernism, though like many explorers in this field, he
only occasionally labeled his work as such (e.g., his contributions to *The
Definitive Guide to the Postmodern Scene* [Kroker et al. 1989]).

By the early 1980s, however, Baudrillard's work increasingly resem-
bled the trends of postmodernity it previously criticized. It signified the
end of modernist politics, the end of history (that is, the end of historical sensibility and progression), the end of the social, and the end of
meaning. Cynical to the point of being postcritical, Baudrillard's work
has come to exemplify rather than question simulated sound bites of mass
media and plastic culture.

Though this trend exposes problems bequeathed to reflexive anthropology, the pattern is taken to its logical conclusion by Baudrillard
himself. His *Cool Memories* (1990a) is a pastiche of slogans and dilettan-
tish self-sell that consciously simulates his earlier writings. Given the end
of the social, people are gone; the only forms that remain are semiotic,
inert, and "pata-physical." A similar trend shows in his *L'Auteur par lui-
même* (*The Author by Himself*)—a reflexive pastiche of his past ideas, translated, ironically, as *The Ecstasy of Communication* (1988b).

Politically, Baudrillard has written a polemic sarcastically attacking
the French left (*La Gauche divine* [1985]). He has also declared the end of
politics, which is relegated to a vanished modernism. But there is no
attack on the political right. We also *Forget Foucault* (1987), for we are in
a world in which "power" is only a modernist anachronism. But being
always more cynical and "lefter-than-thou," Baudrillard has gone full
circle and adopted his object, ending up in agentless apathy on the right.
He becomes a court jester for, rather than a critical agent against, the very
things that he should critique (see the excellent critical discussion in
Kellner 1989:ch. 9).

In *Cool Memories*, we are exhorted to blatant sexism:

> Better than those women who climax are those who give the impression
> of climaxing, but maintain a sort of distance and virginity beneath the
> pretense of pleasure, for they oblige us with the offer of rape.
> (Baudrillard 1990a:6; see also 1990b:19)

In *America* we are admonished that

> the strong cultures (Mexico, Japan, Islam) reflect back to us the image of
> our degraded one.... No such thing in California, where there is total
> rigor, for culture itself is a desert there, and culture has to be a desert so
> that everything can be equal and shine out in the same supernatural form.
> (Baudrillard 1988:126)

Being mostly an East Coaster and more than occasionally anti-American,
I don't resist such characterization out of chauvinism, and indeed
Baudrillard sometimes wonderfully captures the plastic interchangeability of American mass culture. He has a Geertzian verve and nuance on
mainstream America that our own analysts almost completely lack, and it
is a bitingly ironic pleasure to read many of his vignettes, particularly in
the earlier parts of *America*. But even within southern California, what
about Los Angeles's ethnic spectrum? What about the inner cities that
provide the disparaged ground against which American antiseptic living
throws itself into relief? For an ethnographer, the thought is startling that

> all you need to know about American society can be gleaned from an
> anthropology of its [car] driving behavior. That behavior tells you much
> more than you could ever learn from its political ideas. Drive ten thou-
> sand miles across America and you will know more about the country than
> all the institutes of sociology and political science put together.
> (Baudrillard 1988a:55)

Freeways and deserts may be impersonal byways of endless circulation, but the social forces that they both divide and connect are not
considered by Baudrillard. His polarization of West/Rest, United
States/Europe, bad/good, and postmodern/modern leads to a banality
that precludes rather than promotes exposition and criticism.

Though these tendencies are extreme in Baudrillard, he is a caution-
ary bellwether: His work has often been a step ahead of the avant-garde
crowd that has absorbed French theory and funneled it into American
anthropology uncritically a few years later. Postmodern pastiche in writing predisposes us to this problem: A series of disconnected sound bites
makes each one take on the status of an overessentialized and undernu-
anced nugget in order to be meaningful at all. It is this that underlies

what Michael Taussig (1992) calls the wild oscillation between essentialist and constructivist extremes in contemporary cultural theory.

Yet Taussig is himself guilty of essentializing a Western system that
is nervously demonic and contrasting it to a life of utopian healing among
the disempowered (Taussig 1992; cf. 1993). This is the flip side of
Baudrillard's tendency to homogenize and polarize from a non-Marxist
direction. In both cases, Orientalism and Occidentalism are maintained,
but their values are nominally reversed. We can illustrate by taking a
passage from Baudrillard's "What Are You Doing After the Orgy?":

> Black is the embarrassment of White. The obscenity of blackness
> gambles and wins against the obscenity of whiteness. Marvelous Idi Amin
> Dada, who was himself carried triumphant by four English diplomats,
> whose ambassador is received by the Pope. Marvelous Emperor Jean-
> Bedel Bokassa, eating up little black babies, lavishing diamonds upon the
> Western Dignitary! Nowhere else as in Africa does the concept of power
> undergo parody in as Ubu-esque a fashion. The West will be hard pressed
> to rid itself of this generation of simian and prosaic despots. . . . All of
> them Bokassas, all of them Amin Dadas. Incredible, no hope for that
> continent. All the Peace Corps and other charitable institutions will go
> under there. The power of scorn, Africa's contempt for its own authen-
> ticity. (Baudrillard 1983c:46)

The offensiveness of this passage dovetails with its total neglect of the
colonial legacies that racked Africa and paved the way for such regimes.
As a vast generalization, it fails to consider African leaders and countries
that serve as important counterexamples (most recently including South
Africa). This is not to deny the significance or perniciousness of African
banalities of power. But these require an understanding of historical and
social processes by which parodic horror polarizes the postcolonial state
against its people (see Mbembe 1992 and subsequent debate in *Public
Culture*; Trouillot 1990).

Conversely, however, one can also obtain a Taussig-type analogue by
simply reversing "white" and "black," "the West" and "Africa," and
substituting European colonial rulers for African ones:

> White is the embarrassment of Black. The obscenity of whiteness
> gambles and wins against the obscenity of blackness. Marvelous Queen

Victoria, who was herself carried triumphant by four English Diplomats, whose ambassador was received by the Pope. Marvelous King Leopold II, eating up little black babies in the Congo, lavishing diamonds upon the African Dignitary. Nowhere else as in Europe does the concept of power undergo parody in as Ubu-esque a fashion. Africa was hard pressed to rid itself of this generation of simian and prosaic European despots. All of them Victorias, all of them Leopolds. Incredible, no hope for the European continent. All the charitable institutions have long gone under there. The power of scorn, Europe's contempt for its own authenticity.

The point here is not to disparage Taussig, whose early work was scintillating, even explosive, in pushing open the borders of ethnography, literature, and history (e.g., Taussig 1980, 1987). It is rather that essentialisms can easily reemerge from either side. The result in Baudrillard is particularly offensive because, in stark contrast to Taussig, he is misanthropic and sees little hope of redemption.

Man with his humors, his passions, his laugh, his genitalia, his secretions is really nothing more than a filthy little germ disturbing the universe of transparency. (Baudrillard 1988b:38)

For Baudrillard, of course, his comments are outrageous simply because, for him, they can *have* no reference: It is only the *idea* of woman, of America, of Africa, or of man that is being satirized. But this irony grows so thin as to disappear, leaving only its underlying essentialism.

In one of his recent works, Baudrillard suggests that the Persian Gulf War did not take place; it was a virtual video war of simulation on combat screens for combatants and on TV screens for citizens (Baudrillard 1995b; cf. also 1993a, 1993b, 1994a, 1994b, 1995a). Of course, this *was* a simulacrum of war, but it was also linked very directly to disturbing flesh-and-blood effects: the systematic bombing and killing of tens of thousands of Iraqis sprawled concretely on the ground. It is only by crosscutting the tightening spiral of postmodern sensibilities with the asymmetries of power that one may comprehend how war is so virtual for one side and so murderous for the other (see Norris 1993; Kellner 1992). When asked about such warfare ("So you think we are presented with a situation with no victim, no aggressor and no aggression?"), Baudrillard can only respond,

The world, including our social universe, has become objectively indifferent. In an indifferent world, the emergence of behavior without quality, or more indifferent still, constitutes an event. (Baudrillard 1992:192)

The cynical dismissal of humanism, the reemergence of essentialism
through pastiche and sound-bite fragmentation, the pushing of postcritical irony to the point of anticriticism, and the textualism of traveling
signification in the absence of social analysis: These are the problems that
postmodernism, amid its many other potentials, leaves for cultural
anthropology and cultural studies.

Nietzsche and American Cultural Studies

Some of these same problems are evident in the ancestral figure so often
looked to in today's critical theory: Nietzsche, whose poignant contradictions, whose quest for empowered agency in an agentless world, are so
postmodern. There are many wonderful sides to Nietzsche; not only is he
inexhaustible, but his combination of critique and aesthetic is powerfully
eloquent, even in English translation. But amid his nineteenth-century
prescience, Nietzsche's aristocratic conceit and condescension are all too
easily ignored. So too is his rhetoric of trumping all argument by ratch-
eting irony to a yet higher level. In the process, critical substance can be
sacrificed to smugness.

　　In present debates, Nietzschean influence represents the logical
extension—some would say the bastardization—of the postmodern
inflection in cultural studies. To consider this relationship, some background is necessary to show the relationship between the history of
cultural studies and its present incarnations.

Cultural Studies

Cultural studies developed first in England at the Birmingham Centre for
Contemporary Cultural Studies (CCCS) in 1964 under the venerable
leftist Richard Hoggart. During the 1970s, under the directorship of
Stuart Hall, the CCCS pursued an interdisciplinary education that aimed
particularly at middle- and lower-class university students and encouraged them to look critically at the politics and culture of British society.
The early emphasis was significantly ethnographic, including case studies of working-class socialization and actual or potential resistance in

youth subculture and among racial minorities (e.g., Hall and Jefferson 1976; Willis 1977; Hebdige 1979; Hall et al. 1978). A critical appraisal of mass media and contemporary public culture was also important from an early period. Ethnography was often intertwined with critique of English cultural forms that encoded inequalities and made them palatable through television, film, and the press (e.g., Bennett et al. 1981; Hall et al. 1980). Cultural studies journals such as *Screen* and *Screen Education* elaborated critiques and counterpedagogy against these mainstream trends.

Many of the center's research efforts were collaborative and coauthored. They also drew widespread attention. The goal was to create an extensive network that combined scholarship, theory, and grassroots mobilization to resuscitate the political activism of Britain's political left. During the 1980s, racial and feminist issues were increasingly melded with the earlier focus on class relations (e.g., Gilroy 1987; Franklin et al. 1991). But all forms of inequality rested within a context of political resistance; during the 1980s, this meant opposition to the reigning conservatism of Thatcherism in England. Cultural studies dedicated itself to critiquing and countering this statist hegemony, as reflected in works such as *Policing the Crisis* (Hall et al. 1978), *The Empire Strikes Back* (Centre for Contemporary Cultural Studies 1992), *The Politics of Thatcherism* (Hall and Jacques 1983), and *The Hard Road to Renewal* (Hall 1988).

Stuart Hall, who directed the CCCS from 1969 until 1979, has been one of its most influential theorists and spokesmen. A black Englishman of Caribbean descent, Hall drew brilliantly on the work of Antonio Gramsci to underscore struggle as a continuing "war of cultural position" during periods of reactionary ascendancy (e.g., Hall 1986a, 1986b, 1986c). Gramsci had emphasized that domination was a process of hegemonic cultural influence above and beyond brute political power. In this view, it was particularly important to expose reactionary popular influence and uncover how cultural, political, and economic processes led common people to think and act against their shared interests. Theory and action were connected in this task. Critical scholarship was not an elite prerogative but an organic linkage of understanding and awareness between intellectuals and members of the working class. This goal was pursued though the critical pedagogy of the Open University, which included correspondence courses on contemporary culture and critical theory that became widely popular among those not otherwise easily able to pursue a university degree.

During the late 1980s, cultural studies became increasingly concerned with surface forms of public culture. In the process, it placed increasing emphasis on styles of cultural representation and how mainstream logics of representation might be decentered. Gradually its critical theory shaded increasingly into deconstructive aesthetics. The growing European interest in postmodernism during the 1980s dovetailed with these trends. The hegemonies of public culture were still criticized, but more lightly, ironically, and flippantly. Studies abounded of pop culture, celebrities, tourism, and leisure.[6] The political thrust of Gramsci, and of critical theory more generally, was blunted in favor of playful fragmentation. In the process, Gramsci's ideas were used in increasingly vague and sweeping ways; concepts such as "resistance," "articulation," "hegemony," and "war of position" were attributed easily in the absence of sustained social analysis. This analytic slide and its bland outcomes have been effectively documented by David Harris in his underappreciated account of British cultural studies, *From Class Struggle to the Politics of Pleasure* (1992).

The 1980s trends of cultural studies have since been both Americanized and postmodernized.[7] Facilitated by Lawrence Grossberg and others, cultural studies has mushroomed into an interdisciplinary field of huge proportions in the United States and elsewhere. Its growth has been so explosive that Stuart Hall himself admits, "I don't know what to say about American cultural studies. I am completely dumfounded by it" (1992:285). Coming on the heels of postmodernism, American cultural studies quickly became a magnet for scholars who wanted to decenter discourse but retain some commitment to political critique and resistance. In the 1990s, this newer version of cultural studies provides an important space for discourse between scholars whose identity and interest in disempowered forms of expression run against the conservative mainstream in disciplines such as English, philosophy, comparative literature, history, and anthropology. Against such academic hegemonies, cultural studies combines critical sensitivities with a reflexive awareness of authorial position. It now provides a valuable forum for intellectual creativity and academic support among black cultural studies, Chicano/a studies, subaltern and postcolonial studies, postmodern feminism, gay and lesbian studies, screen theory, and the new historicism, among others.

This proliferation has given common ground and political ballast to voices that wish to benefit from postmodernism without being lost in it. But at the same time, it has diluted the social and political edge of cultural studies in its earlier British form. In the process, cultural studies has all but severed itself from ethnography and other forms of detailed sociopolitical or historical documentation. As Nelson et al. uncritically suggest (1992:2), cultural studies now encompasses "textual analysis, semiotics, deconstruction, ethnography, interviews, phonemic analysis, psychoanalysis, rhizomatics, content analysis. . . . Its methodology, ambiguous from the beginning, could best be seen as a bricolage."

From the viewpoint of anthropology, the positive features of contemporary cultural studies also have a major downside. The term itself has become so vague as to mean almost anything. Two cultural studies readers present a more tangible view. The *Cultural Studies Reader* (1993), edited by Simon During, was published in Britain and carries a strong postmodern cast, including selections by Lyotard, Barthes, Foucault, de Certeau, and Soja, as well as younger figures such as Eve Sedgwick, Cornel West, Gayatri Spivak, and Michele Wallace. To these are added more classical Gramscian or critical views by Stuart Hall, Bourdieu, Adorno and Horkheimer, Raymond Williams, and others. Of the twenty-eight contributors, only one, Renato Rosaldo, is an anthropologist. On the American side is *Cultural Studies* (1992), edited by Grossberg, Nelson, and Treichler and published in the United States. This encyclopedic volume is predictably both larger and more American, including 788 pages of contributions by forty-four authors. Most are younger authors "past the post" from a wide range of backgrounds in literature, liberal arts, media studies, communication, critical sociology, humanities, and a range of interdisciplinary programs. Only two (Emily Martin and Renato Rosaldo) are faculty in departments of anthropology.

As a closer analysis of these and many other works would reveal, the interdisciplinary spread of cultural studies has shifted its balance decisively from social theorists and field researchers to literary theorists, critics of public culture, and creative writers. This is not "bad"; disciplinary boundaries are constraining and should always be permeable. Within this movement, however, the field has slid from the study of social action to the study of texts. To make such an assessment is not to reimpose a divorce between things that are acted and those that are "expressed." But this is just what is done when only the representational side of the coin is considered. This one-sidedness precludes a critical understanding of how representation relates to action over time.

If the relationship of thought to action is the pivot of critical theory, this articulation is now neglected in cultural studies. The same is often true in postcolonial studies, which is pregnant with possibilities but often entangled in rarefied deconstruction; its discursive formations can be self-described turmoils of convolution (see Ashcroft et al. 1995; Williams and Chrisman 1994; Bhabha 1994; see critique in Dirlik 1994; Chakrabarty 1992; cf. Jacoby 1995). Reflecting this, the critical substance of Gramsci's thought (like that of Frantz Fanon [1968, 1991], which was initially so important to postcolonial studies), has diminished to the point of being almost vestigial. This trend in cultural studies poses an ironic contrast to cultural anthropology and political economy in the 1990s; these latter fields have become increasingly interested in Gramscian thought and its relationship to concrete cultural and historical conditions.[8]

In style and spirit, cultural studies writing has been decisively post-modernized, especially in its American incarnations. Even the titles can be difficult—"I Throw Punches for My Race, but I Don't Want to Be a Man: Writing Us—Chicanos (Girl, Us)/Chicanas—into the Movement Script" (Chabram-Dernersesian 1992). This is not to dismiss underlying content—which is here a vivid exploration of empowering female identity across the macho masculinity of the Chicano movement (cf. also Anzaldúa 1987). In the process, however, we are easily led down the postmodern path. A disquieting attitude of authorial conceit can result, as in the published remarks of Homi Bhabha in the discussion of his paper, "Postmodern Authority":

> I can't apologize for the fact that you found my paper completely impenetrable. I did it quite consciously. I had a problem, I worked it out. And if a few people got what I was saying or some of what I am saying, I'm happy. (Bhabha 1992:67)

Not surprisingly, there has been a palpable sense among anthropologists that cultural studies has stolen, if not bastardized, their notion of "culture." Yet some of this response has been defensive, jealous, and reactionary. Cultural studies and postcolonial studies *have* gained critical purchase on important fields—and important authors—that cultural anthropology had neglected and refused to take seriously.

These omissions highlight the disempowering effect of mainstream academic culture, even within anthropology. It is in just this regard that a modernist notion of homogeneous culture is particularly problematic: Assumptions of cultural homogeneity mask the representational and social struggle that reveals our own culture to be a site of power and contestation. For modernist cultural anthropology, "culture" was an objective and authentic object of systematic description. For cultural studies, by contrast, it is a maze of representational assertions shot through with power and ripe for deconstructive critique. If cultural anthropology posited the objective study and appreciation of culture systems, cultural studies pursues the positioned critique and deconstruction of cultural hegemonies.

But these ideal types are themselves twisting. Having flirted with postmodernism, cultural studies shies away from substantive documentation, declarative theorization, and social grounding. Revealingly, this is much less true in the longer and more impressive scholarly works of authors such as Cornel West, Paul Gilroy, Teresa de Lauretis, Meaghan Morris, Michele Wallace, and Eve Sedgwick than in their shorter rhetorics of cultural studies inclusion. But social agency remains subordinated to textual concerns; the fight is against discursive hegemonies more than it is about social analysis or political forces. Though the laudable aim is to privilege voices deemed to be otherwise mute or disempowered, cultural studies in practice now often tends toward abstract content and rarefied form. Often its arguments can be understood by only a narrow audience even within the scholarly community. This is exactly the opposite of the public and organic intellectualism championed by Stuart Hall in the correspondence courses of the Open University that resulted in widespread British interest in a critical approach to popular culture in the late 1970s and early 1980s. In some ways, then, cultural studies has done a U-turn.

As a form of critique, discursive deconstruction rests on the assumption that we can resist the hegemony of Western logos and rationality by subverting and defamiliarizing expected forms of expression. As against this rarefied endeavor, however, we also need to learn more about actual inequalities of age, race, nationalism, ethnicity, and class—as well as how they engage processes of expression and representation in the details of social life. The rhetoric of cultural studies can be eloquent, and its conceptualizations as pregnant as they are ephemeral. But these impressionistic insights need to be rigorously documented and clearly communicated in the contemporary world. Amid the roller coasters of prosaic concern, we need to know more about complex cross-currents in which counterhegemony against one type of inequality may actually reinforce other forms of domination. This is what happens in the real world of Bosnia, South Africa, eastern Germany, south-central Los Angeles, Peru, West Virginia, Cambodia, academic anthropology departments, the highlands of New Guinea, and elsewhere.

Nietzsche

The logical conclusion of cultural studies—at least of its emergent American form—is perhaps found in the work of Friedrich Nietzsche (1844–1900). The connection may seem a contentious one, but in the cultural deconstructions of the early 1990s, it almost seemed as though Nietzsche had supplanted Gramsci as the patron saint of cultural studies. The Nietzschean legacy, in which established truths are debunked and bathed in contradiction, includes a frontal and explicit critique of modernity. For instance, Nietzsche's *Ecce Homo* (his description and critique of his own *Beyond Good and Evil [1968b]*), proclaims,

> This book is in all essentials a *critique of modernity*, not excluding the modern sciences, modern arts, and even modern politics, along with pointers to a contrary type that is as little modern as possible. (Nietzsche 1969b:310)

Amid his prescient awareness and wonderful critiques, Nietzsche insists on his own discursive power as a justified conceit. Such a view is particularly evident in *The Gay Science* (1974) and *The Antichrist* (1968c) as well as in his widely read *On the Genealogy of Morals* (1969a). Hence the Nietzschean delight, picked up in postmodern pastiche, of affirming both the thing and its opposite, giving us a jarring series of contradictory viewpoints to undermine the myth of received objectivity. In cultural studies of the early 1990s (as in postmodernism), these oppositions can give only the illusion of greater depth, since surface discrepancies cannot be grounded. Though the Nietzschean agent as superman (*Übermensch*) is overtly absent, there remains a rarefied aesthetic irony serving an ultimate will to discursive power.

Of course, the counterargument is that Nietzsche was snubbing the rationalist tyranny of Kant and Hegel. As stressed by Deleuze (1983), he was giving negation and partiality back their power and will. That this power embodies itself through fragmentation and contradiction can make it rejuvenating and effective—a means of refusing hegemonic logic. But Nietzsche himself held a neoaristocratic conceit based on his own artistic gifts. His own art was empowered; all else was trash. Does the same problem of exclusion hold when trying to appropriate Nietzsche to empower cultural studies? Or to empower postmodern feminism or queer theory or black studies or postcolonial studies—sometimes vis-à-vis each other?

The strength and weakness of feminist appropriations of Nietzsche is evident in what Luce Irigaray writes as an intertextual love affair with him: *The Marine Lover of Friedrich Nietzsche* (1991a; see also Patton 1993; Oliver 1995). In this work, the eloquent French feminist engages Nietzsche as a lover and comrade-in-arms.[9] Her literary journey to become a female self parallels Nietzsche's Zarathustran dictum "Become what you are!"— despite Nietzsche's own reliance on an archly masculine mode. Indeed, Nietzsche's dripping disparagement of women—immoderate even by Germanic standards of his own day—is almost totally ignored by Irigaray. She gets her revenge at the book's end by vaunting her own eroticism against Nietzsche's implicit impotence. Moreover, she asserts that Nietzsche's eternal return is condemned to sameness and death because he is stuck in male *ressentiment*. As such, he is blind to the difference of woman. He cannot as a man give birth to a rejuvenated self (cf. Oppel 1993).

The potentials of using Nietzsche and then trumping him on his own terms are pregnant in Irigaray, but they leave many problems, particularly for less gifted writers. It is disconcerting that Irigaray leaves the feminine in a self-sealed universe of unilateral power. Is this a womanly mirror-world of Nietzsche's patriarchy?

When Nietzsche's conceit moves to a celebration of domination as well as ridicule, he parts company with the principal legacy of cultural studies. His condescensions are invidious and recurrent, and his misogyny swells with vitriol. His work has racist and fascist dimensions as well, though these are more hotly debated. The issue is complex given the contradictory and conflicted nature of Nietzsche's remarks, particularly in his middle-period volumes of juxtaposed aphorisms. Where a larger argument is thematically developed, however, a dominant emphasis emerges, both in his earlier work such as *The Birth of Tragedy* (1968a) and later works such as *On the Genealogy of Morals* (1969a) and *Twilight of the*

Idols (1968c). In these, there is an overriding sense of personal struggle against degeneracy and a hyperaristocratic fight against the contaminating effects of priestly and slave morality.

It is hard to contest the recent view that

> the dazzling beauty of Nietzsche's writings may blind the reader to the explosive character of his opinions. Nietzsche expounded a radical and aristocratic egoism, poured scorn on Platonism, Christianity, modernity, enlightenment, democracy, socialism, and the emancipation of women; denounced the belief in human equality as a calamitous conceit; and ardently championed a rank order of desires, types of human beings, and forms of life. Nietzsche's standpoint, which he describes as above politics, has implications for politics. (Berkowitz 1995:1)

The relative neglect of these problems in recent debates is presaged by the blind spots of deconstructionism and postmodernism. It has also been exacerbated by two of Nietzsche's chief interpreters: Walter Kaufmann in the United States and Gilles Deleuze in France. As Nietzsche's long-standing English translator and apologist, Kaufmann (e.g., 1974) suggests that Nietzsche emphasizes the individual rather than the collective will to power. Thus, for instance, he debunks the state as well as the church. But this does not wash the slate clean. Nietzsche's arrogance makes sexism, racism, and fascism the second-order derivatives of authorial conceit. This authority becomes guiltless and all-powerful in the hands of the aesthetic master. Disparagement is intrinsic to Nietzsche's praise of contradiction and his Dionysian impulse toward violent egotism. Examples are plentiful in his works.[10]

For Deleuze (e.g., 1983), Nietzschean affirmations must be seen in the context of Kantian and Hegelian antecedents that favored consistency and synthesis over contradiction and power. The Enlightenment stressed rationality and logic over poetry and emotion; it left the negative and the antithetical without will or affirmation. But if irreducibility, multiplicity, and contradiction can be important tools for resistance, a critical humanism suggests they should retain grounding by criticizing rather than eulogizing inequality and domination. As Hardt notes,

> Deleuze's reading has made such a profound impression on Nietzsche studies partly because it succeeds in making so much of Nietzsche's

thought while avoiding or effectively diffusing the force of arguments about Nietzsche's individualism and reactionary politics. (Hardt 1993:31)

To claim that Nietzsche is only the product of his times in terms of political incorrectness might be a defensible if timid argument except that his will to discursive power inflects contemporary cultural studies. This is especially true in his use of literary agency to empower condescension. The attempt to empower some voices by trumping others on prior aesthetic grounds is cause for concern. *There is simply no guarantee that the most aesthetically elevated voice will also be the most socially progressive, nor that the most plodding is the most reactionary.* This problem is exacerbated by the fact that Nietzsche has circled into cultural theory through literary and philosophical discourses that privilege textual references over social ones. A random example can be taken from the dust jacket of *Within Nietzsche's Labyrinth* (1990), by Williams College professor of philosophy Alan White:

> In *Within Nietzsche's Labyrinth*, Alan White looks beyond Nietzsche's flamboyant but ambiguous words of praise for violence and oppression in search of subtler "yes-saying" or affirmative teachings, the ones Nietzsche presents with "the voice of beauty," which speaks only to readers with "fingers for nuances." It is this Nietzsche of nuance, the poet-philosopher, the one scholars find so exceptionally frustrating, that White concerns himself with.

Would we accept a similar statement about the patent contradictions—albeit much less poetic, though perhaps no less vehement—of Patrick Buchanan or the white supremacist David Duke? Compare:

> In *Within David Duke's Labyrinth*, Alan White looks beyond Duke's flamboyant but ambiguous words of praise for violence and oppression in search of subtler "yes-saying" or affirmative teachings. It is this Duke with "fingers for nuances," the one scholars find so exceptionally frustrating, that White concerns himself with.

This is not to bastardize the richness of Nietzsche's thought by taking snippets out of context, but rather to show that this is exactly what proponents of Nietzsche frequently do. And as one moves Nietzschean ideas beyond the narrow range of self-reflection to *social* theory, they assert not just arrogance but castigation of other people. Nietzsche's emphasis on obliterating nihilism through self-assertive dominance is, if anything, far greater than his much-emphasized voicing of nihilism per se.[11]

This legacy poses a serious caveat for the contemporary celebration of the end of modernity and the reflexive praise of Nietzschean resistance. Though the postmodern impetus in fields such as cultural studies may praise Nietzsche's critical insights, they have difficulty asserting alternative grounds for authorship in the absence of some kind of humanism—unless the writer is empowered de facto by being a member of a minority or dispossessed interest group. It is important that Nietzschean self-assertion not become grounds for prior privilege— much less prior disparagement—on the basis of *any* type of skin color, gender, or ethnic background. This is *not* to excoriate cultural studies nor to bash multiculturalism (see chapter 8). It is rather to emphasize that *alternative routes and more explicit ethical consideration are needed to ground these highly important intellectual developments.*

Heidegger and Existentialism
The Larger Philosophic Project

Parallel problems present themselves in a different key in the case of Martin Heidegger. Heidegger is now receiving a swarm of reattention, including in anthropology.[12] A more overtly philosophical figure, Heidegger draws upon the nihilism of Nietzsche and the existential angst earlier conveyed by Kierkegaard. Heidegger posits that the everyday existence of man is unauthentic. Simply being in the world swallows up our sense of Being with a capital *B*; it undercuts our self-consciousness about our existence and precludes our ability to comprehend what we really are.

> Thus, inevitably and continuously, the forward driving "I" is sacrificed to the persistent and pressing "they." . . . The driving, integral, all-essential I is hidden, almost all my life, by the daily round. (Grene 1968:460)

In the context of then-current philosophy, it could be argued that Heidegger was trying to take Being out of the realm of pure thought and view it in relation to the lived world. But from a contemporary vantage point, it certainly seems that Heidegger's view of social life is highly negative. This view fuels his drive to isolate Being as an atomized state of self-consciousness that is logically prior to interaction in the world. For Heidegger, as for many existentialists, we become aware of our Being by confronting the most alienated and isolated form of our existential facticity—the dread of our own death. This dread is then traced outward to reveal the alien absurdities of the external world and the autonomy and separation of our existence. To realize human authenticity, in this view, is to detach ourselves from social engagement, from the external "they." The larger goal is to allow the wholeness of human Being to be self-conscious and then, secondarily, to be outwardly actualized. But this self-consciousness is an inverted pyramid balanced on an asocial base.

Heidegger's perspective contrasts diametrically to that of Bakhtin, who suggests:

> I am conscious of myself and become myself only while revealing myself for another, through another, and with the help of another. The most important acts constituting self-consciousness are determined by a relationship toward another consciousness (toward a *thou*). . . . The very being of man (both external and internal) is the *deepest communion*. To *be* means *to communicate*. . . . To be means to be for another, and through the other, for oneself. . . . I cannot manage without another, I cannot become myself without another. (Bakhtin 1984:287)

Against these humanist alternatives, it could be argued that Heidegger, like Nietzsche, should be interpreted as progressive in relation to his philosophical forebears. At one level, Heidegger was trying to break rather than buttress the Cartesian division between self and object. In this interpretation, it is a crass reimposition of this divide to call the Heideggerian subject an egotistic individual. For some, Heidegger's work is squarely within the genealogy of hermeneutic thought that runs from Schleiermacher and Dilthey to Husserl, Gadamer, and Ricoeur (e.g., Palmer 1969). This interpretation could emphasize the potential sociality of "solicitude" in Heidegger's project and argue that he was simply operating on an abstract plane that left empirical or social referents aside as a separate issue (cf. Bernasconi 1993).

Though these countertrends can be productively cultivated, it remains true that Heidegger ultimately allows little place for a humanistic or social view of existence. Heidegger's asociality and ahistoricity are hard to deny, especially given alternative legacies available to him via German phenomenology and humanism (Blitz 1981:ch. 6). For Heidegger, primary engagement with the other as social being results in existential forfeiture. As David Harvey puts it,

> Heidegger refuses to see mediated social relationships with others (things or people) as in any way expressive of any kind of authenticity. Indeed, mediated relationships of this sort are felt as threatening to identity and any true sense of self. (Harvey 1993a:14)

Understanding for Heidegger is not a social or even a mental process but an ontological one. It is not surprising that Heidegger avers the possibility of true Being in the ontologies of other cultural traditions. In contrast to Cassirer, he explicitly denies this possibility for mythic ontologies founded on *mana* (see Mimica 1993:82). Instead, Heidegger remains limited to a restricted if not distorted form of Western ontology, including in his later work. As Mimica suggests,

> Heidegger's subsequent poetical ontology is a dismal failure . . . precisely because it insists on being as an "unveiling" of a primordial structure of human existence, yet it is conducted within the limited horizon of the modern Western world and its cultural-historical matrix, which Heidegger had *selectively* reappropriated and distorted, yet deemed inexhaustible. (Mimica 1993:84)

Rather than appreciating the diverse reality and meaning of subjective experience, Heidegger retreats to an arrogant retrieval of what he personally deems to be the authentic and lustrous disclosures of German and Greek poetry and philosophy. Against these paragons, "the stance of man seems almost a devotional passivity" (Palmer 1969:149). Conversely, as Heidegger himself puts it, "we should *do* nothing, but rather wait" (Heidegger, quoted in Palmer 1969:151). Though one may concur with Heidegger's later critique of modernist technology and of human mastery, these critiques are likewise grounded in a disparaging reduction of subjectivism to "subjectism."

If this is Heidegger's philosophy, his politics and ethics—his pragmatics in the realm of the social—were devoted to the ideals of German Nazism (Farias 1989). Heidegger's work suggested that true philosophy could be conducted, if not only in German, then only in German and Greek. This notion draws heavily upon Nietzsche's early work (e.g., *The Birth of Tragedy* [1968a]). Heidegger's notorious "Letter on Humanism" debunks the humanist tradition and ethics along with it: "Here as elsewhere, thinking in values is the greatest blasphemy imaginable against Being" (1977b: 228).

Egocentricity and emphasis on personal will are highly evident from Kierkegaard and Nietzsche to Heidegger and, more ambivalently, Sartre. The lack of a developed theory of the social is glaring in all of these writers. The failure of effective social theory in Sartre's *Critique of Dialectical Reason*, particularly as attempted in its second volume (1991), is the partial exception that proves the rule. Though striving for social collectivity, Sartre is ultimately unable to escape from the notion (expressed in the work's first volume) that "it is *initially within itself* that free subjectivity discovers its objectivity" (1976:71).

Certainly alternative strands of existentialism could be emphasized. Sartre tries heroically to subsume first humanism and then Marxism within the existential mantle. He pushes hard to go beyond egoistic limitation and confront the realm of the social. And in terms of anthropology's own history, Sartre certainly lands on the humanist side in his celebrated dispute with Lévi-Strauss (Lévi-Strauss 1966:ch. 9; Sartre 1976). Other authors could be considered to widen this horizon further, such as the theological existentialism of Martin Buber, who emphasized the I-thou relationship alluded to by Bakhtin earlier in this chapter. But in the main strands of Kierkegaard, Nietzsche, and Heidegger, the privileged locus of Being is an egotistical consciousness, if not a conceited philosopher. Sartre excepted, it is not coincidental that existentialism from Kierkegaard to Nietzsche to Heidegger leaves the social lives of common people in the dust and often disparaged. In the German tradition of pure philosophy, disparagement easily harmonizes with and promotes social oppression. This is true even though and even especially because it eschews explicit social theorizing in favor of supreme self-consciousness and self-assertion.

Of course, existential self-assertion can also provide an intellectual lever against the collectivizing hegemonies of the modernist church or state. But the present era of late modernity already sees itself as largely cut off from such institutions and from social and ethical commitments generally. In a contemporary context, then, the excesses of an existential will to power are cause for special concern.

Heidegger's case is particularly unsettling and well documented. He did not just appropriate but also expounded and expanded Hitlerian notions of racial purity and anti-Semitism. He enacted these beliefs in academic politics and in 1933 became the powerful first National Socialist rector of the University of Freiburg. His inaugural lecture, "The Role of the University in the New Reich," celebrated the advent of a new and pure Aryan nation. He was not just a passive tolerator of Nazism, but an active proponent of it. His colleagues, including his own mentor, Edmund Husserl, suffered severely as a result of Heidegger's personal drive to purge the university of Jews and those unsympathetic to Nazism.

In 1975 Pierre Bourdieu wrote a stinging indictment of Heidegger and linked the habitus of his philosophy to the social field of German nationalism (see also Farias 1989; cf. Wolin 1991).[13] One need not agree with the excesses of Bourdieu's critique; he reduces Heidegger to the contours of his social milieu. But we can appreciate how Heidegger's refusal of ethics underscores the need for critically humanist sensibilities that connect explicitly to social theory.

And Closer to Home ...

Rarefied aesthetics, egotism, and social disconnection pervade the work of Heidegger, Nietzsche, and Baudrillard. They also infuse the larger field that stretches from existentialism to postmodernism. Alternative readings could find more productive strands in these authors and approaches. Indeed, a richer view of alternative interpretations from fields such as anthropology is greatly needed—as opposed to superficial treatments and bandwagon invocations. But in the current scene, the weaknesses of these approaches get scant attention. Interiority and asocial conceit have troubling ethical implications. It is against this context that a direct consideration of ethics and values—as in a critically humanist perspective—is particularly important.

The present critique is not a simple or reactionary cry that "this work is dangerous." The postmodern impetus, much less the development of cultural studies, has opened anthropology to a host of exciting and creative possibilities. These developments have also provided innovative critiques of previous approaches. Postmodernism, like cultural studies, does not embrace (and is, if anything, *against*) totalizing narratives or authorship. But it is a plain caution to realize that postmodern turns can continue a Western philosophic tradition of rarefying and then fetishizing its own representations.

> The insight that the subject is constituted in language and the notion that there is nothing outside the text have led to the privileging of the aesthetic and the linguistic which aestheticism has always promoted to justify its imperial claims. (Huyssen 1986:208)

In the course of this privileging, the door is left open for social disconnection and authorial arrogance. Fragmented images can predispose new forms of uncritical essentialism.

From a critically humanist vantage point, an empirically grounded and analytically explicit exposure of inequality is a vital complement to existential and postmodern excesses. This antidote can be productively informed by strong ethnography. The academic disenchantment with modern liberalism needs now to be confronted with rigorous studies of social inequality at home and abroad (e.g., Trouillot 1989, 1990; Donham 1990; Povinelli 1993; Lomnitz-Alder 1992; Malkki 1995). Patterns of resistance or self-help merit special attention, including how these may unwittingly reinforce old hegemonies or perpetuate new ones (e.g., Hale 1994; Williams 1991; Ortner 1989; cf. Scott 1985). The Foucauldian workings of discourse, knowledge, and texts can be fruitfully engaged with social action rather than excluded from it (e.g., Lavie 1990; Fischer and Abedi 1990; Messick 1993). Against this, it becomes all too easy to incarnate the state as a simple and undifferentiated reflex of occidentalized evil (see countertrends in Stoler 1991; Sahlins 1992; Dirks 1987; Fox 1985; Comaroff and Comaroff 1991; Thomas 1994).

Diverse genres, plural voices, and creative writing can certainly be useful tools, and it can be effective for the form of writing to harmonize with the content of the argument. But it is a mistake to emphasize voicing over substance, particularly when voicing restricts our understanding to an impressionistic sweep that is rarefied, confusing, or beyond declaration. In such cases, sign value easily becomes its own fetish. In the process, the legacy of postmodernism and cultural studies tends to project resistance thinly and to privilege its more abstract or ephemeral dimensions. It is for this reason that the replacement of detailed exposition and social analysis by pastiche and irony is cause for concern. This is not a conservative or defensive reaction against reflexivity, but an attempt to make it more productive and ethically responsive. The postmodern alternative is to both give up on objectivity and remain ethically ungrounded.

> In challenging all consensual standards of truth and justice, of ethics and meaning, and in pursuing the dissolution of all narratives and meta-theories into a diffuse universe of language games, deconstruction ended up, in spite of the best intentions of its more radical practitioners, by reducing knowledge and meaning to a rubble of signifiers. It thereby produced a condition of nihilism that prepared the ground for the re-emergence of a charismatic politics and even more simplistic propositions than those which were deconstructed. (Harvey 1990:350)

Many cultural anthropologists purport to have either ignored postmodernism or to have left it behind. The cutting edge of cultural anthropology now moves through Gramsci and cultural studies to new border zones of contested representation. But the problems bequeathed to cultural anthropology by the postmodern turn can be uncritically absorbed in the very attempt to avoid grand theory and to be "above" or "beyond" a programmatic analysis of anthropology's intellectual history.

It is now too late to be first past almost any post—be it postmodern, postcultural, postcritical, postmodern feminist, posthistorical, and so on. These many developments are myriad observation posts that will continue to cast creative new images into the future of anthropology. But being so many and so close together, they are also fenceposts with a long shadow. They not only define and defend themselves against already established positions, they inhibit the rigorous social and cultural analyses that are crucial for anthropology.

In the rush to privilege new voices and mute older ones, critically humanist continuities in anthropology are underappreciated even as they are often tacitly drawn upon as a grounding point—one of the few left viable in a world of floating signifiers. Critically humanist sensibilities are not inimical to, but enhance the critique of Western individuality, the questioning of unbridled rationality and objectivity, and the need to relativize Western "being" and authorship. On the other hand, a critically humanist perspective emphasizes a direct exposure and critique of the inequalities that postmodern legacies pretend to address but substantively neglect. It promotes empirical substance, careful documentation of social action and personal belief, systematic analysis, clear writing, and moments of presumed and appropriately bracketed objectivity. When used as a complement rather than as an alternative to these emphases, the defamiliarizing strengths of traveling reflexivity can enrich cultural anthropology rather than depleting or destroying it.

Ethnographic Counterpoint
"Like Money You See in a Dream": Petroleum and Patrols in South New Guinea

In a postmodern era, journeys of exploration don't end; they ratchet their ironies to a higher scale. These ironies are not just discursive, epistemological, or limited to a world of tropes; they have enormous impact on people's lives. The play of signs is a powerful strategy of domination and disempowerment that dovetails easily with Western imperialism and neocolonialism. Postmodern sensibilities easily mock or simply assume these realities rather than delineating them.

The substance of postcolonial image and power is highly evident in Chevron's oil pipeline project in south Papua New Guinea. As portrayed in a front-page story in the *Wall Street Journal* (McCoy 1992), Chevron was aware of environmental concerns and tried hard to "do the right thing" as it built its billion-dollar, 159-mile pipeline through remote and thinly populated parts of the New Guinea rainforest. The pipeline was laid underground—an innovative environmental design that added tens of millions of dollars to the cost of the project. This kept the pipeline less accessible to saboteurs and was supposed to result in the permanent clearing of only 1,500 of Papua New Guinea's 88.8 million forest acres. In addition, Chevron committed $45 million to building roads, schools, and clinics, and another $40 million to building a sixty-six-mile highway through the mountains. "We didn't need that road for our operations, but the people wanted it," said the on-site managing director (McCoy 1992:12). The government of Papua New Guinea has owned a 22.5 percent stake in the project and is expected to collect about $1 billion in taxes, fees, and other payments. For the regional provincial governments, Papua New Guinea is also collecting a royalty totaling 1.25 percent of the value of all oil pumped, a sum projected to be about $25 million at current oil prices. Chevron also advanced an interest-free loan of over half a million dollars to a corporation representing landowners living along the southern end of the pipeline.

In 1935, Australian patrol officer Jack Hides led a daring and arduous patrol of exploration near parts of the area where the pipeline currently lies. Widely viewed as liberal, energetic, romantic, and committed, Hides and his few men (mostly Papua New Guinean constables and carriers) encountered hellish terrain, hostile attack, disease, and starvation. Collectively, they made one of the last long-distance patrols of first contact over a major uncharted region of New Guinea and, indeed, the inhabited world. This heroic view of the patrol was rendered by Hides himself; his colorful account, *Papuan Wonderland* (1936), became a best-seller in Australia.

In their poignant reanalysis, Edward Schieffelin and Robert Crittenden (1991) trace the historical moments through which Hides's ideals were in fact compromised. Schieffelin and Crittenden effectively juxtapose the colonial record of Hides's expedition with the accounts and beliefs of Papuans as derived through meticulous ethnography from each area through which the patrol passed. The result is titled *Like People You See in a Dream*. The scale of patrol violence is documented to have been greater than previously thought. By careful judgments of historical fact, Schieffelin and Crittenden link this violence to the clash of indigenous and foreign understandings. Notwithstanding the ideals he went in with and the story he came out with, Hides became disoriented, bewildered, and wildly uncertain along the way. Schieffelin and Crittenden's account makes the suspicion and resistance of local peoples as ethnographically clear as it was opaque to Hides. Misunderstanding and disillusionment made a dreadful experience of first contact on both sides; the dream was a bad one.

The well-publicized forays of Chevron Oil near many parts of this same area have met with a similar fate more than a half-century later. Despite public-relations efforts, Chevron officials are befuddled. Villagers wielding traditional weapons have violently attacked Chevron officials; vehicles have been seized, roads blocked, and work periodically shut down. James Harrington, Chevron's manager of land and government relations in Papua New Guinea, "figures the conflict will probably interrupt oil production at least temporarily" (McCoy 1992:12). The ominously if appropriately named Hides Gas Project that is associated with the development has also run into stiff local opposition (PIM 1991).

It is almost as ironic as it is expectable that colonial history is here repeated in the neocolonial present. Hides wanted food and safe conduct, but he had little of value that he could or would give to local people. Chevron wants oil and safe conduct; they have spent enormous sums of money, but very little of it has actually gotten to the local people whose lands have been cleared. Of the half-million dollars that went to the southern landowners, all but $25,000 "just disappeared," says a Chevron official (McCoy 1992:12). Agreements were signed and money paid to persons who had little or no accountability to the local groups they supposedly represented.

At the local level, umbrella investment organizations were set up by the company but only on a centralized scale that would have required financial cooperation between villages and clans that were enemies of each other (Kutubu Plan 1989:69–70). The failure of such projects has allowed "the oil company . . . the advantage of being able to ignore political realities in the communities they are dealing with while at the same time appearing to be protecting them" (Weiner 1991:72). Anthropologists Ernst and Burton (1992:8) emphasize in their report for Chevron that "despite their small size and in some cases, demographic precariousness, they (the clans) should be considered as the bases for incorporated local land groups." They further note that

> although they are called clans, the patrilineal groups of the Fasu have little in common with the large clans found in some other parts of Papua New Guinea's highlands. With an average membership of under 25 people (compared with 350 traditionally for the clans around Wabag in the Enga Province), they are probably best considered a different *sort* of thing than merely a different size of the same thing. (Ernst and Burton 1992:5)

These contrasts are not ethnographic minutiae. The very point is that local details can be extremely important. The distinction between small lineages and larger clans is not just a footnote relic of anthropology's interest in kinship. Here it is a key part of why enormous wealth has been wasted in south New Guinea and why Hides's experience gets repeated.

In part because "the clans cannot be related to local organization in any simple way," Ernst (1992:7) strongly recommended that a Papua New Guinean liaison officer spend as much time as possible in the local villages. Given the amount of money at stake and the possibility of misunderstanding, misrepresentation, and misappropriation of funds, he emphasized,

> It is especially important that he not be associated with the compensation provision functions . . . and that he establish as well as is possible that he does not directly represent the interests of Chevron Niugini, but is a resource . . . for the local population. (Ernst 1992:7)

Not heeding this entreaty, Chevron continued to treat clans as if they were pan-local entities for purposes of negotiation and compensation. In parts of the pipeline area, Chevron hired former Australian patrol officers to direct relations with the indigenous population, including some who acted as labor organizers. "The company thus re-created the conditions of colonial paternalism and domination by hiring such individuals, some of whom had notoriously intimidating and racist attitudes towards Papuan New Guineans" (Weiner 1991:73). The specter of Jack Hides has returned—ruder and more powerful than the original.

The mountain highway that Chevron constructed in the north has become a conduit for New Guinea highlanders wanting to infiltrate the Kutubu area. Liquor, theft, poaching, squatting, and rape have been introduced to thinly populated areas unaccustomed to such problems (McCoy 1992). Neither Chevron nor the Papua New Guinean government will pay for teachers to run the new schools that have been constructed; some have already been boarded up. Environmental disruption has been greater than locally expected; fishing resources that were plentiful have diminished due to muddying of the rivers (McCoy 1992). Construction has scared away game animals that were previously hunted, and river people have been left scrambling for subsistence. A road along the pipeline that Chevron says it somehow expected to keep "private" is being opened up. Logging companies are buying timber rights along it; huge swaths of timber may well be clear-cut from the area. And lurking in the future is the possibility of oil leakages or explosions—contingencies that have not been publicly noted, much less discussed with people residing near the project (McCoy 1992; Ernst and Burton 1992:18–19).[14]

Jack Hides had the excuse and the cost of being the first white-skinned person in some of these areas. Liberal ideals aside, there was little way he could have known what awaited him. The chinks in his romantic faith appeared as a result of his confrontations with resistant Others.

What was unleashed was the cultural-cum-physical violence that so often underpins imperial intrusion. Chevron, for all its expenditures, has much less excuse. Its access to information is great, its profits are enormous, and yet the scale of its social destruction is much larger. Certainly there is plenty of blame to go around, including to the Papua New Guinean government, the liaison officers, and some people from the area in question. But if Chevron had been more in touch with local people, more direct in their compensation, and more sensitive to the social impact of changes, the difficulties could have been greatly ameliorated.

Voices of local people and of anthropologists familiar with the area could have helped greatly if they had been listened to. Despite ample possibilities for Chevron to listen, the comments of Ernst and Burton still hold true for most of the groups in question:

> It was clear that among the Fasu, there was a far greater understanding of general Western European derived cultures ... than expatriate Chevron personnel have of Fasu culture. This is unfortunate, for the power to initiate most of the actions in this area rests with Chevron, not the Fasu. (Ernst and Burton 1992:18)

Now that it has effectively paid off government officials and established a try-hard image in the *Wall Street Journal*, Chevron has hunkered down and tried to tough out local opposition. But the extended seizure and closure of the multibillion-dollar Panguna copper mine by indigenous rebels at the other end of Papua New Guinea, in Bougainville, should give Chevron reason to reconsider (see Robie 1989; May and Spriggs 1991; Wesley-Smith 1992). As of early 1996—several years after the initial resistance by local groups—Fasu and Foi peoples who reside near the Kutubu pipeline are making serious threats to attack workers, sabotage the line, and shut down its production altogether if they do not receive outstanding payments owed to them and if their demands for a 5 percent share equity are not met (Robie 1996). As a result Chevron Niugini has been forced to evacuate more than eighty of its staff, together with spouses and children, from the area. It is in their own interest—as well as that of the local people—that officials listen more attentively and respond more effectively to indigenous concerns.

The larger political economy of Papua New Guinea puts this situation in perspective. As of 1994, oil and minerals constituted 79 percent

of Papua New Guinea's total exports (PIM 1994a:27). The oil boom
revenues of 1993 were supposed to be put in the Minerals Resource
Stabilization Fund, which would have afforded the country a dependable
income for years and provided a buffer against transient fluctuations in
oil, gas, and mineral revenues. But national legislation gutted this fund.
Instead of being saved, surplus revenues were liberally allocated.
Spending on government administration skyrocketed, and national taxes
were sharply reduced. At the same time, infrastructural investments and
capital expenditures by the Papua New Guinean government actually
decreased instead of increasing (PIM 1994a: 27). Windfall profits were
dissipated through largess, excess administration, and other siphonings.
The country's deficit ballooned rather than shrank, reaching a massive
810 million kina in mid-1994 (Wesley-Smith 1995:371). By late in the
year, the country was staring into the face of total bankruptcy. Lack of
funds paralyzed many government services; public employees could not
be paid (Wesley-Smith 1995:371). After a change of governments, the
kina was floated on the international currency market and sustained a
quick devaluation of 20 percent (PIM 1994b, 1994c).

Given Papua New Guinea's lack of capital industry and its depen-
dence on imported products, national leaders are increasingly pressured
to sign fast-track contracts with multinational corporations for more
large-scale oil, mineral, and logging projects. Knowing the government's
weakness (and stung by local unrest), corporations bargain more toughly.
Despite plans, public-relations efforts, and stated intentions, government
and corporate interests easily turn a blind eye to environmental degradation and social disruption. The government owns a significant share of
these new projects and is largely dependent on their continued revenue.
Top government officials can receive lucrative personal consultantships
that encourage support of company policies.

Troubling as they are, the problems of the Chevron oil development
project are surpassed by those from other mining and logging operations
in Melanesia. Local opposition to the mining contract at Bougainville
provoked local rebellion, shutdown of the mine, and a violent toppling
of the Bougainville provincial government. The Papua New Guinea
Defense Force attempted to crush rebel leaders by invading the province;
when this was unsuccessful, the state withdrew and blockaded the island
(see Liria 1993). Cut off from external contact or support, Bougainville's
infrastructure collapsed, its food sources dried up, and essential services

ceased. Caught in the middle, the local populace has suffered major hardships (e.g., Sasako 1991; Wesley-Smith 1992). At the other end of Papua
New Guinea, ecological and social problems seethe as a result of the huge
Ok Tedi gold and copper mine (Hyndman 1994; PIM 1994f; Kirsch 1993,
1995). In addition to bringing major disputes over land compensation,
lack of employment, and social disruption, the mine introduced heavy
metals and other sediment that destroyed downstream environments
along the Ok Tedi and the massive Fly River system. Despite this ecocide,
the controlling BHP corporation—with government support—has
refused to build a tailings dam to contain the contamination. Indeed, the
government has recently passed an Ok Tedi Agreement Bill (condemned
by the International Commission of Jurists) that makes it illegal for local
people to claim damages for land affected by pollution from the mine.[15]

The situation is at least as bad in northern Irian Jaya, across the
Indonesian border from Papua New Guinea, where tailings from the
Freeport-McMoRan gold and copper mine at Grasberg have devastated
the ecology of two major river systems. Barred legal recourse, some
indigenous peoples protesting the mine have had their villages burned; an
undetermined number have been beaten and killed by Indonesian military forces, whose actions have been consistently condemned by Amnesty
International. Freeport-McMoran, Inc. admits to being primarily
responsible for the transportation, feeding, and housing of Indonesian
troops in the area, and independent sources confirm that military action
has been liberally aided by the corporation's security personnel and
management (Press 1995; Australian Council 1995; Chatterjee and
Seneviratne 1996; Burton 1995). The United States Overseas Private
Investment Corporation (OPIC) canceled $100 million in political risk
insurance for this West New Guinea mining complex (Bryce 1995). But
as a Fortune-500 company with annual revenues of $2 billion, Freeport
is expanding its operations as well as its public relations at a furious pace.
Its Grasberg site is becoming the largest gold mine and third-largest
copper mine in the world, with total reserves estimated at a staggering
$50 billion. Freeport is the largest single United States investor in
Indonesia, which has recently approved a thirty-year contract extension
for the corporation to mine in that country (Press 1995; Shari et al. 1995).
The Indonesian government owns a 10 percent stake in Freeport's
Grasberg project and works closely with the company in controlling and
restricting access to the mine site, which employs 14,000 people but only

15 percent from the local area. Among its goodwill projects, Freeport plans to build a shopping mall and a four-star hotel near the company town.

Freeport-McMoRan also wields influence in the United States, where it is based. It has recently taken out full-page ads in the *New York Times*; it claims its woes are a fabrication of extremist environmentalists and anthropologists. Anthropologists are singled out in particular for "wanting to create a human zoo in Irian Jaya" (quoted in Burnett 1995). Freeport has hired former CIA Director James Woolsey as a legal counsel, and its influential board of directors includes Henry A. Kissinger and William Cunningham, the chancellor of the University of Texas. Anthropologist Steven Feld has recently resigned his position at the University of Texas in protest over the collusion between Freeport-McMoRan and the university, citing a disregard for human rights in their pursuit of financial gain (Vaughn 1995).

Throughout Melanesia, pressure also mounts from conglomerate Asian logging firms, which push to ease restrictions on the cutting of rainforest timber. Devastation of forest habitats and displacement of people from alienated land are becoming a major problem in Papua New Guinea as well as in the Solomon Islands, Vanuatu, and Irian Jaya (see PIM 1994h; Bennett 1994). Between 1993 and 1994, Papua New Guinea's logging exports jumped 24 percent by official accounts, and the actual rate of increase is believed to be much higher (*Post Courier* 1995b). Recent evidence suggests that unscrupulous Asian logging firms are seducing remote New Guinea peoples into signing contracts that effectively give away their land for clear-cutting (Schieffelin 1995). This will have obviously disastrous consequences for the local population once they have dissipated the funds initially granted them.

With respect to petroleum, new drilling has located additional reserves that are to be developed and linked to the previous Chevron pipeline by 1996 (PIM 1994d). This casts further doubt on the initial plan to keep the Kutubu pipeline pristine. More ominously, a huge liquid natural gas project "four or five times the size of Kutubu" is being developed for exploitation in adjacent south New Guinea areas (PIM 1994e:43, PIM 1994a:28). If developed as planned, this project is now speculated to be the largest oil and gas facility anywhere in the world's southern hemisphere.

In short, the unfortunate consequences of mammoth projects such as the Kutubu oil pipeline are likely to snowball rather than burn themselves out in the future. The exploitative squeeze of development on local people—abetted by dreams of windfall profit on all sides—is likely to get worse. There is now increasing pressure to permit permanent alienation of locally owned land for development purposes with no right to additional compensation after initial contracts are signed. As such, Papua New Guinea's most significant resource—the fact that 97 percent of its land is managed for local subsistence by indigenous owners—may be in jeopardy.

There are seldom simple answers in such situations. Initially, at least, landowners are themselves among those most eager to contract for economic development. Local expectations are often unrealistic, if not utopian. Filer (1990) has argued that land compensation agreements create a time bomb of social disruption and antipathy no matter how much good will is shown by officials and liaison officers. It would be a mistake to suggest that government or company personnel are all penalizing the local people or the national interest. If economic development is eagerly sought by local people, it can be politically manipulated and exploited by them as well. The issues are complex because indigenous beliefs about land affiliation often conflict with ideas of ownership based on permanent residence. Tracks of local spiritual affiliation and proprietorship are diffuse and politically manipulable or extendable, especially in the remote rainforest areas where some of the largest development projects are located. Local groups compete; everyone wants a piece of the action, and no one seems to get enough. At least in the short term, local leaders can be lured by large and immediate cash payoffs to capitulate to corporate interests.

In these circumstances, one cannot assume someone to be a "good guy" or a "bad guy" on the basis of residential location, socioeconomic class, or skin color. But as Hyndman (1994) emphasizes, there is a dominant pattern in New Guinea, as in other parts of the world: Large-scale mining or drilling operations result in massive social problems, political disruption if not rebellion, ecological degradation, and stark stratification between those who profit handsomely and those who are disenfranchised. *Though all parties may be self-interested in different ways, larger structures of force ensure that those entering the fray with economic and political power benefit, while the vast majority of local people become disgruntled, disillusioned, and dispossessed.*

In a postmodern world, it is no surprise that spending a billion dollars, including many millions ostensibly slated for the local population, has not created a harmony of satisfaction in south New Guinea. *The problems raised by postcolonial pastiche and absurdity are not limited to the world of texts and authorship; they engage large-scale structural inequalities and engage a political economy of late modernity that has a huge impact on peoples' lives.* Consequences are not only unintended and ironic; they are enormously real, as is the value of the money that is funneled to a select few and kept from many others. Yet progress marches on. Summing up the situation, the *Pacific Islands Monthly* states that Papua New Guinea "is likely to make $1.3 billion in exports from its newly opened Kutubu oil field; an economic bonanza by anyone's standards" (Garrett 1992:23). Unfortunately, those most affected do not often count as anyone.

Given the practical neglect of political and economic subordination on so many fronts, it is all the more important for anthropologists to expose and critique these trends through our research and teaching. It would be a shame if this critical potential was lost amid the rarefied aesthetics of postmodern discourse.

practices

Beyond Bourdieuian Legacies

Pierre Bourdieu has become the most influential
"critical theorist" in the world of social science.
—Jeffrey Alexander

Theories of practice—most consistently associated with French sociologist Pierre Bourdieu—elaborate on modernist understandings of inequality. Viewed from a critically humanist perspective, the hyperrelativism of postmodernism is countered in practice theories by direct and critical analysis of inequality and domination. This analysis is carried out across a range of cultural and socioeconomic parameters that link individual and collective dimensions of status and stigma. However, practice theories have been less responsive in addressing a full range of subjective diversity, both in the reflexive contestations of representation and authorship and in the cultural complexities of a late modern world. The possibility of cross-pollination between practice theories and postmodern sentiments is thus especially germane for critically humanist sentiments that mediate between reflexivity and objectivism, and between appreciation of subjective diversity and the critical analysis of inequality.

Until recently, perspectives on practice have been opposed to postmodern awareness. Though roughly contemporary, practice theories emerged slightly earlier in the social sciences—during the 1970s and early 1980s—until they were impacted by reflexive concerns in fields such as cultural anthropology.[1] The temporal proximity of these approaches belies their underlying difference; practice theories combine and attempt to resuscitate grand theoretical traditions that postmodern views reject. Viewed historically, theories implicating practice and agency have attempted to meld the strengths of Marx, Weber, and Durkheim or Lévi-Strauss. Though they are synthetic, it is probably too strong or static to describe practice theories as a synthesis, since they maintain an active tension between alternative dimensions of social action. In general terms, practice emerges at the intersection between individual and collective processes, and between symbolic force and material or economic power (see fig. 2). On the one hand, individual practices are seen as constrained and orchestrated by collective structures of cultural logic or organization. But individuals are also seen as agents who reinforce or resist the larger structures that encompass them. Sociocultural life is thus a product of both societal structure and individual agency. Within this recursive relationship, practice theories focus on the way that domination is perpetuated (or altered) by cultural or symbolic as well as political-economic and material forces. In contrast to earlier versions of social constructionism (e.g., Berger and Luckmann 1967), practice theories foreground the critical exposure of inequality and disempowerment.

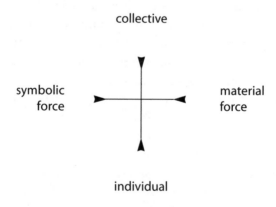

Figure 2

If 1960s anthropology tended to divide the symbolic, the social, and the material, practice theories link these together as complements through the linchpin of practical inequality. The concept of "practice" is key because the concrete actions of social agents become the point through which symbolic and material-economic inequities influence each other. Whereas structural theories relegated the individual actor to obscurity—through an emphasis on superstructural, infrastructural, or social structural determinants—practice theories bring individual action back to center stage; personal agency is kept in play with, rather than reduced to, cultural logic or political economy. Practice theories thus mediate the divide between positivist and critical theory by taking an objectivist stance but foregrounding relations of inequality and domination. As such, they have provided a late and forceful attempt to combine the modernist strengths of symbolic, social, and materialist perspectives, and to unify positivist social science with critical theory.

A contrast with posthumanist or antihumanist critiques is apposite here. More flexible than many modernist approaches, theories of practice have been critically dynamic, if not dialectical—they recapitulate in their very form the complementary aspects of social action they strive to theorize. But where fully reflexive perspectives hold social multiplicity to be chaotic and beyond the range of totalizing theory, practice theories rededicate themselves to master narratives that may comprehend this complexity. It is no wonder, then, that theorists of practice have had little sympathy for postmodernism—as reflected in Bourdieu's (1990b) defense of scholasticism and his protection of sociology as social science, and Giddens's (1990a, 1994) plea to extend rather than curtail the reach of modernist theory. (One might also note Sahlins's sardonic critique of those still *Waiting for Foucault* [Sahlins 1993a].)[2]

Selected Players
Giddens, Bourdieu, Ortner, Sahlins

As illustrated by a quartet of influential figures, theoretical interest in practice and agency has infused a wide range of scholarship in sociology, anthropology, and history.

In Britain, sociologist Anthony Giddens has developed and championed an integrated approach to structure and agency. By the late 1970s, Giddens had already published books on Durkheim, Weber, and Marx and crafted an excellent critical summary of their thought (1971, 1972a, 1972b, 1973, 1979b). Giddens identified convergences in these works and melded them into his own theory, which centered around a dualistic notion of structure and the unintended consequences of social action. For Giddens, structure both shapes social action and is recursively shaped by it (1977, 1979a). In form if not in content, Giddens's work mediated the debate among those who emphasized consciousness and agency, those who emphasized infrastructural determinants, and those who emphasized objective institutional structures in the ordering of social action. In the process, he combined cultural, materialist, and social structural dimensions of social theory.

In 1984 Giddens published *The Constitution of Society,* an omnibus if abstract overview of his "theory of structuration." He has since elaborated this theoretical structure (e.g., 1987) and produced an eight-hundred-page textbook of sociology based on it (1989a). His other recent books reject postmodern influences and provide commentaries on the political, structural, and affective consequences of modernity (1990a, 1991, 1992, 1994a, 1994b). As one of his "theses on the future of sociology," Giddens asserts that "a theoretical synthesis will emerge giving a renewed coherence to sociological debates" (1987:29). Giddens's theory was subject to much commentary in the late 1980s, including in three major volumes published between 1989 and 1991 that discussed and critiqued his work.[3]

In France, Pierre Bourdieu combined Marxist diatribe with a Goffmanesque view of personal strategy and Weberian understanding of how authority is legitimated to perpetuate domination. Armed with a highly distinctive critical approach, Bourdieu cut vigorously across the static objectivism of French structuralism as well as the subjectivism of French phenomenology and existentialism. Bourdieu's work has been particularly prolific and influential. Indeed, it is often considered synonymous with practice theory. As such, it will be considered in more detail later.

In the United States, Sherry Ortner (1984) foregrounded practice in an attempt to transcend lingering 1960s divisions between symbolic and material explanations of culture. In so doing, she highlighted the relevance of Giddens and Bourdieu for American cultural anthropology. Focusing on the individual as the point of articulation between subjective dynamics and objective structures, Ortner harnessed anthropology's rebellion against depersonalized theories of social structures or cultural systems. Drawing upon trends in transactional and processual analysis, she emphasized that agency could be brought into the analysis without giving up the importance of cultural or structural constraint (cf. Barth 1981, 1994). Consistent with this emphasis, her own subsequent ethnography (1989) attended with nuance to the practice of individuals in the process of institution building—the founding of Buddhist monasteries in the Nepalese Himalayas. This reflects Ortner's desire to engage practice theories with ethnographic and historical specifics; she is critical of ethnographic "thinness" in many existing studies of disempowerment or resistance (1995a). Her latest project-in-process (1991, 1995b) comes back to the United States and parallels Bourdieu's own path by attending to the symbolic construction of class in a contemporary Western context.

Extending from the late 1950s to the present, Marshall Sahlins's work has spanned from cultural ecology, to symbolic economy, to structuralism and structural history.[4] Practice has been important to Sahlins as a linking point between structure and event, but he is not a "practice theorist" in a larger sense; his later work resonates with practice theories through a complementary agenda. Particularly during the late 1970s and 1980s, Sahlins combined major theoretical legacies such as French structuralism, American symbolic anthropology, and the Annales school of French history—particularly its relationship between events and encompassing structures.[5]

For Sahlins (e.g., 1985:148f.), the disjuncture between structure and event poses what he calls "the risk of signs in practice": The world may prove refractory to the signs indexed to it. Reciprocally, however, structures may stay relatively constant at the semiotic or cultural level even as the material or social world alters by means of culturally constituted action. Practice can thus be the outcome of structural determinism even as its ramifications transform rather than reproduce the material world that these structures inform and continue to comprehend. For Sahlins, concrete practices and historical events provide the point of entry to these larger processes. Like Ortner (but unlike Bourdieu and Giddens), Sahlins is a dedicated ethnographic empiricist. The practices he describes (particularly the history of Polynesian cultures) are carefully detailed in real events and lives, even as they are theorized at high levels of structural sophistication. Sahlins and Ortner thus engage a more American and more ethnographic notion of practice as individual and eventive— even as they differ concerning the degree to which structural changes can be caused by events per se. By contrast, the theories of Bourdieu and Giddens rely on the structured motivation of abstract individuals rather than the practices or events of specific individuals in cultural-historical circumstances.

As these four authors illustrate, recent perspectives that engage issues of practice, structure, and agency are multifarious; they form permutations on an interrelated set of themes rather than a coherent approach. Sahlins, for one, would rightly bristle at the thought that his structural history could be subsumed under theories of practice. Likewise, Giddens's perspective has a distinctive legacy within critical sociology in England and northern Europe, including a stronger and more abstract theorization of "agency" than of practice per se (e.g., Clark et al. 1990). In American anthropology, practice approaches have probably appeared with greatest coherence in the work of Sherry Ortner and at the University of Michigan, in conjunction with work by historians (e.g., Dirks, Eley, and Ortner 1994).[6] Collectively, approaches to practice engage widening concerns in history, representation, and critical theory. Even as their impact diffuses, the legacy of practice theories remains influential in American anthropology and sociology as well as in European social sciences.

Bourdieu

As a term, *practice theory* is most commonly associated with the sociologist Pierre Bourdieu and his research teams in Paris. Following his experience among the Kabyle in Algeria and his disenchantment with French colonialism in the late 1950s, Bourdieu engaged and then critiqued French structuralism in his ethnographic articles of the 1960s. His powerful 1972 book *Esquisse d'une théorie de la pratique*[7] was published in a much revised English version as *Outline of a Theory of Practice* in 1977.[8] This work has been highly influential in cultural anthropology.

As discussed by Bourdieu himself (1990a, 1990c), his practice theory was forged in the hot debate between the objectivism of French structuralism à la Lévi-Strauss, the subjectivism of French existentialism and phenomenology à la Sartre and Merleau-Ponty, and the Marxism of Louis Althusser, among others. For Anglo-American understandings of Bourdieu, it is important to review this classic French debate between objectivism and subjectivism in the context of Marxism.

Though it may seem odd from an English or American perspective, French thinkers have generally regarded Lévi-Strauss's structuralism as the epitome of objectivism. In several ways, Lévi-Strauss incarnates a line of French thought—from Descartes in the seventeenth century to Durkheim in the late nineteenth century—that adduces mental properties through deductive reasoning and then illustrates their projection in the external world. The objective connection between the mental and the social is not doubted in this reasoning, nor is it believed to be knowable through induction, fact collecting, or hypothesis testing alone. Analysis proceeds by a kind of deductive objectivism that considers itself quite positivistic.

In the mid-twentieth century, Lévi-Strauss emphasized the objective determination exerted by structures of binary opposition in human thought. The playing out and mediation of mental antinomies was ethnographically illustrated by Lévi-Strauss in dualistic structures of kinship and marriage, totemism, myth, and art. Dualisms were socially and aesthetically mediated but were ultimately opposed at a deep cognitive level that was largely unconscious, especially in so-called primitive societies. The significance of individual action or volition was thus minimized in favor of semiotic structures and their patterns of categorical opposition. Philosophically, Lévi-Strauss was positioned as an objectivist opponent to the subjectivism of twentieth-century French existentialism and German and French phenomenology, which gave a larger place to personal will and experience in the determination of social life. Merleau-Ponty's philosophy, for instance, grounded human experience in bodily experience and sensation; Sartre's existentialism emphasized willful engagement with the dilemmas of human existence.

Lévi-Straussian structuralism stood in contrast as well to European Marxism of the 1960s. Though both structuralism and Marxism were objectivist and deterministic, they became sharply polarized over whether structures of mind or those of social and material inequality were determinant in the final instance. Whereas *structuralists* emphasized the importance of *semiotic* structures, classic *Marxists* emphasized the structure of *material* life and *economic* exploitation. Marxism viewed semiotic logics as mental superstructures or ideologies that masked rather than revealed underlying determination. In French anthropology of the 1970s, then, Marxists drew upon structuralism but maintained that semiotic structures were themselves determined by structured modes of material production.

As intellectual Marxism broadened to encompass a more dynamic view of subjectivity and resistance, its critique of Lévi-Straussian structuralism began to dovetail with and reinforce criticisms made by French

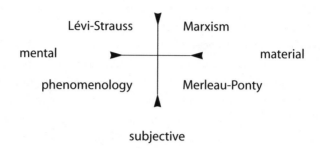

objective

Lévi-Strauss   Marxism

mental   material

phenomenology   Merleau-Ponty

subjective

Figure 3

phenomenology and existentialism. Sartre, for instance, attempted to combine revolutionary consciousness with the historical constitution of free subjectivity, and he launched a frontal assault on structuralism in the process. Whereas Lévi-Strauss's structuralism emphasized synchrony, social stasis, and determinism by unconscious mental structures, Marxism and phenomenology emphasized history, social transformation, and determinism by conscious subjectivity as mediated by material and economic forces.

Emerging during this period, Bourdieu's work located itself at the intersection of the axes that underlaid these intellectual debates in an attempt to mediate and resolve their opposition (see fig. 3). Following Lévi-Strauss, Bourdieu preserved structuralism's strong emphasis on semiotic logic; he did not afford either material structures or mental agency ultimate causality in the determination of social action. But he remained strongly if not archly *critical* of the social inequalities that semiotic structures enforced; indeed, he placed the critique of structural domination at the heart of his analysis. Retaining the stridency of Marxist critique, he directed his attack squarely at French structuralism's tendency to neglect the ideological effect of structures on practical action over time.

Though social norms may present a conservative and unchanging order in a synchronic or logical sense, Bourdieu suggested that this order played itself out in real practices and real time to create real inequalities among real people. That this structure was deeply internalized and largely unconscious to actors made its influence all the more impervious to awareness and all the more difficult to socially confront or overturn.

Bourdieu stressed that structured inequalities play out ubiquitously in the most mundane and habitual aspects of daily life—the division of labor, the physical structure of the house, the rules of etiquette and speech, the daily schedule and monthly calendar, the rules of marriage, and so on. The unequal effects of these practices in the social world were as ingrained, persistent, and difficult as they were important to expose. Practice theory was thus dedicated to the critical illumination of the unequal results of structural orientation as they played out in the lived time and symbolic space of concrete social action.

In Bourdieu's hands, then, practice theory uses a Marxist critique to mediate if not transcend the opposition between objective structure and subjective experience and between mental and material determinants in modernist French thought. On the one hand, the effect of objective structures on action is subjectivized; the very practical and taken-for-granted nature of habitual experience is key. On the other, the subjective impetus of actors is objectivized; larger structures of domination and subordination are brought to light even if (indeed, especially because) their operation may be refractory to the awareness of individuals. In all, Bourdieu combines subjective impetus with objective structure to formulate a theory of practice that is critical, dialectical, and encompassing.

Though not emphasized by most commentators,[9] Bourdieu's subjective component of practice draws heavily upon Erving Goffman's view that interpersonal relations are a competitive game of status and prestige. Bourdieu suggests that individuals in positions of dominance receive disproportionate opportunity to practice and absorb "the rules of the game." They became effective strategizers. Indeed, their advantage is strongest when their strategies are deeply internalized; they appear to have that intuitive feel for success. As such, their acquisition of status through grace, style, and decisive confidence seems at once automatic and natural. Those who are disadvantaged, on the other hand, labor like workers in a contest of privilege whose rules they cannot effectively know; they follow the conservative and plodding "doxa" of mundane social life. Precluded from playing effectively in the game of status acquisition (much less overturning it), they are doomed to an ineffective habitus that reproduces the conditions of their own domination.

For Bourdieu, subordination is as much symbolic as it is economic or political. Rather than trying to determine whether economic or symbolic inequalities are primary, Bourdieu viewed these as complementary kinds of currency or "capital." For instance, a plumber may receive relatively high wages—have high economic capital—but be considered uncouth and have low cultural prestige or symbolic capital. Conversely, an advanced graduate student or young Ph. D. may have high cultural or symbolic capital but receive little remuneration and have difficulty surviving economically.

Bourdieu has been particularly concerned to chart the relationship between symbolic and economic capital. (It can be noted that such relationships have been particularly dramatic and tumultuous in French social and intellectual history. Modern France has exhibited a tendency toward conservative nationalism and centralized political power, but it has also afforded great honor and prestige to radical innovators in intellectual and artistic production.) In many cases, Bourdieu suggests, one form of capital can ultimately be "cashed in" for another. For instance, the artist who trades cultural status to members of the managerial class in the form of art lessons obtains some of their economic capital. Conversely, bourgeois clientele pays the artist money in hopes of gaining cultural refinement and hence symbolic capital. On a larger scale, philanthropists buy cultural prestige by magnanimously giving away financial assets for public causes or in support of the arts. In larger terms, then, if symbolic domination is underpinned by practical inequalities of wealth and power, so too economic and political inequalities are conditioned and legitimated by a cultural system of prestige and cultural value. The mental and the material are thus linked in a dynamic structure that reciprocally configures inequality; neither is reducible to the other.

Bourdieu's corpus of writings has been so extensive and wide-ranging that all but the most dedicated scholars know only a portion of it. He has published almost two dozen books, scores of articles, and copious revisions and translations of his previous work. The many assistants and students who accompany academic renown in France continue to increase Bourdieu's output. Against this is the recursive style of Bourdieu's writing, which seems to recapitulate in every sentence the complex structure of his points of view. These complicated constructions are galvanized and enlarged by Bourdieu's ringing critique of inequality and domination.

Bourdieu does not mince words, and his gaze has been far-flung. In addition to ethnographic studies on the Kabyle of Algeria (e.g., 1962, 1979), Bourdieu has published major critical research volumes on French schooling and university education; contemporary art; photography; advertising; the symbolic distinctions of French class structure across a wide array of social practices and cultural preferences; the prestige structure of French academia; and the origin of the modern intellectual "field" in nineteenth century art and literature.[10] To these are added commentaries and articles (including over fifty in *Actes de la recherche en sciences sociales*) and the published interviews and verbal commentaries that reflect the aura of major figures in French intellectual life (e.g., Bourdieu 1990c, Bourdieu and Wacquant 1992; Bourdieu 1993c).

Bourdieu's influence in the United States has been particularly strong in anthropology and in the sociology of education. In the late 1980s and early 1990s, a large secondary literature on Bourdieu developed in English as well as French.[11] To students familiar with American anthropology and English sociology, however, Bourdieu's arguments are often hard to follow. His critical style is involuted and flits across vast terrain without clear topical breaks. His findings are seldom framed or separated from theoretical pronouncement, and his use of case material, diagrams, and statistics is loosely illustrative at best. However, Bourdieu's ability to penetrate the capital workings of inequality across diverse dimensions can be powerful, and he effectively critiques approaches that would divorce inequality from concrete practices in lived time.

Selected passages can be used to illustrate Bourdieu's style and some of his basic arguments.

ON PRACTICAL LOGIC

For Bourdieu, the practical logic of lived experience is impervious to formal or axiomatic structures of explanation; these ignore the obfuscations of structural ideology and the inequalities that occur in practice. Hence, a Bourdieuian sociology of practice must use academic objectivism at the same time that it turns this objectivism against itself.

> Practical logic, based on a system of objectively coherent generative and organizing schemes . . . has neither the rigor nor the constancy that characterize logical logic, which can deduce rational action from the explicit, explicitly controlled and systematized principles of an axiomatics. (1990a:102)

Probably the only way to give an account of the practical coherence of practices and works is to construct generative models which reproduce in their own terms the logic from which that coherence is generated; and diverse diagrams which, through their synoptic power of synchronization and totalization, quietly and directly manifest the objective systematicity of practice. (1990a:92–93)

The spurious alternatives of social physics and social phenomenology can only be superseded by grasping the principle of the dialectical relationship that is established between the regularities of the material universe of properties and the classificatory schemes of the habitus . . . through which there is a social world. (1990a:140)

HABITUS AND HEXIS

In Bourdieuian practice theory, structured inequalities are at once internalized as a subjective state and objectively reproduced in the unthinking and taken-for-granted dispositions of daily life—the *habitus*. Grounded in routine bodily dispositions or *hexis*, the habitus provides grounding for analysts as well as actors; it concretizes the object of analysis in lived experience and precludes the uncritical abstraction that obscures de facto domination.

The habitus is the universalizing mediation which causes an individual agent's practices, without either explicit reason or signifying intent, to be none the less "sensible" and "reasonable." (1977:79)

Class (or group) habitus, that is, the individual habitus in so far as it expresses or reflects the class (or group) could be regarded as a subjective but non-individual system of internalized structures, common schemes of perception, conception and action, which are the precondition of all objectification and apperception; and the objective co-ordination of practices and the sharing of a world-view . . . founded on the perfect impersonality and interchangeability of singular practices and views. (1990a:60)

Body hexis speaks directly to the motor function in the form of a pattern of postures that is both individual and systematic, because linked to a whole system of techniques involving the body and tools, and charged with a host of social meanings and values . . . —a way of walking, a tilt of the head, facial expressions, ways of sitting and of using implements, always associated with a tone of voice, a style of speech, and (how could it be otherwise?) a certain subjective experience. (1977:87)

DOXA IN DAILY LIFE

The structured but largely unconscious suppositions of habitus are *doxa*—the underlying classifications and rules that enforce status and inequality all the more because they are typically not subject to explicit awareness or critique. These rules and classifications infuse virtually all areas of social life; in a sense, they form its precondition.

> Systems of classification which reproduce, in their own specific logic, the objective classes, i.e., the divisions by sex, age, or position in the relations of production, make their specific contribution to the reproduction of the power relations of which they are the product, by securing the mis-recognition, and hence the recognition, of the arbitrariness on which they are based. . . . This experience we shall call *doxa*, so as to distinguish it from an orthodox or heterodox belief implying awareness and recognition of the possibility of different or antagonistic beliefs. (1977:163–64)

TIME AND STRATEGY

In contrast to a formal model of synchronic structure and reversible exchange, Bourdieu stresses the importance of lived time—the rhythm and tempo of practices that inculcate bodily habits and allow cultural strategies and distinctions to play out through a lived and irreversible sequence. Daily activities or calendrical schedules form the preconditions of this temporal unfolding; they encode as "natural" a particular division of activity, including gendered or age- or class-based asymmetries of production, consumption, and social or spiritual transaction. Within this context, activities such as marriage and exchange, which appeared as reciprocal alliance and social integration from a structuralist point of view, in fact reveal a highly pragmatic and irreversible history of status rivalries, honor gained and lost, and strategic deployment of economic and political capital.

> To restore to practice its practical truth, we must therefore reintroduce time into the theoretical representation of a practice which, being temporally structured, is intrinsically defined by its *tempo*. . . . To substitute

strategy for the *rule* is to reintroduce time, with its rhythm, its orientation, its irreversibility. . . . [P]ractices [are] defined by the fact that their temporal structure, direction, and rhythm are *constitutive* of their meaning. (1977:8–9)

The matrimonial game is similar to a card game, in which the outcome depends partly on the deal, the cards held (their value itself being defined by the rules of the game, characteristic of the social formation in question), and partly on the players' skill: that is to say, firstly on the material and symbolic capital possessed by the families concerned, their wealth in instruments of production and in men . . . ; and secondly on the competence which enables the strategists to make the best use of this capital. (1977:58; cf. 1976)

OCCUPATION, CAPITAL, AND CLASS

Since the early 1960s, Bourdieu has been particularly concerned to analyze the relationship between cultural and economic capital in French society. The symbolic space of cultural domination teems with status distinctions that are subtle and taken for granted—for instance, status differences between upper-class and lower-class tastes in matters of music, food, sports, books, politics, and the arts. In *Distinction* (1984), his massive study of French cultural capital, Bourdieu's argument is punctuated by insets of informant statements, advertisements, statistical tables, graphs, and complex conceptual diagrams.

The analyses presented in this book are based on a survey by questionnaire, carried out in 1963 and 1967–68, on a sample of 1,217 people. The survey sought to determine how the cultivated disposition and cultural competence that are revealed in the nature of the cultural goods consumed, and in the way they are consumed, vary according to the category of agents and the area to which they applied, from the most legitimate areas such as painting or music to the most "personal" ones such as clothing, furniture, or cookery. . . . Two basic facts were thus established: on the one hand, the very close relationship linking cultural practices (or the corresponding opinions) to educational capital (measured by qualifications) and, secondarily, to social origin, (measured by father's occupation). (1984:13)

Those who have acquired the bulk of their cultural capital in and for school have more "classical," safer cultural investments than those who have received a large cultural inheritance. For example, whereas the members of the dominant class with the highest qualifications (the *agré-gation* or a diploma from a *grande école*) never mention certain works or certain painters typical of middle-brow culture . . . , have considerable knowledge of composers, and prefer the *Well-Tempered Clavier* or the *Firebird Suite*, the highly educated members of the working and middle classes often make choices which indicate their respect for more "scholas-tic" culture (Braque, *Concerto for the Left Hand*). (1984:65)

ON EDUCATION AND THE UNIVERSITY

Secondary schools are a major site of French cultural distinction and sta-tus reproduction. Bourdieu stresses that French education privileges those whose parents have economic and symbolic capital. Class-biased techniques of pedagogy and examination affirm the "natural" ability of these students to attend prestigious schools, which in turn facilitates their entrance to a major university.

In the present state of the [French educational] system, the exclusion of the great mass of working-class and middle-class children takes place not at the end of primary schooling but steadily and impalpably, all through the early years of secondary school, through hidden forms of elimina-tion. (1988a:154)

The whole logic of an academic institution based on pedagogic work of the traditional type and ultimately guaranteeing the "infallibility" of the "master," finds expression in the professorial ideology of student incapac-ity, a mixture of tyrannical stringency and disillusioned indulgence which inclines the teacher to regard all communication failures, however unforeseen, as integral to a relationship which inherently implies poor reception of the best messages by the worst receivers. (Bourdieu and Passeron 1990:111)

The structure of the university field reflects the structure of the field of power, while its own activity of selection and indoctrination contributes to the reproduction of that structure. (1988a:41)

FIELDS OF ARTISTIC PRODUCTION

Like institutional education, so too do the arts present a field of forces and struggles for Bourdieu; the meaning of a given intellectual product is shaped by the larger structure of contests for prestige that contextualize it.

> The literary or artistic field is a *field of forces*, but it is also a *field of struggles* tending to transform or conserve this field of forces. . . . The meaning of a work (artistic, literary, philosophical, etc.) changes automatically with each change in the field within which it is situated for the spectator or reader. This effect is most immediate in the case of so-called classic works, which change constantly as the universe of coexistent works changes. (1993b:30–31)

> The struggle in the field of cultural production over the imposition of the legitimate mode of cultural production is inseparable from the struggle within the dominant class (with the opposition between "artists" and "bourgeois") to impose the dominant principle of domination (that is to say—ultimately—the definition of human accomplishment). (1993b:41)

REFLEXIVITY

Given Bourdieu's critique of objectivist ideologies, it is not surprising that he is critical of the objectivizing impetus in academics. For him, academics tend to reproduce the conservative ideology of their own academic culture without exposing the practical structures of domination that these ideologies keep hidden. Bourdieu stresses the need to incorporate both a critical view of academic structures and a practical view of their subjectivity. At the same time, however, Bourdieu asserts that his own perspective can be uniquely objective and scientific; only his reflexive sociology can free itself of obfuscating shackles and discern the combined subjective and objective truths of academic and wider social practice. Bourdieu's reflexivity is strongly positivist and different from postmodern views that emphasize the impossibility of objective understanding.

> Like every science, sociology accepts the principle of determinism understood as a form of the principle of sufficient reason. The science that must give the reasons for that which is thereby postulates that nothing is without a reason for being. (1993c:24–25)

In the social sciences, the progress of knowledge presupposes progress in our knowledge of the conditions of knowledge. (1990a:1)

It is one and the same thing to find oneself inevitably involved in the struggle for the construction and imposition of the legitimate taxonomy, and, by raising oneself to the second degree, to take as one's object the science of this struggle. (1990c:180–81)

We can expect the progress of reason only from a permanent struggle to define and promote the social conditions that are most favorable to the development of reason. (1990b:389)

Appreciations

Bourdieu's work has been very influential and has cross-pollinated major strands of modernist theory. It has also retained a highly distinctive and critical edge, as opposed to blander attempts to combine or amalgamate approaches. Bourdieu's work has effectively galvanized the critical intensity of Marx, the Lévi-Straussian exposition of *a priori* structures, and the Weberian desire to mediate objectivist and subjectivist understandings within sociology. In addition, Bourdieu has put domination in play through the notion of symbolic as well as economic capital. Terms such as *habitus, doxa, hexis, strategic field, symbolic capital,* and *practical logic,* not to mention *practice* itself, are now basic concepts in anthropological parlance. Foreshadowing later trends, Bourdieu's work of the 1970s exploded the barrier between foreign or legitimately "ethnographic" contexts and the critical analysis of Western public culture, modern institutions, and academic structures. This makes his work relevant for the cultural anthropology of late modernity, which exhibits an increasing awareness of the connection between the foreign and the Western, the village and the city, and the ostensibly simple and the manifestly complex. His reflexive critique of theory and academic scholarship significantly predated the mid-1980s American interest in reflexive ethnography, even if these developments are not truly comparable. That Bourdieu's writing is difficult stimulates the debate between those who wish to dismiss it altogether and those who feel obliged to penetrate it more deeply. His expression and empirics can be a productive challenge for those wishing to refine his ideas or apply them more systematically in specific contexts.

From a critically humanist perspective, Bourdieu's particular strength is his exposure and critique of alternative forms of inequality; he opens these up to new levels of theoretical awareness and understanding. Bourdieu enables this critique through an array of concepts that penetrate the complementarity between symbolic and economic domination. In the process, his work exposes the embeddedness of domination and how refractory it can be to awareness or resistance. Bourdieu shows how domination is often most present in areas of social life where it is least expected: our underlying axes of cultural classification, our most basic and physical patterns of movement, and our most mundane patterns of everyday habit. That these things go without saying has made the subordinations they encode all the more resistant to analytic exposure.

Bourdieu's corpus of work has grown enormously, both in topical sweep and in sheer size, yet his writings retain an analytic lens that is both sophisticated and powerful. During a period in which many social theorists have despaired of their ability to forge larger and more coherent directions, Bourdieu's work remains influential: It reminds us that grand theories can make important contributions and chart unexplored potentials.

Practical Criticisms

In several respects, the strengths of Bourdieu's theory are also its weaknesses. From a critically humanist perspective, Bourdieu's insightful expositions and critiques of inequality harbor a negative complement: They are thin in their appreciation of cultural and subjective variation. Bourdieu does maintain a dynamic relationship between symbolic and economic domination, but he has much less concern for cultural and subjective diversity. What are the ethnographic and historical specifics that make sociocultural systems different over time and space? How have cultural formations changed, proliferated, and differentiated? What are the diverse ways in which people may resist or attempt to subvert structures of domination? Amid the drumbeat of domination, Bourdieu's appreciation of diversity, nuance, and cultural richness seems rather muted; the world of cultural variation is faded and sapped of significance. Ethnographic and historical details are presented more to illustrate Bourdieu's theory than to explore or appreciate the circumstances at hand. Cultural and historical variation can get ground up in the hegemonic totality of Bourdieu's theoretical mill.

Notwithstanding the qualifications in his prose, then, Bourdieu's theory is ultimately totalizing. It reconfirms the excesses of high modernist paradigms: a tendency to be overly categorical, too quick in self-justification, not open enough to alternative forms of understanding, and liable to turn empirical observations into props for theoretical assumptions. Despite equivocations, reflexive analyses, and qualifying complexities, Bourdieu defends his sociology as an objective science that must be protected against all other alternatives. In the process, it shuts itself off from intellectual growth and enrichment. To detractors, Bourdieu pretends to be a lone giant when pretensions to intellectual giantism are anachronistic or passé (see Marcus 1990).[12]

Apart from postmodern critiques and the common wish to topple a theoretical eminence, Bourdieu's dismissal of alternatives does seem rather quick (e.g., 1990c). Given that his perspective has already incorporated major strands of modernist social theory, it is perhaps natural that it resists further innovation. And the disciplinary rivalry between French academic fields does not lend itself easily to theoretical or empirical openness. But it remains true that the central features of Bourdieu's thought have undergone surprisingly little refinement or development over the last twenty-five years, even as they are increasingly spun out through recombinations, republications, and topical accretions. In the face of other alternatives, Bourdieu launches predictable counterattacks: The criticism is deemed to be either too objective, too subjective, or blind to the full nuance and insight of his own theory.[13] He fortifies his walls at the same time that he builds his castle.

Of course, this does not undercut the potential of Bourdieu's original project; it is wrong to bypass a theory simply because it is grand or resistant to change. But the problem is deeper if this resistance is empirical as well as theoretical. It is on this point that Bourdieu's lack of appreciation for cultural and subjective diversity becomes most telling. Baldly put, Bourdieu's empiricism is weak. His evaluations often seem based on assertion rather than careful factual deliberation; their theoretical strength is often their factual weakness. In his empirically strongest projects, such as *Distinction* (1984) and *Homo Academicus* (1988a), there is richer *illustration* of his analysis. But it remains hard to deepen our understanding of specifics, as opposed to simply accepting or rejecting Bourdieu's own point of view.

If this weakness is evident within Bourdieu's work, it is also evident in what he excludes. Bourdieu fails to truly engage a range of cross-cultural variation in subjectivity, belief and action—both between and within cultures. Much of this variation may not fit so comfortably with Bourdieu's axes of symbolic and economic capital and their various related incarnations. Bourdieu's categories are less empirically responsive for being powerful; his strong critique of inequality needs to be widened—both empirically and theoretically—by a fuller and more honest confrontation of cultural and historical variation.

These criticisms, it should be noted, are somewhat mitigated by a recent and as yet untranslated volume in the Bourdieuian corpus: *La Misère du monde* (1993a). This is a huge collaborative work of multivocal ethnography—a detailed rendition by teams of French sociologists of the grievances, prejudices, and "miseries" of contemporary French blue-collar workers, shopkeepers, immigrants, petty officials, dispossessed teenagers, unemployed workers, and so on. Mobilizing his large cadre of students, Bourdieu has documented a plethora of plaintive and sometimes reactionary voices among French common folk; the work is a compendium of their opinions. These voices explode the thin surface of French public life and expose the daily cauldron of discontents and frustrations that cross from city to suburb and back. The stories are often riveting; they remind one of the laboring discontents of Americans chronicled so well in Studs Terkel's classic book *Working* (1974).

Consistent with the fragmented voices now common in American cultural anthropology, Bourdieu's *Misère* has a chopped-up quality that is overlain with critiques that are as heavy in tone as they are light in analytic substance. Accordingly, the larger structures that predispose and then reflect personal discontent are but thinly analyzed by Bourdieu and his team, even as these are theoretically damned. Bourdieu himself conducted and wrote up several of the interviews as well as supplying the critical introductions to some of the volume's many sections and, of course, the introduction to the work as a whole.

Their great potential notwithstanding, the substantive accounts in *Misère* are an apparent exception that ultimately confirms Bourdieu's larger tendency. The work is markedly thin in analyzing, conceptualizing, or carefully theorizing the diversity of dissatisfied voices that it so poignantly records. These are not teased apart so much as grossly subsumed by Bourdieu himself. The result is therefore consistent with the larger weaknesses of Bourdieu's perspective, as discussed earlier. However, Bourdieu's support of a new generation of critical ethnography on diverse segments of contemporary French society remains highly significant. It may have an important legacy: to diversify, energize, and "ethnographize" the future of French sociology. As such, it may expand theoretically beyond Bourdieu's own categories.

It is important to note (although it may be surprising) that Bourdieu's influence has *not* been particularly strong in French *anthropology*, which still largely considers sociology to be a disciplinary competitor. Many French anthropologists still embrace Lévi-Strauss's intellectual ancestry, though they now tend to articulate structuralist concerns to a range of materialist and psychoanalytic issues as well as to myth and social structure.[14]

Leaving aside these recent French developments, the general weaknesses of Bourdieu's approach from a critically humanist perspective can be concretized and summarized in five areas. Many of these caveats pertain to the work of Anthony Giddens as well. Though it is not possible to treat his work in detail here, the tendency for theory to be powerful in abstraction but weakly engaged with the specifics of cross-cultural diversity and cultural history may also be mentioned in Giddens's case.

First, though Bourdieu emphasizes practice (and Giddens emphasizes agency), there is little ultimate emphasis on the creative impact that individual actors may have. The abstract or average individual is highly theorized, but the actions and practices of real individuals have little analytic nuance. Ultimately sociological, these theories are relatively thin in their understanding of individual and cultural subjectivity.

Second, despite their emphasis on time and process, these theorizations of practice and agency have little feeling for historical change or transformation, including their specifics. Though practice and agency are analytically highlighted, they work primarily to maintain inequality rather than to resist or alter it.[15] The contemporary notion of practice thus bears surprisingly little relationship to the Marxist notion of praxis. If the theoretical approach of Bourdieu (and Giddens) is deficient in engaging human diversity across cultural space, it is also deficient in explaining concrete changes over historical time. Bourdieu is unconvincing in his response to this criticism.

> The problem of change. I do not see where my readers could have found
> the model of circular reproduction which they attribute to me (structure

→ habitus → structure). Indeed, I could show how the opposition between statics and dynamics, structure and history, reproduction and transformation, etc., is totally fictitious, in so far as it is the structure which constitutes the principle of the strategies aimed at preserving or transforming the structure. (1990c:118)

The implication still lingers that structure determines the behavior of its own future incarnations.

Third, the theoretical paradigms of Bourdieu (and Giddens) have a narrow and insufficient appreciation of human motivation. There has been a marked tendency for theories of structure and practice to attribute motivation to political and economic self-interest, at least in the final instance. Though these theories give strong weight to agency, the subjective power of agency tends to be confined to "schemas" or "strategies" of domination and "interest" over various "rules" and "resources." Without a grounding in cultural variation, these terms easily harbor Western assumptions, namely, that interest is self-interest and that it invariably tends toward economic and political domination.

Bourdieu and Giddens attempt to transcend motivational reductionism by making cultural categories the condition as well as the consequence of inequality in the social distribution of resources. And in fairness to Bourdieu, his notion of symbolic capital was itself developed to combat economic reductionism:

The use I make of the notion of interest, which can call forth the accusation of economism against a work which, from the very beginning (I can refer here to my anthropological studies), was conceived in opposition to economism. The notion of interest—I always speak of *specific* interest— was conceived as an instrument of rupture intended to bring the materialist mode of questioning to bear on realms from which it was absent and into the sphere of cultural production in particular. (1990c:106)

This rebuttal is important. Ultimately, however, Bourdieu's attempt to widen economic or material reductionism has been seriously limited by motivational concepts such as "game," "strategy," and "capital," which it has borrowed for purposes of critique. In the final analysis, Bourdieu's symbolic capital still tends to result in or be exchanged for economic or political capital. As Harker et al. note, "Politics . . . is seen as a ghostly *deus ex machina* which works unseen behind the facade of appearance . . . as the *ultimate* form of capital, for which all other lesser currencies are finally cashed in" (1990:211).

Fourth, the strong attention Bourdieu gives to inequality in general actually masks diverse forms of inequality that are not isomorphic with symbolic or economic capital. There is little specific analysis of gendered or sexual inequality, of racism, ethnocentrism, or nationalism. For Bourdieu, such inequalities ultimately boil down to generic symbolic or economic and political concerns, and these turn out to be two sides of a single capital coin. Though much is made of domination in a general sense, it is inequality of wealth and power in the service of rank or class distinction that is ultimately emphasized. Domination based on gender, sexuality, race, ethnicity, or nationality is either neglected or blurred within more encompassing categories. Though this was also frequently true of Marx, such a weakness is more excusable for a social theory developed in the 1840s and 1850s than it is for one developed in the social and intellectual context of the 1960s, 1970s, and 1980s. Bourdieu's totalism is highly compromising in this regard. In particular, the *variable* relationship that different forms of inequality have to one another becomes difficult to analyze. The complexity and confusion that appear in Bourdieu's charts in an attempt to spatially diagram various forms of capital underscore rather than ameliorate this difficulty. Ultimately, Bourdieu's analysis cannot easily grasp the conflicting interests of individuals as they strategize, compete, or resist inequality across *different* social fields and in *different* cultural logics.

Fifth and finally, the notion of structure is vague in Bourdieu's work and abstract in Giddens's (Sewell 1989, cf. 1993). On the positive side, practice theories use a dual notion of structure—structure is both constitutive *of* and constituted *by* action. This provides an effective way to subsume and transcend theoretical polarizations between objectivism and subjectivism and also between base and superstructure. But in the modernist attempt to trump these oppositions within a single theory, the notion of structure enlarges; it reifies to fill the conceptual vacuum where superstructure and infrastructure were located. Even if structure is now a constitutive or constructive process rather than a static entity, it still tends to be self-fulfilled, tautologous, and "functional" in the work of Bourdieu and Giddens. Bourdieu himself describes his theory as a kind of "constructivist structuralism" or "genetic structuralism" (1990c:123;

Honneth et al. 1986:43).[16] Despite all the qualifications and emphases on process, structure still persists as a large and vague black box.

This trend can be seen in a larger comparative and historical context vis-à-vis parallel incarnations of "culture" and "structure" (and now "hegemony") in cultural anthropology from the 1950s through the 1980s. The anthropological concept of structure that was associated with British structural-functionalism was enlarged to accommodate dimensions of Lévi-Straussian semiotic structure and, during the 1970s, Marxist concepts of structural domination. In the 1980s, a rejuvenated notion of structure emerged from practice theories to combine these notions; structure was exposed as a powerful ideology as well as a principle of classification and a social glue. By the late 1980s and early 1990s, however, cultural anthropologists had become wary of structure in *any* guise and wary of culture as an overly integrated and positivist entity. Recently, then, neo-structure has been increasingly replaced by terms such as "hegemony." And "culture" is replaced by notions such as "imaginary" or "ethnoscape."[17] But like their predecessors, these terms now threaten to blanket the large terrain they are supposed to illuminate; as reified categories, they hide the variation that underlies them.

American Engagements

Even if Bourdieu is taken as an archetype of practice theory, his strengths and weaknesses have not translated directly to American-Anglo concerns with structure and agency. Relative to French sociology, American cultural anthropology is bolstered by a stronger tradition of detailed ethnography and a richer appreciation of cultural diversity in political and economic history. From a critically humanist perspective, American attempts to apply and diversify Bourdieuian practice theory (and Giddens's theorization of agency) have been quite important.

There is a long and productive relationship in anthropology between European grand theory and the pragmatism of American ethnography. Though the analogy could be pushed too far—and is difficult to assess as it approaches the present—there are several historical junctures at which an American emphasis on ethnographic particularism has provided refinement or important critique for grander European theorizations. This is evident in Boas's move to relativize and combat the speculative excesses of

Victorian evolutionism in the 1890s and early 1900s; Murdock's move to empiricize the rather formal British and French notions of social structure during the 1950s; and Geertz's move to particularize and localize Weberian interpretive sociology during the 1960s and 1970s. Analogous, perhaps, is Ortner's move to localize the generalities of Bourdieuian practice theory in the 1980s and 1990s.

In the current instance, American anthropologists have embraced diversity in temporal as well as spatial terms; there is special interest in historical change and variation as well as in ethnographic specifics of practice in diverse cultural contexts. As part of this process, current developments in American cultural anthropology reflect the influence of cultural studies and Gramscianism; American approaches to practice increasingly include critical analysis of cultural contestation and representational politics. Bourdieu's influence remains part of this mix but is in no sense preeminent. Indeed, it would be possible to view this same confluence in American cultural anthropology through the lens of Gramsci, as will be discussed later, or perhaps through the cultural politics of Frantz Fanon, as opposed to considering it through the context of practice theories per se.[18]

All these strains meld in the combined concern with culture, power, and history that is now prominent in American cultural anthropology. Indeed, programs that emphasize this triumvirate of issues have grown and spread quickly in the United States: permutations on culture-power-history present a dominant institutional trend in American cultural anthropology today, from coast to coast.[19] This trilogy is also reflected in important monograph series, including one edited by Ortner, Dirks, and Eley and another edited by Bourdieu, Bloch, and Comaroff. Jean and John Comaroff at Chicago have been influential in developing a flexible if sometimes loose version of critical theory in the analysis of culture and history (see Comaroff 1985; Comaroff and Comaroff 1991, 1992, 1993).

Against such alternatives, Bourdieu's theory seems conceptually rigid and ethnographically and historically restricted. The Bourdieuian themes that do carry lasting influence in American anthropology include his seminal insights concerning symbolic capital, his stress on the uncritical or unselfconscious nature of habitus in practice, and his insistence that the strategic play of structure be considered over lived time. The resonance of culture-power-history approaches to these theoretical initiatives is reflected by their concern with representation and power while rejecting postmodern excesses. The Comaroffs, for example, advocate a "neomodern" approach, which effectively captures the spirit of these trends:

> The human world, post-anything and -everything, remains the product of discernible social and cultural processes; processes partially indeterminate yet, in some measure, systematically determined; ambiguous and polyvalent, yet never utterly incoherent or meaningless; open to multiple constructions and context, yet never entirely free of order—or the reality of power and constraint. It is in this sense that we affirm, by prefix and predilection, our commitment to *neo*modern anthropology. And to the conviction that, far from being opposed to (or detachable from) theory, ethnography is instrument in its creation—and hence is indispensable to the production of knowledge about all manner of social phenomenon. Indeed, we would argue that no humanist account of the past or present can (or does) go very far without the kind of understanding that the ethnographic gaze supposes. (Comaroff and Comaroff 1992:xi)

Such current perspectives engage a historical understanding of domination and symbolic power while flirting cautiously with a fully reflexive or deconstructive view. Though recent attempts have been made to include Foucauldian concerns within the culture-power-history nexus, exactly how this juxtaposition can be put together theoretically remains to be seen (see Dirks et al. 1994; Stoler 1995). The need for this expansion reflects the gradual dissolution of a practice theory paradigm in cultural anthropology, even as underlying issues of cultural as well as political and economic domination and their relation to practice remain highly important.

In actual usage, Bourdieu's relentless critique of inequality is now employed selectively, like an occasional punctuation mark, in American cultural anthropology. A bright spark, Bourdieu is cited to galvanize and lend stridency to the parts of analysis that hammer on inequality in general and symbolic domination in particular. In contrast to Foucault's, Bourdieu's acknowledged influence in anthropology has likely begun a slow if steady decline. But it is important that the fruits of practice for an ethnographically responsive critical humanism not be lost sight of amid the rush to promote antitheoretical fashions.

Practices, Spaces, and Places in Late Modernity

The current legacy of practice and structural history in American cultural anthropology is too diverse and close to home for me to easily characterize, but two junctures bear particular note. The first concerns space and place; the second concerns the relationship between objectivity and authorship. Both relate to important issues of agency, and both emphasize the need for greater diversity in conceptualizations of culture and power. From the standpoint of a critically humanist perspective in anthropology, both these Bourdieuian weaknesses can be compensated for by extending and deepening the American commitment to detailed ethnography in an era of late modernity.

Though practice theories have brought issues of time to the study of structures, they have dealt much less successfully with issues of space and place. Practice theorists have considered spaces and places in their abstract structure (as in Bourdieu's [1977] classic analysis of the Kabyle house) or as a path of movement or displacement by individual agents (as in Ortner 1989). But the analytic expansion of space and location to include imagined or discontinuous space suggests new kinds of cultural and practices (e.g., Appadurai 1990). How are structures of practice spatially and locationally configured? Where on the very empirical ground does one structure or practice leave off and another begin?

The same difficulty confronts notions of "culture," "field," "hegemony," or, more recently, "imaginary." It remains unpopular to consider the locational dimensions of such constructs. (Q: "Where does one hegemony leave off and another begin?" A: "That's the wrong question; these are only heuristic or analytic distinctions.") But we must begin to ask such questions if we are to refine our understanding of heuristic constructs, or, perhaps better, to deconstruct them in a less than totally destructive manner. The line papered over by these concepts—the line between abstract structure and embodied agency—is pragmatically revealed by making comparisons: Is it indeed possible or desirable to compare one "field" or "hegemony" or "imaginary" to another? We can now take for granted that cultures cannot be defined by discrete or stable traits. Nor can they be uncritically compared within the analytic space of a synchronic region or network. Yet it is just this possibility that the reification of concepts such as "structure of practice," "hegemony," "field," or even "imaginary" ultimately imply.

The answer is increasingly that these concepts should be desubstantialized; they should be viewed more as processes than as entities. But this assessment—which I fully agree with—still leaves concrete issues of comparative space in abeyance. It leaves guiding concepts ungrounded in a physical sense as well as an analytic one.

The issue is galvanized as the legacy of practice is confronted with postcolonial if not postmodern constructions of identity. Like inequalities, identities are now recognized to cross and transect disparate localities (e.g., Lash and Friedman 1992; Featherstone et al. 1995). Sociocultural theorists such as Harvey (1990, 1993a) link the proliferation of dispersed identities to the time-space compression of postmodernity. These themes also resonate in cultural anthropology (e.g., Gupta and Ferguson 1992; Rouse 1991; Shore 1996: chs. 5,6). Practice engages diverse forms of identity that do not boil down to a shared location.

In most regions of the world, these processes are prominent and sometimes dramatic. Melanesia and New Guinea in particular serve as a case in point. Twenty-five years ago, it was common to hold the heuristic illusion that linguistic or political units were relatively self-contained in parts of New Guinea. In the context of the 1990s, however, such a notion seems laughable. Known by reputation as a site of rich tribal ethnography, Melanesia has long since entered a world of village-town hybrids, evangelical transformations, postcolonial politics, and the continuing if continually compromised pursuit of economic development. Classic Melanesian monographs were typically grounded in village-based ethnography. Assuming the homogeneity if not autonomy of indigenous local culture, they often focused on kinship or descent, leadership structure, ritual organization, or topics such as subsistence intensity, sexual antagonism or pollution, socioeconomic exchange, or symbolic construction.

Rich as this work has been, it needs to expand and accommodate new developments. The site of Melanesian ethnography has appropriately grown from the village to include the school, the church, the courts, the disco or cinema, the store, and relatives or *wantoks* in towns or urban centers, as well as the mines, the parliament, and the multinational corporations seeking huge logging or mineral rights. Melanesian studies now embrace a host of topics that articulate "traditional" concerns with deep postcolonial tensions concerning access to national resources and development, fundamentalist Christianity, law and order, and the mediation of ethnic identities maintained between village and town, between regions, and in some cases between nations.[20] These identifications range from wage remittances from distant relatives to women's church groups, business investment cooperatives, violent gangs of dislocated young men, and political affiliations that resist regional or national government. Personal and collective identity is increasingly forged as a creative discordance among local, regional, and sometimes millennial identifications and aspirations. Indigenous languages are compromised and in some cases relinquished amid the spreading *lingua franca* of Melanesian pidgin (Kulick 1992). Kinship obligations compete with the drive for individual wealth and prestige as incipient class divisions informed by migration and urban living grate against deep allegiances based on natal kinship and affiliation. Marriage intertwines with business (*bisnis*) through the inflation of bridewealth payments (Marksbury 1993). Women of traditional virtue are judged not just against standards of female pollution but those of Christian propriety. Even in reasserting local custom (*kastom*), status conflicts of a postcolonial nature emerge at the core of politics and representation.[21]

These developments rebound in complex relation to the attempts of Melanesia's independent states to create national identities in the face of social and political fragmentation (Foster 1995b). Media, art, tourism, and language reflect this mix of the local with the national and even the global.[22] The tensions of this cauldron are easily engaged by problems as diverse as town and urban migration; vandalism, robbery, sexual abuse, a skyrocketing incidence of sexually transmitted diseases, ecocide and land alienation by multinational mining and logging corporations, local warfare, rebellions against the regional or national government, and political turmoil and corruption.

Equally important and much less emphasized are the ways in which indigenous people assert meaning, dignity, and resilience or resistance amid these problems. The fact that most people still spend most of their time cultivating their gardens should not be lost sight of. Indigenous practices and indigenous beliefs are far from dead; indeed, they resurface with creative regularity. More than a simple retention of custom, traditions are actively re-created as they are reproduced. The tensions and problems of postcolonialism are legion, but the practical ways in which people find continuities and creative spaces as they engage the possibilities and constraints of change—how they expand and elaborate their received senses of practice and agency—have only recently been opened to understanding and theorization by cultural anthropologists.

Contemporary configurations of practice and agency are thus both understudied and ripe for detailed investigation. This research may be stimulated by theoretical analysis or by programmatic critique but needs in the final instance to be engaged by substantive ethnography of actual social situations. How do different fields of prestige get constituted and become juxtaposed with each other in individual lives? What forms of meaning and dignity form amid the plethora of established and emerging inequalities? Which competing forms of postcolonial practice are most deeply motivating and which are most consciously strategized about? How are traditional forms of gender, age, and ethnic domination reproduced even as they are greatly transformed and in some cases subverted?

In the postcolonial present, we may not be able to effectively delineate "systems" or "cultures" or "structures" or "hegemonies" or "ethnoscapes" along analytic boundaries much less spatial ones. But we can study the contours of practical experience whereby individuals construct alternative goals and identities. We can study how they employ limited resources to negotiate competing sources of symbolic capital. The abstract space of postmodernism or the textualized space that continues to haunt cultural studies can be effectively concretized by looking at the locational construction of identity and inequality in the practices of individuals. That these practices mediate between conflicting identities and aspirations injects a dynamism that practice theories originally lacked; it makes processes of choice and change intrinsic rather than residual to social practice. It opens up rather than closes a rich and emergent understanding of agency. And it grounds these processes in the experience of actual individuals, as opposed to the abstract individuals of general theory.

If American anthropology of the early twentieth century turned the homogeneous concept of "Culture" into the relative appreciation of "cultures," perhaps in a period of late modernity it can now turn the general notion of "Practice" into the richer ethnography of "practices." The difference between these two twists on anthropology's spiral is that power and inequality are now considered central rather than irrelevant to the creation of difference.

Practices of places and spaces also emerge on a larger scale. Positing the existence of regional or national or transnational contours may be a separatist reification (Bourdieu 1991a:223). But these remain ethnographic facts of great importance. The deterritorialization of nation-states and diasporas, not to mention "tribes," has been consistently complemented by a bloody reterritorialization that is amply evident in Bosnia, Rwanda, Kuwait, and many other areas. It is also evident on a smaller scale in Papua New Guinea's reconquest of its insular province of Bougainville, with its huge copper mine. As any New Guinean seeking land compensation or political leverage will tell you, concrete notions of place and space continue to matter very much. The way that regional or global processes are selectively interpreted and actively appropriated or subsumed within existing local asssertions and divisions remains extremely important.

The fluid nature of contemporary identities—what Appadurai (1993) describes as postnational social formations—requires concrete documentation in economic and social terms as well as in imaginary ones. If the analytic demands of such spaces are more complex than they were for people once thought to be without history, they remain as important on the sociological ground as they are in more dispersed airwaves of affiliation. When practices are viewed in actual spatial locations and not just as microcosms of a neo-capitalist world, the specific features that inflect the relationship between power and culture come into clearer view. Postmodern geography and its marriage with the ripples of world systems theory have been highly stimulating in British and Scandanavian critical theory of the 1990s (e.g., Friedman 1994; Lash and Urry 1994; Bird et al. 1993; Featherstone et al. 1995; Miller 1995; Heelas et al. 1996; Keith and Pile 1993; Hannerz 1990; Soja 1989). But these studies remain both ethnographically and historically underspecified; there is little detailed treatment of concrete conditions or real people. Though global notions of space help refine our understanding of late modern diversity, the current tendency is still too often either to collapse these differences into a singular and undifferentiated Space—the abstract space of late modernity—or to reduce spaces, deconstructively, to a reflex of our own representations.

Ethnography can be used to turn Space into spaces at the same time that it turns Practice into practices. Field research can consider the location that practices take and the variable relationship they have with multiple identities and affiliations. This task can draw upon the strengths of practice theories without being confined by their limiting assumptions. The study of political economy and history that practice theories have pushed ahead in the United States need not be inimical to the study of composite identities and cultural contestations, particularly in a period of

late modernity. The ethnography of practices links concrete agency to
the study of how publics, imaginaries, and their associated aspirations are
locationally promoted, negotiated, or rendered superficial.

On a larger scale, many suggest that the late modern world mixes
global homogenization with the flexible or hybrid accumulation of cultural fragments. In the present perspective, this linked antinomy stems
from the developmental interface between local practices and their
appropriation of larger economies of images and capitals.[23] Practices
serve as a fulcrum between the local and the global as well as between the
material and the referential. As Bourdieu identified and others now
explore, practice provides a point of entry to consider how actions and
identities proliferate over time. Large-scale spatial diversity is the end
result of this spiraling outcome: Small initial variations telescope through
practical and symbolic reinforcement into large cultural and political-
economic differences. The chaos theory of spatial divergence or fractal
identity may or may not turn out to be important for anthropology
(Appadurai 1990:20–21). But its potential for critically humanist sensibilities is not so much to permit the objective comparison of sociocultural
forms as to illuminate larger structures of relationship between cultural
diversity, on the one hand, and social inequality, on the other. In a period
of late modernity, small-scale structures of local agency and large-scale
ones of political culture and economy can be concretely documented,
analyzed, and theorized in the context of each other.

It may be asked whether anthropology's engagement with practices
and spaces must invariably be pluralizing; is a grander and more singular
theory intrinsically improper? This question can itself be reframed in
more pragmatic and productive terms. The question may not be one of
abstract principle—are master narratives still possible? It may rather be a
practical one: Given our current intellectual context—our present state of
empirical and theoretical understanding—what emphasis is likely to be
most productive and most compelling? In the case of practice and space,
I would argue, we are at a historical moment of knowledge in which
practical correctives to vaguer and more speculative theorizations are in
order. This countermove is both intellectually important and conve-
niently able to draw upon the traditional strengths of American cultural
anthropology. This is not to debunk or preclude the possibility of more
general analysis, much less the larger directions that cultural anthropology continues to maintain. It is rather to emphasize that we need now to

analyze practices and spaces more concretely under diverse contemporary conditions and via more diverse kinds of cultural capital.

Practices of Authorship

The above agenda raises a final key issue: power and history in authorship. Though Bourdieu is highly attuned to the politics of disciplinary voicing within academia, his and other versions of practice theory tend to be uncritical of their own objectivity and of the source material they draw upon. Despite a stated emphasis on reflexivity and recursion, theorizations of practice tend to close up in self-justification rather than open out to the value of alternative facticities or orders of representation (contrast Said 1978; Guha 1988a, 1989; Chatterjee 1993). The possibilities of reinterpretation—as well as resistance—are hence underplayed. Though the goal is critical theorizing, the critique in practice theories has neglected the historical process by which the images, facts, and figures of its own knowledge are established and re-created over time.

Taken in appropriate doses, reflexive engagements can facilitate rather than compromise the ethnography of practices across spaces. What is the historical cartography of analytic interests over a comparative range of ethnographic places and over specific periods of time? How can such awareness be used to promote rather than paralyze the comparative study of practices—not just ours, but theirs?

To take a simple example from Melanesia, the history of "warfare" in this part of the world encompasses (a) collective violence that was indigenous and ostensibly prior to Western influence; (b) reciprocating violence between Europeans and Melanesians during the early colonialism of the mid-nineteenth century; (c) asymmetrical violence whereby Melanesians were "pacified" by Western powers during the late nineteenth and early twentieth centuries; (d) Melanesia's engagement in World Wars I and II; (e) the violence that sometimes attended so-called cargo cults; (f) violent dispute over postcolonial nationhood (for example, the Fijian coup or the Bougainville secession); and (g) the ongoing local violence of gangs or *raskols* in contravention of postcolonial authority and social control. Crosscutting these realities is the highly selective rendering by Western observers in different parts of Melanesia at different times, that is, the organization of foreign observation and writing that has configured the history of violence and warfare in Melanesia as an object of knowledge.

Even a preliminary history of this warfare (Knauft 1990b) reveals shifts of authorial as well as ethnographic difference (cf. Prakash 1995). These entail at least:

- *warfare of Melanesian savagery*—as portrayed and projected by seafaring explorers and traders from the late eighteenth to the early twentieth centuries
- *innocent warfare of heathen resistance*—portrayed by missionaries as a natural Melanesian response to nefarious labor recruiting in the nineteenth and early twentieth centuries
- *civilizing warfare of colonial pacification*—as portrayed by colonial governments and their agents
- *cathartic and socially functional warfare*—as portrayed by Western ethnographers between the 1930s and the 1950s for indigenous groups nominally under colonial control
- functionalist *"global" warfare* between Americans and Japanese in Melanesia during the early 1940s—as portrayed by Western military historians and journalists with little reference to the experiences of Melanesians themselves
- *violence of religious and millenarian rebellion*—portrayed by anthropologists and colonial officers as part of Melanesian "cargo cults" during the post–World War II era
- violent and yet *ecologically adaptive warfare* in the highlands of New Guinea during the 1960s and 1970s—as portrayed by materialist anthropologists
- *resurgence of "tribal warfare"* in the New Guinea highlands on the cusp of the transition from colonialism to postcolonialism—as portrayed by modern ethnographers of the 1970s and 1980s
- feared *"raskol" violence* by gangs of disenfranchised youth—portrayed especially by journalists and reported in newspapers in the wake of colonial withdrawal and national independence
- the *postcolonial rebellions* by local groups against the nation-state and/or multinational corporation development projects—portrayed especially by journalists as disruptive resistance against budding national governments and their political viability

The association of these "warfares" with particular historical periods and particular parts of Melanesia is partly a function of intellectual history, including the shifting interests of Western interpretive lenses and the different kinds of alterity that have been acceptable or desirable to project onto Melanesians (cf. Lindstrom 1993). Many types of collective violence were in fact scattered much more widely over time and over the spaces of Melanesia than written histories attest. As such, the way that "violence" has played off the political imagination of savagery, pacification, colonialism, or a neophyte postcolonial state is crucial to grasping its full significance in our own historical record.

Increasingly, these issues are being considered by Melanesians themselves, not just as informants but as authors (see critiques by Hau'ofa 1975, 1994; Iamo 1992; Waiko 1992). The current literature soberly reminds us of the thickness of the line that continues to separate interpretations by Western academics from those by Melanesians themselves.[24] At the same time, Melanesian voices—constituting perhaps one-sixth of the world's languages—are anything but monolithic; to encourage indigenous authorship is not to say that indigenous voices are in harmony, nor that we must necessarily agree with all of them. There can be major difference between elite indigenous views and the perspectives of those who are less educated or less economically advantaged. It would be shortsighted to replace older essentialisms, in which natives are objects rather than subjects of authorship, with new ones that would replace anthropology's representation of non-literate voices with indigenous authors assumed ipso facto to be both representative and uniquely authentic.

These issues will be returned to in later chapters, but their relevance for the theorization of practice may be mentioned here. The legacy of practice theories needs to begin engaging the complexities of representation and history in practices of authorship itself. These authorial practices need to be put alongside rather than against the practices studied "out there." This requires a commitment to refine rather than renounce our strategies of objectivity. A critical genealogy of authorship can enable rather than impede this finer empiricism. In the process, the legacy of "practice" can be made more productive: it can embrace historically reflexive moments without being overwhelmed by them. Though Bourdieu paves the way for this possibility, he is defensive rather than concrete and open-minded in actualizing it. It is not necessary to choose between critically analyzing our own representations and those of others; the one can facilitate the other.

To consider this issue further, we turn next to Foucault . . .

moments of
knowledge and power

Foucault and Alterities of Sex and Violence

In retrospect, Michel Foucault (1926–1984) may well be seen as the most important Western theorist at the interface between modern and post-modern sensibilities. Viewed from a critically humanist standpoint, Foucault has been particularly important in prying open the relationship between knowledge and power; he lays open the underpinnings of representational domination in Western modernism and provides a powerful critique of Western modes of knowing. Though his work does less to expose a range of alternative cultural perspectives, Foucault's relation to perspectival and broader cultural diversity brims with possibilities. Particularly in his midperiod and later works, Foucault explores the creative role of diverse or subversive subjectivities at the eccentric margins and historical recesses of Western imagination. From a critically humanist perspective, it is productive to ask how power and culture relate to each other in Foucault's work—what implications they can have for articulating a critical study of power with the appreciation of cross-cultural subjectivity and resistance.

For Foucault, Western knowledge is not a means of enlightenment but a basis for classificatory imposition that has broad historical structure. In the modern era, this epistemic power has had the invidious effect of dividing types of people and institutionalizing subordination and stigma through the projection and classification of difference. Because these categorical understandings have been basic to modern Western knowledge—integral to its *episteme*[1]—they are deeply internalized and subjectified. Indeed, these conditions of knowledge are central to the way we constitute ourselves as subjects. Foucault suggests that resisting this power is particularly difficult; what seems to be opposition against power or authority is often just a superficial reshuffling of terms or allegiances at the level of content. This leaves intact the deeper axioms of knowledge upon which subordination is based. Though it remains hard if not impossible to step outside such assumptions or collectively subvert them, it is possible to see how extreme or eccentric practices push against their limitations; one can scout the radical world that is otherwise unthought and unsaid. Both in history and in the present, Foucault suggests, the boundaries and margins of discourse give clues that individuals can consider as they extend the possibilities of alternative subjectivity.

Foucault's move to critique and historicize Western knowledge-as-power has been highly influential in cultural anthropology. So too are his assessments that power and resistance entail each other; that master plans of opposition reproduce the epistemic premises they seem to oppose; and that the envelope of the unthought and the unsaid is best expanded at the epistemic, social, and sexual margins. Like the influence of French predecessors such as Durkheim and Lévi-Strauss in earlier decades, Foucault's impact in American cultural anthropology of the 1990s is both penetrating and diffuse. Like them and perhaps Bourdieu, Foucault forces us to look at the world through a brilliantly different perspective. That some of the more recent turns in cultural anthropology have backgrounded an explicit sense of their intellectual history increases the importance of recognizing Foucault's persistent influence.

Foucault's work leaves a large question of application: How are analyses geared for a critique of Western knowledge and power to be applied in Third World and Fourth World contexts, in postcolonial and postindustrial circumstances, and across the global range of cultural and epistemic variation? In what ways is a Foucauldian perspective able to stretch from its moorings to address subjectivities that are nonwhite, nonmale, nonliterate, or non-Western (see Stoler 1995; Young 1995a, 1995b)? Similar questions were asked of Marxist thought in anthropology during the 1970s. These questions are particularly important from a critically humanist vantage point that juxtaposes the exposure of domination and the critique of power against the play of cultural diversity.

The dominant trend in anthropology has been to invoke Foucault as a dependable and general-purpose critic of Western epistemic domination. Foucault informs critiques of colonial or neocolonial knowledge-as-power and our own complicity as social scientists in this nomination. He also sets the stage for the current concern with decentered discourse and discursive resistance in the face of power. For example, Foucault's (1975, 1980b) celebration of the epistemic margins foreshadows the current value placed on hybrid cultural developments and the interest in fragmented or eccentric voices of disempowered people (e.g., Taussig 1987; Lavie 1990; Tsing 1993; Lavie and Swedenburg 1996; Grossberg et al. 1992). The implicit hope is that Foucault's relationship between power and subjectivation will expose countermoves that are possible against the reigning Western episteme. As discussed below, however, the celebration of these representational tactics often leaves an essential divide between those discourses assumed to be subordinate and those assumed to reflect Western dominance.

Though Foucault was more interested in knowledge-as-power than in social action per se, his works do seem to encourage a war of subjective positioning. In this respect, Foucauldian perspectives have potential linkage with practice theories and Gramscian views of culture (see chapter 6 of this book; cf. Dirks et al. 1994). Foucault stressed the importance of subjective diversity in the resistance against power, and he pursued his analysis by means of historical and cultural specifics. The exploratory value of Foucault in contemporary anthropology would thus seem naturally related to detailed and critical ethnography.

For various reasons, however, Foucault has more often been used for rhetorical support than concretely engaged in the ethnographic trenches. This is partly due to the historical conditions that accompanied the movement of Foucault's ideas across the Atlantic. In American anthropology of the mid-1980s, Foucault's work both informed and was contextualized by the reflexive consideration of ethnography found in the works of George Marcus, James Clifford, Paul Rabinow, Michael Taussig, and others.[2] This connection was reinforced by Rabinow's important role in introducing Foucault to the mainstream of the American humanities and human sciences (e.g., Rabinow 1984; Dreyfus and Rabinow 1983).[3] Along with the most popular of Foucault's books, such as *Discipline and Punish* (1979) and the first volume of *The History of Sexuality* (1980a), Rabinow's authorship and editorship helped establish a Foucauldian beachhead that has since spread in cultural anthropology.

Though other works about Foucault's thought and life have since proliferated, their daunting variety and specialization give them less influence in anthropology than one might have anticipated.[4] And the great attention given to Foucault's midcareer studies by anthropologists has led to relative neglect of his earlier and particularly his last projects. Rabinow (1984:27) notes that his own emphasis is biased in these respects. For several reasons, then, Foucault's influence in American cultural anthropology is as selective as it is deep, belying the originality, complexity, and variety of his writings. Anthropology's Foucault tends to emerge as the precursor to reflexive ethnography and associated general critiques of knowledge-as-power. Notwithstanding Foucault's own commitment to historical detail, rigorous ethnography is frequently left outside this picture.

It is not my purpose here to detail a Foucauldian genealogy in anthropology; rather, it is to engage three Foucauldian moments in a dialogue with concrete ethnography, in particular, the ethnography of the New Guinea south coast. Epistemic critique is thereby engaged with cultural diversity. Ethnographic specifics up front pave the way for an increasingly general theoretical discussion later on; ethnographic richness informs Foucault's perspective as well as the reverse. In the process, the common opposition between Foucauldian critique and ethnographic documentation can be penetrated to refine both sides of their uneasy relationship. In particular, reflexive moments that look inward to our own forms of knowledge can stimulate rather than preclude reciprocal moments that appreciate the substance of ethnographic diversity. Moments of perspectival critique and those of bracketed objectivity can be mutually empowering rather than mutually deconstructing.

Since sex and violence are prominent both in significant portions of Foucault's historical work and in the ethnography of south coast New Guinea, they provide a substantive as well as an analytic point of linkage; as charged issues, they help to move Foucauldian concerns into substantive ethnography and to lever theoretical reassessments of Foucault from a non-Western vantage point.

Theoretic and Ethnographic Interlocutors

Foucault focused on the structure, disjunction, and sedimentation of Western knowledge, particularly in seventeenth- to nineteenth-century Europe and, late in his career, in Greek and Greco-Roman antiquity. Within this arena, three phases of Foucault's work are especially prominent. Foucault's early studies assessed how the human subject came to be constituted in the modern human sciences (e.g., 1970, 1972). This work considered the broad structures of presupposition that have underlain modern Western knowledge and representation. His midcareer interests increasingly applied these insights to a historical critique of Western institutions such as the asylum, the medical clinic, and the prison. Here, the twin face of Western knowledge-as-power showed itself through the classification of deviance, sickness or criminality, and the bodily institutionalization or "carceration" of these categories through "dividing practices" of institutional stigma and control (e.g., 1965, 1973, 1979). Foucault's final work complemented his studies of epistemic structure and institutional power by considering subjects' relationships to themselves. These self-relationships were increasingly considered through what were termed "technologies of the self." Foucault undertook this latter project particularly in the historical context of Greek and Greco-Roman antiquity (1984, 1985, 1988). As Gilles Deleuze (1988) has suggested, these three overlapping Foucauldian agendas consider how subjects are constituted in the first instance via knowledge, in the second instance via power, and in the third instance through the ethics of self-relationship. In the latter two moments, Foucault was fundamentally concerned, among other things, with constitution of the self through sexuality or violence.

The language-culture areas of the south coast of non-Austronesian New Guinea stretch for some 2,500 km across what is now Irian Jaya and Papua New Guinea, from the Asmat language families in the west across the Kolopom, Marind-anim, Trans-Fly, and Kiwai regions to the Purari and Elema in the east (see map 1).[5] From classic ethnographic sources, this region appears particularly "flamboyant" in matters of sexuality, ritual, and violence (Knauft 1993a). Sexual customs included a diverse array of extramarital heterosexual relationships, ritual promiscuity, serial sexual intercourse, and various forms of anal, oral, and masturbatory homosexuality. Violence was often internalized through painful or fright-

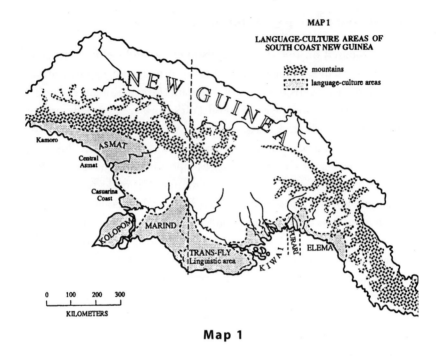

Map 1

ening ordeals of initiation and was projected outward through head-hunting, cannibalism, and/or human sacrifice as part of elaborate fertil-ity cults. In myriad permutations, south coast New Guineans were aggressively testing the limits of human sexuality and violence. Given his personal as well as academic interest in extremes of sex and violence, Foucault might have been quite interested in south coast New Guinea had he known more about it.

I: Objectification and Sexualization of the New Guinea South Coast

Following Foucault, we can consider south coast New Guinea first as an object of knowledge in the human sciences—as an object of Western epis-temic gaze. Beyond the general temptation to exoticize New Guineans, the ethnographic construction of this region has passed through several phases. This reflects a more general pattern: The modernist creation of alterity contains gradations, tears, and discontinuities; it is far from uniform. Colonialism and ethnography, like modernism, have been neither monolithic nor monolithically evil. For the early Foucault, however, shifts that occur within long epistemic periods of a century or more are largely insubstantial—in contrast to the historical rupture and radical disjuncture between one long episteme and another. In the context of cultural anthropology, this view needs to be refined to illuminate smaller shifts in knowledge, including the ethnographic construction of different world areas over different periods of time. To pursue this refinement, the specifics of history and its historiography cannot be escaped. In the present context, this means penetrating the discursive context of ethnographic history in western Melanesia.

Of Savages and Sex: Beyond Simple Tropes

Literate constructions of south coast New Guinea in the nineteenth century reflected the remoteness of the region and the small but competing interests of Western constituencies—those few missionaries, traders, and government officers headstrong enough or ambitious enough to broach the region. Their early accounts reveal frustration at the swampy and seemingly impenetrable coastline, the consistent lack of profitable or exploitable resources, and the violent hostility of the indigenous population (e.g., Bevan 1890; Strachan 1888; Chalmers 1895; see Langmore 1974). The natives, accordingly, were seen as wild and occasionally monstrous.

> Perpetual murders and intertribal butcheries of the most revolting nature, arising from frivolous or superstitious pretexts, are of almost daily occurrence within the protectorate. . . . [T]here is overwhelming evidence to prove that the Papuans are by nature both treacherous and bloodthirsty. (Bevan 1890:276, 293)

> They are one and all cannibals, frightfully cruel and terribly treacherous. Headhunting seems to be their only occupation, and the practice of offering up human sacrifice on even the most trivial occasion prevails throughout. (Caley-Webster 1898:135)

Well into the twentieth century, books about Melanesian peoples catered to the lay readership in Australia and England by emphasizing themes that had by then receded from most other parts of the Pacific: savages, cannibals, and headhunters. In the 1920s and even later, books on south New Guinea peoples had titles such as *Adventures in Cannibal-land*,

Among the Headhunting Savages and Cannibals, My Friends the New Guinea Headhunters, Cannibal Caravan, Years Among the Cannibals, Among Papuan Headhunters, and so on.[6]

Though Christian missionaries of the period shared the general Western belief that Papuans were a "degraded people," they believed that the Papuans could be "raised" through peaceful example and religious instruction.[7] As such, the missionaries were strongly at odds with the foul-mouthed, drunken, and unscrupulous practices they perceived to exist among irreligious Western traders, and they blamed the traders for provoking Melanesian attacks. Conversely, however, missionaries were more ill-disposed than traders to indigenous sexual customs, which they deemed particularly heathen. The missionary position thus defined itself vehemently against "debauchery," "perversion," "filth," and presumed "bestiality." Some indigenous rites were deemed "so unnatural" as to be "simply unprintable," even in standard monographs of the 1920s.[8]

It was the task of patrol officers to control the vices that had been publicized by colonial constituencies—by missionaries against non-Western forms of sex and by traders against non-Western forms of violence.[9] This task was magnified by the geographic, economic, and social intractability of the region to European intrusion. Colonial governments were loath to fund administration in south New Guinea. British and then Australian presence in the eastern half of the region was extremely thin, and the Dutch neglected most parts of their West New Guinea colony well into the twentieth century.[10]

While colonial control solidified in other areas of Oceania from the 1880s through the 1920s, the south coast of New Guinea remained an archetype of unenlightened Melanesia, the Black Islands. In earlier periods, the entire region had been shaded dark on the map and labeled simply "the Islands of the Bad People."[11] But by the early twentieth century, this primitiveness took on a distinctive cast relative to other peoples deemed more completely Pacific. Gaugin's Polynesia held an aura of bounty, beauty, and eroticism that evoked attraction if not dignity and status.[12] Aboriginal Australia boasted the propriety of a sacred social and spiritual order, at least to the scholarly community.[13] South New Guinea, by contrast, was seen to be lacking in moral and aesthetic as well as economic development. In 1920, the descriptive compendium of the Kiwai and Trans-Fly areas by the intrepid colonial officer Wilfred Beaver still intoned that the region was "a land of disappointment, a land where nothing happens as you anticipate, where the Unexpected usually occurs and the Impossible is achieved" (Beaver 1920:18).

For the young discipline of British anthropology, however, this lack of colonial development made the region especially attractive as an early site for field research. Native customs were not only in place, they seemed primitive and flamboyant. As literate and educated Victorians on the far edges of colonial empire, the first wave of ethnographic observers—through the first decade of the twentieth century—had much in common with Melanesian missionaries They both tended to believe that Papuans were lowly but not hopeless people.[14] While missionaries wished to salvage native souls before they were degraded by guns, liquor, and profanity, early anthropologists worked to preserve ethnographic customs on paper before they were altered—to save them for science rather than to transform them for God. Both constituencies were linked by their opposition to Western traders, labor recruiters, and other commercial interests, who were perceived to have a negative and adulterous influence on Melanesians. Liberal for their day, missionaries and scholars worked from the 1870s to the 1910s to reduce the impact of the Queensland labor trade and keep its worst excesses from spreading. A significant amount of what is historically recorded about Melanesia from this period is filtered through the lens of diatribes against Western adventurers and labor recruiters, who were widely viewed as debauched and unscrupulous. These sea-rovers enticed or kidnapped Melanesians and sold them in indentured servitude if not slavery to plantation owners in Queensland and Fiji.[15] Combined with the bloodshed, disease, depopulation, and disruption that afflicted eastern Melanesia, the criticism of blackbirding (as this labor trade was dubbed) helped convince colonial officials that traders and recruiters were a political liability and should be kept *out* of areas further west, including the New Guinea south coast.

In 1884 the British colonial office proclaimed a protectorate over the Papuan quadrant of New Guinea. Reluctantly taken, this step was the result of Australian demands for an English presence and fear of competing German interests. To the ire of Australia, however, this annexation was also designed to inhibit commerce; the colonial administration severely restricted or completely prohibited trade in guns, liquor, and Papuan bodies in British New Guinea. Highly resented by traders (e.g., Bevan 1890), these prohibitions were nonetheless continued and expanded after the colony was transferred to Australia and became the Territory of Papua in 1906.[16]

Despite the gap between laws and realities in significant parts of the new colony, colonial restrictions were largely effective along the south coast, where there was little economic impetus in any event.[17] Apart from trade in bird of paradise feathers and a few abortive attempts to raise coconuts, this overdetermined brake on commercial development facilitated the persistence of indigenous practices. These included customs of sex and violence that, to European eyes, were more extreme than the vices of the Western recruiters and traders that Papuans were ostensibly being protected from. Deemed primitive and authentic, however, native customs became important topics of academic study at the same time that colonial administrators were charged with controlling or suppressing them.[18]

Between the 1910s and the 1930s, the south coast of New Guinea became a hotbed of ethnographic observation. Stuffed heads still attracted attention (e.g., Haddon 1923). Overall, however, the classic ethnographies of the region are exceptionally rich. Indeed, the "tribal ethnography" of the region's constituent societies is quite likely as inclusive as that recorded for any comparably sized coastal region in the world, rivaling even the works published on the groups of the northwest coast of North America by Boas and others.

This anthropological interest was presaged by A. C. Haddon's voyage of 1888 and his Cambridge Expedition to the Torres Strait a decade later. For almost forty years after that, Haddon worked from his Cambridge position to cultivate interest in and the publication of ethnography from coastal and island regions of New Guinea. It was over this period that south coast monographs grew to include the voluminous work of C. G. Seligman, Gunnar Landtman, Wilfred Beaver, Paul Wirz, F. E. Williams, and numerous papers and introductions by Haddon himself.[19] As Michael Young (1988:4) suggests, Haddon was "arguably the most influential British anthropologist in the first two decades of the century." Strongly influenced by Haddon's "Notes and Queries" anthropology, south coast ethnography documented the rich genera of customs and myths as a kind of natural history. This emphasis was not accidental; Haddon's original training was in zoology, and, like other early anthropologists such as Tylor and Boas, he was dedicated to the establishment of anthropology as a respectable science.[20] In the resulting ethnography, subjectivity was suspended and replaced by a plethora of particular, separate, and impersonal beliefs and customs.

> The old-fashioned monograph, then, which aims at an all-round description of any given people or culture, is something like a long and perhaps ill-assorted *menu* from which the anthropological diner is invited to take what tempts him. It is open to question whether this is the best method of dishing up one's results. . . . But, for good or ill . . . [this] method has been adopted here. (Williams 1936:x)

This perspective informed the huge monographs on south coast societies, including some of those written subsequently by Dutch researchers concerning western parts of the south coast.[21]

As ethnographic text, this dry facticity provided a scientific neutral zone that described native customs in detail and arranged them in institutional categories. This strategy served both to valorize anthropology as an academic science and to protect native customs from condemnation by traders, missionaries, and colonial officers (Knauft 1993a:ch. 2). If natives were depersonalized and made static through objective description, and if this inscription facilitated nominal colonial control (which it certainly did), indigenous customs were at the same time richly detailed and put outside the realm of common disparagement.

Seen in retrospect, the primary south coast ethnography slightly predates the later British interest in social structure, politics, and economics.[22] Hence, the interests of British structural-functionalism, which were to become so important in central and eastern Melanesia through the influence of Bronislaw Malinowksi and Raymond Firth, were much less evident along the New Guinea south coast, which received a lasting stamp from Haddon's view of anthropology as a kind of ethnographic catalog.[23]

With the growth of newer theoretical interests between the 1930s and the 1960s, however, the New Guinea south coast became an ethnographic as well as an economic backwater, even within Melanesia. While the profile of British functionalism and structural-functionalism grew, Massim and Sepik areas of Melanesia to the east and the north claimed the bulk of ethnographic attention by the 1930s. The 1930s also saw the discovery by Westerners of over one million inhabitants in the mountain-ringed valleys of interior New Guinea. These tribal populations constituted the largest remaining group of "uncontacted" indigenous peoples in the world, and they attracted enormous Western interest. Following the hiatus of World War II, anthropological fieldwork exploded into the New Guinea highlands.

Overshadowed by these developments, the south coast of New Guinea was left behind; its ethnographic profile faded. Today, virtually all the significant monographs published about south coast groups are based on primary research more than thirty years old. With the exception of Robert Maher's *New Men of Papua* (1961), no academic monographs frontally consider the impact of colonial or postcolonial developments on the people of this coastal region (but cf. Hammar 1995).[24] Supplanted for decades by other areas, the south coast of New Guinea was neglected as an area for ethnographic fieldwork. As an object of Western knowledge, it is now often considered to be "history."

It is crucial to expose and analyze the pairing of particular theoretical lenses and historical interests to particular world areas over time if we are to comprehend their status as academic knowledge (Appadurai 1986). The epistemic stamp put on a given world area stems from the overlay of perspectives that have become affixed to it over time (Fardon 1990). A historical view of ethnographic production is particularly important when viewed against the continuing trend in ethnology for information from different regions to be compared without considering the differing theoretical and historical lenses through which divergent accounts have been collected (see the general critique in Knauft 1993a:ch. 6).

In the present case, it is evident that the classic monographs of the New Guinea south coast were viewed very differently by the 1970s and 1980s. Gender and sexuality claimed increasing attention. Works such as Foucault's *History of Sexuality, Volume 1* (1980a) became increasingly influential. Melanesian anthropology witnessed growing interest in what were considered extreme customs of "sexual antagonism" and "female pollution," particularly in the New Guinea highlands.[25] During the 1980s, this literature was complemented by Gilbert Herdt's publications on Melanesian sexuality and psychology.[26] Based on rich fieldwork among the Sambia of interior southeast New Guinea, Herdt brought Melanesian sexuality to center stage and launched a detailed comparative assessment of homosexuality in the southwest Pacific.[27] With its flamboyant sexual practices, south New Guinea (now expanded to include adjacent areas inland) was resuscitated and became the ethnographic centerpiece for the comparative characterization of ritual homosexuality in the Pacific.[28]

Particularly in the 1980s context of gender-bending, gay and lesbian awareness, and AIDS, Herdt's work on ritualized homosexuality in Melanesia generated massive interest. Indeed, there was a palpable rush to extend and concretize his emphasis through secondary ethnology. In the process, several authors reconfigured the older south coast ethnography and extrapolated well beyond Herdt's original concepts. By the mid- and late 1980s, numerous "homosexual societies" or even "sperm cultures" were posited for precolonial south New Guinea.[29]

> The broadest contrasts among Melanesian cultures emerge, then, from a comparison between the so-called semen groups of the Lowlands and the Highland cultures in which semen is not the ritualized stuff of life. (Lindenbaum 1984:342)

> Homosexual societies [in New Guinea] are thoroughly "egalitarian" in ethos. . . . No homosexual society has a ceremonial exchange system based on intensive, surplus production. (Feil 1987:178–79)

Homosexuality had become a metonym for south New Guinea, which was thought of as the semen belt of Melanesia. If the Other of the New Guinea south coast had first been a debauched savage and then a neutered cluster of objective traits, was he now homosexualized?

The portrait of south New Guinea as "homosexual" begs Foucault's critique against sexual essentialism. Not only are singular sexual practices a questionable basis for characterizing an entire society (much less a whole region) but the designation of homosexual societies made "society" a male province, since female homosexuality has been only rarely known in this region. This essentialism has been empirical as well as analytic and has helped skew the facts. At the height of the 1980s interest in homosexuality, the actual extent of the practice is now known to have been significantly overestimated for south New Guinea.[30] Along the south coastal rim, ritual homosexuality was in fact far less prevalent than the occurrence of ritual *heterosexuality*, that is, extramarital or promiscuous sexual intercourse between men and women conducted as part of fertility cult celebrations during periods of ritual license. As this example illustrates, reflexive awareness can facilitate rather than compromise more refined empirical analysis. By understanding a particular ethnographic lens, we can compensate for its biases more effectively; we can look through it more clearly (Knauft 1993a: chs. 3–5).

Like earlier phases of natural history descriptivism, however, the emphasis on south coast homosexuality during the 1980s had important rhetorical and strategic value against then-prevalent alternatives; its contribution needs to be considered in the academic context of its time. First, Herdt's work gave academic credentials to the ethnographic study of sexual practices; these became a more legitimate focus of fieldwork. Second, it valorized *homo*sexuality. Given that anthropology has not been immune to homophobia, this was a signal accomplishment. Third, homosexuality itself was now relativized; Melanesian homosexuality provided a contrast to homosexuality in the West. Specifically, Herdt suggested that Melanesian homosexuality contrasted to Western gay lifestyles in that it was (a) ritualized and prescribed rather than open to personal choice, (b) universal rather than a minority practice among young men, (c) transient to heterosexuality instead of being a lifelong sexual orientation, and (d) asymmetric between elder and junior males rather than being potentially reciprocal between same-age partners.[31] Though these contrasts are polar and somewhat overdrawn, they illustrated important cross-cultural variation in homosexuality and helped convey to a larger Western readership the cultural naturalness of striking diversity in sexual practices.

Now in the 1990s, it seems expectable and appropriate that this view is being superseded by Herdt himself in more refined study of Melanesian psychosexualities as well as in his new work on gay identities in the United States and his global purview on the range of nonnormative sexual alternatives.[32]

The larger point is that ethnographic characterizations need to be considered in the pragmatic context of their own period as well as against more contemporary and ostensibly absolute standards of correctness. We easily embrace the myopia of the present when criticizing our representational past. This context needs to be remembered when considering anthropology of the 1970s and 1980s as well as the anthropology of the 1930s or 1890s.

With the benefit of hindsight, even the most current characterizations of sexual diversity will eventually seem problematic (see Weston 1993a, 1993b). This is inevitable insofar as the goal is to continue stretching our awareness of human possibilities against the constraint of existing categorical assumptions. Currently there is strong interest among gender theorists in polysexual diversity and the potential power of marginality in forging resistant selfhood.[33] As foregrounded by Judith Butler (1990, 1993a), the deconstruction of essentialized gender or sexual identity focuses attention on the potentials of sex/gender performances, self-presentations, and new identities.[34] In Melanesia, as in many other world areas, a new generation of fieldworkers is beginning to provide fascinating and poignant accounts of postcolonial diversity in sexual expression, sexual work, and—just as importantly—the persistence of gendered discrimination and sexual domination.[35] Critiques of sexual essentialism in the characterization of Melanesia need to engage these emerging developments at the same time that they move beyond a simplistic or homogenizing view of the region's ethnographic history.

Genealogical Present(s)

In terms of Foucault's agenda, a critical history of ethnographic trajectories constitutes a first moment: a genealogy of how subjects have been created and continue to be created through changing criteria of ethnographic "knowledge." Though genealogical critique is now a well-worn path in anthropology, it can be invigorated by taking a more detailed and concrete view of ethnographic histories than is often attempted. The work of authors as diverse as Stocking (1987), Stoler (1995), Young (1995a), Clifford (1988), Said (1978, 1993), and Guha (1988a, 1988b, 1989, 1992) is valuable in this respect. Foucault's own genealogical rigor was not distracted by the complications that result when the style of writing make a parody or a farce of the complexity of historical material (Boon 1990).

Views of the past harbor a tension between establishing a history of events and the Foucauldian drive to critique the epistemic suppositions that underlie historical narratives. As Foucault foreshadowed in his final studies of Greek and Greco-Roman antiquity, epistemic shifts may be diverse and fine-grained rather than totalizing. A nuanced analysis reveals this process in concert with the historical and areal specifics of anthropology's past (e.g., Fardon 1990; Manganaro 1990). Foucault's first moment need not be sealed off from historical specifics and need not presume epistemic continuity over a century or more; rather, it can forge a critical genealogy that exposes specific assumptions across distinct geographic and temporal fields. This project highlights how peoples and places are categorized in the present relative to the past. It also shows the inclusions and exclusions of authorship that the historical field has instantiated. As such, illuminating the configuration of past representations and present constitutions is a prerequisite to finding more progressive approaches for the future. If Foucault's genealogical analysis is Western and generalist, it can be useful for cultural anthropology by being made both more geographically diverse and more temporally nuanced.

As Fernando Coronil (1992a, 1992b), Ann Stoler (1991, 1995), Nicholas Thomas (1994), and James Carrier (1992, 1995) have all emphasized, there remains a lingering tendency in anthropology to collapse the great diversity of ethnographic and related writing—as if anthropology has had a singular Occidental gaze upon a singular colonial object. An emphasis on discursive forms to the neglect of their political and economic conditions reinforces this problem.

In postcolonial awareness, a critical examination of the social and cultural circumstances of authorship becomes an especially important part of our genealogies. In the present case, it is painfully obvious that almost the entire corpus of writings referred to above has been authored in the final instance by white observers rather than Melanesians themselves (contrast Kyakas and Wiessner 1992). What conditions have determined the dearth of indigenous scholarly voices in Melanesia? (See Hau'ofa 1975, 1994a; Morauta 1979; Knauft 1995b.) And what patterns of postcolonial authorship privilege men over women, wealthy over poor, or some ethnic groups over others? More broadly, what underlies the contrast between Melanesian scholarly traditions and those of African academics or subaltern authorships from India? Historical differences between ethnic and gendered circumstances and places need to be judged with an eye toward expanding a whole range of diversity in future authorships—indigenous as well as Western. All these implications resonate with the reflexive historicity of Foucault's critical agenda as applied within the heart of ethnography.

Not surprisingly, however, there is also a danger of essentializing indigenous authorship in the constitution of postcolonial identities;[36] this trend is itself subject to critical examination. Commentators such as Kwame Appiah (1991), Arif Dirlik (1994), Dipesh Chakrabarty (1992), Stuart Hall (1996), Carole Davies (1994), Ella Shohat (1992), Anne McClintock (1992), and Russell Jacoby (1995) have all noted that evocations deemed "postcolonial" are themselves prone to projective reification. Like Western anthropologists, postcolonial authors do not necessarily stand for their ostensible constituencies. This sharpens rather than diminishes the need to document the contours of diversity— in terms both of indigenous authorship and specific content—and the need to evaluate what scholarly and tactical value these variants have in the changing present (see Appiah 1992). A combined genealogical and historical commitment remains crucial if we wish to see what purpose specific representational strategies did or did not serve in the past, which strategies have already served their purpose in the present, and which tactics can now be extended or bent to create more productive views in the future.

II: Power, Institution, Resistance

A second, complementary strand of Foucault exposes the way subjects are constituted through invidious "dividing practices," particularly as these are institutionalized through knowledge as power. This emphasis is highly evident in Foucault's works such as *Birth of the Clinic* (1973), *Discipline and Punish* (1979), and *Madness and Civilization* (1965), which accentuate the oppressive organization of Western institutions such as the clinic, the prison, and the asylum. Power is at center stage as *pouvoir*, that is, power as an actually instituted and reproducible relationship of force.[37] As opposed to many Americanist readings, Foucault is interested in the epistemic "how" of power rather than its social "what" or "why;" he stays resolutely nominalist in analyzing how institutional categories of separation and division operate as categories of knowledge. As stressed by Feher (1990), Foucault remains a genealogist, not a social scientist.

This moment of Foucault poses difficulties for anthropology. The epistemic history of the relationship between knowledge and power is often hard to chart accurately within non-Western contexts, particularly in the absence of written records. Moreover, ethnographers often feel obliged to defend rather than critique the indigenous epistemes that underpin others' institutions. To criticize the knowledge of foreign peoples can be perceived as offensive—and it can reduce the chances of getting a research visa for a return visit. It also works against the utopian and romantic impetus that valorizes cultural diversity. As noted in earlier chapters, this liberal and empathic impetus has been influential and strategically valuable to professional anthropology almost since its inception.[38]

It is thus easier to follow Foucault's lead and link dehumanizing social divisions to the intrusion of power/knowledge from the Western state (e.g., 1973, 1975, 1979, 1980c). Against the state as colonial or neocolonial bastion, local voices are easily seen to provide a pastiche of marginal resistance. This point of view effectively highlights the counterhegemonic dimensions of subaltern expressions. However, it does less to illuminate indigenous structures of knowledge and power or their larger development over time.

This is not to minimize or downplay state power, which has often been pernicious. In the current anthropological climate, however, the emphasis on decentered resistance carries its own risk of essentialism. Notwithstanding the complexity of its portrayal, the celebration of hybrid marginality can be ironically predictable. Conversely, it becomes a bit too easy to lay all ills at the doorstep of the panopticon of the state. As Michel-Rolph Trouillot (1991) has noted, this unwittingly leaves the non-Western Other dangerously close to a utopian slot that is more noble than realistic. This reflects a lingering tendency to polarize traits across a static divide between the West and the Rest. At extremes, the Occidentalized Leviathan becomes as great a reification in the anthropology of the 1990s as the Orientalized tribe was in the anthropology of the 1950s.

Dividing Practices: Melanesian and Colonial

If one is interested in domination, it is hard to ignore structures of knowledge and power in areas such as south New Guinea, where some groups heartily killed their neighbors, where youths were often traumatized by their elders in violent initiation practices, and where females were forced into serial sexual intercourse, sometimes at a young age and in a way that could compromise their health and fertility. All this took place with minimal help from agents or forces of state control. Melanesian bodily inscriptions could institutionalize categorical social divisions through traumatic nose-bleeding, penis-bleeding, tongue-bleeding, finger-lopping, burning, rubbing with nettles, food taboos, forced feeding, scarification, teeth-blackening, widow-strangulation, bodily adornment, sex via vaginal, anal, oral, or dermal penetration, and, after death, endocannibalism, exocannibalism, exhumation, relic disembodiment, or anointment by or drinking of cadaveric fluid (Knauft 1989a). Dizzying arrays of bodily practices could radically empower men over women, elders over juniors, political dominants over political subordinates, or one clan or ethnic enemy over another. As these practices clearly indicate, the will to cultural power need not encompass the Occidental will to knowledge to present a strong field of carceral forces.

Foucault conceptualizes "the carceral" in his analysis of the early modern penal system.

> By operating at every level of the social body and by mingling ceaselessly the art of rectifying and the right to punish, the universality of the carceral lowers the level from which it becomes natural and acceptable to be punished . . . . [T]he great carceral continuum . . . provides a communication between the power of discipline and the power of the law, and extends without interruption from the smallest coercions to the longest. (Foucault 1979:303)

Carceration through cultural belief and action was of course not the same in indigenous south New Guinea as that exposed by Foucault in the gaze of Western modernity. Among other things, it was not based on Western law or bureaucracy, and it did not entail surveillance based on detachment. But its was omnipresent if not omnipotent in its own way, and it often operated through the privileged knowledge of senior men. Status divisions could be totalizing, dominating, and internalized down to the deepest core, and they could be inscribed in bodies in a profound and sometimes pernicious way. In precolonial Melanesia, these divisions were the primary means of constituting subjectivity—the *a priori* idioms of contrast through which persons transacted their individual and collective selves (cf. Strathern 1988). Habitus that is invidious needs no master designer even in the absence of colonial oversight.

None of this denies or minimizes the impact of Western colonialism or the imposition of categories of knowledge and power through ethnography itself. Along the south coast of New Guinea, the indigenous customs most subject to colonial suppression were also central to Papuan ontology. As linked dimensions of primordial myth and classification, ritual sexuality and headhunting were keystones of a cosmological cycle that entailed the cultural creation of life force through ritual sexuality and the redress of its loss through the headhunting of enemies (Knauft 1993a:ch. 9).[39] These Melanesian elaborations on sex and violence were anathema to the order that colonialism was dedicated to creating. Along the New Guinea south coast, missionaries and colonial officers zealously committed themselves to the suppression of orgiastic rituals and head-hunting.[40] Given the cultural importance of these features, their demise altered if not transformed indigenous structures of knowledge and power. This fact was actively exploited by colonial authorities and missionaries to dismantle local beliefs and customs considered pagan or uncivilized.

Along the south coast of New Guinea, the period of effective colonial control lasted from the early twentieth century to 1975 in Papua New Guinea and virtually to the present day in West New Guinea via Dutch and then Indonesian control. Indigenous practices and the assumptions of knowledge and power that underlie them were progressively compromised over this period. Cultural dimensions of change have been particularly important, since the number of colonial intruders has generally been small and their economic impact has been minimal until recent decades. Nevertheless, indigenous beliefs were changed by the suppression of warfare, the slow but steady spread of Christianity, and the sporadic wage labor available on coconut plantations. These developments alternately informed and reflected local crises that have been as cultural and epistemic they have been political and economic (cf. Maher 1981). Prominent Papuan responses have included so-called cargo cults and movements, which have simultaneously embraced and reformulated Western assumptions about knowledge-as-power.[41]

Colonial organization, and the classificatory epistemology that supported it, entailed enormous power asymmetries between Western whites and Melanesian blacks. But these power asymmetries confronted those previously in place. Given the current trend to emphasize intrusive practices of domination and division, it is important not to neglect those that were already present. The indigenous men's house had its own power of classification, domination, and bodily inscription. Flanked by enemy skulls, sacred ancestral carvings, and traumatizing elders, young men could be reborn through awe and terror to a world in which age, sex, and tribal enmity were markers of life force and selfhood that were violently wrested and brutally maintained. Details are complex (see Knauft 1993a), but the intensity and diversity of practices are striking.

Among Asmat and Kiwai, the taking of an enemy head was an important prerequisite for marriage and attaining adult male status; among Asmat, the tally of heads taken was a crucial dimension of male prestige and success. Bitter fights sometimes broke out even within victorious

Asmat war parties over possession of an enemy corpse (Zegwaard 1959). For many south coast groups, and particularly the Purari, the severed head of a child, woman, or old person served as well as that of a man for purposes of life force incorporation. Asmat and Kolopom sometimes tortured their victims before dispatching them. Among Purari, enemy bodies were fully cannibalized and the heads "fed" to large wicker monster embodiments in order to rejuvenate ancestral spirits (Williams 1923a). Among Kiwai, decapitated heads were struck against the central longhouse post and their blood smeared to consecrate it (Landtman 1927:ch. 2). Likewise, Asmat consecrated their elaborately carved ancestral *bis* poles by anointing them with the blood and chest fat of slain victims (Eyde 1967:347). Racks of enemy skulls were a crucial source of ritual power and clan honor among eastern Kiwai (Haddon 1918).

Among Marind-anim, scores of heads were captured in long-distance headhunting raids. The children of decapitated adults were abducted and resocialized through radical and prolonged initiation rites until they were considered Marind-anim. Marind-anim subjected their own young women to frequent bouts of serial sexual intercourse with between five and thirteen Marind-anim men. (The sexual secretions that dripped from the woman were collected for a variety of ritual purposes.) The vaginal irritation and infection caused by this repeated sexual trauma rendered a significant proportion of Marind-anim women sterile even prior to Western introduction of venereal diseases.[42] Among Kolopom, prepubescent girls were used in sexual intercourse by their prospective fathers-in-law and the latter's clan mates; sexual fluids obtained were rubbed on the groom-to-be to aid his growth and sexual development (Serpenti 1984). Female status was particularly low among Kolopom, Asmat, and Trans-Fly peoples, where women had few property rights, exercised little marital choice, and could be subject to stringent pollution beliefs and sexual or domestic violence (Knauft 1993a: ch. 5). Boys could be subject to traumatic initiations that in various groups involved threatened death, beatings, anal intercourse from adult men, and prolonged separation from mothers and other women.

Though all these practices were subject to colonial influence, it would be pointless to argue that the intensity of south coast violence, much less sex, was primarily a product of the colonial encounter.[43] In the same breath, however, the variability, beauty, and intrinsically social nature of the region's practices and beliefs must also be noted. In terms of gender,

Elema women exercised a high degree of spousal choice; Purari women gained high prestige from taking lovers; and Kiwai women gained elaborate power through vaginal life force and magic (Knauft 1993a: ch.7). It appears that many Purari and Kiwai women engaged in extramarital intercourse with pleasure and esteem; ritual sexuality formed a venue of creative and sometimes lucrative experimentation. Women were incorporated as participants in great pageants of cosmological reenactment among the Marind-anim and had grades of initiation parallel to those of men. Girls' initiation was untraumatic and that of boys benign among south coast groups such as Purari, Elema, and probably Asmat. Victimization of enemy groups for bodies and heads was minimal among Elema, Kolopom, and Trans-Fly peoples. Among Purari, headhunting required only a single victim for an entire large village on the occasion of infrequent ceremonies; killing could be statistically rare at the same time that it was cosmologically central.

South coast fertility cults were particularly impressive in their aesthetic embodiment. Purari concretized their ancestral spirits in large sacred effigies kept in special rooms at the rear of the community's large longhouse (Williams 1923a). Elema ritual cycles revolved around the production of ornate *hevehe* masks, which could be over twenty feet high and yet light enough to be paraded around the village by wearers who assumed their mythic identities (Williams 1940). These masks were created in a special large longhouse and paraded by the hundreds at climactic ceremonies. Asmat carved incarnations of ancestral fertility in elaborate fretted *bis* poles, canoe prows, shields, and houseposts (Schneebaum 1990). Marind-anim performers donned a multitude of stunning costumes to reenact primordial myths (Baal 1966). Kiwai totem clans venerated ancestral spirits in elaborate pageants of costumed dancing (Landtman 1927:ch. 27). All these embodiments were a source of great pride, enjoyment, and social affiliation among the men and women of several communities. Indeed, they configured collective identity through contexts of exchange and spirituality that throw into question Western assumptions about the "self" as a separate and autonomous entity (cf. Strathern 1988; Mauss 1967).

Along the south coast of New Guinea, the tie among the violent, the sexual, and the aesthetic was not just an epistemology but an ontology of fertility based on the giving and taking of life force. Existence and being were themselves at issue. The life force of existence was charged in sexuality, cultivated in labor and productivity, and taken in killing. It was its own world of being, knowing, and power. In contrast to the cosmologies of Foucault's classical Europe, which substantialized power as sovereignty, or Western modernity, which operationalized it as knowledge, New Guinea cosmologies encoded power as transaction and exchange. Power was subjectified in lines of gender, age, and ethnicity. It reverberated through endless cycles of growth and fertility that included the exchange of life force in ritual sexuality; the negative exchange of headhunting; and the shared embodiment of life force in sacred costumes, trophies, or relics. It divided men from women, old from young, clan from clan, and enemy from enemy despite and indeed because of the exchange between them. Paradoxical from a Western point of view, division was defined through the transaction of complementarity.

Stated Inequalities: Crossing Essential Divides

Cutting across typical appropriations of Foucault, south New Guinea makes it obvious how age, sexual, ethnic, and material divisions can be subjectified, embodied, and instituted through epistemic-cum-social violence without as well as with the state. Foucault would agree that it is an empirical question how these divisions are different under different regimes of subjectivity and power. It is time for anthropology to analyze these variations and their permutations more vigorously. This is by no means to minimize power-as-knowledge imposed from the West. Rather, it means appreciating how such intrusions are actively engaged by indigenous powers that have their own internal legacies of bodily and institutionalized inscription. The critique of Western knowledge and power becomes all too easy if indigenous subjectivities are juxtaposed en masse against a homogeneous bloc of Occidental opposition.

Likewise, dividing practices in early or precolonial contexts have crosscut each other in complex ways. And conflicts between different forms of resistance can be endogenous as well as imposed. Along the south New Guinea coast, Asmat egalitarianism was highly developed among men and precluded rank leadership. But it was violently competitive and facilitated both an extraordinary rate of male homicide and very low status for women (Knauft 1993a:ch. 5). Among Purari, by contrast, women had great autonomy and status in marriage, sexuality, and control of wealth. But the male status system included strong asymmetries of political rank, including hereditary chieftainship; Purari villages became fortresses focused around central chiefs and polarized in enmity against each other. Trans-Fly peoples fought to resist ethnic and military encroachment from the Kiwai to their east and especially the Marind-anim to their west; yet their resistance seems to have rigidified their authority structure and intensified the domination of elder men over women and youths (Knauft 1993a:ch. 8). As these examples illustrate, resistance along one axis of inequality may facilitate oppression on another, even under circumstances that remained in large part outside colonial reach. Following Foucault, practices must be analyzed in close relationship to their epistemic and ontological underpinnings. These relationships are not simple; they need to be carefully teased apart and documented in each case.

These issues become especially poignant under postcolonial circumstances. The institutionalization of postcolonial regimes of power and knowledge is a joint product of the ghost of colonialism and, as importantly, the power and knowledge of preexisting local and regional regimes. The refraction of these hybrid powers and knowledges into postcolonial dividing practices and institutional initiatives—and counter-initiatives—is particularly important and complex.

Given these developments, terms of resistance are at least as internally conflicted in a late modern as in a premodern world. In situations of fragmented and displaced identity, the fight against some inequalities is bound to reinforce others. This is patently evident in postcolonial circumstances of personal uncertainty, much less political turmoil. What is important here is not just the relativism of different dividing practices, but the developing relationship between their different types of difference. As cultural modes of being, the epistemologies that underlie these divisions are neglected rather than illuminated by juxtaposing a simple hegemony of Western political economy and knowledge against a utopian view of indigenous Others. What holds for knowledge also holds for power; dividing practices are neither as monolithic as a Eurocentric model implies nor as easy to contest as a simple model of indigenous resistance, discursive refusal, or fragmentation might suggest.

III: Subjectivity and Power

The most neglected side of Foucault's work, and perhaps now the most important for anthropology, is his concluding emphasis on subjectivation and technologies of the self—how it is that subjects constitute themselves as subjects. Before considering this issue, two notes are necessary concerning Foucault and the politics of gender and sexuality. First, Foucault's work has had an uneasy and sometimes troubled relationship with feminism.[44] Both theoretically and pragmatically, Foucault was not particularly responsive to feminist concerns, as reflected in his statements about rape (see Macey 1993:374–75). And despite his genealogical critique of sexual desire, Foucault is still often considered in the masculine line of great European philosophers that included Kant, Hegel, Nietzsche, Husserl, Heidegger, and Sartre. For various reasons, as Meaghan Morris (1988:55) put it, "Foucault's work is not the work of a ladies' man." As presaged by Butler (1987), however, feminist scholars of the 1990s have increasingly revalued Foucault's relevance for the deconstruction and reconstruction of gender and sexuality (see Ramazanoglu 1993; McNay 1993; Butler 1993b).

Especially during the 1970s and 1980s, Foucault also came under attack from the gay community. The publicly guarded nature of Foucault's own homosexuality (especially in light of its private intensity)[45] was a political target for those promoting the exposure or "outing" of gay men. Prominent gay spokesmen also criticized the antiessentialism, relativism, and social constructionism of Foucault's work—as if there is nothing "essential" about being gay.[46] Foucault's refusal of high-profile politics and his failure to come out of the closet more fully compromised his reputation, particularly in the wake of his death from AIDS in 1984. It may be long debated whether Foucault's public closet of sexual identity was the logical outcome of his relentless nominalism—including a consistent refusal of the social and collective in favor of the epistemic and personal—or whether his nominalism and lack of disclosure were both symptoms of a deeper escapism. In the context of recent developments in queer theory and the crumbling of the gay/lesbian divide, however, appreciation of Foucault has increased in the 1990s. David Halperin has even called for a gay hagiography of "Saint Foucault" (Halperin 1995).

In the final years of his life, when he was in poor health, Foucault recast the projected second and third volumes of *The History of Sexuality* into an original and detailed study of ancient Greek and Greco-Roman technologies of selfhood (1985, 1986). As biographer James Miller (1993:33ff.) has suggested, Foucault's sensitive and even Apollonian description of self-constitution through dietetics, physical regimen, and disciplined care provided a complement to the Dionysian pain/pleasure that he actively explored in his sexual life and endured in a more sinister vein in his battle with AIDS (see also Macey 1993:ch. 16). In what sense Foucault's last work is personally or politically redemptive is an open and provocative question.

Foucault's final works imply that subjectification can be a creative as well as an active process—that subjects may fashion themselves to expand upon, if not resist, historically received structures of knowledge and power. In Foucault's early and mid-period work, by contrast, the potentials for resistance or effective change seemed minimal. De Certeau (1984:ch. 4), among others, criticized Foucault for neglecting the role of tactical resistance in practices of everyday life. But Foucault's later work suggests that a newly empirical economy of power relations consists "of taking the forms of resistance against different forms of power as a starting point. . . . Rather than analyzing power from the point of view of its internal rationality, it consists of analyzing power relations through the antagonism of strategies" (Foucault 1983:211). He thus favors "a reactivation of local knowledges—of minor knowledges—in opposition to scientific hierarchization" (Foucault 1980c:85). It is through "the reappearance of these local popular knowledges" that "historical contents allow us to rediscover the ruptural effects of conflict and struggle that the order imposed by functionalist or systematizing thought is designed to mask" (Foucault 1980c:82).

Foucault's interest in historical memoirs reveals his intellectual trajectory. In midcareer works such as *I Pierre Rivière* (the memoirs of a nineteenth-century convicted killer) and *Herculine Barbin* (the memoirs of a nineteenth-century hermaphrodite), Foucault foregrounded the power of state nomination and classification.[47] The resistance of Rivière—who murdered his mother, brother, and sister and wished fervently for his own death—seems as violent and troubling as it is fascinating. (Barbin ultimately committed suicide.) Moreover, these memoirs are presented in flat verbatim; they are unanalyzed and underdiscussed by Foucault. On the personal side, correspondingly, Foucault's Maoist affinities of the early 1970s favored actions that were violent, uncreative, and terroristic (Foucault 1980c:ch. 1; Miller 1993:chs. 6, 7).

But in his last work, Foucault shifts from violent intensity toward ethical pleasure through a delicate and more compassionate technology of selfhood. Developing these interests through a historical study of Greek and Greco-Roman subjectivation, Foucault sought to explore "the transformations that one seeks to accomplish with oneself as object" (1985:29). As opposed to an ethics governed by rules and prohibitions, he was interested in voluntary and deliberate practices which change and transform life, providing it with a stylistics or an "aesthetics of existence" whereby life becomes a work of art (1985:ch. 1). Foucault relativized his views and suggested that

> techniques of the self, I believe, can be found in all cultures in different forms. Just as it is necessary to study and compare the different techniques of the production of objects and the direction ... [of] government, one must also question the techniques of the self. (Foucault 1984:369)

This emphasis practically invites ethnographic explorations of cultural and sub-cultural diversity in subjective self-fashioning. In contrast to the perspectives of classic symbolic or psychological anthropology, however, this self-construction of subjectivity foregrounds the tension between individual will and epistemic structure to explore the envelope of the unthought and the unsaid. In this respect, Foucault's last work forms a bridge between the psychology of selfhood and the current awareness by cultural anthropologists that disempowerment allows spaces for creative marginality (e.g., Lavie 1990; Tsing 1993).[48] Foucault's goal was not only to critique the limits imposed on us but to experiment with the possibility of pushing creatively beyond them (Foucault 1984:50).

The uncharted area in this agenda concerns agency and social practice. Foucault began to address this issue at the end of his life, when he suggested that

> it is not enough to say that the subject is constituted in a symbolic system. It is not just in the play of symbols that the subject is constituted. It is constituted in real practices—historical analyzable practices. (Foucault 1984:369)

However, as many have suggested—and as Freundlieb (1994) has emphasized—Foucault's corpus as a whole only thinly addresses issues of human agency or practice. Though thoughts are real, and though saying is a form of acting, innovations in thought and subjectivation have a highly variable relationship to social and political action. Deleuze's (1988) elaboration upon Foucault is helpful in this regard. Deleuze suggests that issues of desire, power, and resistance become particularly significant when considering the "pleats" or "folds" that form the boundaries of the self. In this view, the division between the self and others is formed jointly by lines of power imposed externally and the active pushing of the self against these. Though the subject may not change the total field of force outside, s/he can reposition his/her own identity to bend lines of power and create an altered space for self-configuration. As Elspeth Probyn (1993:129) puts it, "The act of 'pleating' or 'folding' (la pliure) is thus the doubling-up, the refolding, the bending-onto-itself of a line of the outside in order to constitute the inside/outside—the modes of the self." Taking care of the self as opposed to simply "knowing oneself" involves practices that are at once practical, political, and sexual (Foucault 1984:130).

Like ethnographers, Foucault was highly aware that subjectivation is historically, socially, and epistemologically contingent. Amid the accelerated sign-images of the late twentieth century, Foucault (1983) suggests that subjectivation becomes the dominant site of struggle for power; we become increasingly enmeshed in forces that incite our own relationship to ourselves. Insofar as power and resistance are complements for Foucault, resistance through creative subjectivation becomes progressively important as we engage the pressures of late modernity.

Subjectivation and Resisting Generality: The Case for Examples

Ethnographic specifics from non-Western contexts expand our awareness of the potentials and complexities of subjectivity as resistance. For south coast New Guinea, as for much historical ethnography, the first point is a negative one: Classic sources often neglect subjective experience. What this necessitates, however, is not despair but more penetrating ethnography to illuminate these potentials in the recent past and the present. Ethnographic examples become cases in point.

Among Asmat of the Casuarina coast of south New Guinea, homosexual relations between men secretly persist despite government and missionary opposition. Pairs of adult men dedicate themselves to each other as permanent bond-friends (mbai) (Schneebaum 1988).[49] Bond-friend partners express their closeness through reciprocity in fellatio, anal intercourse, or mutual masturbation, and though they may be physically affectionate with other men, homosexual orgasm should be exclusive within their relationship. In contrast to this *private* bonding, the *public* and ritualized aspects of homo- and heterosexual partnership that were highly developed among Casuarina Asmat have been *eradicated* by Catholic missionaries. Extramarital sexuality has thus been driven underground, privatized, and made intensely homosexual among men. Schneebaum quotes his main informant, Akatpitsjin:

> Having a *mbai* [homosexual bond-friend] is like having a *papisj* partner, a [heterosexual] exchange partner. We all have our *mbai* here. Pastor has stopped us from *papisj*, from exchanging wives, but we still have our *mbai*. He does not know this. (Schneebaum 1988:193)

Viewed in the Foucauldian perspective elaborated by Deleuze (1988), the persistence of Asmat homosexuality in the postcolonial era bends the line between external power and internal desire to create a new space for self-assertion by Casuarina Asmat men. This homosexual bonding presents a space of radical resistance to and infringement upon the sexual taboos of the Catholic priests, as well as being the secret usurpation of the priests' own most implicit homosexual desires. Given preexisting patterns of homosexuality among Casuarina Asmat men, their current practices do not assert homosexual bonding as a new phenomenon. Rather, they illustrate a subtler change in what Foucault (1985:27) identifies as the *way* in which the individual as ethical subject establishes his or her *relation* to the rule—for instance, a change in the meaning and context of sexual relations. Just as ethics are contested through codes and behaviors, they are also tactically contested by *repositioning the meaning of the self vis-à-vis ethical standards.* These relational changes can be both nuanced and dramatic since they recontextualize action within force fields of knowledge and power.

Similar processes are evident in contemporary gender struggles in the United States. Kath Weston (1991) shows how American lesbians and gays powerfully reconstruct the notion of "family." In the process, values of love, help, and enduring solidarity are appropriated but repositioned. As such, they create a new and valorized ethical space for families constituted through choice and friendship rather than through blood or biogenetic connection (contrast Schneider 1980).

Among Gebusi, well inland from the New Guinea south coast, I knew two young men, Dawhi and Godiay, who were age-mates undergoing age-grade indoctrination. Adult men copiously inseminated the adolescents so that they would grow large and strong and attain full masculinity (Knauft 1986, 1987b). However, Dawhi and Godiay engaged each other in reciprocal fellatio as well as being recipients of semen from older men. Moreover, they displayed their sexual affection for each other in a series of ribald, hilarious, and very public jests. At one level, the displays of Dawhi and Godiay could be taken as public resistance against the formal but only loosely enforced asymmetry between initiated and uninitiated men—that adolescents should resist the pleasures of orgasm and receive semen from older men instead of enjoying its release with each other. Since there was no explicit penalty *against* age-mate homosexuality, however, Dawhi and Godiay were not so much breaking a cultural rule as exploring a realm of sexual pleasure across the grain of standard practices.

At another level, the homoerotic display of Dawhi and Godiay could be taken as resistance to the heterosexual marriage that was expected to follow their initiation. Both young men stated clearly that they didn't want or need women because they had each other as lovers. Indeed, their opposition to women was sexually antagonistic if not misogynistic. When images of heterosexual intercourse were evoked by the male spirit medium during men's spirit séances, Godiay and Dawhi took the lead to incite the male audience to displays of violence against women. They even shot arrows into the longhouse roof as a graphic indication of how violent sex with women would be. One man, who was particularly brutal with his own wife, joked with approval that he would slice off a woman's breast.

The point here is that pushing subjectivation as resistance in areas of sex, violence, or other forms of desire is not in itself necessarily progressive or reactionary, liberating or fascist. It can be either or both.[50] The result needs to be assessed pragmatically depending on social context, a point with which Foucault would likely concur. This assessment should not just consider the degree of stigma, coercion, or inequality within an undifferentiated notion of inequality, but should analyze the relation between different axes of knowledge and power as culturally constituted—for example, between sexual domination and inequalities of gender, ethnicity, age, race, or class. Resisting one of these axes of inequality may simultaneously reinforce other forms of domination.

Subjectivation in the Postcolony

In postcolonial circumstances of competing or combined epistemes, subjectivity and agency become particularly complex. Though Foucault does not consider these dynamics, they practically jump out as Foucauldian relevancies in a late modern world. As Mbembe and Roitman (1995) have elaborated, and as Fanon (1991) foreshadowed, postcolonial socioeconomic and political crisis is integrally bound up with crises of subjectivity. In many parts of Melanesia, for instance, the tension between giving and keeping has been an intrinsic if often underappreciated dimension of traditional exchange and affiliation (e.g., Bercovitch 1994; Weiner 1992a). Under conditions of a cash economy, wage labor, and commodity possession, collectively constituted notions of subjectivity and identity—what Marilyn Strathern (1988) calls the Melanesian "dividual"—become especially difficult. Demands for reciprocity and contribution in collective exchange or remittances home compete against the personal value placed on commodity ownership, the raising of one's own bridewealth, or the importance of capital accumulation.[51] New forms of elite or incipient class inequality come in tension with strong allegiances of kinship and clanship (Errington and Gewertz 1995:chs. 2, 5; Strathern 1984, 1993; Connell and Lea 1994).

These tensions can also have a poignantly gendered and sexual dimension. Under pressure for cash and consumption, masculinity in Melanesia undergoes new stresses and developments. These include circuits of migration between rural and urban areas, the attractions of theft and criminality, the importance and yet difficulty of continuing education, and the opportunities and complications of serial sexual relationships (Fife 1995; Goddard 1995; Nihill 1994). Discrimination against and victimization of women can extend in tandem with the frustrations of these new circumstances (e.g., Zimmer-Tamakoshi 1993a, 1993b). Along the south coast of New Guinea, indigenous patterns of sexual exchange, spouse-sharing, or ritual sexuality abut newer practices that commoditize sex and enforce a moral divide between marriage and prostitution or sex work (Hammar 1992, 1995 in press). It is evident in several parts of New Guinea that exchange of cash or gifts for sex is increasingly common in town and city environments and is increasingly used as a degrading marker of female status.[52] Status distinctions based on postcolonial notions of ethnicity, race, religion, and class easily compound those of gender and sexuality to overdetermine the notion of a *disco meri*, loose woman, or prostitute (*pasindia meri* or *pamuk meri*). Women can be tainted with the diffuse aura of such stigma insofar as they are seen as geographically mobile, un-Christian, greedy for money, or uncaring about kin, as well as for having multiple sexual partners per se. All these attributes may imply or be seen to reflect sex-for-cash relationships.

The difficulties of postcolonial subjectivity are well known, along with the excesses of patriarchal power that they can be heir to. As Mbembe (1992) has noted in an African context, the legacy of colonial "commandment" easily dovetails with excesses of violence once Europeans have left. The subjectification of colonial violence, as vignetted by Taussig (1987), can easily come back to roost in what Mbembe calls the "anxious virility" of postcolonial atrocities and obscenities.

This has occurred to some degree in the Indonesianization of West New Guinea (Gietzelt 1988; Monbiot 1989; May 1986). It is less pronounced in Papua New Guinea, where authority structures have stayed relatively decentralized and where the colonial encounter was relatively nonviolent and nonalienating of land (at least when considered on a global comparative scale). But if an African-style banality of power is not imminent in Papua New Guinea, huge and increasing problems of corruption, ecocide, insurrection, guns, drugs, lawlessness, gendered abuse, and sexually tranmitted diseases do raise the possibility of an ultimate slide down some parallel path.[53]

If this is one potential side of the story, however, it is not the only one. On a more positive and equally important note, these calamities run up against the bulk of common people, who creatively forge subjectivity in everyday experience and practice. It is especially important here to recall Guha's (1989) proviso that governance that is partial and based largely on coercion rather than consent is typically *not* hegemonic in the original Gramscian sense; its subjectivities are not fully internalized by most of the population, who are only ostensibly its subjects. This point, so applicable to colonial history, rebounds importantly in postcolonial situations as well, as Fanon (1968:chs. 3, 4) again foreshadowed. Not withstanding difficulties, then, New Guinea and other postcolonies are full of creative and resilient development. As Appiah reminds us, again in an African context, resilience persists in even the most dire circumstances:

> Despite the overwhelming reality of economic decline; despite unimaginable poverty; despite wars, malnutrition, disease, and political instability, African cultural productivity grows apace: popular literatures, oral narrative and poetry, dance, drama, music, and visual art all thrive. The contemporary cultural production of many African societies, and the

many traditions whose evidences so vigorously remain, is an antidote to the dark vision of the postcolonial novelist. (Appiah 1991:356)

As Foucault illustrated in his studies of Greek and Greco-Roman subjectivity, creative elaboration of self-relationship does not depend on a Nietzschean banality of power or the Dionysian excess that is celebrated by Deleuze and which is more influential in Foucault's earlier work. Certainly a body dominated by or saturated with waves of violence and pain—what Deleuze and Guattari (1987:ch. 6) so graphically describe as the rammed intensity of a sadomasochistic "body without organs"—may be used to push open the envelope of the unsaid and undone. And this is certainly an option that Foucault himself explored.[54] But this is not the only route. Nor, similarly, does the crisis of subjectivity encouraged by a postcolonial banality of power lead down a simple path. The later Foucault illustrated with delicacy that the care of the self and the use of pleasure need not be less important, nuanced, or creatively intense for being less violent or draconian. In this respect, I suggest, it is important to embrace a critically humanist perspective and break decisively from the Nietzschean will to power that Foucault first sought in pain and violence. To do otherwise flirts with a stance that is ultimately asocial if not unethical.

The epistemics of desire in the context of social power lead us back to rather than away from agency and practice. Here one must respond to Spivak's assertion against Foucault and Deleuze that "it is impossible for contemporary French intellectuals to imagine the kind of Power and Desire that would inhabit the unnamed subject of the Other of Europe" (1994:75). But despite Spivak's eloquence, we are not limited to a European imaginary, nor even her own. Once again, ethnographic portrayal of lived experience can be helpful. Powers and resistances that tend to be taken for granted in the West can be defamiliarized against agents and objects of desire in other cultures and in other parts of our own. We must listen and record more carefully and vigorously, not less so. Cultural anthropology is now well positioned to open up agency and subjectivity in unfamiliar epistemic contexts and refract them socially and politically through different lenses of gender, age, race, sexual, religious, or class inequality. This throws into relief the specific practices as well as the epistemic tensions of others. It also helps clarify their relationship to our own relationship to ourselves.

Conclusions

Foucault's perspective can be refined and levered to new positions through detailed ethnography. It may be asked how we can maintain the rigor and focus that ethnography has desired while de-siring ourselves from an uncritical assumption of Western power and knowledge. It is not facetious to answer that the voices of others provide a world of answers. Foucauldian engagement with ethnography can shed important critical light beyond Eurocentric biases, asocial limitations, and textualism.

Foucault's various moments have significant implications for critically humanist sensibilities in cultural anthropology. All of his analytic phases open new vistas on inequality and domination. But all merit a greater attention to and appreciation of cultural diversity. Foucault's early view that Western epistemes endure over long periods of time can be pluralized to provide a greater appreciation of variations in the constitution of knowledge. Rather than being divorced from refined historical analysis, epistemic diversity can be particularized in both spatial and temporal terms—in alternative cultural contexts and over decades rather than centuries. Epistemic critique can engage rather than refuse the nuances of temporal and cultural diversity.

Foucault's middle-period exposure of knowledge and power in Occidental "dividing practices" has informed scintillating critiques of colonialism and representation in fields such as cultural anthropology. But this awareness can now be extended to address the bodily and institutional force of others' epistemic assumptions, in addition to those of the West. Alternative forms of knowledge and power have long reached out to interlace themselves with Western and other colonial legacies. Examining the hybrid interface of epistemic powers that stem from different modes of knowledge and subjectivity is crucial to understanding the complexities, hegemonies, and resistances of a late modern word. These include knowledges and powers concerning race, religion, ethnicity, and nationality, as well as those of sex, gender, class, and projective deviance or illness.

The workings of subjectivity are extended and refined in Foucault's last work on technologies of the self. This perspective can provide nuance on changing contours of subjectivation in the context of power and history—including in colonial and postcolonial circumstances. If Foucault's nominalism still leaves his work in an uneasy relationship with the analysis of social action, his latter projects provide fertile ground for extending this connection. Subjectivity diversifies in close if not dialectical relationship to larger structures of epistemic domination. This connection engages thematic moments that critically humanist sensibilities attempt to keep in tension: an appreciation of subjective diversity and critical exposure of changing inequalities. If Foucault's work galvanized these issues with brilliance, a critically humanist ethnography can both concretize his contributions and extend them in important ways.

gramsci and bakhtin

Dialogues Against Hegemonies

Along one prominent line of reasoning, Antonio Gramsci (1891–1937) is the most important Marxist theorist of the twentieth century and Mikhail Bakhtin (1895–1975) the greatest twentieth-century theorist of literature. Both men were centrally concerned with the relationship between subjective diversity and resilience or resistance against totalizing forms of control or domination. Gramsci considers this relationship through a trenchant critique of cultural hegemony as the basis for class-based inequality. Bakhtin, on the other hand, illustrates how aesthetic forms and communication provide an irrepressible dynamic that cuts across homogenizing strains and subverts authoritarianism. From a critically humanist perspective, Gramsci and Bakhtin begin from complementary vantage points; whereas Bakhtin foregrounds the value of subjective diversity, Gramsci emphasizes critiques of inequality. Given how effectively their perspectives articulate critically humanist sensibilities, it is particularly fruitful to analyze them in relationship to each other.

The personal backgrounds of Bakhtin and Gramsci contextualize their work and its striking reemergence in cultural theory during the 1970s and 1980s. Though differing in political orientation, intellectual goals, and nationality, Gramsci and Bakhtin each cut their intellectual teeth as passionate and critical young writers in the late 1910s and early 1920s. Both studied language and philology at the university level, and both were highly concerned with the theoretical relationship between language, literature, culture, and social action. Both men were caught up in the wake of the 1917 Russian Revolution, which, for critical thinkers presented both opportunity and enigma. Instead of occurring in Britain, France, or Germany, which had developed economies of wage-earning and industrial capitalism, the revolution occurred instead in Russia, which was economically backward and on the feudal fringes of Europe. The seeming failure of classic Marxism—as then understood—to predict revolutionary outbreak in Europe created both a conundrum and a stimulating challenge for the political avant-garde.[1] How deeply flawed were existing views of Marxism? What were the features of ideology, belief, and symbolism—the cultural superstructure—that had prevented the revolution from occurring in the developed West? Could the intelligentsia that had galvanized revolution in Russia be turned to advantage elsewhere? Just as important, how could the seizure of state control modeled by Lenin be kept from the nightmare of fascism or totalitarianism?[2] And what was the historical role of the rich intellectual developments that took place in Europe and Russia in the late nineteenth and early twentieth centuries?

For leftist intellectuals of the 1920s—and especially those on the eastern and southern margins of Europe—these questions informed fresh analyses of consciousness, representation, and language. Many believed in the power of ideas to a degree difficult to fathom today. The intellectual was a passionately engaged figure, debating, instructing, and working for a better society. Gramsci edited an Italian leftist journal of political and cultural critique, lectured workers in Turin, and spent a year and a half with party leaders in Moscow before returning to head the Italian Communist Party (PCI) in 1924. An astute cultural critic and theoretician as well as a political organizer, he struggled to keep the potential of a workers' revolution alive in Italy. Despite his supposed immunity from political arrest as a member of parliament, Gramsci followed the grim legacy of previous PCI leaders and was imprisoned in 1926.

Bakhtin was far more cautious; he avoided those in power, kept a very low profile, and survived by means of humility. However, he spearheaded a scintillating cadre of intellectual eccentrics. The so-called Bakhtin circle debated critical philosophy, art, and religion and explored avant-garde and classical music, drama, and literature. Anticonformist, members of the circle gave lectures and performances to enthusiastic audiences in small Russian towns such as Nevel and Vitebsk between 1918 and 1924 and expanded their brilliant eccentricities in Leningrad for several more years. Most of its members, however, were dead a decade or so later because of Stalinist purges, concentration camps, or physical ailments exacerbated by war and its shortages (Clark and Holquist 1984:264). Bakhtin himself was arrested in 1929 and sentenced to exile. But like Gramsci, Bakhtin remained optimistic about the potentials of progressive communication even in the face of overwhelming state persecution.

If Bakhtin's intellectual commitment was ultimately to literature and language while Gramsci's commitment was ultimately to politics, both men transcended this division by stressing the intrinsically social nature of human existence. For both—in resonance with the writings of the young Marx, which had not yet been published—an implicit kind of species-being allowed for open-ended experience, communicational positioning, and intersubjective awareness.[3] Transubjectivity was irrepressible and could ultimately lever open even the tightest constraints on language, representation, and politics. Faith in this possibility persisted for both men despite brutal personal oppression and isolation, and neither was in good health to begin with.

In many respects, the works of Gramsci and Bakhtin—as separate as they were from each other—need to be seen in the context of parallel personal struggles. Born in undeveloped Sardinia, Gramsci was sickly since early childhood.[4] Among other difficulties, he was severely hunchbacked because of spinal trauma resulting from a childhood fall, and he had periodic internal hemorrhaging. "The doctors had given me up for dead, and until about 1914 my mother kept the small coffin and little dress I was supposed to be buried in" (Gramsci, quoted in Ransome 1992:56). The political imprisonment of Gramsci's father from 1898 to 1904 left Gramsci's mother and her seven children destitute; she worked as a seamstress. Deformed and ill, Gramsci was tormented by his schoolmates, felt himself a drain on his family, and was a loner, notwithstanding the support of his mother. "The isolated existence I have led since child-hood . . . did me great damage. . . . [F]or a very long time, I have believed it was absolutely, fatally impossible that I should ever be loved" (Gramsci, quoted in Ransome 1992:58).

As a young adult, Gramsci suffered from nervous and gastric disorders, needed a special diet, and attempted to conquer physical weakness through intellectual work. Excelling in his studies, he managed an impoverished and solitary existence away from home at secondary school and at the University of Turin (though he was unable to sit for his last exams). Gramsci found purpose and meaning in leftist political activism and journalism; he published his first article at age nineteen. Following a psychological and physical breakdown, Gramsci rededicated himself to revolutionary struggle and argued for a complete socialist renovation of working-class education. In 1916 he suggested:

> Culture is organization, discipline of one's inner self, a coming to terms with one's own personality; it is the attainment of higher awareness. . . . [O]nly by degrees, one state at a time, has humanity acquired conscious-ness of its own value and won for itself the right to throw off patterns of organization imposed on it by minorities at a previous period in history. And this consciousness was formed not under the brutal goad of physio-logical necessity, but as a result of intelligent reflection, at first by just a few people and later by a whole class, on why certain conditions exist and how best to convert the facts of vassalage into the signals of rebellion and social reconstruction. (Gramsci, quoted in Ransome 1992:72)

From 1919 until his arrest in 1926, Gramsci worked with the Italian Communist Party to organize the workers and mediate the party's complex relationships to organized labor and the Socialists, not to mention the Fascisti. Moving to Moscow in 1922, Gramsci became part of the Communist inner circle through his astute political analysis and strategies. Though he also suffered another breakdown, he met Julia Schucht in a sanatorium outside Moscow and married her later that year. Gramsci moved alone to Vienna in late 1923, returned to Moscow for a difficult personal visit with his wife and son in 1925, and returned to Rome as head of the Italian Communist Party in 1926. His short tenure was marked by one biting speech in parliament, but the increasing Fascist crackdown on dissidents forced his family, which had joined him, to

Switzerland. Remaining in Italy, Gramsci anticipated his own arrest but felt it his duty to stay on: "A captain must be the last to abandon his vessel."[5] After a show trial, he was sentenced to twenty years and five months in prison.

Left without medical care or proper meals, Gramsci's plight in prison became torturous; it turned into an extended death agony. Over this period, "his teeth fell out, his digestive system collapsed so that he could not eat solid food, his chronic insomnia became permanent so that he could go weeks without more than an hour or two of sleep at night; he had convulsions when he vomited blood, and suffered from headaches so violent that he beat his head against the walls of his cell" (Hoare and Nowell-Smith 1971:xcii). His wife's deep depression increasingly kept her from corresponding with him, and the letters and packages sent by his sister-in-law, Tatiana Schucht, became Gramsci's main source of personal support. By 1927, however, Gramsci had written of his intention to work intensively and systematically while in prison on subjects that could give "focus and direction to my inner life" (Ransome 1992:106). The Fascist prosecutor had declared, "For twenty years we must stop this brain from functioning."[6] In defiance, it became Gramsci's mission to develop himself on paper.

After nine years without medical intervention, Gramsci had arteriosclerosis, angina, gout, and tuberculosis in his back as well as his lungs. After a physical and nervous collapse in 1932, outside efforts to press for his release were intensified, but the Fascist authorities refused unless Gramsci conceded defeat and submitted his own petition for clemency. Despite his condition, Gramsci refused.[7] He resumed work on his notebooks after a stay in a prison hospital and continued despite another breakdown in 1935. He ultimately outlived his prison sentence, which had been changed to expire in the spring of 1937, but by this time he was too ill to move. He died on April 27, 1937, six days after obtaining his freedom. He was forty-six, had spent eleven years in prison, and had never seen his second son.

It was during his painful demise that Gramsci filled the 2,848 pages of his thirty-three *Prison Notebooks*. These constitute the bulk of his intellectual corpus. Within this wealth of jottings, critiques, and allusive commentaries, one finds Gramsci's seminal work on hegemony, civil and political society, passive revolution, historical blocs, organic intellectualism, the Italian state, the modern prince, and the place of literacy, popular culture, and media in consciousness, as well an astute analysis of capitalist mass production (Fordism) and topics of cultural critique in Italian intellectual and artistic history. Gramsci's notebooks make virtually no statement of his personal experience or sufferings; his tone is penetrating, objective, and amazingly free of railing or exaggeration. This supreme will of trenchant analysis in the face of personal agony was Gramsci's final and enduring act of resistance, resorted to only in the absence of the political action he longed for but could no longer undertake. He lived the maxim of the leftist journal he had helped found: "Pessimism of the intellect; optimism of the will."[8]

Gramsci never knew if his writings would elude the prison censors or if they would be read. Much of his prose is cryptic in an attempt to avoid censorship or confiscation. While making funeral arrangements, however, Tatiana Schucht, Gramsci's sister-in-law and indefatigable supporter, managed at great risk to herself to smuggle out Gramsci's notebooks and safeguard them until secret transport to Moscow could be arranged. Her own story of dedication to Gramsci and his legacy is just beginning to be appreciated.[9]

BAKHTIN'S LIFE AND INTELLECTUAL CORPUS ARE SLIGHTLY LESS TORTUROUS but no less amazing than Gramsci's. Bakhtin was afflicted beginning at age sixteen with osteomyelitis—a painful bone disease that periodically crippled him. In 1918, at age twenty-three, Bakhtin and his wife escaped the hunger, privation, and threat of Russian government persecution in Petrograd and moved to Nevel, a rural town of four sawmills and thirteen thousand inhabitants some three hundred miles to the south. Bakhtin taught in a gymnasium and headed the local school board (Clark and Holquist 1984:38). Gradually attracting a small band of eccentric but brilliant intellectuals, Bakhtin lived in Nevel and nearby Vitebsk for six years and then spent five years in Leningrad. Cautious of persecution, unwilling or unable to extend professional connections, and much less ambitious than his colleagues, Bakhtin labored in poverty. He had difficulty finding work or marketing his writings, several of which were published under the name of (or with the vague coauthorship of) sympathetic colleagues.[10] His book *Problems of Dostoevsky's Poetics*, which awaited publication for seven years, was finally printed under his name in May 1929.

By this time, Bakhtin had been arrested in Leningrad on thin charges of subversive religious activity; a positive review of his book made little impact (Clark and Holquist 1984:143). After detention for several months, Bakhtin's leg condition was complicated by nephritis, and he was transferred to a hospital where he underwent an operation. Bakhtin was then given a virtual death sentence by the court: ten years in a prison camp on the Solovetsky Islands. Pleas reduced this sentence to six years of exile in Kustanai, a town in Kazakhstan with a severe climate, a minimal cultural life, and a population of some thirty-four thousand (Clark and Holquist 1984:253). At Kustanai conditions were hard, but Bakhtin was a survivor. "Despite his impracticality, he somehow managed to get through even the most adverse circumstances. His ability to survive was due in part to his equanimity, his sense of humor, and his capacity for accepting gracefully any interlocutor" (Clark and Holquist 1984:254).

Bakhtin's wife found odd jobs; he himself once worked as an accountant for a cooperative, gave lectures such as "The Organization and Techniques of Commerce and the Annual Financial Plan," and published an economic article titled "Experience Based on a Study of Demand Among Kolkhoz Workers." Starvation and Stalinist purges racked Russian Kazakhstan during the 1930s, but despite Bakhtin's poverty and increasing unemployment, he continued to write, the work interrupted only by a stream of cigarettes and endless pots of tea brewed by his wife. During the 1920s and 1930s, Bakhtin's intellectual writings piled up in notebooks, reworked and elaborated for himself but with little thought of publication. Ever circumspect, he even refused to write letters.

In 1936 Bakhtin was transferred to Saransk, a larger town in Mordovia but with a literacy rate of only 13 percent. Now allowed to teach, Bakhtin became "virtually a one-man world literature department" (Clark and Holquist 1984:259). Though his course load was "incredible," he found time to write. In the following year, however, most of his fellow faculty members were purged. Bakhtin's low profile again saved his life; he escaped and moved to Savelovo, a small rail center on the Volga River. Here he was once again jobless, and increasingly severe osteomyelitis led to the amputation of his right leg in 1938, further reducing his mobility and chances of employment. However, Bakhtin wrote prolifically, basing his analysis on smuggled books and his own prodigious memory (Clark and Holquist 1984:262).

The persecution of Russian intellectuals lifted on the eve of World

War II, and Bakhtin finally submitted his dissertation on Rabelais to the Gorky Institute, which expressed interest in having him lecture there. His book manuscript *The Novel of Education and Its Significance in the History of Realism* was also scheduled for publication. But the manuscript was destroyed in the war when the Soviet Writer archive was bombed. And during the ensuing privations and war shortages, the insouciant Bakhtin used his only remaining draft for tobacco paper, smoking it page by page, beginning at the end. (Only the first section of the work remained by the time it was discovered, in the 1960s.) As for his dissertation on Rabelais, new suspicions prevented its acceptance. In June 1952, after more than a decade, this work was finally passed but was awarded only a lower "candidate's degree," a slight that Bakhtin "passed off with a shrug" (Clark and Holquist 1984: 325). Bakhtin dismissed such calamities and tossed his remaining manuscripts carelessly aside. But his own stature within the small cultural community of Saransk gradually grew; Bakhtin was able to pitch his lectures at any level he wished and became enormously popular as a teacher. Out of caution and because of his own worsening health, he shunned opportunities to move to more central institutions (Clark and Holquist 1984:331).

During the 1960s, literary revivals in Moscow led Russian scholars to renew their interest in Bakhtin's 1929 book on Dostoevsky. Believing he was long dead along with the rest of the Bakhtin circle, they were ultimately amazed to discover him alive in out-of-the-way Saransk, a rare survivor of the Stalinist purges. It slowly became evident, moreover, that Bakhtin had a trove of path-breaking manuscripts that lay moldering. Ever wary of publication, Bakhtin only reluctantly relinquished his work for dissemination. He admitted privately to having authored several earlier books that were increasingly realized to be stunning examples of his lifelong intellectual perspective. These included *Freudianism*, the famous *Marxism and the Philosophy of Language* (both published under Volosinov's name), and *The Formal Method in Literary Study* (first printed under the name of Medvedev).[11]

Bakhtin's growing fame in the late 1960s and early 1970s came when his health and energy were declining. He finally moved to Moscow in late 1969. His wife Elena died a mere two years later, her last thoughts being how to get tea for her husband. Bakhtin's remaining intellectual zest was sapped by grief, though he received a constant stream of acolytes. Even so, his last writings are impressive in their ripe summary of his thought

(Bakhtin 1986b; cf. Clark and Holquist 1984:341). Bakhtin finally died in early 1975 after gently refusing the last rites from a priest. One of his last requests was to be told once again his favorite story, the tale in the *Decameron* "where miracles are performed at the tomb of a man regarded as a saint, but who had in fact been a dreadful rogue" (Clark and Holquist 1984:347). The dialogism that is the hallmark of Bakhtin's intellectual corpus—the open-ended, common, and nontotalitarian capacity of language for surprising voices, reversals, and prankish vitality despite all domination—pervaded his authorship, his life, and his playful and self-effacing death.

Gramsci and Bakhtin
Legacies and Appropriations

The lives of Gramsci and Bakhtin have intellectual importance in addition to their pathos and drama. In personal history and genius, both figures were ripe for being influencing French and English theorists during the late 1970s and 1980s. It was during this period that their work finally emerged in belated translation. The first full edition of Gramsci's *Prison Notebooks* was not published in Italian until 1965; an important selection in English translation was edited by Hoare and Nowell-Smith and published in 1971.[12] Bakhtin's books were first published in translation during this same period,[13] and his salvageable manuscripts were translated into English in several installments during the 1980s.[14] During the late 1980s and 1990s, the corpus of secondary books and articles on Bakhtin and Gramsci has skyrocketed.

At least as important as the timing of this publication, however, has been the specific appeal of Gramsci and Bakhtin to Western intellectuals in a context of late modernity. Marginalized voices from the eastern and southern fringes of Europe, their work has an openness and an optimism that have been particularly fresh for French and Anglo intellectuals—who have often come to doubt the reasons for their own authorship. The tactical struggles of Gramsci and the dialogic dances of Bakhtin shoot through their lives as well as their work. Neither reached or could intend authorial closure. Both wrote in widening circles of evolving personal notebooks, double-voicing themselves to elude the censor's pen, writing for the sake of the idea rather than the fame of academic production. Trained scholars, both pursued a relentless philological method that works over ideas to open them out rather than finalize them. Both emphasized the emancipatory potential of shifting and repositioned representations. And both were committed teachers and listeners who were respected and appreciated by common people. As such, their work engages the contemporary importance of intellectual and social position and the awareness of culture as a shifting contestation. But amid this fluidity, their perspectives each retain a remarkable groundedness. Even in the cynical 1990s, who can deny the commitment, integrity, and perseverance of Bakhtin and Gramsci in the face of punishment, isolation, poverty, suffering, and the ever-present specter of death? Theirs was a passionate mission of intellectual reaching in and reaching out despite the enormous odds against success or even written survival. Intellectualism *did* matter, and analytic utterance *could* be a powerful act of resistance. For academics safe in their houses and doubting their credentials, such authorship was authentic and compelling as well as brilliant.

It would be wrong to mythologize Bakhtin and Gramsci. Even within European intellectual circles, alternative figures of the period could also be mentioned—Walter Benjamin, Georg Lukács, Theodor Adorno, the latter Ludwig Wittgenstein, Hannah Arendt, and Rosa Luxemburg, among others. Between the 1970s and the early 1990s, increased interest in these and other authors resonated with a wider appreciation of critical, disempowered, and subaltern voices. But to historicize Gramsci and Bakhtin from a late modern context is as much to appreciate their status as it is to explain it. Both were dedicated to objectivist analysis and not paralyzed by their own prescient insights concerning historicity and the openness of authorship. Both were committed to vigorous scholarship about the very shiftiness of subjectivism, and neither was enamored of textual analysis or clever authorship for its own sake. For both men, intellectualism was ongoing work of the most profound and deeply social kind—an active engagement that linked representation and experience and that used dialogue, critical debate, and theory to galvanize intersubjective awareness.

The differences between Bakhtin and Gramsci are also significant; Gramscian insights are linked more to political issues, while those of Bakhtin relate more to literary ones. Where Bakhtin illuminates the possibilities of utterance and voicing, Gramsci struggles against the reactionary realities of political culture and class structure. If Gramsci's war of position strained ultimately toward confrontation (including the political confrontation that kept him in Italy and led to his arrest), Bakhtin's softer dialogism provided playful and multivocal tactics of continuation through decades of adversity and oppression. Where Gramsci uses metaphors of martial arts and realpolitik, Bakhtin uses those of humor and philosophical if not religious sublimity. Gramsci was censured to omit Marx, while Bakhtin was censured to include him.

One can approach the thought of Bakhtin and Gramsci through their concepts that have been most influential in fields such as cultural anthropology. Gramsci distinguishes between the openly *coercive* force of *political society* and the deeper and more penetrating *hegemony* of cultural and historical force in *civil society*—that is, the cultural dispositions and social institutions that predispose consent to (if not compliance with) politically repressive regimes. While the social life of workers may provide them the opportunity for revolutionary action, this potential can be subverted by a hegemony of reactionary beliefs and dispositions. Gramsci holds, then, that one needs to respond with a constant *war of position* against the hegemony of the reigning *historic bloc*. This positional struggle is a tactical deployment through cultural as well as social and political skirmishes. By such means, political consciousness is marshaled, augmented, and preserved through inauspicious periods of *passive revolution* until a later and more appropriate time for ultimate confrontation by means of physical force. This later and decisive confrontation is the *war of maneuver*—an open warfare of political liberation, as epitomized by the Russian Revolution.

Gramsci analyzes the cultural means by which twentieth-century capitalism subverts egalitarian and communitarian understandings. These cultural hegemonies included not just Italian Fascism but new ideologies of labor, gender, and the work force that ensure worker discipline and compliance in mass production—what Gramsci termed *"Taylorism"* or *"Fordism"* (after Henry Ford). Though he was ultimately most concerned with Italy, Gramsci was highly attuned to the historical specifics of politics and culture that informed the *subaltern status* of disempowered groups as geographic or class peripheries within nation-states or empires. For Gramsci, the analysis of language use, literacy, and literature was immensely important to see how cultural biases and their associated politics developed and were disseminated in different cultural and national traditions.

Against bourgeois hegemonies, Gramsci strove to identify working-class interests and analyze how these resonated with or were undercut by artistic and cultural developments. Not limited to the elite, cultural developments could resonate with common people and workers in a more organic philosophy. The scholar's task was to cultivate the potential of such common but nascent sensibilities—to become an *organic intellectual.* As such, Gramsci was highly attuned to—and in some ways originated—the notion that culture is a primary site of political and educational struggle.

On the surface, Bakhtin looks more like a linguistic and literary scholar than a political theorist. His interests foreground features such as *speech genres,* the *structure of the modernist novel,* the *philosophy of language,* and the presuppositions of time and space—*"chronotopes"*—that inform literature at different historical periods. But these concerns link to larger issues. Bakhtin is ultimately a social philosopher—a theoretician of communication as the foundation of being and experience. He holds transubjectivity through *dialogue* to be the basis of human relationality and existence. His emphasis on *socially situated utterance* rather than on formal and depersonalized aspects of language reflects Bakhtin's renowned emphasis on the *dialogic aspects of communication.* These stand in systematic opposition to the *monologic discourse* of repressive authoritarianism—as was painfully evident in the official dogma and discursive tyranny of Stalinism. Bakhtin's celebration of *hybridity*—the mixture of different linguistic consciousnesses within a single utterance—connects directly to issues of intersubjective meaning: how it is that subjective diversity changes and enriches one's being.[15] With great nuance, Bakhtin penetrates the complex diversities of *voicing,* the assumptions of audience or *addressivity,* and the combination of multiple voices in *heteroglossia.* He stresses that there is an intrinsic dynamic between experiential *"insidedness"* and interpersonal *"outsidedness"* in human communication and understanding.

Bakhtin exposed and analyzed dialogic imagery over the history of Western literature in specific genres of time, space, and social connection. These include the carnivalesque hilarity and grotesque reversals of sixteenth-century popular festivals, as portrayed by Rabelais (Bakhtin 1968); the polyphonous dialogue among self-developing characters in Dostoevsky's poetics (1984); and the exploratory self-actualization of the Germanic *Bildungsroman*—the late eighteenth- and early nineteenth-century biography of personal emergence and education (1986b). Through appreciative rendering, Bakhtin modifies his style and his analytic distinctions to coax out the features of voicing and intersubjectivity most salient to each of these literary world views.[16]

In his moral and aesthetic philosophy, Bakhtin stresses *answerability in art*—the duty of the artist to move beyond formalism and reductionism, preserve diversity, and embrace the social nature of communication as an interactive process. Transubjectivity provides the processual basis for human being. This theme is reflected equally in Bakhtin's early and important *Philosophy of the Act* (1993), in his pragmatic analysis of linguistic meaning (*Marxism and the Philosophy of Language* [1986a]), and his collected later essays on speech genres (1986b). Bakhtin's work develops a theory of emergent communication that is at once powerful, deeply subtle, and often implicit. For Bakhtin, there is an ever-present tension between *centripetal* forces, which attempt to dominate and unify voices, and irrepressible *centrifugal* forces, which drive creativity and diversity.[17]

BAKHTIN AND GRAMSCI HAVE BEEN INTRODUCED SELECTIVELY TO THE Western humanities and social sciences over the last two and a half decades. Though most books on Gramsci view him through the lens of Communism and Marxism,[18] his writing on literature, language, and religion makes up a large and even preponderant portion of his prison notebooks—most of which are still untranslated into English. It deserves to be emphasized that "language and linguistics have recently come to be seen not as a marginal subject in the *Prison Notebooks* but as occupying a central place in their overall theoretical construction" (Forgacs and Nowell-Smith 1985:164). Bakhtin's work, on the other hand, has been explored predominantly by literary and language specialists, who have less understanding of the humanist strains of the early Marx—as opposed to Marxism—that resonate effectively with Bakhtin's perspective. In critical theory, by contrast, Bakhtin's work has often been invoked through a totalizing lens, as if every conceivable variant of hybridity, dialogue, heteroglossia, or the carnivalesque indicates discursive resistance against oppression.[19] Bakhtin himself would have been the first to debunk such generalization: The meanings of utterances are highly variable and depend on their historical and cultural context.

Interpreters and translators have magnified the difference between Bakhtin as a literary theorist and Gramsci as an analyst of politics and culture. (Bakhtin has been presented to the Anglo-French world by literary analysts such as Michael Holquist and Tzvetan Todorov; Gramsci has been popular among Marxist historians and was introduced, brilliantly, by leftist figures such as Raymond Williams and Stuart Hall.) From a critically humanist perspective, however, it is evident that both Bakhtin and Gramsci see living and writing and theorizing as a linked process of active social engagement—a progressive mosaic of social affiliation, trenchant intellectualism, and instigation. This process is reflected in the style as well as the substance of their work—the productivity of recursive hermeneutics, the resulting openness of the fragment, and the momentary insight that illuminates a larger empirical field. In lieu of a bleached master narrative or schematic grand theory, Bakhtin and Gramsci develop their views through diverse examples drawn from their encyclopedic reading and prodigious memory of European history, culture, and art. Though Gramsci would have recoiled at Bakhtin's seeming political timidity, and Bakhtin likewise at Gramsci's risky activism, the one struggle picks up where the other leaves off. In either case, received formulas do not work. Bakhtin's wonderful faith in dialogue and Gramsci's poignant critique of hegemony have been rich for late modern anthropology. Too seldom, however, has their openness been used as a lever upon their own texts to read them in fresh ways. To read Gramsci and Bakhtin in the direct context of each other helps to underscore their complementarity. In the process, they illustrate how to mediate the lingering divide between the poetic or expressive and the political or economic that still often inflects fields such as cultural anthropology.

Gramsci and Bakhtin
A Dialogue

Following brief introductions, Bakhtin and Gramsci can speak in a dialogue of passages they themselves have authored.

INTRODUCTION

> **Todorov:**   Mikhail Bakhtin is the most important Soviet thinker in the human sciences and the greatest theoretician of literature in the twentieth century.[20]

> **Forgacs and Nowell-Smith:**   Gramsci is the greatest Marxist writer on culture, and the one from whom there is most to learn.[21]

Emerson: Bakhtin did not write "essays." The formal structure and streamlining of the critical essay, at least as we know it in the English-speaking world, is simply not his mode. He is often at his most provocative in the tiny fragment, in his jottings for future projects not yet worked out or beyond hope of publication. . . . Available evidence suggests that Bakhtin did not conceive even his published books as concise, self-sufficient theoretical statements.[22]

Forgacs and Nowell-Smith: The Notebooks of Antonio Gramsci have the character very much of what has come to be called an "open text." They do not have imprinted on them those features of hierarchy and directness of argument which characterize works written for publication in book or pamphlet form. This "openness" of Gramsci's text to different readings, based on different hierarchizations of the argument, is particularly remarkable in the context (in which Gramsci belongs) of Marxist political writing. Although there is a coherence to them, this coherence is not linear; it is established through multiple branchings out. They require a different sort of suspended attention, an openness of reading to match their openness of writing.[23]

HUMAN NATURE AND PHILOSOPHY

Gramsci and Bakhtin are distinctive in emphasizing the irreducibly social nature of existence; human relationships are the heart of "being." Accordingly, a philosophy that strays from socially engaged understanding is idealistic and untenable.

Gramsci:*   What is man? We maintain that man is a process, and, more exactly, the process of his actions. "Human nature" is the "complex of social relations." It includes the idea of becoming; man "becomes," he changes continuously with the changing of social relations. Human nature denies "man in general."[24]

Bakhtin: Life can be consciously comprehended only as an ongoing event, and not as Being *qua* a given. Aesthetic activity is powerless to take possession of that moment of Being which is constituted by the

---

* Subsequent passages are quoted verbatim from the works of Gramsci and Bakhtin except for light editing to improve smoothness and flow; page number citations are provided in the note keyed at the end of each passage. Passages do contain unmarked ellipses, sometimes major, occasionally including constituent sections drawn from different manuscripts or notebooks. All emphases are original.

transitiveness and open event-ness of Being. Being cannot be determined in the categories of nonparticipant theoretical consciousness—
it can be determined only in the categories of actual communion, i.e.,
of an actually performed act, in the categories of participative-
effective experiencing.[25]

Gramsci:　　The humanity which is reflected in each individuality is
composed of various elements: 1. the individual; 2. other men; 3. the
natural world. But the latter two elements are not as simple as they
might appear. The individual does not enter into relations with other
men by juxtaposition, but organically, in as much, that is, as he belongs
to organic entities. Thus Man does not enter into relations with the
natural world just by being himself part of the natural world, but
actively. These relations are not mechanical. They are active and
conscious. So one could say that each one of us changes himself, modifies himself to the extent that he changes and modifies the complex
relations of which he is the hub.[26]

Bakhtin:　　Only that which is itself developing can comprehend
development as a process. A theory needs to be brought into communion *not* with theoretical constructions and conceived life, but with the
actually occurring event of moral being—with practical reason. A life
that has fallen away from such answerability cannot have a philosophy:
it is, in its very principle, fortuitous and incapable of being rooted. All
attempts to force one's way from inside the theoretically cognized
world into actual Being-as-event are quite hopeless.[27]

THE INTRINSICALLY SOCIAL NATURE OF EXISTENCE

The socially engaged nature of existence puts the immediacy of human
relations at the heart of analysis. This entails a necessary connection
between self-actualization and collective realization.

Bakhtin:　　I am conscious of myself and become myself only while
revealing myself for another, through another, and with the help of
another. The most important acts constituting self-consciousness are
determined by a relationship toward another consciousness (toward a
thou). The very being of man (both external and internal) is the *deepest communion*. To *be* means to *communicate*. To be means to be for
another, and through the other, for oneself. A persona has no internal
sovereign territory, he is wholly and always on the boundary: looking
inside himself, he looks *into the eyes of another* or *with the eyes of another*.

I cannot manage without another, I cannot become myself without another.[28]

Gramsci: Man is to be conceived as an historic bloc of individual and subjective elements and of mass and objective or material elements with which the individual is in an active relationship. That ethical "improvement" is purely individual is an illusion and an error: it cannot be realized and developed without an activity directed outward, modifying external relations both with nature and with other men, in the various social circles in which one lives, up to the greatest relationship of all, which embraces the whole human species. For this reason one can say that man is essentially "political" since it is through the activity of transforming and consciously directing other men that man realizes his "humanity," his "human nature."[29]

Bakhtin: Pure, solitary self-accounting is impossible. A word is a bridge thrown between myself and another.[30]

ON FORMALISM AND REDUCTIONISM

Consistent with their emphasis on social embeddedness and cultural and historical practices, Gramsci and Bakhtin each eschew scholastic abstraction for its own sake and are highly critical of reductionism.

Gramsci: One may term "Byzantinism" or "scholasticism" the regressive tendency to treat so-called theoretical questions as if they had a value in themselves, independently of any specific practice.[31]

Bakhtin: In asserting that the literary work is external to consciousness, the formalists did not cleanse it of the subjectivity and fortuitousness of individual perceptions. Instead, they severed it from all those spheres in which the work becomes historically real and objective—from the unity of the ideological horizon, from the objective reality of social intercourse, and from the historical timeliness and importance of the epoch contemporary to the work.[32]

Gramsci: It is essential at all times to demonstrate the futility of mechanical determinism. Even historical materialism could not but be a mainly critical and polemical phase of philosophy.[33]

Bakhtin: Marxists often do not fully appreciate the concrete unity, variety, and importance of the ideological environment, and move too quickly and too directly from the separate ideological phenomenon to conditions of the socioeconomic environment. Material aesthetics is incapable of founding artistic form.[34]

Gramsci: A common error in historico-political analysis consists in an inability to find the correct relation between what is organic and what is conjunctural. This leads to presenting causes as immediately operative which in fact only operate indirectly, or to asserting that the immediate causes are the only effective ones. In the first case there is an excess of "economism," or doctrinaire pedantry; in the second, an excess of "ideologism." In the first case there is an overestimation of mechanical causes, in the second an exaggeration of the voluntarist and individual element. The distinction between organic "movements" and facts and "conjunctural" or occasional ones must be applied to all types of situation; not only to those in which a regressive development or an acute crisis takes place, but also to those in which there is a progressive development or one towards prosperity, or in which the productive forces are stagnant.[35]

ON NIETZSCHE

Bakhtin and Gramsci had a clear awareness of Nietzschean excesses, including authorial indulgence and lack of social commitment implied by an ungrounded will to power.

Bakhtin: Participation in the being-event of the world in its entirety does not coincide, from our point of view, with irresponsible self-surrender to Being, with being possessed by Being. The aspiration of Nietzsche's philosophy reduces to a considerable extent to this possessedness by Being (one-sided participation); its ultimate result is the absurdity of contemporary Dionysianism.[36]

Gramsci: That all those Nietzschean charlatans in verbal revolt against all that exists, against conventionality, etc., should have ended up by accepting it after all, and have thus made certain attitudes seem quite unserious, may well be the case, but it is not necessary to let oneself be guided in one's own judgments by charlatans. In opposition to fashionable titanism, to a taste for wishful thinking and abstraction, one must draw attention to a need for "sobriety" in words and in external attitudes, precisely so that there should be more strength in one's character and concrete will.[37]

LANGUAGE, COLLECTIVE EXPERIENCE, AND POLITICS

For Gramsci as well as Bakhtin, language was a central basis for collective experience; it provided unique opportunities for reflecting and shaping social awareness. Though the point was more developed for Bakhtin, both authors showed how language and literature instantiated world views and particular ways of life.

Gramsci: Philosophy is a conception of the world and above all a cultural battle to transform the popular "mentality." Given all this, the question of language in general and of languages in the technical sense must be put at the forefront of our enquiry. "Language" is essentially a collective term which does not presuppose any single thing existing in time and space. If it is true that every language contains the elements of a conception of the world and of a culture, it could also be true that from anyone's language one can assess the greater or lesser complexity of his conception of the world.[38]

Bakhtin: Only to the degree that a literary work can enter into that kind of integral, organic association with the behavioral ideology of a given period is it viable for that period (and of course, for a given social group). Outside its connection with behavioral ideology it ceases to exist, since it ceases to be experienced as something ideologically meaningful.[39]

Gramsci: Our research is thus into the history of culture and not literary history; or rather it is into literary history as part or an aspect of a broader history of culture. Every language is an integral conception of the world and not simply a piece of clothing than can fit indifferently as form over any content.[40]

Bakhtin: The process of assimilating real historical time and space in literature has a complicated and erratic history, as does the articulation of actual historical persona in such a time and space. We will give the name *chronotope* to the intrinsic connectedness of temporal and spatial relationships that are artistically expressed in literature. The chronotope defines genre and generic distinctions. The chronotope as a formally constitutive category determines to a significant degree the image of man.[41]

Gramsci: Language = history, and non-language = the arbitrary.[42]

Bakhtin: Literature is inseparable from the totality of culture and cannot be studied outside the total cultural context.[43]

RENAISSANCE TO RABELAIS TO RESISTANCE

Gramsci and Bakhtin were highly aware that "humanity" has been a dynamically developing construct over the course of modern European history.

As part of this dynamic, both emphasized popular folk understandings as a key countervailing force against ruling-class interests and ideologies.

Gramsci: What does it mean that the Renaissance discovered "man," that it made him the center of the universe? Does it mean that before the Renaissance "man" was not the center of the universe? One could say that the Renaissance created a new culture or civilization, in opposition to the preceding ones or as a development of them, but one must "limit" or "specify" the nature of this culture. Man was not "discovered," rather a new form of culture was initiated, a new effort to create a new type of man in the dominant classes.[44]

Bakhtin: This requires an essential reconstruction of our entire artistic and ideological perception, the renunciation of many deeply rooted demands of literary taste, and the revision of many concepts. At the time of the Renaissance the dual tone of popular speech was waged in a tense struggle against the stabilizing tendencies of the official monotone. This struggle, of course, continued during the following centuries, but it acquired new, complex, and sometimes hidden forms.[45]

Gramsci: From the 14th century to the 16th popular poetry is remarkably important, since it is still tied to a certain energetic resistance on the part of those social forces which arose with the reawakening of the reform movement occurring after the year 1000 and culminating in the communes. After the 16th century these forces have degenerated utterly and popular poetry declines until we reach its current forms in which popular interest is satisfied.[46]

Bakhtin: We cannot understand cultural and literary life and the struggle of mankind's historic past if we ignore that peculiar folk humor that always existed and was never merged with the official culture of the ruling classes. We see that in Rabelais freedom of laughter, consecrated by the tradition of popular-festive forms, was raised to a higher level of ideological consciousness, thanks to the victory over linguistic dogmatism.[47]

Gramsci: Folklore should be studied as a "conception of the world and life" implicit to a large extent in determinate (in time and space) strata of society and in opposition to "official" conceptions of the world that have succeeded one another in the historical process. The folk conception of the world is not elaborated and systematic because, by definition, the people (the sum total of the instrumental and subaltern classes of every form of society that has so far existed) cannot possess conceptions which are elaborated, systematic and politically organized and centralized in their albeit contradictory development. It is, rather, many-sided because it includes different and juxtaposed elements.[48]

Bakhtin: We have tried to understand Rabelais precisely as part of the stream of folk culture, which at all stages of its development has opposed the official culture of the ruling classes and evolved its own conception of the world, its own forms and imagery. In spite of their differences in character and tendency, the carnival-grotesque form exercises the same function: to consecrate inventive freedom, to permit the combination of a variety of different elements and their rapprochement, to liberate from the prevailing point of view of the world, from conventions and established truths, from clichés, from all that is humdrum and universally accepted. This carnival spirit offers the chance to have a new outlook on the world, to realize the relative nature of all that exists, and to enter a completely new order of things.[49]

Gramsci: We have established that philosophy is a conception of the world and that philosophical activity is not to be conceived solely as the "individual" elaboration of systematically coherent concepts, but also and above all as a cultural battle.[50]

DOSTOEVSKY

Though Bakhtin's book on Dostoevsky was his most sustained and celebrated early accomplishment, Gramsci independently echoed Bakhtinian themes concerning the self-actualization of Dostoevskian characters through social relationship and struggle.

Gramsci: In literature (art), sincerity and spontaneity are opposed to calculation or mechanical procedures.[51]

Bakhtin: In Dostoevsky, consciousness never gravitates toward itself but is always found in intense relationship with another consciousness. Every experience, every thought of a character is internally dialogic, adorned with polemic, filled with struggle, or is on the contrary open to inspiration from outside itself—but it is not in any case concentrated simply on its own object.[52]

Gramsci: There is a strong national-popular feeling in Dostoevsky, an awareness that the intellectuals have a mission towards the people. By contrast is the traditional attitude of Italian intellectuals towards the people—the meaning of "literature for the humble." This is not the relationship contained in Dostoevsky's expression "the humiliated and offended."[53]

Bakhtin: Dostoevsky's characters are not voiceless slaves but *free* people, capable of standing *alongside* their creator, capable of not agreeing with him and even of rebelling against him.[54]

Gramsci: Dostoevsky's people may be "objectively" made up of "the humble" but they must be freed from this "humility," transformed and regenerated. For the reactionary Italian intellectual, by contrast, the expression "the humble" indicates a relationship of paternal and divine protection, the "self-sufficient" sense of his undiscussed superiority. It is like the relationship between two races, one considered superior and the other inferior, like the relationship between an adult and child in the old schools or, worse still, like that of a "society for the protection of animals" or like that between the Salvation Army and the cannibals of Papua.[55]

Bakhtin: In Dostoevsky's polyphonic novel there is a *fully realized and thoroughly consistent dialogic position*, one that affirms the independence, internal freedom, unfinalizability, and indeterminacy of the hero. For the author the hero is not "he" and not "I" but a fully valid "thou," that is, another and other autonomous "I."[56]

LANGUAGE AND POLITICS

The mediation of linguistic and social difference was key to meaning, creativity, and human resilience for Gramsci and Bakhtin. Though Gramsci was more explicit in his political critique and Bakhtin more refined in his linguistic analysis, both emphasized the importance and irrepressible nature of linguistic diversity.

Gramsci: Are the life and taste of an age something monolithic, or are they not rather full of contradictions?[57]

Bakhtin: Words are always filled with content and meaning drawn from behavior or ideology. The social *multiaccentuality* of the ideological sign is a very crucial aspect. By and large, it is thanks to this intersecting of accents that a sign maintains its vitality and dynamism and the capacity for further development. A sign that has been withdrawn from the pressures of the social struggle—which, so to speak, crosses beyond the pale of the class struggle—inevitably loses force, degenerating into allegory and becoming the object not of live social intelligibility but of philological comprehension.[58]

Gramsci: Besides the "immanent grammar" in every language, there is also in reality a "normative" grammar (or more then one). This is made up of the reciprocal monitoring, reciprocal teaching, and reciprocal "censorship." But this "spontaneous" expression of grammatical conformity is necessarily disconnected, discontinuous, and limited to local social strata or local centers. . . . The number of "immanent or spontaneous grammars" is incalculable and, theoretically, one can say that each person has a grammar of his own.[59]

Bakhtin: The social diversity of speech types and the differing individual voices are those fundamental compositional unities with whose help heteroglossia can enter; each of them permits a multiplicity of social voices and a wide variety of links and interrelationships (that are always more or less dialogized).

The artistic image of a language must by its very nature be a linguistic hybrid. What is hybridization? It is a mixture of two social languages within the limits of a single utterance, an encounter, within the arena of an utterance, between two different linguistic consciousnesses, separated from one another by social differentiation or by some other factor.[60]

Gramsci: Alongside this actual "fragmentation," however, one should point out the movements of unification, with varying degrees of amplitude both in terms of territory and "linguistic volume." Written "normative grammars" tend to embrace the entire territory of a nation and its total "linguistic volume," to create a unitary national linguistic conformism.[61]

Bakhtin: Every concrete utterance of a speaking subject serves as a point where centrifugal as well as centripetal forces are brought to bear. The processes of centralization and decentralization, of unification and disunification, intersect in the utterance. Every utterance participates in the "unitary language" and at the same time partakes of social and historical heteroglossia—the centrifugal forces.[62]

Gramsci: One must speak of a struggle for a new culture, that is, for a new moral life that cannot but be intimately connected to a new intuition of life, until it becomes a new way of feeling and seeing reality and, therefore, a world intimately ingrained in "possible artists" and "possible works of art."[63]

Bakhtin: Language, in the process of its practical implementation, is inseparable from its ideological or behavioral implementation.[64]

HEGEMONY AND MONOLOGISM

Gramsci's influential concept of hegemony resonates strongly with Bakhtin's notion of monologism; whereas the former is a totalizing cultural domination and control of subjectivity, the latter is an authoritarian suppression and denial of socially engaged and creative dialogue. The larger context of these points of view—strongly developed by Gramsci and implicit in Bakhtin—is a critique of domination. Both men emphasized the importance of creative positioning through diversity as a counter to authoritarian control.

> **Gramsci:**   Regardless of the name they assume, restorations of political regimes, especially those of the present epoch, are repressive. The psychology behind such an intellectual expression is based on panic, on a cosmic fear of unintelligible demonic forces which can only be controlled by a universally repressive force. In its acute phase, the memory of this panic lasts a long time and governs people's wills and feelings. Freedom and creative spontaneity disappear.[65]

> **Bakhtin:**   The authoritative word demands that we acknowledge it, that we make it our own; it binds us, quite independent of any power it might have to persuade us internally; we encounter it with its authority already fused to it. It is a *prior* discourse. The tendency to assimilate such discourse takes on an even deeper and more basic significance in an individual's ideological becoming, in the most fundamental sense. Authoritative discourse performs here no longer as information, directions, rules, models, and so forth—but strives rather to determine the very ideological interrelations with the world, the very basis of our behavior; it performs as an *internally persuasive discourse*.[66]

> The domain of ideology coincides with the domain of signs. They equate with one another. Wherever a sign is present ideology is present, too. Everything ideological possesses semiotic value. The word is the ideological phenomenon par excellence.[67]

> **Gramsci:**   What we can do, for the moment, is to fix two major superstructural "levels"; the one that can be called "civil society," that is the ensemble of organisms commonly called "private," and that of "political society" or "the State." These two levels correspond on the one hand to the function of "hegemony" which the dominant group exercises throughout society and on the other hand to that of "direct domination" or command exercised through the State and "juridical" government. The functions in question are precisely organizational

and connective. The intellectuals are the dominant group's "deputies" exercising the subaltern foundations of social hegemony and political government. These comprise:

1. The "spontaneous" consent given by the great masses of the population to the general direction imposed on social life by the dominant fundamental group; this consent is "historically" caused by the prestige (and consequent confidence) which the dominant group enjoys because of its position and function in the world of production.

2. The apparatus of state coercive power which "legally" enforces discipline on those groups who do not "consent" either actively or passively. This apparatus is, however, constituted for the whole of society in anticipation of moments of crisis of command and direction when spontaneous consent has failed.[68]

Bakhtin: The struggle and dialogic interrelationship between the authoritative and the internally persuasive are what usually determine the history of an individual ideological consciousness. There is a struggle constantly being waged to overcome the official line with its tendency to distance itself from the zone of contact with various internally persuasive discourses. Our ideological development is an intense struggle within us for hegemony among various available verbal and ideological points of view, approaches, directions and values.[69]

CONSCIOUSNESS AND COLLECTIVITY

The complex and often compromised relationship between social collectivity and individual consciousness was especially important to Gramsci and to Bakhtin.

Gramsci: The active man-in-the-mass has a practical activity, but has no clear theoretical consciousness of his practical activity, which nonetheless involves understanding the world in so far as it transforms it. His theoretical consciousness can indeed be historically in opposition to his activity. One might almost say that he has two theoretical consciousnesses, or one contradictory consciousness: one which is implicit in his activity and which in reality unites him with his fellow-workers in the practical transformation of the real world; and one, superficially explicit or verbal, which he has inherited from the past and uncritically absorbed. But this verbal conception influences conduct and the direction of will, often powerfully enough to produce a condition of moral and political passivity.[70]

Bakhtin: Ideological differentiation, the growth of consciousness, is
in direct proportion to the firmness and reliability of the social orientation. The stronger, the more organized, the more differentiated the
collective in which an individual orients himself, the more vivid and
complex his inner world will be.[71]

Gramsci: Consciousness of being part of a particular hegemonic
force is crucial as the first stage towards a further progressive self-
consciousness. This is why it must be stressed that the political development of the concept of hegemony represents a philosophical
advance as well as a politico-practical one. The superstructures of civil
society are like the trench-systems of modern warfare. A war of position is not in reality constituted simply by the actual trenches, but by
the whole organizational and industrial system of the territory.[72]

OF WHAT USE CAN ETHNOGRAPHY POSSIBLY BE IN A LATE CAPITALIST
OR EARLY POSTMODERN WORLD IN WHICH OTHERS SHOULD SPEAK FOR
THEMSELVES, IN WHICH OUR OWN AUTHORSHIP IS IRREVOCABLY
COMPROMISED, AND IN WHICH THE FORMS OF OUR OWN EXPRESSION
UNAVOIDABLY REINFORCE THE HEGEMONY OF WESTERN POLITICAL-
ECONOMIC AND CULTURAL DOMINATION? WHY NOT RENOUNCE
ETHNOGRAPHY?

Though neither Bakhtin or Gramsci addressed this specific question, they
often wrote as if they had.

Bakhtin: Entry as a living being into a foreign culture, the possibility of seeing the world through its eyes, is a necessary part of the
process of understanding it; but if this were the only aspect of this
understanding, it would merely be duplication and would not entail
anything new or enriching. In order to understand, it is immensely
important for the person who understands to be *located outside* the object
of his or her creative understanding—in time, in space, in culture.

   The moment of empathizing is always followed by the moment of
objectification and then a *return* into oneself. And only this returned-
into-consciousness gives form, from its own place, to the individuality
grasped from inside as a qualitatively distinctive individuality.[73]

Gramsci: Is a philosophical movement properly so called when it is
devoted to creating a specialized culture among restricted intellectual
groups, or rather when, and only when, in the process of elaborating
a form of thought superior to "common sense" it never forgets to

remain in contact with the "simple" and indeed finds in this contact the source of the problems it sets out to study and to resolve? Only by this contact does a philosophy become "historical," purify itself of intellectualistic elements of an individual character and become a "life."[74]

Bakhtin: Does the author not always stand *outside* the language as material for the work of art? Any truly creative voice can only be the *second* voice in the discourse. The writer is a person who is able to work in a language while standing outside language, who has the gift of indirect speaking.[75]

Gramsci: Why not shatter? Unhinge?! All you would really be doing is cutting yourselves off from the people, from their consciousness, their solidarity. It is you yourselves you are shackling. It is yourselves you are reducing to slavery. You are alienating yourselves from every bond of solidarity between you and the people, even the bond of shared humanity which links one with another.[76]

Bakhtin: To think about the consciousness of other people means to *talk with them; otherwise they immediately turn to us their objectivized side*: they fall silent, close up, and congeal into finished, objectivized images. An enormous and intense dialogic activity is demanded of the author.[77]

WHY SHOULDN'T WE DISMISS THE IMPORTANCE OF AUTHORSHIP AND INTELLECTUALISM?

Both Gramsci and Bakhtin were avid in their defense of engaged intellectual activity. As we are living in a period that sometimes debunks the importance of sustained critical thought, their remarks on this issue are particularly important.

Bakhtin: The author is not required to renounce himself or his own consciousness, but he must to an extraordinary extent broaden, deepen, and rearrange this consciousness (to be sure, in a specific direction) in order to accommodate the autonomous consciousness of others.[78]

Gramsci: Fatalism is nothing other than the clothing worn by real and active will when in a weak position. Pessimism is the most serious danger we are facing at the moment—because of the political passivity, intellectual torpor, and skepticism about the future such pessimism induces.[79]

Bakhtin: Our era is characterized by an extraordinary complexity and a deepening in our perception of the world; there is an unusual growth in demands on human discernment, on mature objectivity, and the critical faculty.[80]

Gramsci: Nothing can replace the individual thinking mind or establish from scratch intellectual and scientific interests where people are only interested in café chit-chat or think that the aim of life is enjoying oneself or having a good time.[81]

Bakhtin: Being a representative does not abolish but merely specializes my personal answerability.[82]

And Anthropology

As many have suggested, Bakhtin and Gramsci are highly relevant for the complexities of late modern cultural anthropology. Their works encourage an openness to common voices, a sensitivity to cultural and historical complexity, a deep understanding of subjective subordination, and a trenchant awareness of countervoicing and resistance. Taken together, they forge a critical humanism that articulates an appreciation of subjective diversity with keen understanding of how domination operates and how it can be subverted.

Bakhtin and Gramsci preserve connection across intersubjective divides. They do not pretend to erase or transcend the border between self and other; rather, they turn it from a boundary into a frontier, deepening our exposure of inequalities, on the one hand, and valuing the potentials of social experience and intersubjective understanding, on the other. In contrast to postmodern legacies, neither shirks the importance of rigorous scholarship or the responsibility of authorship; their grasp of personal positioning increases rather than saps their commitment to life and work. Neither is interested in texts for their own sake apart from cultural and historical context. And neither gives in to flippant, superficial, or self-indulgent authorship. Without relinquishing intellectualism, their writing is refreshingly open, shuns recipes, and is welcoming to creative dialogues of analysis and application.

Gramsci pursues his interpretations with greater political conviction, and Bakhtin with more literary playfulness; as such, they act almost as a check and balance on each other's excesses. These excesses—which are more evident in their larger corpus than in the dialogue above—include an ultimate rigidity of political agenda for Gramsci and a looseness of literary accommodation for Bakhtin. From a critically humanist standpoint, Bakhtin treads more lightly in his critique of inequality, and Gramsci in his appreciation of cultural diversity. Taken together, however, they resonate wonderfully with each other and with the complexities of contemporary circumstances. The postcolonial world is replete with fragmented identities, hybrids, and deeply conflicting inequalities. Gramsci and Bakhtin provide theoretical perspective and conceptual tools for penetrating the cultural representations and political contestations now central to cultural anthropology. At the same time, they promote rather than paralyze our intellectual dedication to ethnography and analysis—our ability to reach out with rigor as well as compassion across the intersubjective divide.

If the cultural and political are linked, this linkage can be both scholarly and humanizing in cultural anthropology. Insofar as intersubjective understanding entails moments of outsidedness—of being an interlocultor and yet having one's own perceptions and one's own voice—objectification is intrinsic to understanding. *As in good ethnography, the dialectic between empathy and detachment, insideness and outsidedness, should be actively engaged rather than disparaged or cut off from either human experience or analytic reflection.* This is not to deny the conflicts posed by representation but rather to be self-conscious about them. In the present case, for instance, is it a disservice to Gramsci and Bakhtin to pull their voices out of their own context and put them directly together? A close reading of their dialogue lessens this problem, but it remains a real one. Where is the fiery political rhetoric of Gramsci or the extended literary nuance of Bakhtin? And yet the resonance between Gramsci and Bakhtin remains important for cultural anthropology; it illustrates how to bridge debates that pit cultural interpretation against critical theory or evocative writing against empirical analysis. Together, Bakhtin and Gramsci provide powerful support for a critically repositioned humanism in cultural anthropology. In both cases, high human purpose and common culture are intrinsically connected. Bakhtin shows how representation and communication remain playful and resilient forces in the face of monologic domination. Gramsci cuts across cultural and historical hegemonies with a critique of their underlying dynamic. If art and cultural dialogue find their apotheosis in the progressively political for Gramsci, the progressively political finds its apotheosis in art and dialogic culture for Bakhtin. Artistic and political answerability are two sides of the same coin.

If all interpretations are selective, the present one may be no less slanting than the tendency to cohere Bakhtin and Gramsci as great thinkers juxtaposed across a few famous concepts—perhaps "hegemony," "war of position," "civil society," and "historic bloc," for Gramsci, and "dialogue," "heteroglossia," "hybridity," and "carnivalesque," for Bakhtin. In fact, each writes in ways that are suggestive rather than programmatic or reified.[83] The dialogue of own emergent culture can benefit from fresh combinations of trenchant voices, past as well as present (cf. Tedlock and Mannheim 1995). The artificiality of the above-quoted dialogue marks the constructivist limits beyond which a more ethnographic engagement of this process may take place. In the process, we can learn more deeply from non-Western voices. One such opportunity is provided by the dialogic emergence of contestation and change in Gebusi spirit mediumship.

Hegemonies and Dialogues in Gebusi Spirit Mediumship

It is by now a basic move to read rich and discordant images as hybrid resistance against hegemonies of gender, age, ethnicity, or class. Particularly in contexts of aesthetic innovation and creative performance, the voice of the disempowered can be seen as the colonial subject protesting colonialism, the woman resisting patriarchy, the indigenous believer crying out against state religion, the youthful agent defying gerontocracy, or the spiritual gift economy resisting the market.[84] Accordingly, the decentering of state or Western logics through contradictory or disordered discourse can be taken as a symptom of subordinating pressures and a resistance against their domination.[85]

This link between creative dialogue and resistance—crucial as it is—is often conflicted. Moving past important basic insights, the relation between dominating impositions and local responses is a thicket of complexity (Gal 1995; cf. Scott 1985, 1990). In a given circumstance, it can be difficult to sort out exactly what is progressive and what is reactionary—or even what criteria of power or asymmetry one should use to imply such assessments. To confront these issues, we can consider a new genre of spirit séance that was developed by a spirit medium named Wahiaw in a remote Gebusi settlement of Papua New Guinea's Western Province during the early 1980s. His innovation is all the more striking against the backdrop of alternative spiritual belief and practices.

Dialogic and Hegemonic Context

Occurring about once every eleven days and lasting all night, Gebusi séances each entail up to a hundred songs. These songs are authored by the medium's spirits, sung by them through the medium's body, and chorused in beautiful harmony by the assembled men of the settlement. To ride Gebusi séance songs is to take a train of radically fragmented images: arcane, evocative, and erotic. They telescope the past, present, and future, as well as the spaces of the spirit world and those of the Gebusi landscape. Song lines do not form a connect-the-dots picture so much as a poetic collage of overlapping and resonating flashes. Subsequent images recontextualize, ironize, or eroticize previous ones. As if to collapse the Melanesian premodern with the academic postmodern, Gebusi séances merge obscure and arcane vocabulary with larger themes that are ultimately predictable if not taken for granted by the audience.

Gebusi spirit séances foreground the lewd adventures of the medium's spirit women, who cavort in the spirit world and joke sexually with the Gebusi men present. These voicings and their chorused echo among the men prompt banter and infectious repartee. As well as teasing each other, men joke directly back to the spirit women, who can respond with further provocations in subsequent song lines. Dialogic as well as multivoiced, Gebusi séances are shot through with humor, play, and aesthetic creativity. As the "second voice of discourse,"[86] they are at once melodic, profoundly meaningful, funny, and arousing.

In terms of gender, however, this deep aestheticism is also hegemonic. Not only are Gebusi women excluded from the séance, but the agency of the spirit woman, who forms the ideal image of female beauty and sexuality, is controlled by the men; she is voiced by a male medium, echoed by the male Gebusi chorus, and responded to in autocommunication between the men's chorus and their own banter. Spirit women are bold and sexy; they not only flirt with seduction, they consummate it. The fantasy ends abruptly, however, in the lives of real Gebusi women. Like their spiritual counterparts, young women are encouraged by cultural ideals to be attractive, coy, and flirtatious. These same themes are reinforced by the lascivious idioms of the spirit séance itself, which women listen to from the other side of the thin sago-leaf wall that separates their collective sleeping quarters from those of the men.[87] But Gebusi women can be beaten by brothers and with impunity by husbands if they are suspected of flirting or, especially, adultery (Cantrell n.d.).

The spirit woman, in contrast, flirts and fornicates at will even as she remains the medium's spirit wife and the center of acclaim.[88] Her excesses fuel sexual impetuousness among men in the audience: "I'm too horny to wait for a woman." In day-to-day experience, a Gebusi woman alone is considered an invitation to rape.[89]

In addition to heavy joking and homoerotic horseplay at the séance, a man aroused by the spirit woman may seek sexual release with a younger man or boy, who sucks him to orgasm outside the longhouse. Though most séances are not accompanied by homosexual trysts per se, homo-erotic joking pervades virtually all of them. This action redirects what Gebusi men themselves suggest is heterosexual desire. Such male homo-sexual appropriation of sexuality parallels men's structural appropriation of female reproduction, for instance, their belief that boys need to receive masculine life force through insemination in order to attain adult masculinity (see Knauft 1986, 1987b, 1989b).

Despite and indeed because of its charged emotional context, Gebusi spirit séances provide the fluid context—and often the sugar coating—for serious and potentially grave sorcery accusations. Between about 1940 and 1982, virtually one-third of all adult Gebusi deaths have been homi-cides, and the bulk of these have been the execution of persons within the community suspected of sorcery.[90] These killings are legitimated and typically instigated by the pronouncements of the medium's spirits during séance inquests, including those that entail a high degree of sexual joking and repartee. In the eroticized aura of the séance, the structural tensions of sexual frustration that accompany marriage-related disputes easily inform men's collective acceptance of the target—male or female—that the medium's spirits have suggested as the sorcery suspect. These accusations draw on gender hegemonies and appropriations; just as men appropriate the voice of the spirit woman in their singing, and just as they appropriate the spirit woman's desire in their sexual joking, so too they maintain a gendered monopoly on violence that can draw upon the energy of sexual frustration and direct it as aggression against the person suspected of sending sorcery. In short, the multivocal dialogue of the Gebusi spirit séance combines rich aestheticism with the cultural hege-mony of gender domination and violent scapegoating.

Though the killing of sorcery suspects is in no sense reducible to spir-itual imagery alone, this violence is effectively instigated by the sexual and social imagery of the séance (Knauft 1985a:ch. 8, 1989b). The structural tensions of Gebusi society revolve around the mandate for sister exchange in marriage despite practices of kinship and social affiliation that reduce both the practical possibilities for completing such marital exchanges and the means to acknowledge or ameliorate anger in cases of nonreciprocity. The projection of hostility and the justification of aggression against the sorcery suspect are a prominent result. In the context of the spirit séance, male license in fantasy informs men's habitus of violence in fact. A definitive spiritual verdict, if there is one, typically appears self-evident. Traditionally, men would sometimes proceed at dawn—immediately following the conclusion of the séance—to ambush and execute the suspect.

Acceptance of the spirit medium's verdict is encouraged by the heightened arousal and sexual tension that accompany the event. Gebusi audiences are not dupes; to push this issue is to miss the point. Rather, there is a deep and mutual resonance among the superconscious associations of the entranced spirit medium, the deepest and most unstated fault lines of Gebusi marital and sexual practice, and the unexpressed or inexpressible sensibilities of audience members, which come out as bawdiness and aggressive displays of sexual humor. The chronotope of sexual frustration and sorcery attribution that bridges these domains is hegemonic. It is the application of this chronotope to the situation at hand that the spirit medium makes explicit.

The sociological side of this shared reality is highly evident; the séance is a public event attended by the men of the various clans in the settlement. During the séance itself, they typically accept and unify around the spirits' identification and indictment of the sorcerer. Indeed, men find it difficult to discuss or confront these most serious issues in the absence of spiritual guidance; the mandate for accusing or executing a sorcery suspect almost invariably comes from the omniscient voice of the spirits in séances. This voice seems obviously true in retrospect, even if it is often not predictable ahead of time.

Innovations and Mythic Proportions

In his new séance genre, Wahiaw cut across existing hegemonies. At one level, he elaborated the festivity and entertainment value of the séance in lieu of its sorcery and divinatory function. Indeed, some of Wahiaw's most important séances were sung as replacements for expected sorcery inquests. Instead, Wahiaw engaged a new set of tensions that seethed just beyond the Gebusi horizon: the proliferation of trade goods, the development of wage labor, and their conflict with Gebusi notions of kinship and exchange. These developments are poised to complicate Gebusi men's control over violence and sexuality. For instance, they glimpse a shift from direct male violence as a means of settling disputes over sorcery and marriage to the possibility of paying goods or money to compensate aggrieved parties.[91] In the process, the potentials of using material compensation in disputes and as bridewealth at marriage suggest the possibility of a more general shift from direct reciprocity through violence to delayed reciprocity through economy in matters of exchange.

Wahiaw's séances were innovative in form as well as content. Like standard séances, his new songs were sung spontaneously by his spirits and chorused line by line by the assembled men. But unlike regular séances, his story lines and characters formed a coherently evolving mythic drama. Gebusi mythic narratives (*gisagum*) are not normally "invented"; they are a stock set of stories handed down from elders to juniors in public tellings. Wahiaw's mythic narratives, however, emerged as innovations, directly from the spirits. In effect, he altered the aesthetic genre of the séance to imbue spontaneous spirit world images with new and even epic proportions. Wahiaw's stories were not just remembered, they were retold by audience members to others afterward in the form of standard *gisagum* narratives. Transformed from transient song to lasting myth, they have become an enduring part of the Gebusi narrative corpus.

Wahiaw's innovations are illustrated in two contrasting *gisagum* that he sang over a short period of time. In the first, Wahiaw's songs developed standard mythic themes of a handsome and upright male hero whose propriety ultimately rewards him with marriage to a beautiful young woman. Wahiaw put a poignant twist on this tale by introducing a trade-store gift between the man and his hopeful partner as a pivotal thematic element. Indigenous gifts are common between Gebusi friends and need not normally be returned. But because the trade-store good also qualifies as a new kind of personal property that is ultimately inalienable, the young woman in Wahiaw's story feels obligated to come back to the hero and give back his gift once she has been promised away in sister-exchange marriage to an ugly suitor. Her reappearance gives the hero the chance to break off her onerous marital commitment (which was never consummated) and draw her back to himself. The narrative ends with the happy reunion of the original couple.

In this *gisagum*, the anomalous status of the trade-store good as both gift and commodity serves as something like an elastic band that allows the actors to stretch their relationship apart and yet be pulled back together again. In point of fact, the hero's trade-store gift *is* elastic—a band of stretch cord sewn into the woman's bark cape. The trick of the story is the creative use of the trade item, not as a bald foreign intrusion but as a good that can be selectively manipulated to play upon *both* the affective connection of gift- giving and the impersonal nature of commodity ownership. The narrative thus hybridizes an autonomous Western individual, who abides by the commodity contract, with what Marilyn Strathern (1988) describes as the indigenous Melanesian "dividual"—a transacted or transindividual identity based on gifts and exchange.[92] In the process, the woman and her lover are able to subvert the rules of sister-exchange marriage and assert their own union without negative consequences.

Wahiaw's second *gisagum*, by contrast, marks a more radical transformation of mythic themes. The story begins with four young cousins (two boys and two girls) who are enticed down a hole by an old woman; they are kidnapped and disappear. Their parents search and search for the lost children but cannot find them; they ultimately give up, except for the mother of the younger girl. Eventually she finds the hole the children have gone through. Climbing into it, she descends a tall underground waterfall and emerges, like Alice in Wonderland, on the other side of the millennial looking glass.

Much of the narrative takes place in this lower world—a Gebusi place of danger and notoriety. But the lower world in the narrative is a revelation of cargo. The woman finds a huge Western-style house, fully furnished, where she is welcomed by another woman. (The audience is amazed and exclaims its desire to live there, too.) After digging a few net bags of sweet potatoes,[93] the women get into the lower-world woman's new truck and drive to the patrol post. (More exclamations by the audience.) Shaking with fear, they are admitted through a long series of rooms and doors until they enter the office of the chief patrol officer, who is surprisingly termed *kogway wi*, or "culture mother." The officer is a gruff, fearsome, and yet generous benefactor with a nose as big as a house post; he swivels all day in his office chair and alternately gives orders and grants favors. To the young woman's amazement, he gives them metal patrol boxes full of clothes and money in exchange for their mere bags of sweet potatoes. (The Gebusi audience exclaims in awe.) The primordial giver of Gebusi culture has become the giver of commodities.

The women drive back to their Western house, where they count their money and try on their new clothes under the light of their pressure lamp before washing with soap, eating a full meal of store-bought goods, and going to bed on a mattress with sheets under the cover of a mosquito net. (Such stuff is high fantasy for Gebusi; the audience goes wild.)

The women continue to supply the patrol officer with bags of sweet potatoes in return for trunks of clothes and money. When the young woman asks for her missing child, however, the officer becomes angry; all four children are under contract to work at the patrol post, and their absence is the price of the goods the woman receives in trade. The children are indentured, and the very process of earning them back ensconces the girl's mother in the same material seductions that separate her from the children. Michael Taussig's *The Devil and Commodity Fetishism* (1980) could hardly have found a better example.

Over time, the familial separation works its toll on the young woman, despite her ever-increasing wealth. The patrol officer keeps putting her off, taking her sweet potatoes, giving her trunks of money and clothes, and writing letters that say the children's employment is not yet up. (The Gebusi audience gets provoked: One man yells he would rip up the letters; another proclaims that the woman was living as though she were in jail, even if she *did* receive clothes and money.)

After years of waiting, the patrol officer gives the woman a letter telling her that her former husband has given her up for lost, married another woman, and started another family. As the woman reads (she has learned to read), her tears soak the letter until it disintegrates in her hands. She has lost not only her child but her upper-world husband as well. (The Gebusi audience loudly laments her plight.)

The next day, however, the four years of the children's contracts are up, and they are returned to her. Moreover, she is given the patrol boxes full of goods and money that each of the children has received; as the faithful parent of the younger girl, she becomes the mother of all the children. In their new truck and with all their rich possessions, the four young adults and their de facto mother drive back up to the upper world. Finding their old house fallen down and the clearing covered with weeds, they set up their lawn chairs, relax, and wait until the woman's ex-husband emerges from the bush. His former wife berates him for his unfaithfulness; how could he have given up on his wife and child? Unlike the standard narrative hero, who bears privation to maintain his romance (as in the first narrative), he has been unfaithful and must suffer the consequences. The woman then opens a final letter the patrol officer had given her; it invites her back down to the lower world to live. The woman and her children thus leave their natal kin and drive back down to the patrol post with all their possessions, leaving the still-impoverished traditional village behind forever. Down below, the patrol officer welcomes the family back and gives them all big houses full of Western amenities. The woman's sons and daughters all marry outsiders in balanced exchange. In addition, her new sons-in-law give her huge bridewealth gifts—a practice Gebusi themselves have strongly avoided. The tale ends with a Gebusi heaven-on-earth at the patrol post. (The audience exclaims what a fine way to live that would be.)

AS A NEW KIND OF MORALITY TALE, WAHIAW'S SECOND NARRATIVE portrays the tension between indigenous and wage economies. What starts as kidnapping proceeds through loss, the dark alienation of wage labor, and spousal abandonment. One plumbs the deep sorrow that is pervasive in Papua New Guinea as the result of separation between relatives in town and those in the village. This pathos is perhaps the new "sorrow of the lonely" in a Papua New Guinea that is now postcolonial (cf. Schieffelin 1976).[94] Nevertheless, all doubts are resolved and washed away through myth as the wage economy persists; what starts as pain ends in millenarian luxury. By the myth's conclusion, new families have been reconstituted, wealth abounds, and morality has been maintained. By contrast, the indigenous village has faltered in its commitments; poor and disparaged, it is left behind in the bush.

Variations on a Dream

Wahiaw's two narratives are complements—two sides of an ambiguous currency. Each recognizes the moral tension that poses the desire for Western goods against the desire for social and moral affiliation.[95] But in the first narrative, the trade good *resolves* indigenous romance and brings it to fruition as traditional marriage within the village. It uses the propriety of the material contract to cement rather than explode this local world. In the second narrative, by contrast, wealth, contract, and family are clearly bought at the *expense* of village life. Wahiaw's two myths embrace highly contrastive outcomes. As Michael Lambek (1993:14) puts it in an African spiritual context, "Varying views of the world, even different senses of what knowledge is, can be held concurrently. People's attitudes to knowledge cannot be reduced to ideological formulae."[96] This diversity provides the spark for alternative courses of action—for instance, to absorb Western goods within a village economy or, as in the second myth, to leave village relations behind entirely. In everyday practice, such tensions are currently at the heart of cultural contestation in Melanesia—the desire for wealth and prestige, on the one hand, and the wish for the propriety of kinship and exchange relations, on the other.[97] This tension also informs more radical attempts at millenarian or political-spiritual transformation—what used to be referred to as Melanesian cargo cults (Burridge 1960; Lawrence 1964; Worsley 1968). These poignant initiatives have bubbled and erupted in Melanesia in various guises for well over a century, and they show no sign of abating (e.g., Lattas 1992; Whitehouse 1995). The changing cultural and economic dimensions of possession—possession in its spiritual as well as in its material sense—are central to this process.

Engaging these themes, Wahiaw's second narrative goes against many dominant—some would say hegemonic—aspects of Gebusi culture. It puts forth a female hero rather than a man to triumph in the world of trade goods and wage labor. She engages Western wealth not out of greed but out of devotion to her young daughter and her cousins. Moreover, the exchange of persons for wealth—both the children laboring for the patrol officer and the grown children marrying for bridewealth—suggest an implicit change in the Gebusi person-for-person model of reciprocity. In contrast to a world that legitimates male control over women in sister-exchange marriage and over violence in sorcery accusation, material exchange in Wahiaw's myth forestalls and eventually overcomes these negative possibilities; tensions are resolved through delayed material compensation without recourse to either violence or sexual domination. (It is notable, for instance, that the patrol officer does not attempt to engage the lone young woman sexually or make her his wife.)[98] Ultimately, then, Wahiaw mediates opposed logics of exchange—intrusive versus indigenous—while transcending the limitations of each; moral propriety and equivalence are made consistent with material wealth rather than being at odds with it.

Wahiaw's innovative challenge to both traditional and intruding forms of power is especially remarkable given his personal circumstances. His village was extremely remote; its population had used stone axes into the mid-1960s.[99] Even by the early 1980s, outmigration and development were very slight; there were no accessible trade stores or schools, and no one from Wahiaw's area spoke pidgin or any other contact language. As if to cap this marginality, Wahiaw himself had long been crippled. He had to be laboriously carried to give séances in neighboring hamlets, and it is likely that he had never even seen the Nomad patrol post. Though there was an incipient development project north of Nomad in late 1981, his own settlement was too distant to benefit from it.[100] Wahiaw's exceptional vision of wage labor, commodities, and their tension emerged from tranced visions that had virtually no basis in personal observation or experience; they were elaborated from others' fleeting accounts by using the powerful imagination of his own spirits.

Wahiaw's prescient awareness expands upon views that consider hybrid resistance in the face of Western and indigenous hegemonies. First, it illustrates the power of aesthetics to actively reach out and embrace change. Changes do not just impose themselves like Captain Cook, arriving like Leviathan on a self-contained island of culture. Not only is change desired poignantly, sometimes achingly, but it is generated actively, sometimes as its own seed, from the heart of most distant cultures themselves.

Second, it suggests that indigenous views of change are often more multilayered and nuanced than our own. They comprise different voices and different opinions, not only between individuals but even in a single individual (such as Wahiaw) over a short period of time. They illustrate the ambiguity, tension, and what Gramsci called the contradictory consciousness of embodying *both* sides of a material and moral dichotomy. And yet their alternatives do not shy from bold choices; they can empower both sides of a conundrum with cultural force and value. That Western trade goods and wage labor are the thin point of a massive wedge of social disruption was highly evident to Wahiaw, notwithstanding his isolation. At the same time, these problems are subsumed through millenarian incorporation rather than denied; they are not resisted in any simple sense.

Third, Wahiaw's narratives point up to the need for an ethnography of processes of change that is more nuanced and detailed, not less so. Amid complex tensions, it is all too easy to assume resistance against some behemoth—counterhegemony by locals against the state, or the Rest against the West. This is wishful thinking that neither Gramsci nor Bakhtin succumbed to. At the other extreme, the culturalist alternative improperly assumes an essential core of indigenous identity that reproduces itself even as the world around it changes. As Wahiaw demonstrates, this is also fundamentally inadequate. Finally, in the transformation view, spiritual life catapults itself into modern if not postmodern traveling cultures. Or, more cynically, it simply trades in received identities, making culture a sad parody of its previous self, now lost in tourism, or traded for cases of beer, a Toyota truck, or an African banality of power. But this final view also misses the point; it underplays the force of long-standing beliefs that do not go away even as they fragment, reposition, and change.

If these characterizations are simple, it remains true that many current perspectives on culture and hegemony fail to penetrate *the deep ambiguity and profound tension of living agents as they wrestle morally and socially with inequalities of change.* A continuing commitment to rigorous ethnography is crucial in this regard. A more focused and nuanced attention to these rocky realities can encourage both an appreciation of aesthetics and a critique of power.

It is important to retain the relativist moment that appreciates idioms without reducing them into resistance. But if we are to expose and critique inequality, this moment needs to be matched by others that shun an excess of relativism. Gramsci suggests that contradictory consciousness juxtaposes the true practical fellowship of lived experience against the subverting hegemony of cultural ideology. One of the tasks of a critically humanistic approach is to climb inside this schism—to alternately appreciate the subjectivities and critique the inequalities that engage hegemonies in the absence of easy answers.

Wahiaw's vision cuts across indigenous and Western hegemonies alike: gender domination, sexual domination, the violence and scapegoating of unrequited reciprocity, and the sacrifice of kinship for the luxuries of material possession. But his own alternatives are ideal and far removed from practical conditions, which present huge impediments to Gebusi lived experience. Even with respect to male violence, the substitution of wealth exchange for person-for-person reciprocity is no panacea—as continuing domestic, criminal, and intergroup violence in the New Guinea highlands make clear. Apart from these practicalities, the way that wage labor might reengender domination or magnify other forms of inequity is not considered by Wahiaw. He acknowledges the problems of wage labor but leaves them aside in his utopian ending.

The limits of Wahiaw's critical awareness—as incredible as it is from his restricted position—reflect a theoretical insight: that even the most perspicacious and sensitive intuitions engage rather than avoid new hegemonies. These may be altered or repositioned but they are unlikely to fade away. Futures are always hazy from the vantage point of the present, and even the best-laid plans have unintended consequences in practice. As Bakhtin and Gramsci both imply, the best one can hope for is an ongoing spiral of awareness and contestation. Though this result is discouraging if the goal is a static or final resolution, it becomes much less so if the struggle is considered meaningful in itself.

Like the Dostoevskian author who refines the complexities of living dialogue, Wahiaw goes beyond stock authorial images; his marvelous personae have their own autonomy and divergent spirit, respected apart from Wahiaw himself. This subjective diversity in inner voicing provides a key way to explore and reflect upon practices and inequalities by appropriating and remodeling them. The consequences of innovation are harder in the real world than in the world of the imagination. But that utopias remain mythical and that inequalities reengage is not, as Bakhtin and Gramsci remind us, reason for despair. The story is not over. For every new twist of domination and presumption, there is another space for aesthetic evaluation and critical response.

Dialogues against hegemonies are located in specific sociocultural and historical contexts. But if the specifics of counterposition are central to their dynamic, then rigorous ethnographic and historical documentation becomes all the more important. Without this, it becomes all too easy to let analysis spin off into either the romance of relativism or the romance of resistance. The complexities of position in the face of the new and the taken-for-granted underscore the importance of rich ethnography for a critically humanist anthropology that articulates an appreciation of diversity with a critical exposure of inequality. Like Gramsci's and Bakhtin's voices, Wahiaw's is trenchant and helpful in this regard.

gender, ethnography, and critical query

Bakhtin, Gramsci, and Foucault (not to mention Nietzsche and Heidegger) are dead white European men now enshrined in the Western intellectual tradition. By itself, this fact should not relegate them to contemporary obscurity, particularly within a critically humanist perspective that foregrounds the ability of an engaged intellectual to understand across difference. Given the intellectual power of figures such as Bakhtin, Gramsci, Foucault and others—not to mention Marx, Weber, and Durkheim—the goal should not be to debunk modernist authorship but to critically learn from it and complement it with voices of alternative insight and value. It is in this latter regard that famous traditional ancestries—and the longer male genealogies that invariably precede them—need not be accepted as hegemonic in a field such as cultural anthropology. There are many important but historically underplayed insights by women, diasporic writers, subalterns, and others whose writings are now increasingly being brought to light from disempowered crevices. Their creativity has often been undervalued but now provides personal experience and antitheory to lever open or explode received wisdoms. These views provide insights on disempowerment that often escaped understanding in the work of more classical writers. In the rejection of modernism, an anticanonical canon of champions from the outside creates new paragons at the same time that it avoids old ones. This discovery and praise of alternative authorships neither escapes tropes of heroic modernism nor is condemned to insignificance because of this lack of escape.

Beneath surfaces, there seems no reason to polarize newly discovered voices against those more venerable in the study of critical theory. Indeed, creativity is as likely to be found in the potential dialogue as in the conflicts between these authorships. Charles Lemert's (1993) mixture of readings, *Social Theory*, is an apt example: Juxtaposed effectively against segments from Marx, Durkheim, Weber, Freud, Simmel, Keynes, Parsons, Fromm, Goffman, Habermas, Foucault, and Bourdieu are selections by W. E. B. DuBois, Lenin, Gandhi, Martin Luther King Jr., Virginia Woolf, Aimé Césaire, Frantz Fanon, Audre Lorde, Cornel West, and Vaclav Havel. Caveats are inevitable (only eighteen of the eighty-eight selections are by women), but the mix of critical authors has been opened up in ways that neither bury the venerated nor deify the radical.

In the present account, the authors and grand theories of previous chapters are ripe for countervoicing. For a critical humanism that seeks to appreciate diversity, this diversity can be discovered in authorships as well as in the peoples we study among. In both respects, diversity can reflect upon subjectivities of disempowerment that are pronounced in the late modern world and neglected or underanalyzed in received modernist theory. The trick, however, is to combine the expanding edges of diverse awareness with the most productive legacies of our modernist past.

The preceding chapters of this book can be productively re-viewed through the lens of gender and sexuality. Other axes of inequality would be equally appropriate. One could adopt a postcolonial critique, a racial or ethnic revaluation, or perhaps an ecological rereading. Some of these have been alluded to or will be considered in the following chapter. But regardless of where one starts, it is almost a truism that inequalities intertwine. The question is not whether "class," "gender," "sex," "race," or "ethnicity" is primary and other forms of inequality secondary. Rather, it is increasingly agreed that the categories themselves need to be de-essentialized and reconstructed—as Judith Butler (1990, 1993a) and others have argued for gender and sex; as Kwame Appiah (1992) and Paul Gilroy (1993) have suggested for race; as Brackette Williams (1989) and Arjun Appadurai (1990) have suggested for ethnicity; as authors from Gayatri Spivak (1987) to Trinh Minh-Ha (1990, 1991) and Chandra Mohanty (1991a, 1991b) have suggested for gendered subaltern identity; as authors from Benedict Anderson (1983) to Homi Bhabha (1990) and Partha Chatterjee (1993) suggest for nationality; and as the early Baudrillard (1975), among many others, suggested for Marxist notions of class. The dreary alternative is what Nancy Hewitt (1992) describes as the "intersection" model of inequality: Inequalities such as class, gender, sex, race, ethnicity, or nationality compete against one another to occupy the center of theory debates. The contenders collide at the critical cross-roads; all are weakened, and only the strongest survive. The unfortunate result is that disempowerments become antagonistic to each other's critique. But neither is it sufficient to collapse all of these into a single discursive resistance—as if diverse forms of disempowerment could be combated by simply refusing the canons of Western logos.

Against these dual pitfalls, the relation between dimensions of inequality may be recast as an ethnographic question. How should diverse cultural understandings of inequality force us to rethink our notions of gender, sex, ethnicity, race, religion, and age, much less class? How do disempowerments resonate with and transform each other? In what ways and under what conditions does resistance along one dimension of inequality conflict with or reinforce other inequalities? Resistances, like powers, often fail to harmonize. Though postmodern sensitivities are symptomatic of this fact, they need to move beyond self-contained analysis and plumb the concrete worlds of others' experiences. How inequalities may be resisted, how they combine, or how they reinforce each other is an empirical question as much as an epistemic one. The definition, relationship, and relative importance of different dimensions of inequality should not be assumed a priori but rather allowed to emerge from specific ethnographic and historical practices. Recent studies of gender and sexuality in anthropology foreground this investigation, as do postcolonial or subaltern studies, diasporic interests, and cultural studies more generally. But recent gendered analysis in anthropology has been especially strong in its *ethnographic* exploration of these issues. This chapter examines this distinctive lens and then uses it to consider prior directions in feminist anthropology and present developments in postmodern feminism and queer theory.

Recent Gendered Ethnography

It is always risky to suggest specific examples of a recent academic trend, much less to cohere them. The danger of lumping people under labels and of reifying the result is as great in anthropology's analysis of itself as it is in anthropology's analysis of foreign peoples and cultures (Appadurai 1988). The present analysis is intrinsically problematic in this respect. For the heuristic purpose of seeing larger directions, however, it could be said that a recent wave of ethnographies inflected by issues in the study of gender now constitute one of cultural anthropology's sharpest cutting edges. On the one hand, these works expose the complexity and intensity of gendered disempowerment; on the other, they penetrate the experience and voicing of gendered diversity, including that of the ethnographer. The effective weaving of these complementary themes is particularly germane for the wider cultivation of critically humanist scholarship in contemporary anthropology. The works considered below form a snapshot within a larger field of shifting interests. If this larger field of gendered and sexual concerns continues to move as quickly in its scholarly future as it has in its recent past, the present account will at best date a moment in time rather than presage its future. This increases rather than decreases the importance of gradually stepping back and considering recent trends of gender in ethnography within a larger historical and transdisciplinary context.

Gendered ethnography need not imply ethnography either by or about women, even though it tends as yet to overlap significantly with both of these. Most recently, it connotes detailed ethnography that uses insights about gender derived from late 1980s and early 1990s theorizations (or anti theorizations) about culture and representation. In so doing, these works focus on issues of experience and power and connect them directly with the ethnography of gendered voicing. In this process, gendered inequality informs innovative ethnographic perspectives on many areas of life. Though women's lives are often central in these ethnographies, they are central as a vantage point on diverse topics rather than being a separable arena of content that is set off—and potentially marginalized—from the rest of cultural anthropology. That recent gendered ethnographies are as yet less influential among male anthropologists and the study of male-dominated activities—quite notably excepting important studies of alternative male sexualities—is both unfortunate and in the process of changing.[1] In the future, indeed, a burgeoning critical literature on masculinity and on the relationship between alternative forms of gendered experience is likely to make creative mincemeat of any such generalization.

For the moment, it is important to stress that recent developments in female-gendered ethnography are, in larger terms, not a new trend. They draw on a long legacy of works by female anthropologists, the wives of male anthropologists, and other female authors who have been undervalued or neglected in anthropology's received ancestries, including Gladys Reichard, Zora Neale Hurston, Ella Deloria, Laura Bohannan, and Jean Briggs, among others.[2] However, there is a significant new development: The influence of such legacies upon recent work is now *recognized* to be important. Moreover, these works are recognized to be important in *theoretical* as well as ethnographic terms (e.g., Behar and Gordon 1995). Reciprocally, the movement of gendered ethnography into the mainstream of cultural anthropology is now accompanied by more explicit and penetrating theoretical critiques. This combination of rich ethnography and current theory draws upon but goes beyond the postmodern emphasis on "writing culture." As many have noted (and as discussed later), the emphasis on ethnographic reflexivity that entered cultural anthropology in the mid-1980s initially did so with little acknowledgment or inclusion of women's contributions to ethnographic and theoretical innovation.

Any list of recent gendered ethnographies is provisional; it teases a recent past rather than launches a history. My reading is selective, and I may have left out important works as a result of inattention or ignorance. Of the many important strands of feminism within cultural anthropology, this book privileges recent theoretical angles and is limited to a restricted segment within these. Many arenas of feminist ethnography—including those that focus on health, reproduction, domestic economy, colonial history, activist movements, popular perceptions, and so on—are presently underemphasized. Even so, it is not hard to find a corpus of works that foreground recent developments in cultural and critical theory and grapple importantly with issues of disempowerment and gendered voicing. Even if one narrows the purview to but a single monograph per selected culture area completed between 1990 and 1994 on the basis of primary field data, a global range of important exemplars is easily evident:

- Lila Abu-Lughod's *Writing Women's Worlds* (1993); see also her *Veiled Sentiments* (1986) [North Africa]
- Ruth Behar's *Translated Woman: Crossing the Border with Esperanza's Story* (1993) [Central America]
- Dorinne Kondo's *Crafting Selves: Power, Gender, and Discourses of Identity in a Japanese Workplace* (1990) [East Asia]
- Corinne Kratz's *Affecting Performance: Meaning, Movement, and Experience in Okiek Women's Initiation* (1994) [East Africa]
- Smadar Lavie's *The Poetics of Military Occupation: Mzeina Allegories of Bedouin Identity Under Israeli and Egyptian Rule* (1990) [Mid-East]
- Elizabeth Povinelli's *Labor's Lot: The Power, History, and Culture of Aboriginal Action* (1993) [Australia]
- Gloria Raheja and Ann Gold's *Listen to the Heron's Words: Reimagining Gender and Kinship in North India* (1994) [South Asia]
- Nancy Scheper-Hughes's *Death Without Weeping: The Violence of Everyday Life in Brazil* (1992) [South America]
- Anna Tsing's *In the Realm of the Diamond Queen: Marginality in an Out-of-the-Way Place* (1993) [Southeast Asia]
- Kath Weston's *Families We Choose: Lesbians, Gays, Kinship* (1991) [United States]
- Nicole Polier's "Stella's Stori: Colonialism, Christianity, and Conflict in the Life of a Papua New Guinea Migrant Woman" (under review) [Melanesia]

To these can be added ethnographic but nonmonographic works by senior scholars such as

- Margery Wolf's *A Thrice-Told Tale: Feminism, Postmodernism, and Ethnographic Responsibility* (1992)

This list could certainly be expanded. There is nothing sacred about culture area designations and omissions, nor is there anything profane about other works that might also be added—including some by male as well as female authors (e.g., Lancaster 1992; Parker 1991; Herdt and Boxer 1993; Herdt and Stoller 1990). Indeed, the wealth of additional possibilities underscores the larger point about the current importance of recent gender (and sexuality) to the theorization of culture and power.[3]

Though admitting the permeability of boundaries and the mushrooming of potential additions, the dozen works specified above provide a convenient if delimited point of departure for considering specifics. In all of these works, a critical, gendered position on representation and power is key to how the ethnography is theorized and presented. But, these works do not uniformly flag themselves as being "about women"; this is important, and it keeps them from being confined to the category of "anthropology of women" or "women's ethnography." Topically limited issues such as the evaluation of "female status" have been left behind even as there is a staunch and salutary commitment to maintain rather than relativize a critique of gendered inequality. That the relationship between feminist and postmodern agendas is productively variable in these works illustrates a grappling with important theoretical issues rather than the duplication of foregone conclusions. By considering these ethnographies, some current trends in anthropology's culture of gender can be elucidated—first in terms of their strengths, and then in terms of their limitations and potentials.

Contributions

The ethnographies configured above all engage critical theory. But they shy from theoretical closure and programmatic trumpeting. They present women's voices richly but tend, at least in most cases, to avoid textual noise and to refuse authorial cacophony. They consider their own authorship with openness and nuance but are usually wary of the confusion that can result from radical reflexivity. One of the strongest features of these works is their dedication to drawing out and documenting women's diverse experiences. The ethnographer becomes an accompaniment to women's voices rather than drowning them out. Reflexive insights and creative forms of textual presentation emerge dialogically in the text rather than being asserted a priori.

All these works bring the hybrid nature of women's experiences to center stage as a lens upon wider dimensions of social life and representation. This is not a simple pastiche of fragmented identity so much as the half-in/half-out dimension of women's experiences at the borders and boundaries of power in matters of family, employment, politics, and writing. Women come across as uniquely able to "off-center" power relations. They do this not so much through bald resistance as by playing on their boundary status to be both influential and slightly beyond the full reach of male institutions. While women's marginality and peripherality are illuminated, their position is neither degraded nor viewed as having a single route up. Women maintain dignity and meaning through the use of creative trapdoors, mazes, and chambers of refuge that may include other women even as they are confined and oppressed in a larger sense.

The doubly or triply disempowered position of women—their subjugation by ethnic, racial, or class as well as gendered discrimination—becomes a special challenge for creativity and persistence. Women forge dignity, meaning, and influence in conditions crying for criticism—as exploited Japanese confectionery workers (Kondo); half-crazed but mindful spirit mediums and madwomen (Tsing, Lavie); domestically secluded Islamic wives or maidens (Abu-Lughod); wives-to-be undergoing creative domestication through female initiation (Kratz); disparaged dykes (Weston); disenfranchised postcolonial foragers (Povinelli); battered wives (Behar); dowered daughters-in-law (Raheja and Gold); victims of rape and incest (Polier); or underappreciated ethnographers (Wolf). In Tsing's ethnography, the agile resistance of a marginal woman—the diamond queen incarnate—is the titular theme; for Lavie, the decentering power of hybrid marginality is epitomized by formidable women (chs. 4, 6). Even in the worst conditions of poverty, sickness, and the repeated deaths of their children, women persist, at least at moments, to flaunt vitality in the face of adversity (Scheper-Hughes). Despite tragedies and sorrows, there is will and endurance. In many cases, this persistence is mixed with women's marvelous sense of humor and irony about the absurdities of power. There is a palpable sense of women's resilience.

Women are actively listened to in all of these works. Female voices are cultivated and crafted as sources to learn from; the writing emerges organically from below, rather than being imposed from above. This contrasts to a traditional ethnographic tone—archetypally masculine—in which voices are trotted out to verify authorial assertions based on theoretic or analytic assumption. The portrayal of the particular has been a strength of cultural anthropology since Geertz, and in some sense since Malinowski and Boas. But gendered ethnography of the early 1990s has the special strength of rendering women's diversity through sensibilities that are neither parochial nor pedantic.

Deconstructive tendencies are hence tempered by the importance and meaning of women's experience. Genealogies of power and representation are engaged and reengaged with real people. It is women's lives themselves that come across as rich, creatively fragmented, and decentering. This is not some newfangled theoretical invention, but a reality that women have long engaged—an astute influence upon power and a peripheral resistance against it. As Margery Wolf (1992) critically theorizes, this fact itself highlights how women's voices have been muted and theoretically devalued in anthropology.

Both tactical and meaningful, these perspectives offer much to critical sensibilities that have been either stung or stimulated by anthropology's reflexive turn. All the monographs in question have been influenced by reflexive considerations. Some, such as Polier, Scheper-Hughes, and Wolf, explicitly critique postmodern influences; others, such as Lavie, Kondo, Tsing, and Behar, consider them more favorably. But all partake to some degree of Abu-Lughod's desire to acknowledge authorial positioning without compromising the accounts of women themselves. Postmodern nihilism has little place here. Rather, the space between the baldly critical and the merely cynical is a dynamic and sometimes progressive site, both in women's lives and for those who write about them. In the course of their experiences, women appropriate the zone afforded them and rework it to provide new or more rewarding configurations. Women are shown in what Linda Alcoff calls their positionality:

> The concept of woman as positionality shows how women use their positional perspective as a place from which values are interpreted and constructed rather than as a locus of an already determined set of values. (Alcoff 1988:434, emphasis omitted)

As a result, "the position that women find themselves in can be actively utilized (rather than transcended) as a place from where meaning can be discovered" (ibid.).

In recent gendered ethnography, women's initiatives house this positionality as a tension between risk, potential, and unintended outcome. The consequences of women's idioms and actions are difficult to foresee once they engage new avenues of influence and power; women can find themselves in a losing race if they confront modernity or postmodernity on others' terms. Most if not all of these works highlight the complexities of resistance and the unforeseen, unintended, and sometimes undesirable effects of going outside the domestic mainstream in attempting to broach its constraints. They emphasize the plurality of women's experiences and suggest that generalizations (such as those I am now making) are best limited to issues of gendered process rather than specific beliefs or practices.

Gender is not contained as an isolated axis of domination in any of these works. Instead, gendered disempowerment provides a connection and linkage point to other inequalities.

- In *Crafting Selves*, Kondo shows how Japanese gender asymmetries enforce female subordination, obedience, hard work, and economic austerity. Women's experience is fragmented and crafted between gendered domination of domestic life and the duties of wage employment, both of which are deeply internalized. These values articulate with the generational control that Japanese parents exert over grown children and the personal as well as economic control of workers by patriarchal management. These are put into context by the culture of working-class labor relations in Japan and the history of women's subordination in part-time employment.

- Abu-Lughod's work on female poetry and narrative among Egyptian Bedouins reveals how women elaborate aesthetic nuance and meaning in a cloistered domestic environment structured by patriarchy and eldership. Parts of her work illustrate how the very desire to circumvent senior men can put young women and men in the vise of wider ethnic and class asymmetries as disposed by the Egyptian state.

- Polier reveals multiple discriminations in the life of a Papua New Guinean migrant woman, who faces gang rape, prostitution, disparagement, and squalid living conditions when she breaks the strictures of her tribal village and moves to a neocolonial mining town. Having forged a self-made existence, Stella's fragmented life is paralleled by her remarkable narrative of shifty resilience and evangelical revival in the face of difficulty.

- Weston's analysis of lesbians and gays in San Francisco illustrates the tensions among sexual affiliation, social community, and the economic disempowerments that stress and threaten these bonds. These tensions play out vis-à-vis the straight world and in natal family relationships as well as within the lesbian and gay community.

- Tsing's work in a remote area of Indonesia shows how marginality plays with, transgresses, and yet ultimately maintains itself within stigmatizing gendered hegemonies, on the one hand, and ethnic or national ones, on the other. For the eccentric older woman who is the incarnate "Diamond Queen," Dayak resistance against the Indonesian state is also directed against norms of gender, kinship, and sanity itself.

■ Raheja and Gold show how North Indian women use aesthetic forms to reimagine gender and kinship and open cracks of subversion across hierarchy and gendered subordination. These potentials persist in rituals, narratives, and songs even though they are seldom pursued or acted out by North Indian women in the normal rounds of everyday life.

■ Lavie's study of Sinai Bedouins under Israeli occupation illustrates the ironies of allegorical identity amid the idiosyncrasies and absurdities of military domination. Eldership and patriarchy intertwine with foreign intrusion to create a byzantine nexus of power and shifting resistance. These complexities allow spaces for some women to brazenly confront and manipulate their oppressors, but they can also compound one another to drive women mad.

■ For Kratz's Okiek women of west-central Kenya, female initiation is both the assertion of womanhood's value and an institutional acquiescence to gendered and ethnic domination. Women's rituals and narratives are richly elaborate at the same time that they are located within larger structures of male authority, inequality based on age, and ethnic stigma. These strictures become pragmatic as well as ideological in the meanings that ensue after women's initiations have been completed.

■ For Scheper-Hughes, Brazilian women's pain becomes stoic in the face of relentless hunger, disease, and the deaths of their children. These hardships are directly linked to religious, biomedical, and political factors that reproduce women's poverty and restrict their access to resources and medical care.

■ For Povinelli, colonial history and its legacy in land alienation provide the context for labor and politics among Belyuen Aboriginals of north Australia. Belyuen women serve as public spokespersons as well as economic managers and providers amid the gendered Otherness of Australian race relations. Women physically instantiate their identity through food gathering and other activities on their traditional land while also negotiating vis-à-vis the stores, courts, and officials that constitute the larger context of state power and neocolonial domination.

■ As the *Translated Woman*, Behar's Mexican "Esperanza" exudes independence and refuses marital domination; her status is both reflected and reinforced by her experience as a poor peddler and reputed witch. Rife with marital and domestic discord, Esperanza's life embraces attendant disputes of property, inheritance, and land. Faced with the pathos of violent hardship and bittersweet successes, she is herself ultimately caught as an agent in cycles of domestic and generational authority.

As a more detailed account could reveal, the articulation of gender to ethnic, racial, national, and class discrimination is nuanced and diverse in these works. Specifics are not assumed, but articulations between gendered and other inequalities repeatedly emerge. In some instances these inequalities reinforce each other, while in others they work at cross-purposes, leave interstitial openings, or pit opposition to one form of subordination against the reinforcement of others. In some cases, women's marginality is empowering; in others, including for Scheper-Hughes's impoverished Brazilian women, it is devastating. But more often it is both at the same time. This complexity underpins the allure mixed so powerfully with stigma in Lavie's Bedouin madwoman, Tsing's Malaysian diamond-queen shaman, Polier's born-again Papuan prostitute, Abu-Lughod's willful schoolgirl, Gold's Rajasthani storyteller, and Behar's Mexican peddler witch. The diverse vitality of women's experience across complex subordinations is opened up rather than bleached of significance. Theoretically, this means wrestling with but ultimately steering between radical deconstruction, on the one hand, and yawning theoretical deduction, on the other.

More generally, then, the movement from gender to considerations of class, racial, or ethnic inequality is surprisingly integral to these works. The reverse is not as frequently the case: Many ethnographies that take the inequality of class, race, ethnicity, or colonialism as their point of departure do *not* open out as easily to a comprehension of gendered disempowerment (or sexuality) on either empirical or theoretical grounds.

Current trends in gendered ethnography are cautious in assessing how gendered positions alter or accommodate larger structures of power; the critique of these hegemonies is both contingent and empirically grounded. As delineated by Marilyn Strathern (1987), this caution is reinforced by the long-standing tension in feminist anthropology between the relativism of cultural anthropology and the unifying if not universalizing strains of feminism. As these ethnographies reveal, the tension between general critique and empirical exception reflects real-world complications. The attitudes of Japanese part-time confectionery workers reinforce structures of economic and domestic domination at the same time that their "crafted selves" provide an implicit critique of these structures. Okiek female initiates in west-central Kenya engender their subordination as wives-to-be even as they perform and elaborate a rich culture of womanhood. Women in Uttar Pradesh submit to male-controlled marriage even as they comment ironically upon it. Bedouin women perpetuate their domestic confinement and separation from political power even as their separation creates a space for female dignity and meaning. The Diamond Queen (Tsing), the madwoman (Lavie), and the Papuan *fani meri* (Polier) remain subordinated within patriarchal or neocolonial or national powers. The same is true of the aberrant and perhaps suicidal woman who forms the focus of Wolf's portrayal. Brazilian women studied by Scheper-Hughes are so economically and emotionally crushed that they can become hardened even to the deaths of their own children. It is only where women have a greater political auton-omy within their community that there is widely organized resistance— as among the lesbian and gay communities studied by Weston and the female spokeswomen portrayed in Aboriginal north Australia by Povinelli.

Caveats and Potentials

The ethnographies considered above contain many more nuances than I can credit here. Indeed, my implicit creation of an "ideal type" of recent gendered ethnography may easily be critiqued as a male hegemonizing move. (I should emphasize that I welcome the dialogue that could emerge from such a critical engagement.) My present purpose is not to reify this corpus but to highlight some of the common strengths and value of these works, and to explicate (further below) how they present an advance on complementary trends in and out of cultural anthropology. From a crit-ically humanist standpoint, what is particularly special about them is the way they combine a valorization of gendered diversity with a critique of gendered inequality.

Limitations and possibilities can be confronted in the same potentiat-ing vein. If my characterizations give short shrift to anthropology's large legacy of comparative materialist, political-economic, and symbolic assessments of female status, the same could often be said of the monographs in question. This is not simply because these works are topically distinct "life experiences of women." Indeed, one purpose of considering these disparate works as a cluster is that they explode the life history category on both presentational and theoretical grounds. As part of this expansion, they sketch a path toward larger social and political analyses. This is a trend that has been effectively mined by historians such as Carlo Ginzberg (1980, 1993) and Joan Scott (1988). It can be argued, however, that this path needs further accentuation in recent gendered ethnography—for instance, connecting women's experiences theoretically to larger historical trends and political-economic forces.

Though evocations are rich and the finger is frequently pointed to these larger issues, their exposition is highly variable in recent gendered ethnography. Where women's voices have taken over the bulk of the work, as in Behar's *Translated Woman* and Abu-Lughod's *Writing Women's Worlds*, the lack of larger political and economic analysis seems to be a distinct weakness. More generally, there is a tendency for gendered cultural ethnography to authorially echo rather than analytically elaborate the tactics of women themselves as they shake up power through play, irony, or disjunction. The same is true of the attempt to shift gendered ethnography from empirical to literary considerations (Behar and Gordon 1995). If narrative is now re-emergent in feminist ethnography, it remains important to historicize and theorize the tactics that can inform discursive strategies and the detailed ethnography that should continue to document them. The goal in this respect is not to *de*-theorize gender but to *re*-gender theory (see Lutz 1995).

If women's narrative or allegorical performance is a constrained kind of practice, the extent of this constraint and its political and economic dynamics deserve larger analysis across a world of structural continuities and new developments. Among the ethnographies above, larger patterns of political and economic hegemony tend to be considered in inverse proportion to the focus on women's voices per se.[4] For all the emphasis on the texture, color, and emotion of women's lives, only a few of the works in question give systematic consideration to who possesses how much of what, how long women work at what tasks, and how the mix of labor, property, and politics works in larger economic and political terms. Rich portrayal of experience is sometimes left in structural limbo. And some of the attempts to close this gap (for instance, that by Scheper-Hughes) make this leap too easily and simply. Perspectives that imply a

simple "women against tyranny" edge cover up much about the complexities of women's lives. Recent gendered ethnography is just beginning to
carefully theorize and critically analyze the structures of gendered power
and inequality within which women's multiplicities are located. In this
respect, important new theoretical developments in the conceptualization
of gender and power will undoubtedly exert increasing influence in years
to come (see Yanagisako and Delaney 1995; Schneider and Rapp 1995;
Ortner 1990a; Collier and Yanagisako 1987).

The ethnographic consideration of gender has the potential to mediate chunks of the large debate that still vaguely distances political economy from the textual and interpretive concerns of literary criticism and
the legacy of postmodernism in cultural anthropology. Works such as
Kondo's *Crafting Selves*, Tsing's *In the Realm of the Diamond Queen*, Polier's
"Stella's Stori," Lavie's *Poetics of Military Occupation*, and Kratz's *Affecting
Performance* create paths that are open to careful analysis of political economy.[5] Povinelli's *Labor's Lot* is particularly distinctive here. In this work,
identity and political economy are focused and brought together through
a female-centric view. In the process, it becomes self-evident that Belyuen
women spearhead the opposition to alienation of their Aboriginal lands—
even though the gendered dimension of this process is not analytically
stressed (but see Povinelli 1991, 1994, 1995, n.d.). Povinelli's work is also
the main one of those presently considered to document the empirical
aspects of labor, wealth, and land utilization—right down to quantitative
tables—as well as women's rich and disjunctive contestation of postcolonial experience (see also, in a different context, Boddy 1989).

What these works collectively open up is a greater articulation
between gendered experience and the larger structural forces through
which inequality is predisposed. The role of gender in postcolonial, late
modern, and transnational arenas of cultural contestation is highly
important. Feminist ethnography is now moving beyond simpler "Third
World women are exploited" models to a more complex awareness of
gendered compromises and contradictions in the experience of transnational economy (e.g., Ong 1987, 1988, 1991a, 1991b; Freeman 1993; D.
Wolf 1992; cf. Mies 1986, 1988). Economically and materially grounded
accounts of gendered identity remain important for understanding diversity across late modern contexts. Correspondingly, the rural dispositions
that still underpin gender relations for so many women and men should
be emphasized rather than neglected amid the potential overlay of

newer-edged alternatives. The fascinating but more shifty or abstract formulations found in journals such as *Public Culture, Genders,* and *Cultural Studies* can be drawn upon but need to be refined and concretized in this respect. This necessitates a commitment to renewed ethnography and attention to continuities and subtle changes as well as more dramatic ones in the development of gendered experience.

The question of authorship—of Western women "speaking for others"—is a thorny issue that should be raised here (e.g., Mohanty 1991a, 1991b; cf. Spivak 1994). This question is crucial to ethnography in general; it is not in any sense relegated to being a "women's issue" (see chapter 8 of this book for a more general view). But women ethnographers have been at the forefront of those considering this problem. The question is deepened by the complex and important feminisms that are not just Western but distinctively local and regional in diverse world areas (Stanton and Stewart 1995; cf. Enloe 1990). Within this panoply, whose feminism does one espouse? Even within countries, there can be a complicated relationship between local women and their own country's feminisms. Who is to speak for whom? Does a female ethnographer who has a long-standing affiliation with local women have more or less authority to represent them than a woman who is a citizen of their country and a passionate defender of women's rights but who may share little with these particular women by way of class background, domestic constraint, or personal experience? Gender is easily complicated by crosscutting agendas based on socioeconomic or ethnic inequality. Moreover, researchers may have their own mixed or bicultural identities. As anthropologists such as Kirin Narayan (1993), Lila Abu-Lughod (1990a), and Kamala Visweswaran (1994) have all pointed out, the pigeonholing of an ethnographer as either "insider" or "outsider" is simplistic; it limits creative new perspectives that partake of multiple vantage points. If Bakhtin is right that some degree of "outsidedness" is intrinsic to dialogue and to meaningful communication, then the issue is not so much to expunge outsidedness but to manage it sensitively. Conversely, the value of indigenous voicing or authorship need not debunk the value of ethnography as a dialogic process. Recent gendered ethnography has been at the forefront of pursuing an important anthropological goal, namely, to understand across difference with nuance. The encouragement of indigenous authorship can itself be an important part of this process (e.g., Kyakas and Wiessner 1992).

From a critically humanist perspective, complementary issues emerge concerning the pragmatic aspects of resistance. Under what conditions can women's potentially subversive voicing take on efficacy and import as collective action? The social and cultural results of agency—its practical effectivity—are important to discern and not reducible to imaginary or discursive terms. If the call for a more refined notion of agency has regularly echoed in cultural anthropology in recent years, this call is now ripe for receiving detailed ethnographic replies (e.g., Ahearn 1995; cf. Knauft 1995c). Recent directions in gendered ethnography are at the forefront of response to this invitation. The rich accounts of women's experience in person-centered ethnographies (e.g., Trawick 1990) can provide a powerful lens on nuances of identity and social action at the microlevel. How do notions of "agency" relate to local constructions of action, will, and purpose?

Though recent gendered ethnographies are wonderfully inductive in this respect, they can be analytically and theoretically expanded. In terms of practice, what are the gendered concepts and actions that mediate between women's voicing in a narrative or expressive mode, the illocutionary force of women's voicing as pronouncement, and their public acts of behavioral confrontation and defiance? What are the pathways that potentiate the link between *voice* and *action*? And what are the pitfalls? For instance, women's personal choices may be ostensibly increased in the postcolonial context of changing marital options, economic opportunities, or newly imagined identities. But this potential for increased female agency can be effectively constrained or subsumed by tightening forms of gender domination at the workplace, the store, or the less-than-traditional home. How are women's newer twists on agency simultaneously expressed and compromised in wage work, residential relocation, economic consumption, and changing values and practices of domesticity? And how are received gender asymmetries reproduced and actively reinstated—at the same time that our analytic attention may be attracted to their apparent change? A number of recent feminist discussions (mostly from a nonanthropological viewpoint) tend to equate the degree of individual agency exerted by women with their personal activism and efficacy (e.g., Gardiner 1995; Mann 1994; Eduards 1994; Apter and Garnsey 1994). In what ways is this universally true and in what ways does it presume Western cultural assumptions about the autonomous individual as the primary locus of effective action (cf. Grewal and Kaplan 1994)?

The ethnographic consideration of gender is well placed to explore all of these questions with theoretical power as well as empirical rigor.

More broadly, the theoretical understanding of gendered and political-economic hegemonies can be articulated with sensitive portrayals of how gendered experience actually emerges through lived action. The paths explored by recent gendered ethnographies are poised to reduce the oscillation between pessimistic views of inescapable domination and optimistic ones of ubiquitous subversion. Recent initiatives in gendered/feminist ethnography are appropriately cautious and textured in part because of their awareness of deeper complexities. The potential here is to meld political-economic analysis with experiential nuance. In the process, the hybrid nature of gendered margins can be drawn upon while opening them up to realms not reducible to signification per se.

Gender/Feminism in Anthropology
Legacies and Disjunctures

Contemporary directions in the ethnographic consideration of gender can be viewed against the backdrop of preceding trends. It is evident that feminist anthropology has many roots and legacies (see overviews in di Leonardo 1991; Moore 1988, 1994a; Behar and Gordon 1995; Morgen 1989; Mukhopadhyay and Higgins 1988; Strathern 1987; cf. Tong 1989). During the 1970s, feminist anthropology burgeoned particularly in relation to then-current interests in Marxist and symbolic anthropology.* During this period, the issue of male/female inequality became important for anthropological theories of domination and oppression, including in precapitalist societies. At the same time, gender was posited as a key axis of domination through cultural meaning and symbolism. As creative as they were modernist, a bounty of works explored these perspectives through the anthropology of women in the mid–1970s and 1980s. Prominent examples include Michelle Rosaldo and Louise Lamphere (1974), Rayna Reiter Rapp (1975), Sherry Ortner (1974) Eleanor Leacock (1981), Alice Schlegel (1977), Ester Boserup (1970), Karen Sacks (1979), Ernestine Friedl (1975), June Nash and Helen Safa (1976), Peggy Sanday

---

* My characterizations are brief and simple; their purpose is only to provide broad comparisons and contrasts.

(1981), Susan Borque and Kay Warren (1978), Susan Rogers (1975), Marilyn Strathern (1972), and Annette Weiner (1976). During the 1980s in particular, there was a flurry of monographs on the symbolic construction of gender, as encouraged by Ortner and Whitehead (1981), among others. All this work has had an influential legacy in feminist anthropology, as reflected in Moore's (1988) overview and di Leonardo's (1991) collection.

Beyond anthropology, many humanities and social science fields benefited both empirically and theoretically from the ethnographic study of male/female inequality and gendered symbolism. The linkage between ethnography and feminist theory drew heavily upon Marx and then Weber, Lévi-Strauss, and Geertz to consider whether patriarchy was universal, if the status of women had regularities or explanations cross-culturally and over developmental time, and what variations were evident in gender as a cultural system. In economic and political and then increasingly in symbolic terms, these issues effervesced during the 1970s and 1980s, even though they have now mostly run their course. Increasingly in the 1990s, the task of comparing domestic units, modes of production, or women's symbolic or semiotic position is swamped by complexity. Not only are subordinations, mediations, and resistances recognized as fluid, but this fluidity is itself theoretically important. Coherent accounts of gender as a symbolic system or totalizing comparisons about women's status have become problematic. Programmatic accounts about gender are increasingly supplanted by partialities, evocations, and the importance of (re)positioning gendered voices.

Feminist theory in anthropology now mediates between critiques of women's disempowerment and tactics of voicing and representation. This last strain was introduced to anthropology in the 1980s through the influence of James Clifford, George Marcus, Paul Rabinow, Michael Taussig, and others (see chapter 3 of this book). But this reflexive inauguration was rightly and repeatedly critiqued by respected female anthropologists for its failure to include feminist and womanist perspectives. Margery Wolf (1992), Lila Abu-Lughod (1988, 1991), Catherine Lutz (1990, 1993, 1995), Sherry Ortner (1993), Ruth Behar (1993b), Micaela di Leonardo (1991), Deborah Gordon (1988), and Kamala Visweswaran (1988) all pointed out that anthropology's reflexive turn was masculinized at the same time that it was elevated to the status of theory. It thus continued to disenfranchise the aesthetic creativity of female ethnographers and indigenous women themselves. Hybrid genres of women's writing that had long been at the margins of anthropology—from Zora Neale Hurston to Laura Bohannan to Meaghan Morris—were theoretically bypassed by Clifford, Marcus, and others, who implied that their own prosaic off-centering was a new (male) discovery.

One consequence of anthropology's recent his-story of critical reflexivity has been a cautious relationship between recent gendered ethnography and critical deconstruction. This contrasts to approaches in other humanities fields that seized the postmodern critique of gender and sexuality more quickly and frontally. In larger historical terms, *recent gendered ethnography is wedged creatively between a past of modernist feminism within its own discipline and a present of postmodern critiques of gender and sexuality outside of it.* This is reflected in an important wave of critical studies on women's health and reproductive technology as well as in the gendered ethnographies considered earlier in this chapter (see Ginsburg and Rapp 1995; Lock and Lindenbaum 1993; Strathern 1992; Martin 1987; Inhorn 1994). The dichotomy that gendered ethnography now mediates is in some ways analogous to that described by Linda Alcoff between cultural feminism and poststructural feminism:

> The cultural feminist response to Simone de Beauvoir's question, "Are there women?" is to answer yes and to define women by their activities and attributes in the present culture. The poststructuralist response is to answer no and attack the category and the concept of woman through problematizing subjectivity. Each response has serious limitations [but] . . . a few brave souls are now rejecting these choices and attempting to map out a new course that will avoid major problems of the earlier responses. (Alcoff 1988:407)

Gendered ethnography is presently on the cusp and the cutting edge of this frontier. But to put this relationship into greater perspective, the poststructural side of the coin needs fuller examination.

Gendered Critique and Post-positivist Persuasion

Along one line of argument, critical deconstructions of gender outside anthropology are now as important as anthropology's own theorization of

gendered inequality was during the 1970s and 1980s. Gender and feminism have moved to a post-Foucauldian era. As in the former period, a
bevy of germinal works springs easily to mind, such as those by Linda
Alcoff (Alcoff and Potter 1993, Alcoff 1988), Rosi Braidotti (1994),
Judith Butler (1990, 1993a), Seyla Benhabib (1992), Teresa de Lauretis
(1987, 1994), Jane Flax (1990, 1993), Nancy Fraser (1989, 1992), Diane
Fuss (1989, 1991, 1995), Donna Haraway (1989, 1990), Trinh Minh-ha
(1990, 1991), Meaghan Morris (1988), Linda Nicholson (1990), Elspeth
Probyn (1993), and Eve Sedgwick (1990, 1993a, 1994), to name a few. By
building on gendered deconstructions begun a few years earlier by well-
known authors such as Hélène Cixous, Luce Irigaray, Julia Kristeva,
Gayatri Spivak, and Monique Wittig, these works present a major corpus
of post-positivist writings on gender, feminism, and lesbianism.
However, with a few notable exceptions, such as works by Marilyn
Strathern (1988, 1992), Henrietta Moore (1994a, 1994b), and Kamala
Visweswaran (1994), these studies have until recently resonated largely
outside anthropology's own feminism. This distance is now closing fast.
The potentials and pitfalls that gendered ethnography now mediates—
between feminist anthropology and the critical retheorization of gender
and sexuality in other humanities fields—is becoming an increasingly
important issue.

As retheorized, gender and sexuality can be deconstructed as part of
a tactical repositioning. Along the way, this move exposes basic assumptions and biases in philosophy, literary criticism, history, the arts, and the
sciences. In contrast to fading postmodernism, the critical deconstruction
of gender and sexuality continues with gusto across a multidisciplinary
front. No deep excavation is needed to discern major figures, such as
those listed above, who view gender or sex beyond the modernist past.

Recent history provides context for this trend. During the 1980s,
gendered theories of representation had a productive opposition to male
French theorists such as Derrida, Foucault, and Lacan.[6] Deconstruction,
genealogy, and the sexualized feminine as psychic Other served as light-
ning rods for feminist criticism. Prominent deconstructions set the trend:
The male postmodern was appropriated, torn lusciously to shreds, and
self-consciously trumped through the lens of sex and gender. Derrida
himself had included a major critique of phallo(go)centrism—the notion
that the phallus is the primary signifier of identity—in his influential *Of
Grammatology*. Along with his critique of logocentrism (the primacy of

the word) and phonocentrism (the primacy of voice-consciousness), this critique was central to his deconstructive analysis. Spivak (1987:148) notes that the gendered side of deconstruction was largely neglected by male antihumanists, especially in the United States. But its poststructuralist and postmodern influence drew in rather than repulsed a new field of feminist scholars.

Critical (anti)theories of sex and gender "past the modernist post" don't constitute a definable or coherent field. Disagreement is legion within the compass of post-positivist feminism and queer theory.[7] Topically, critiques of sex and gender range from the subaltern to the psychoanalytic and consider everything from mass culture to literature to historiography to philosophy—sometimes combining many of these. This crossing between fields—as if camping from one to the other—is itself important; a strength of critical retheorizations of sex and gender is their recourse to topics without being topicalized. They use sex and gender as a theoretical point of leverage for wide-ranging issues. As Eve Sedgwick puts it with respect to queer theory:

> A lot of the most exciting recent work . . . spins outward along all dimensions that can't be subsumed under gender and sexuality at all: the ways that race, ethnicity, postcolonial nationality criss-cross with these *and other* identity-constituting, identity-fracturing discourses. (Sedgwick 1993a:9)

As reflected by Sedgwick and other theorists, gendered and sexualized postings—assertions strongly influenced by but not reducible to postmodernism—are reflexive without being self-destructive. They avoid the paralysis of authorship that plagued much masculinist postmodernism. Girded by passion and commitment, they remain committed to a diffuse belief that progressive change, however indefinable or shifty, is possible beyond the setting horizons of random critical refraction. These approaches critique and chew up the great male thinkers tottering between the modern and the postmodern—Nietzsche, Foucault, Derrida, Lacan, Heidegger—at the same time as they draw upon them. In the process, a regendered view emerges on literature, sexuality, popular culture, psychic development, and processes of representation and signification.[8] Personal experience or standpoint is accorded value even as its theoretical edifice may get dizzyingly abstract. Emphasis is placed on the re-creation of meaning, resistance, and identity by women, lesbians, and gays via the fragments and pastiche that have long been at the margins of masculine modernity. For instance, the work of Judith Butler (1990, 1993a, 1993b, 1994) foregrounds the potential of resignification and performance. For Donna Haraway (1990), the optimism that attends a cyborgian war of position is fueled rather than diminished by the ceaselessness of its reengenderment. Hybrids abound. There are "nomadic subjects" (Braidotti), "fragmented thinking" and "disputed subjectivity" (Flax), "performative troubling" (Butler), "resituated selves" (Benhabib), "paradoxical perversities" (de Lauretis), "multiply contexted positionality" (Alcoff), "re-sexed selves" (Probyn), "unruly practices" (Fraser), and the general "queering" of gender and sexuality. Sedgwick suggests that

> queer can refer to: the open mesh of possibilities, gaps, overlaps, dissonances and resonances, lapses and excesses of meaning when the constituent elements of anyone's gender, or anyone's sexuality, aren't made (or *can't be* made) to signify monolithically. (Sedgwick 1993a:8)

For Butler,

> If the term "queer" is to be a site of collective contestation, the point of departure for a set of historical reflections and futural imaginings, it will have to remain that which is, in the present, never fully owned, but always and only redeployed, twisted, queered from a prior usage and in the direction of urgent and expanding political purposes. (Butler 1993b:19)

David Halperin suggests,

> As the very word implies, "queer" does not name some natural kind or refer to some determinate object; it acquires its meaning from its oppositional relation to the norm. . . Queer is by definition *whatever* is at odds with the normal, the legitimate, the dominant. . . . . It is an identity without an essence. "Queer" demarcates not a positivity but a positionality vis-à-vis the normative—a positionality that is not restricted to lesbians and gay men. . . . "Queer," in any case, does not designate a class of already objectified pathologies or perversions; rather, it describes a horizon of possibility whose precise extent and heterogeneous scope cannot in principle be delimited in advance. It is from the eccentric possibility

occupied by the queer subject that it may become possible to envision a
variety of possibilities for reordering the relations among sexual behaviors, erotic identities, constructions of gender, forms of knowledge,
regimes of enunciation, logics of representation, modes of self-constitution, and practices of community—for restructuring, that is, the relations
among power, truth, and desire. (Halperin 1995:62)

The distinctive thing about queer understandings as opposed to other
movements of deconstruction, defamiliarization, or textual surrealism is
their explicit purpose, which is to expose, confront, and decenter a deep
and pernicious inequality: sexism in general and heterosexism in particular. Its goal is to combat self-destruction by working through and beyond
the shame and disempowerment ensconced by these deep-seated
inequities. What is begged, however, is how the power of floating signifiers articulates with social, political, and economic inequalities.

And Anthropology?

Where does recently gendered and sexualized *anthropology* fit in? None of
the postpositive feminist or queer theorists mentioned earlier are really
anthropological, much less ethnographic. The important recent contributions of Marilyn Strathern (e.g., 1988, 1992) are a major exception, but
even this work tends to deconstruct gender in ways that can compromise
rather than encourage the pursuit of detailed ethnography. Postmodern
feminism has come largely out of philosophy, history, literature, or
cultural studies rather than anthropology. Its insights tend to be text-
based and to arrive through literary or philosophical lenses. This cast on
gender and sexuality is increasingly becoming detached from the 1970s
and 1980s feminist anthropology that stressed coherent symbols and
meanings or statuses and roles. This contrast is effectively marked by the
difference between Henrietta Moore's 1988 review of mostly modernist
feminism in anthropology (*Feminism and Anthropology*) and her scintillating 1994 book *A Passion for Difference*, which takes a more interdisciplinary and more decentered view of gendered differences and subjectivities.

There is arguably a structural as well as a temporal shift from
modernist feminist scholarship—which gave such a high profile to
anthropological research—to feminism influenced by postmodern or

even "postfeminist" sensibilities (e.g., Stacey 1987; Mann 1994).[9] For a relatively small field such as anthropology, it is easy to forget that gendered deconstruction and reconstruction engages a much larger canvas of faculty positions, books, and symbolic capital in disciplines such as English, history, and philosophy. One need only peruse the nonanthropological book list in gender or sexuality from a publishing house such as Routledge or Beacon or Columbia or Duke for an illustration of this point. At the same time, departments of English, literature, history, or philosophy are often more conservative as wholes than are departments of anthropology. Their avant-garde is hence more driven to critical networks *across* disciplines, and these networks can be sizable.

Certainly there are advantages to anthropology's own history in the study of gender. For one, it remains important to avoid tropistic grandstanding, literary involution, or deconstructive breakup. We need to keep antitheory from turning into antimatter. In light of current trends, the deconstruction of gender in anthropology risks becoming a new version of fragmentary ethnography—a fin-de-millénaire "Notes and Queeries." Against this possibility, the strengths of careful social and cultural documentation associated with classic feminist anthropology need to be rediscovered and reinvigorated even as the field expands to engage new sets of theoretical influence. It is by retaining these past strengths that a genealogical view can most productively explore new perspectives on sex and gender. Works by Butler, Haraway, Kristeva, Irigaray, Spivak, Minhha, and others can be as frustrating and difficult as they may be provocative and stimulating. But like the works of Foucault and others that they attempt to supersede, these approaches are anthropologically relevant even though (and indeed because) they are ethnographically open. They can be bounced off cultures and places they never considered, and novel understandings as well as important critiques can result. If some of these authors descend to the obscurity of postmodernism, their implications remain fresher and more progressive than those of postmodern apathy.

Postpositivist feminism and its literary corollaries do resonate with newer directions in the anthropology of gender and sexuality (e.g., Behar and Gordon 1995; Cole and Phillips 1995; Moore 1994; Strathern 1992; Ginsburg and Rapp 1995; Weston 1993a). On pedagogic and tactical grounds, it is important that such new developments be seen through the lens of post-Foucauldian womanist and queer theory as well as through the more masculinist history of postmodernism, symbolic analysis, or political economy within anthropology. The distinctive contributions of feminist and postpositivist feminist writers—not just in voicing, but in alternative content and innovative theory—can form part of cultural anthropology's current genealogy.

This advocacy does not suggest bandwagon acceptance of new approaches; these need to be critiqued and winnowed through substantive fieldwork. In the same way that feminism afforded grounding against postmodern disconnections during the 1980s, so too can feminist ethnography substantialize the contributions and avoid the excesses of postmodern feminism and experimental women's fiction in the 1990s. The apparent fragmentation of gendered identity can be more effectively understood through detailed, concrete, and rigorous ethnography. This can include rather than neglect the changing empirical aspects of economic and social organization and larger patterns of political economy. The powerful but still textual or philosophical insights of postmodern feminism and literary experimentation benefit enormously when viewed critically against the concrete circumstances, voices, and experiences of women, sexual provocateurs, and others who have been enculturated differently than we have been.

That the feminist concerns of white Western women cannot stand for women of color (much less for gays, bisexuals, or third sexes) underscores the enlargement that an anthropological diversity of sex and gender can bring.[10] The relationship between consciousness, agency, and the deconstruction and reconstruction of gender or sexuality is culturally mediated. How do *other* people conceive, instantiate, and manage these relationships? Recent and theoretically nuanced exchanges between postmodern feminists, as in Benhabib et al. 1995, are sapped by their limp failure to include non-Western perspectives (contrast Mohanty 1991a, 1991b). Even Linda Nicholson (1995:2) admits that this failure turns any claim these authors might want to make on feminist theory into "a kind of arrogance." There are echoes here of Clifford and Marcus's (1986:20) brief angst in their failure to centrally include the voices of women writers in reflexive anthropology. But if anything, recent gendered ethnography has been particularly good at affording indigenous women voice and dignity through textual dialogue. This can be a natural link to cultivating indigenous or genuine dual authorship (e.g., Djebar 1993; Kyakas and Wiessner 1992; cf. Abu-Lughod 1993).

The relationship between recent waves of gendered ethnography and reflexive critique is by no means antagonistic. Among the recent monographs discussed earlier, those by Abu-Lughod, Behar, Kondo, Lavie, and Tsing all frontally consider and selectively draw upon reflexive concerns within anthropology. With the benefit of overview, it is evident they resonate with postpositivist critiques of gender and sexuality as well. They reveal women's experiences and expressions to have queer potential vis-à-vis patriarchal order. Gendered ethnographies and postpositivist feminism both emphasize gendered or sexual hybridity, positionality, and the subversive or decentering effects of performative re-signification. Other similarities include the refusal to be topicalized around women's experience alone and a commitment to gender or sex as a point of departure for cutting across categories of analysis and theoretical genres.

There are also important differences between the gendered potentials of ethnography and the legacy of postmodern influences in feminism. Rich ethnography of gendered diversity provides a social grounding that is largely absent in the more literary and textual concerns of feminism outside anthropology and past the post. Gendered ethnographies are highly attuned to how women's re-significations may be accommodated or co-opted by patriarchal or socioeconomic or other hegemonies, even as these structures still beg larger analysis. There is greater awareness of continuities, including traditions of gendered propriety that women assert and defend through proud conservatism. Against this background, modernist innovation poses distinct threats as well as potentials. The realpolitik of longstanding values informs a healthy theoretical skepticism about the potentials of performance as a universal *jouissance*. It guards against what Abu-Lughod (1990a) calls "the romance of resistance." Finally, gendered ethnography reflects the actual experiences of women of color, especially those who are not part of an elite within their society. Flights of fancy are less strained in recent gendered ethnography than in the gendered and sexualized theorizations of philosophical and literary academics.

What those outside anthropology still treat more boldly than those inside is, first, the issue of sexual as well as gendered and reproductive inequality, and, second, how gendered positioning can itself reposition dominating structures of subjectivity, representation, and knowledge. In recent gendered ethnography, the critique of these structures is less direct and poignant than in the postcritical rethinking of sex and gender.

Conclusions

It complements rather than diminishes the recent theoretical influence of figures such as Bourdieu, Foucault, Gramsci, or Bakhtin to read across their grain through fresh lenses of gendered awareness. Gendered ethnography and postpositivist theorizations of gender outside anthropology are highly important in this respect. (The same could be suggested, analogously, for approaches that cut across modernist theory to permute variously as cultural studies, subaltern studies, diasporic studies, or postcolonial studies.) The élan of their innovation rather than their difficulties of textualization and abstraction have been emphasized here (contrast chapter 3 of this book).

Gendered ethnographies of the early 1990s resonate in several ways with refigurations of gender and sexuality outside anthropology. But concrete ethnography is increasingly vital to this larger field; the diversity of gendered experience across a full range of both nonmodern and late modern contexts provides a crucial complement and a hard testing ground for the performative reimagining of gender and sexuality. Anthropology's study of gender needs to draw more strongly upon its own work of the 1970s as well as others' work of the 1990s in this respect.

Both ethnographically and theoretically, sexuality is becoming more important in cultural anthropology—along with critical studies of reproduction, health, and medicine. Queer theory, among others, may be productively used and critiqued as part of these developments. Among other things, cultural varieties of heterosexual relationship and associated male gender identity remain understudied—and undercritiqued—in the anthropological study of gender.

The lingering gap between broad-scale political economy and fine-grained gendered experience provides special space for creative work. Tracing the relationship between gendered power and other idioms of division—including those of nationality, race, class, age, religion, and ethnicity—is particularly important as a middle ground in this regard (see Yanagisako and Delaney 1995; Stoler 1995). The analysis of such articulations is likely to intensify as themes now prominent in cultural studies and postcolonial and diasporic studies engage gendered consideration of political economy, on the one hand, and of agency and personal identity, on the other. The empirical legacy of anthropology's feminist history in areas of female labor, status, reproduction, and health can be increasingly drawn into this analysis.

Growing interest in gender and sexuality is likely to continue eroding the lingering distinction between particularism and theory within cultural anthropology—and the accompanying privilege of theory as a grand and typically male narrative. Gendered and sexualized perspectives are important not just for topical understanding but for reformulating theoretical and antitheoretical initiatives. Theorizing gender promotes the regendering of theory. As reflected in the monographs considered, these developments draw on rich and substantive ethnography. As such, they open to an empirical as well as experiential rethinking that anthropological studies of race, ethnicity, and nationalism may also be positioned, in their own ways, to pursue. These strands broaden and interconnect our understanding of how inequalities and representations develop, proliferate, and transform.

For critically humanist sensibilities, the currently developing relationship between gender and ethnography is especially encouraging. It grounds cultural anthropology in the nuanced diversity of gendered experience while contextualizing it richly across disempowerments and contestations. Ethnographically and theoretically, this situated understanding can be extended to more refined analyses of microdynamics and to larger analysis of political and economic articulations.

multicultural speaking

Beyond Essentialism and Relativism

The world is white no longer, and it never will be again.
—**James Baldwin**, *Stranger in the Village*

Black women are treated as though we are a box of chocolates presented to
individual white women for their eating pleasure, so that they can decide for
themselves and others which pieces are most tasty.
—**bell hooks**, *Teaching to Transgress*

Can the subaltern speak?
—**Gayatri Spivak**, "Can the Subaltern Speak?"

These natives can speak for themselves
—T-shirt worn by gay activist protesting lack of gay speakers at a session on
culture and AIDS at the 1992 AAA meetings in San Francisco

A new kind of cultural worker is in the making,
associated with a new politics of difference.
—**Cornel West**, "The New Politics of Difference"

"Aw, Ah don't pay all dese ole preachers no rabbit-foot." ...
"They ain't no different from nobody else." ...
"Yeah; and hard work in de hot sun done called many a man to preach."
—**Zora Neale Hurston**, *Mules and Men*

Multicultural concerns bring issues of diversity and disempowerment together in a powerful and reflexive way. As such, they form a key point of engagement for critically humanist sensibilities that articulate appreciations of diversity with critiques of stigmatizing difference. What is multiculturalism? At one level, it is simply the existence of multiple ethnic or cultural groups within a society. But more commonly, it is the valorization of these differences—a belief that the expression of ethnic and cultural diversity should be not just respected but socially and politically encouraged within a community.[1]

In American society, multicultural concerns are now large and important. Multiculturalism inflects the curriculum in public schools from the primary grades on up; it infuses debates over reading lists and intellectual canons across many if not most college campuses; and it engages issues of experience, inequality, and representation at the highest echelons of academic theory and scholarship. Under the umbrella of multiculturalism, a mountain of academic books has emerged. A subject search of the term reveals 182 scholarly volumes on multiculturalism in Emory's respectable but by no means exhaustive research library. Of these, 66 were published between 1992 and 1994 alone. Amid this enormous groundswell, anthropology's contribution has been paltry at best; almost none of the above books were authored by anthropologists. More so than cultural studies, multiculturalism has skirted anthropology at the same time that it has spread widely across educational curricula. The irony is greater because cultural diversity has been one of anthropology's principal concerns.

Not surprisingly, anthropologists often lament that multiculturalism fails to acknowledge their importance. As alluded to by the then president of the American Anthropological Association Annette Weiner, it is easy to feel that anthropology's key concept of "culture" has been taken over by activists and educators who advocate multiculturalism but know neither the empirical diversity of cultures nor the scholarly research that comprehends them (Weiner 1992b). Multicultural activists and educators, on the other hand, easily find anthropologists reactionary in defending a limited if not anachronistic notion of "culture." Reputations die hard, and modernist anthropology has often assumed that culture is a largely self-contained and undisputed system. Within this perspective, cultural diversity was tacitly assumed to be (a) a system of objective differences between equivalent social entities, (b) ultimately symbolic rather than political in nature, and (c) best understood by professionals who collected data and dispassionately analyzed them in a university setting that was removed from the field of research.

Advocates of multiculturalism, by contrast, generally hold that cultures are not discrete and autonomous but emerge from power relations that subordinate cultural identities and define them as stigmatized groups. Cultural identities are defined by their relationships to dominant hegemonies; they are not objectively neutral as symbolic systems but by their very nature are political and disputed. Accordingly, the representation of culture relates in an important if not direct way to the politics of cultural contestation, including within the academy. At home as in the field, then, the professional cannot be neutral and detached but should actively promote the viewpoints and voices that are most disempowered and underrepresented. From this perspective, we anthropologists often fail to question our own received assumptions about "culture" in teaching and scholarship. We continue to project culture as an external attribute to be considered "out there" but not in our own practices. From a multicultural perspective, anthropologists' neglect or refusal of cultural politics at home is hypocritical.

Given that politics and positioning are part of multiculturalism, issues of personal identity and representation come quickly into play. Indeed, it is hard to begin illuminating issues of multicultural debate without considering the place of the speaker or author. Is one speaking—as anthropologists have typically done—as an expert outsider who asserts to know culture through assumptions of detached objectivity? Or does one speak from inside personal experiences of stigma and disempowerment?

On the ground and in the classroom, multiculturalism is associated— at least in perception—with the activist representation of minority groups by persons who foreground their identity as victims. Multiculturalism foregrounds disempowered voices "in the text," but it also foregrounds minority inclusion in the ranks of faculty and administrators who control the context of instruction. Are these people predominantly white, male, straight, American, and middle- to upper-class? Or do they include, in addition to women, blacks, Hispanics, Asians, persons of color from other world areas, and gays and lesbians? It is in part because of such questions that anthropologists—especially the majority of us who have difficulty defining ourselves as "victims"—easily become an enemy rather than a friend of those advocating multiculturalism in the classroom.

At least in practical terms, issues of personal experience, victimization, and identity politics are at the core of anthropology's relationship to multiculturalism. This fact tends to be papered over or confused in the highly rarefied or postmodern theorizations that have often provided multiculturalism's point of entry into anthropology to date—for instance, as piggybacked with cultural studies (e.g., Grossberg et al. 1992; Kanpol and McLaren 1995; Shohat and Stam 1994; Trend 1996). In the pragmatics of education—from kindergarten on up—the identity statuses of the instructor, the students, and their larger community have become key points of multicultural contestation. Before analyzing identity politics more closely, this practical dimension of multiculturalism needs to be put in our own historical and cultural context.

Histories and Mediations

In the heat of contemporary debates, it is especially important to see how multiculturalism has been influenced by political and national forces. Though having international dimensions and many previous incarnations, "multiculturalism" as a named phenomenon has had a particularly high profile in the United States during the 1980s and early 1990s. This period can be considered in relationship to larger patterns of American racial categorization and minority response. Di Leonardo (1994) has suggested that the post-World War II era in the United States has seen *whiteness* congeal as an increasingly salient racial category in the American imaginary (cf. Frankenberg 1993; see Winant 1994).[2] When considering the racial categories that are now officially and unofficially used in the United States—White, African-American, Hispanic, Asian, Native American, and "Other"—it is worth recalling that many American ancestries now subsumed under "white" used to be considered separate ethnic groups if not separate races. Irish, Poles, Italians, Jews, and so on were strongly and often invidiously distinguished in the United States during earlier decades. But increasingly during the last half-century, many of these European identities have collapsed into a larger, more explicit, and more hegemonic racial category: the racialization of the American mainstream as "white" in contrast to "blacks" and "persons of color."

From the late 1960s through the 1970s, this consolidation of whiteness was arguably both crosscut and polarized by the civil rights movement and other activisms that attempted to empower nonwhite minorities.

But these counterforces did not remain intact. The 1980s witnessed a marked retrenchment and move to the political right in the United States, as reflected in the dominance of Reaganomics, the waning of left-wing protest movements, and a diminished sense of activism and minority progress, including among African-Americans. Michael Dyson (1995) has suggested that the identity politics of multiculturalism arose particularly during this period—the 1980s—in an attempt to counteract the decline of collective minority activism and social progress (see also Aronowitz 1994). In important respects, then, *the identity politics of multiculturalism has emerged in the United States as an individualistic defense by blacks and persons of color against newly coherent and democratized white racial hegemonies.*

Given this history, it is easier to see why multiculturalism in the United States has not been concerned—at least in the first instance—with anthropology's global representation of cross-cultural diversity. Rather, it has focused on those groups that have been most disempowered within the specifically American cultural scene and in the stories of value told in American education. Prime among the mix of underprivileged voices are blacks, as well as Hispanics, Native Americans, and other minorities, such as Asian ethnicities, depending on their representation and disempowerment in the local community. The push to increase these voices in course readings, in the student body, and in faculty composition has become a hot point of debate in anthropology, as it has for other disciplines. From a critically humanist perspective, these issues should be matters of theory, conceptualization, and critical analysis as well as personal politics. If ethics and theory are linked in cultural anthropology, as I think they must be, then we must also analyze and theorize the ethics of our own practices. This task is made more difficult by polarization between modernist anthropology and multiculturalism, and yet again by the postmodern rarefaction of multicultural identities. A dialogue across these differences seems crucial.

On the surface, there seems little reason why multiculturalism's present cannot dovetail with anthropology's past. For critically humanist sensibilities, the contestation of representation and identity articulates moments that appreciate cultural diversity with those that critique inequality. This linkage can be at the heart of theory as well as politics, particularly in the cultural anthropology of late modernity.

Such contests can be considered briefly on a large scale before examining them closer to home. In the contemporary world, communities of identity increasingly crosscut modernist units such as nations and what used to be called homogeneous cultures. Proliferating as a human network, communities of identity are increasingly constructed, imagined, and remembered across disparate spaces and times. Both locally and globally, identities proliferate and diversify through migration circuits, diasporas, specialized interest groups, and use of media, commerce, and new categories of kinship and remembrance. (See Appadurai 1990, 1993; Lash and Friedman 1992; Featherstone et al. 1995; Bird et al. 1993; Fischer and Abedi 1990; Keith and Pile 1993; Miller 1994, 1995; Rouse 1991, 1995; cf. Harvey 1990; Friedman 1994). These communities are both targets of economic and political influence and principal arenas of responding to subordination and resisting inequality. Both in American society and around the world, culture is not just a construction but a cluster of diverse collectivities negotiated vigorously against a background of practical pressures and ideologies. As many have noted, cultural diversity is a central site of political struggle in a late modern world.

On objectivist grounds, the kinds of issues raised by multiculturalism should be increasingly important to an anthropology of contemporary conditions. And given the difficulty of asserting subaltern or minority identity against the grain of political, economic, and cultural hegemonies, disempowered voices and experiences are a particularly important and valuable part of this diversification. And yet the world of the academy is not the same as the world outside.[3] Some would even argue that the cutting edge of the humanities and liberal arts has now established a reverse hegemony, in which minorities and subalterns are encouraged to speak with less regard to their scholarly performance, rigor, or clarity of thought than those who are not in these categories. Of course, reactionary responses typically ignore the deeper, more pervasive, and more conservative realities of symbolic capital in the university. Identification *can* provide a key vehicle for experientially based insight and understanding. And this potential has been woefully neglected in academia and needs to be remedied. At the same time, however, a given type of personal identification does not *by itself* confer trenchancy of scholarly understanding or insight, nor does it confer identification beyond what is actually shared on the basis of personal experience. The relationship between different forms of disempowerment or identification—including class background and gender as well as race, sexual orientation, or subaltern nationality—remains an open and highly important question.

Even as one accepts the larger importance of multicultural goals, then, the question of authorship and identity reemerges rather than being put to rest. This question rebounds yet more powerfully on anthropologists insofar as we have not been personally subject to the disempowerment of those we write about.

Hitting from the Margins
Multiculturalism and Identity Politics

The tension between insiders and outsiders quickly engages the debate between cultural relativism and identity politics. While cultural relativism lives in a world in which cultures are ultimately separate but equal, multiculturalism places special value on voices and the pain of disempowered peoples, particularly as they struggle to counteract oppression. As discussed in chapter 2, the assumptions of value neutrality that long formed the essential core of cultural relativism in anthropology are in fact highly problematic. They leave cultural relativism ethically ungrounded and make it vulnerable to regressive political co-opting under the rubric of value-neutral scientism. By itself and uncomplemented by other motivations, value-neutral cultural relativism is, in my view, untenable.

But if cultural relativity houses a bias toward uncritical neutrality, identity politics houses a complementary bias toward essentialism.* Viewed from a critically humanist perspective, essentialism makes simplistic or universalizing assumptions about domination and uncritically assumes the possibilities or impossibilities of resistance based on a particular form of collective identity. If the potentials of personal experience are to be fully appreciated, the problems of identity politics cannot be shied away from; they should be confronted directly and openly, just like those of cultural relativism. This necessitates a fuller critique of identity politics before moving on to recontextualize its import and potential for critical pedagogy.

---

* By "essentialism," I mean a pejorative generalization that embraces and reinforces a stigmatizing division between those groups of people who are relatively disempowered and those who are not. This stigma can work in either direction. It is important to note that generalization per se need not be pejorative or stigmatizing and need not be essentialist. In contrast to essentialism, generalization remains a crucial moment of academic discourse.

Essentializing Problems

As important as it can be, the attempt to claim a special voice on the basis of minority racial, sexual, or ethnic identity carries problems, as many have noted. Actively or tacitly, the speaker gives voice on behalf of a larger disempowered group. Yet a single person often does not share the diverse backgrounds and experiences of this larger group. An elite minority spokesperson often has less current day-to-day experience of raw discrimination than the bulk of the group's members. This belies the importance of diversity and of creative contestation within the disempowered group.

But lest the politics of representation be thought to emerge primarily from the speaker him- or herself, it should be emphasized that an author may be taken as a spokesperson when not intending to do so. He or she can thus be pressured to bear what Kobena Mercer (1994:ch. 8) calls the "burden of representation" that is often expected of minority intellectuals. Particularly within academia, it is often the larger *non*minority audience who elevates the victimized spokesperson to an intellectual eminence. This dynamic of expectation is often central to the bandwagon process whereby a minority spokesperson is built up or fetishized. Such heroic elevations are often unrealistic and can unwittingly heighten people's deepest biases—including the suspicion that minority intellectuals are overrated—even when it is the nonminority audience itself who does the overrating.

It is particularly important to emphasize that numerous authors in the contemporary florescence of black studies have themselves not only identified and critiqued these problems but explored how to supersede them. Increasingly, black cultural studies is deconstructing identity politics and replacing it with a deeper critique of race itself as a disempowering category. For instance, Paul Gilroy favors

> a pluralistic position which affirms blackness as an open signifier and seeks to celebrate complex representations of a black particularity that is *internally* divided: by class, sexuality, gender, age, ethnicity, economics, and political consciousness. There is no unitary idea of black community here, and the authoritarian tendencies of those who would police black cultural expression in the name of their own particular history or priorities are rightly repudiated. The ontologically grounded essentialism is replaced by a libertarian, strategic alternative: the cultural saturnalia

which attends the end of innocent notions of the essential black subject. (Gilroy 1993:32)

Of course, deconstruction begs reconstruction, and Gilroy does not fall into the trap of assuming that a critique of essentialism precludes larger forms of generality. He ultimately favors an "anti-anti-essentialism" that he develops as a novel and yet cohesive literary understanding of the "black Atlantic"—namely, the connections of black literary understanding that have resonated among the Americas, Africa, and Europe. That this new conceptualization contains its own new boundaries and blind spots is at once to be recognized and to be taken in perspective as a widening of previous and more limited notions of black intellectual history.

A resonating move is found in the work of Patricia Hill Collins (1990), who on the one hand levers open black literature by foregrounding the diversity of gender, sexuality, and nationality across race, but then returns to general characterizations of black feminist literature. Against the many perspectives that had failed to see a corpus of contributions in the history of black female authorship to begin with, this construction is important, even as it now sets a new standard of generalities that can themselves be critiqued and gone beyond.

Stronger attempts to de-essentialize race as an analytic category have been developed by black studies writers such as Kwame Appiah (1992), Kobena Mercer (1994), Michele Wallace (1990), Cornel West (1993a), Michael Dyson (1993, 1995), and Gilroy in his more recent work (e.g., 1994; cf. also 1987). West's argument provides a convenient point of departure by linking the critique of racial categories to the earlier Gramscianism of Stuart Hall:

> Any notions of "the real Black community" and "positive images" are value-laden, socially-loaded and ideologically-charged. To pursue this discussion is to call into question the possibility of an uncontested consensus regarding them. Stuart Hall has rightly called this encounter "the end of innocence or the end of the innocent notion of the essential Black subject . . . the recognition that 'Black' is essentially a politically and culturally *constructed* category." (West 1993a:19)

This recognition is echoed by Wallace, who suggests that black racialization is unproductive on political as well as intellectual grounds:

Not only does reversal, or the notion that blacks are more likeable, more compassionate, smarter, or even "superior," not substantially alter racist preconceptions, it also ties Afro-American cultural production to racist ideology in a way that makes the failure to alter it inevitable. (Wallace 1990:1)

Wallace argues that attempts to dignify and uplift blacks as a collective group, however well intentioned, remain limited within the structure of a binary division between negative and positive stereotypes. This simply reverses rather than gets outside racist formulations; it passively accepts the terms of the racist debate.

For Kobena Mercer,

The profusion of rhyzomatic connections of the sort that constitute an evolving black queer diaspora community implies another way of conceiving "the role of the intellectual," not as heroic leader or patriar- chal master, but as a connector located at the hyphenated intersection of disparate discourses and carrying out the task of translation . . . in a new conception of the hybridizing role. (Mercer 1994:30)

Within this context, it becomes problematic to generalize a group on the basis of a particular experience of pain and disempowerment. As Brackette Williams states in a recent critique of bell hooks's work,

If we are provided only with untheorized relentless descriptions of painful experiences, we cannot understand them. Understanding is even more elusive when painful experiences are rendered simplistic by too little attention to intragroup variations that do not fit the traditional view of authentic beginnings, however close they may be to the "woundedness, the ugliness" of it all. . . . We hear Dr. hooks cry, but it is neither suffi- cient to hear divas continually crying nor to insist, as she does, that "We need to cherish and honor those among us who emerge as 'stars'." (Williams 1994:151)

Identity politics based on victimization tends to reify and reinforce boundaries based on singular features of identity, such as race, gender, sex, or class. They implicitly accept the dominant ideology of typecast identity and reinforce the very division between the victim group and others that is ostensibly being criticized. Even if successful, the empowerment of the group through the identity of difference encourages a situation of "separate but equal." And encouraging an identity of victimization can unwittingly reinforce and internalize a cycle of dependency in the very attempt to combat it. Given the difficulties of identity politics and the link between them and multiculturalism, Dyson (1995) advocates going beyond multiculturalism to a "postmulticultural" position that contests the underlying categories of multiculturalism itself. At the same time, Dyson, like the other black authors quoted above, retains the goal of empowering disempowered voices in a larger and more profound sense. It is simply the use of essentializing means such as identity politics that is criticized.

The significance of Dyson's perspective is thrown into relief by contrasting it with a related "posting" that may appear to be similar but which is in fact quite different: the "postethnicity" advocated by historian David Hollinger in his *Postethnic America* (1995). Dedicated to his Berkeley colleagues and purporting to go "beyond multiculturalism," Hollinger wants to subsume the appreciation of multiple identities—and people's right to assert them—under the umbrella of a newly rejuvenated United States nationalism. This nationalism is to be based on a cosmopolitanism that elides pluralism, restricts fragmentation, and discourages the development of "ethnic enclaves." Though Hollinger is at pains to stress that this national unification is to be "voluntary" rather than forced, the issue of power—and, more important, disempowerment—is strikingly absent. The implications of Dyson's and Hollinger's postings are thus opposed: One wants to empower minority points of view in ways that go beyond existing racial and ethnic divisions, while the other wants to reduce if not suppress the representation of diversity.

As we point out the weaknesses of identity politics, it becomes all the more crucial to avoid the conservative slide represented by Hollinger. We need to find alternative routes through which minority voices may be empowered. Within the university, it is also important to remember (in contrast to Hollinger), that identity politics can result as much from the mainstream drive to create essential categories of Otherness as from self-assertion by minorities. Critiquing this situation, Virginia Dominguez (1994) suggests that affirmative action initiatives based on race or ethnicity often reflect our own academic "taste for the Other"; they reinforce the kinds of racial divisions they should try to transcend. But, again, this disagreement with affirmative action is not the same as one drawn from a more politically conservative position (e.g., Schlesinger 1994; Ayres 1995). The larger point for Dominguez is that disempowered voices should be valued; their inclusion should be organic rather than mandated. The conservative viewpoint, on the other hand, is that such voices should not be mandated because they need not be included. The former view criticizes the formalization of racial and ethnic boundaries but encourages minority and disempowered voices through alternative tactics that are less essentializing (e.g., Dominguez, 1994:346). In contrast, the latter view criticizes the assertion of minority identity in order to replace it with yet greater insistence on norms and values that are already hegemonic and subordinating (such as those of the U. S. nation-state). Though superficially similar on a selected narrow issue, these points of view move in opposite political directions. From a critically humanist perspective, it remains important to critique and combat disempowerment even as tactics that essentialize these divisions are themselves also critiqued as problematic.

In a dialogic perspective, it is clear that identity politics denies the intrinsic outsidedness—not to mention hybridity—that Bakhtin rightly saw as a necessary condition of intersubjective understanding. It also undervalues the diversity of insidedness that can lever new insights from positions of internal marginality. To draw a boundary around an essential group compromises its intersubjective humanity, even if this boundary is drawn by adherents from the inside as well as by those on the outside. In the reflexive context of ethnographic fieldwork, this would imply the dubious notion that only blacks can study, understand, or speak concerning blacks, that only gays can speak for gays, or that only battered women can speak for battered women (see Kuper 1994). Though seldom acknowledged, this also promotes the unfortunate conclusion that only straight white men can study, understand, or speak about straight white men.

Within the university, this problem is pragmatic as well as theoretical. Some of the sharpest infighting has been within the ranks of leftist intellectuals themselves over the type and form of identity—subaltern, feminist, womanist, lesbian or gay, racially localized or more racially diasporic—that should be privileged or afforded greatest voice. Conferences, edited volumes, and journal ripostes on some of the most interesting issues in critical theory can inflict posthumanist dueling scars of surprising viciousness within their own limited ranks.[4] Those who could forge complementary critiques become enemies. As Mercer argues,

> The worst aspects of the new social movements emerged in a rhetoric of "identity politics" based on an essentialist notion of a fixed hierarchy of racial, sexual, or gendered oppressions. By playing off each other to establish who was more authentically oppressed than whom, the residual separatist tendencies of the autonomous movements played into the normative calculation of "disadvantage" inscribed in welfare statism. . . . In this zero-sum game the only tangible consequence of diversity was dividedness. (Mercer 1994:262)

If identity politics sidetracks the search for less essentializing means of minority empowerment, the same can be true of discussions that try to assert one form of disempowerment as more fundamental or important than another. In a given instance, how does one tell which of several alternative disempowered identities—race, ethnicity, sex, gender, age, nationality—is most compelling? As they assert rights and prerogatives, advocates of these positions easily come into conflict. Yet it is amply evident from anthropology's own history that finding acceptable standards (much less disinterested ones) to comparatively assess different kinds of inequality is a perplexing if not dubious task. This task becomes all the more questionable as identities and affiliations multiply and criss cross in the hybrid circumstances of a late modern world. Under such conditions, the search for an authentic or genuine voice of disempowerment becomes all the more problematic. It can also backfire. In the university, for instance, it can be a disservice for minority scholars to be grandstanded prematurely at an early stage in their development. What is gained temporarily in the public-relations value of quick recognition—the satisfaction of our "taste for the Other"—can be outweighed by a plethora of distractions, demands, and expectations that can sap the minority individual's potential for a more profound and ultimately more powerful career trajectory. If one is really interested in promoting minority scholarship—as we must be—this needs to be a sustained, organic, and long-term commitment, not one based on superficial praise or gyrations.

The renowned difficulties of postcritical writing both reflect and fuel the problems that surround the politics of identification. Critical (anti)-theorists are often encouraged to speak from personal experience. But they are also pressured to be antiessentialist. The author can thus feel obliged to write as a shifting target; the prose convolutes in flashy confusion to avoid attack. This double bind of identity and disavowal has not subsided with the highwater mark of postmodern authorship per se. Rather, the postmodernization of critical writing continues in cultural studies, postcolonial studies, and multiculturalism (e.g., Grossberg et al. 1992; Ashcroft et al. 1995, cf. 1989; Kanpol and McLaren 1995; Shohat and Stam 1994). In certain respects, the politics of identity and the postmodern politics of nonidentity are mutually disenabling.

Progressive Potentials

Notwithstanding such difficulties, it would be all too easy to write off the importance of disempowered identity and insider experience within it. This is exactly what the reactionary reification of political correctness would be happy to do. The critique of identity politics can all too easily lead us back to an uncritical positivism. And this denial of positionality would make us all the more ripe for unselfconscious conservatism. A more refined position that acknowledges the contributions as well as the drawbacks of identity politics is thus necessary.

bell hooks, among others, would be one of the first to emphasize the distinctiveness rather than the uniformity of insider experience. She would likely attack the present account for using some respected black intellectuals to attack the identity politics of others. Such a strategy of "watching them fight it out" reflects and perpetuates a white spectatorial gaze (hooks 1992a). It also reinforces a cruel assumption: that identity is not a "problem" among whites but only among essential dark Others. It is important here to let hooks speak for herself when she responds to Diana Fuss's (1989) critique of essentialism:

> According to Fuss, issues of "essence, identity, and experience" erupt in the classroom primarily because of the critical input from marginalized groups. Throughout her chapter, whenever she offers an example of individuals who use essentialist standpoints to dominate discussion, to silence others via their invocation of the "authority of experience," they are members of groups who historically have been and are oppressed and exploited in this society. Fuss does not address how systems of domination already at work in the academy and the classroom silence the voices of individuals from marginalized groups and give space only when on the

basis of experience it is demanded. She does not suggest that the very discursive practices that allow for the assertion of the "authority of experience" have already been determined by a politics of race, sex, and class domination. Fuss does not aggressively suggest that dominant groups— men, white people, heterosexuals—perpetuate essentialism. In her narrative it is always a marginal "other" who is essentialist. (hooks 1994:81)

To take hooks's criticism seriously and reflexively, we can reframe the question by considering a form of identity politics that is commonly disowned: essentialism within university departments. Specifically, we can consider the politics of anthropology as a typically small and often relatively weak departmental identity within the structure of university power. First, however, it is important to distinguish such gentle forms of disempowerment from those that hooks describes. The latter exist on a wholly different and larger order of magnitude; the disempowerment of blacks and other minority groups has caused incredible pain and suffering and has been both historically pernicious and deeply ingrained. Against this, the disempowerment of some university departments vis-à-vis others seems mockingly meek, compartmentalized, and "academic." And yet this itself underscores the point: If identity politics through strategic essentialism can be found even in normal academic practice, it is it any less defensible for those who have been deeply stigmatized? Are they to be held to a higher standard?

Anthropology can be taken as an example. Both in numbers and in political clout, anthropology often serves in the university as the tacit "foreign Other" or "weak sister" against bigger and better-funded social science departments of economics, political science, and psychology, and the much larger humanities departments of English or history. This imbalance occurs despite (or rather because of) anthropology's coverage of the entire non-Western world, whereas the other social sciences and humanities still focus largely on the West.

As mentioned, anthropology's disempowerment is minor in relative terms. But even in this example, if anthropologists were able to reframe their minority status within the university into a kind of moral and symbolic capital that would allow them to lever greater funding, positions, and profile, would we criticize them for doing it? Given the frequent lack of cross-cultural perspectives in other departments, wouldn't we like to argue that all undergraduates should take anthropology courses as part of a university-wide cultural diversity requirement? Would we stigmatize our senior professors for vigorously asserting the need for more faculty lines in our department in this regard? And if anthropologists were criticized by the other social sciences for being "essentialist" and drawing a boundary around our own limited interests—thus failing to see the ostensibly more "scientific," "objective," and "rational" views promoted by economics, political science, or mainstream Western history—wouldn't anthropologists be justified in criticizing Eurocentrism and its positivist hegemony in rejoinder?

One could change the specific tropes depending on one's particular interests, but the analogy is clear: We all practice identity politics under certain conditions. But because "identity politics" is a stigmatized epithet, we deny the term in reference to ourselves. Indeed, *it is a distinctive sign of empowerment in the rules of the game that one is supposed to be successful through strategies that are justified "objectively" and that do not **need** to rely on tropes of self-interest or victimization* (cf. Bourdieu 1988a). In fact, we not only deny but are highly motivated to deny the self-interest of our own identity politics. And if it becomes a mark of failure in the game of power to advertise one's minority status, so too the attribution of "identity politics" to others becomes all the more stigmatizing and disempowering. This disguises the fact that the seeds of such politics are sown widely, if not universally, among us. It is both more convenient and more beneficial to be in the *un*marked category of political advantage.

If these arguments apply in a relatively benign example such as the relationship of anthropology to other academic fields, they apply at least as strongly in cases of greater inequality.

Speaking of, Speaking about, Speaking for

As the above example illustrates, the problems of identity politics should not let us off hooks's hook too easily. Apart from logical justifications, we still need a pragmatic and critically humanistic way to encourage minority voices in scholarly representation. So the conundrum is reengaged in a more refined way. An alternative tack is to suggest that one should be empowered to speak by the depth of one's personal experience and background. As hooks puts it,

> The "passion of experience" ... is a way of knowing that is often expressed through the body, what it knows, what has been deeply

inscribed through experience. This complexity of experience can rarely be voiced and named from a distance. It is a privileged location, even as it is not the only or even always the most important location from which one can know. (hooks 1994:91)

At one level, at least, this doesn't appear much different from what anthropologists do all the time. Personal experience underwrites the privileged credentials that are afforded to anthropologists on the basis of long-term fieldwork—the prestige of what Geertz (1988) calls the extended "I-witnessing" of ethnography. If anything, hooks's admonition raises Geertz's experience-near ethnography to a higher and more reflexive key by embracing the passion of experience from inside a position of personal disempowerment. It also goes beyond Geertz's problematic assumption that ethnographic voices are unmediated to the ethnographer, much less to the reader of the work. In contrast, inside positioning puts us more intimately in touch with the judgments, values, and sensibilities of those speaking for themselves—and particularly with the features of contestation central to their own identity and "culture." While a variety of voices are important—including insider, outsider, and a creative mix of hybrid perspectives—there is little question that insider voices need cultivation and respect as authors as well as informants.

The deeper issue is that "speaking for" depends on audience and context. In academics, it is best limited to those areas in which one really does have the most experience and the ability to represent it in an intellectually trenchant manner. Problems increase as one generalizes experience or expertise to areas outside one's understanding or beyond one's means of effective expression. Given this mandate, how does the anthropologist confront the problem of using one's training and experience to speak about other people? The most obvious and neglected answer, I think, is to conduct more detailed and sensitive fieldwork—to expose oneself more fully to the lives and experiences one wishes to represent.

Linda Alcoff (1991) is helpful in clarifying the general conditions under which "speaking for others" is most justified. We sometimes do wish to empower representatives. And sometimes representation presumes distance or expertise that does not mirror our depth of personal experience—as when a lawyer represents our case to a judge. Even when not specifically empowered, anthropologists often use their voices to defend or justify the beliefs or customs of local people who are not present and not otherwise easy to have represented. This is a long-standing pattern in cultural anthropology that needs to be continued, even as it needs to be undertaken more sensitively and self-critically than before. It is more problematic to speak for others if they have not actively supported or encouraged this voicing. Indeed, it is important for anthropologists to consider this issue when choosing a field site. Conversely, it is also important to increase the opportunities for people to speak for themselves.

As Alcoff emphasizes, the problems of speaking are mitigated by talking as much as possible *with* or *to* others rather than speaking *about* them. This fosters interchange rather than spectatorship or academic hubris. It also reduces rather than essentializes the difference between groups and promotes interchange in place of mutually exclusive discourse. Speaking with and to is what cultural anthropologists generally do in the course of their fieldwork. But the lesson is also important to transport back to the university. Numerous reasons exist there as well why "talking with" is an important complement to "talking about." Though geographic distance remains an impediment, there are increasing potentials in a late modern world—through burgeoning forms of media, electronic communication, and transport—for voices from the field to be connected in dialogue with anthropology's field at home. This indigenous commentary is an increasingly important part of cultural anthropology.

Alcoff's emphasis on Bakhtinian dialogue in the context of academic politics dovetails effectively with an important distinction drawn by Terence Turner (1993) between what he terms "critical multiculturalism" and "difference multiculturalism."[5] Whereas the latter essentializes differences through identity politics, *critical* multiculturalism pluralizes groups and crosscuts them; it encourages a diversity of voices to participate in a democracy of discussion and debate. Turner favors critical and dialogic multiculturalism because it retains a progressive push without reifying or reinforcing a separation between groups. It uses outsidedness not as a point of division but as a stimulus for wider awareness and understanding. In this regard, the critical multiculturalism discussed by Turner fits well with the reflexive side of a critically humanist perspective: It combines a respect for diversity with a continuing critique of inequality and disempowerment.

What needs to be more highly developed in Turner's and Alcoff's emphases on participatory democracy—and in many current discussions of critical pedagogy[6]—is an up-front consideration of social power. This issue builds upon but goes further than an emphasis on discourse, voicing, or a rejuvenated concept of "dialogue," "culture," or "citizenship." The key problem is that participatory democracy is not always progressive for those in the minority. For instance, on many if not most college campuses of the 1990s, a democracy that gives equal input to all would as often favor conservative ideas of white majorities as it would empower minority opinions. That all are empowered to speak does not mean that all are empowered when final decisions are made. The power structures of most universities (not to mention the boards of trustees or regents, who are shielded from public scrutiny) are typically to the political right rather than to the left of minority groups. In a critically humanist perspective, one cannot assume that inequality will be combated automatically through the voicing of diversity; the one does not entail the other.

Though this issue may appear hinged to semantic distinctions, slippage on this point makes a large practical difference. The problem breaks surface whenever a specific issue pits the importance of a raw "majority rules" attitude against the desire to ensure an outcome that is progressive for women or minorities. A wide-open process does not preclude a power struggle in the end game. This hoary issue has been debated in social contract theory ever since Rousseau blurred the gap between absolute democracy—the most votes—and the more diffuse spirit or underlying sentiment of the group—its "general will." The latter, which is supposed to capture the true, authentic, and progressive feelings of the group, may be in conflict with a specific and narrowly framed electoral tally. An analogous tension exists between a multiculturalism that is "critical" and one based on "difference"—between a general sense of respect for diversity and a specific instance in which minority rights must nonetheless be protected through self-assertion. In much current writing on this issue, the tension between critical and difference multiculturalism is not resolved so much as smoothed over in the apparent hope that the former will supplant the latter—that open discussion and dialogue will lead to power sharing so that opposition on the basis of difference will not be necessary. What happens when dialogue does *not* alleviate disempowerment, however, remains an open question. In this case, the salutary attempt to "de-essentialize" categories of difference can become a rarefied or textualized privilege of academic expression—and one patently disconnected from realities of public opinion and action outside the university.

The tension between dialogue and disempowerment links back to a key dynamic within critically humanist sensibilities, that is, the dynamic between the appreciation of diversity and the critique of inequality. Like the check and balance between these complementary values, the irresolvable tension between difference and dialogue in multiculturalism should be openly admitted, contextually analyzed, and tactically managed. It seems better to be open about this opposition than to cover it up; it should not be swept under the rug. The task of promoting full and open democracy and de-essentializing difference is not always consistent or logically harmonious with attempts to work against the grain of disempowerment. Though dialogue is crucially important to understanding, it does not preclude activism that pushes strongly for one side. Terence Turner himself has been at the forefront of this latter issue in cultural anthropology. Among other examples, he has been a strong advocate of land rights for Amazonian peoples and has encouraged and publicized Kayapo video recording as an "indigenous media" that asserts to the Brazilian state—as well as to conferences of professional anthropologists—their opinions and rights (e.g., Turner 1992). This is both an engaged activism and one that facilitates local people's speaking for themselves. As Turner's case illustrates, dialogue and political essentialism based on minority interest are related moments rather than mutually exclusive alternatives.

In an era of late modernity, the relationship among media, power, and politics cannot be left to itself to work "naturally." This is as true in the university as it is in the Amazon. Democracy does not lay vouchsafed in some kind of sacred Habermasian trust. Rather, it needs to be tactically pushed to allow greater influence for those who have been, and are, disempowered. The key question, however, is how to do this without unduly compromising respect for cultural and subjective diversity—how to do it without undue recourse to essentialism and identity politics. The empowering moment that asserts the identity and rights of those who have been disenfranchised needs to be utilized but also tempered by counterposing moments that reach out to appreciate alternative opinions and diversity both within and outside the group. Though these are alternative sides of a critically humanist perspective, they are not the same thing, either practically or analytically.

Power, Theory, and Practice

How does one orchestrate the balance between cultural relativism and essential critique based on minority interest? How do we know exactly when to shift from one to the other? The answers to this question cannot be absolute; they depend on pragmatic context. In the present instance, I am concerned with critical pedagogy—how to teach cultural anthropology and engage in appropriate and progressive academic practice from a critically humanist perspective. With respect to this goal, the essentialist moment of claiming special privilege on the basis of personal disempowerment needs to be tempered. In a late modern era within academia, recourse to an "inner essentialist core"—whether it is based on racial, gendered, sexual, ethnic, socioeconomic, or national identity—is ultimately shortsighted as a device for achieving influence and progressive change within academia. This very pragmatic conclusion can be reached either from a liberal perspective, in which the university is a relatively open place at which identity politics is unnecessary, or a radical one, in which the university is so pervaded by hegemonic epistemology that it is a hopeless arena for change except by persons who accept its minimum criteria of scholarship. In either case, a frontal war of opposition to basic standards based on identity politics is impractical and unlikely to be effective. The Western university remains a place where respect for diversity in scholarship is perceived to be relatively high, and in which claims to personal privilege tend to be ineffective when not backed up by academic accomplishment, particularly in the long run. That the political climate in the United States may be moving further to the right does not contradict and may reinforce this assessment.

What remains more important than ever is what Gramsci called wars of continuing position. Wars of position afford opportunities for marshaling and encouraging resistance against disempowerment in the absence of sufficient power to overwhelm it directly. To pick a simple example in the academic context, alternative journals and presses can present an opening in the edifice of scholarship. Insofar as the token of scholarly advancement is still often taken to be publication, the political process whereby new press outlets are represented to faculty and deans as "scholarly" can be particularly important.

To emphasize wars of position is not to retreat or to refuse confrontation. Nor is it to deny the importance of strategic collectivity—the importance of circling the wagons and strategizing for the sake of collective action. It is rather to stress that *essentialism on the basis of identity is, in our present academic practice, better seen as a transient tactic than as a principal means of combating inequality.* That identity politics does little to valorize diversity makes it problematic as a dominant strategy on ethical as well as practical grounds. But collective conflicts and the identity politics that they often entail are not totally eliminated. Rather, they become byproducts of a struggle of progressive positioning.

This view draws upon Gramscian dynamics but repunctuates them in the context of micropractices rather than macrosolutions. In Gramsci's strategy, wars of position marshal and preserve working-class forces until they are galvanized in an open war of direct force. This latter struggle is an all-out war of maneuver to seize power from the state—a political revolution. In synoptic terms, Gramsci advocates wars of position (P) that string along until they result in an ultimate war of maneuver (M): $P \rightarrow P \rightarrow P \rightarrow M$. In unfortunate cases where the first revolution is unsuccessful (for instance, revolutionary forces are co-opted by a Louis Bonaparte or a Joseph Stalin), the initial cycle is presumably reengaged until a more progressive and ultimate overthrow is attained: i.e., $P \rightarrow P \rightarrow P \rightarrow M_1 \rightarrow P \rightarrow P \rightarrow P \rightarrow M_2$. As was the case for Marx, the ultimate Gramscian purpose, whatever its length, is to culminate in climactic revolutionary victory.

The present view, by contrast, does not see essentialized opposition as an ultimate end or even as a celebratory vehicle. Likewise, it gives up on utopian hopes for revolutionary conclusions, which often harbor brutal excesses and unintended consequences even when they are "successful."[7] Instead, moments of essential opposition are seen as transient and in important ways undesirable, if sometimes necessary; they become byproducts of progressive positioning. From this perspective, *a continuing war of position does not need to justify itself by essentialized ends.* This does not mean the absence of frontal confrontations or showdowns between rival forces. Nor does it deny the importance of identity politics or the significance of an individual's arguing on behalf of a group. It expands upon critical multiculturalism by accepting the politics of difference as a pragmatically necessary moment from time to time. But this moment is clearly recognized to be ineffective as well as internally compromised as a dominant strategy. Essentializing confrontations, however important they may be in a specific situation, should be the means toward a progressively contested position and not sufficient or desirable in themselves. The moment of essentialism and collapse into a collective identity is not striven for, even though it is accepted pragmatically when necessary. It is a transient feature in a larger war of position that fights against and deconstructs these very same essentialisms. What results is not a Gramscian Marxism with no guarantees; it is a guarantee of Marxism beyond the post (cf. Laclau and Mouffe 1985).

This perspective encourages positional struggles along diverse axes of inequality—axes of inequality that Gramsci recognized but was unable to effectively incorporate. Each struggle has its own oscillation between tactical positioning and temporary confrontation. The larger goal is a continuing war of position against all forms of inequality. Keeping this larger goal in mind—and strategizing about it dialogically—helps reduce the polarization between one axis of resistance and another. It helps avoid internal competition between alternative strategies that critique and combat inequality. It also helps encode a key complementary goal—of valorizing diversity both within and between perspectives.

On a conceptual level, such reframings of Gramsci emphasize pragmatic equivalence as a continuing and organic practice—including on the microlevel, in everyday social relationships. Equivalence is a dynamic and oscillating social process entailed by complementarity between appreciation of diversity and critique of inequality. In this respect, equivalence contrasts with simple equality, which is static and ultimately asocial. The pluralizing features of equivalence are effectively emphasized by Laclau and Mouffe in their discussion of radical democracy, which shares many features with the point of view developed above:

> There are a variety of possible antagonisms in the social, many of them in opposition to each other. The important problem is that the chains of equivalence will vary radically according to which antagonism is involved; and that they may affect and penetrate in a contradictory way the identity of the subject itself. (Laclau and Mouffe 1985:131)

This perspective enables a diversity of contestations, as Henry Giroux (1992) has emphasized in his delineation of critical pedagogy (see also Trend 1996; cf. Rosaldo 1994). Persons are valorized to work against the grain of inequality along whatever axes of disempowerment they are best positioned and temperamentally suited to expose, analyze, and combat.

Though Laclau and Mouffe's perspective has stayed rather abstract (Laclau 1994; Mouffe 1992, 1993), it does not preclude a more substantive view. Drawing on her detailed work on black feminists, for instance, Patricia Hill Collins suggests:

> Replacing additive models of oppression with interlocking ones creates possibilities for new paradigms. The significance of seeing race, class, and gender as interlocking systems of oppression is that such an approach fosters a paradigmatic shift of thinking inclusively about other oppressions, such as age, sexual orientation, religion, and ethnicity. (Collins 1993:617)

Back to Practicalities

A post-Marxist perspective on practice can easily drift into the theoretical ozone. In real social practice, positioning against interlocking inequalities is given the acid test when they directly oppose one another. In the university as elsewhere, it is not uncommon for different axes of disempowerment and self-interest to wind up on different sides. In an academic context, for example, a dean may have money for one new faculty position. Though the anthropological preference seems clear if the choice is between Chicano/a studies and chemistry, it becomes more cloudy if the choice is between Chicano/a studies and African-American studies. Or worse, the dean has announced that one of these two positions will be cut.[8] Constituencies come into de facto opposition as they argue their respective cases. Though the appropriate answer is, of course, to make the pie of positions larger or refuse the question, we do live in a pragmatic world of structural constraints and practical choices. Rather than depersonalizing my opponent across a divide of difference, I can continue to respect someone who works to reduce inequality even though I may disagree and work against him or her in a transient confrontation on a specific case—that is, because of a particular background, set of abilities, and connections that lead me to privilege a different axis of resistance in that instance—for example, race as opposed to gender, sex as opposed to ethnicity, class as opposed to age, or even anthropology as opposed to sociology. It is, one hopes, the broader common commitment to expose and critique inequality that is shared, even as differences along this front are respected in a spirit of critical relativity.

The larger war of position that opportunistically embraces tactics against all forms of disempowerment ultimately takes precedence over transient polarizations. This larger view augurs for competing forms of resistance to be managed more productively and negotiated more strategically. It is hopeless to wish for a static resolution on this score. But respect and larger purpose can be shared beyond the ineffectual cry that valorizes either a single narrow interest, on the one hand, or the ethereal fragments of postmodern identity in general, on the other. As Brackette Williams (1994:151) notes, it is important to locate the key sites of practical maneuvering for change in the thicket of existing inequalities.

It is here that the other side of a critically humanist perspective—respect for cultural and subjective diversity—re-enters the picture and becomes important. It enters now in a new key—not as pure relativism, but as a moment that counteracts the essentialism of interest group politics. It is difficult to specify in advance exactly how and when these alternating moments—the critique of inequality and the valorization of diversity— should be employed. It remains a contextual and tactical decision in each case. But a good way to combat an *excessive* dose of one of these alternatives is to *complement* it with the other.[9] Neither by itself is ultimately defensible. If unchecked, relativist accommodation to power realities in the "system as given" becomes a version of sucking up and selling out. Frontal critique of domination is called for. Conversely, counterproductive fights over essentialized inequalities beg a pragmatic assessment: first, when it is best to tactically reposition and preserve one's capital, and, second, whether there are larger diversities that deserve greater respect. "Respect," as such, cannot be knee-jerk or uncritical. It is time for caution if respect works asymmetrically or in a consistently upward political direction, that is, as ingratiation. It is the positive assertion of equivalence, the refusal to condone disempowerment, and the appreciation of diversity that merit respect, even though the context and style of these assertions and refusals differ in each case.

Dialogue Revisited

Working from the critical side of the coin, Gramscian perspectives can reach out from critiques of inequality to engage a respect for cultural and subjective diversity. Reciprocally, this dialogue can also be initiated by approaches that foreground an appreciation of subjective diversity but stretch toward a critique of disempowerment. This complementary process has been emphasized historically in cultural anthropology at least since Boas: The appreciation of cultural diversity has provided a key link to the combating of ethnocentrism, racism, and sexism. This track has sometimes been taken when it was politically shortsighted or futile for anthropologists to make more theoretically explicit critiques of disempowerment. As discussed in chapter 1, for instance, Marxist scholarship was actively purged from many Western universities, especially in the United States, before these were opened to critical theory during the 1960s and 70s.

In terms of more recently discovered genealogies, Bakhtinian perspectives appreciate subjective diversities that reach out despite oppression and censureship toward critiques of inequality and domination. Amid his consummate sensitivity to literary and discursive diversity, Bakhtin's nuance was dedicated to valorize the irrepressible ability of human communication to counter and crosscut discursive hegemony. Hence his emphasis on the dialogic, heteroglossic, and polyvocalic forces that frustrate monologue and autocracy. On a theoretical plane, Bakhtin combated the structuring totality of Freudianism, formalism, structuralism, and, most ironically, Soviet renditions of Marxism itself. Dialogic positioning was also evident in Bakhtin's response to his own persecution—not only in his role as the guiding force of "the Bakhtin intellectual circle" but as exile, farm accountant, secondary-school teacher, community college lecturer, private scholar, and, surprisingly at the end, Moscow celebrity. In all these capacities, Bakhtin put his values into practice through appreciative discourse with diverse people while cultivating his insights, remarkably, in the one space that remained—his private writing. Bakhtin was not striving for power, status, or renown. He was simply and irrepressibly resilient in manifesting the value of dialogue against suppression. Far from Gramsci's revolutionary, Bakhtin was nevertheless an extremely important and in his own way exemplary kind of organic intellectual. That he had such a pleasant sense of self-effacing humor, and not just irony, is all the more gratifying in a late modern age that easily gyrates between egoistic sobriety and narcissistic abandon. In the conflicts over progressivism, political correctness, and conservatism, one often misses the Bakhtinian ability to take oneself not so seriously.

The point here is that there are many routes to organic intellectualism. Bakhtin would be the first to satirize any attempt to sanctify his own persona. More substantively, Bakhtin's approach lacks the direct critique of inequality that is prominent in the work of W. E. B. DuBois, contemporary black cultural studies,[10] post-positivist feminism, and other critical pedagogies, not to mention Marx. Many works and lives of progressive positioning are worthy of respect. Some of them cultivate the intrinsic double consciousness of the organic intellectual better than does Gramsci's stress on culture as a martial art or Bakhtin's emphasis on progressive aestheticism. The goal is not to enshrine singular examples as more authentic than others; any list can be critiqued as having omitted or underemphasized certain candidates or groups. It would be wrong to re-essentialize the issue by dividing the world into squares and mandating equal coverage by different constituencies. The larger point is that works from *various* cultural positions can be chosen to illustrate the diversity of articulations between the critique of disempowerment and the respect of human diversity. Specifics are historically, contextually, and temperamentally contingent rather than absolute.

Pluralizing the discussion can bring it back home again. In anthropology, this means ethnography: the concrete attempt to live across difference and to rigorously document this difference in a way that valorizes diversity and critiques inequality and domination. It can also mean academic politics—the ability of organic intellectualism to persist in the academy. The university is certainly a real place, and the thoughts and activities of academics have real effects on students, on colleagues, and on the type of knowledge that is valued or cultivated. Insofar as one is committed to anthropology as a profession, the supposed ivory tower involves a lot of real work dealing with real and diverse people. Pushing against inequalities while trying to appreciate voices that deserve respect, being rigorous in knowing the facts and doing one's homework, retaining a sense of humor, risking attempts that attract criticism and court failure, and being willing to admit mistakes: In all these senses critically humanist sensibilities need not see the organic intellectual die an academic death. Given the increasingly reactionary stances of many politicians, students, and even educators, the present is certainly not a time to lose one's nerve or opt out of the fray. Against this negative possibility, the articulation between respect for diversity and critique of inequality may help multiculturalism become a more pragmatic and more personal reality.

Personalizing One's Position

Where do I, personally, stand? For whom do I speak? And why, for most anthropologists, are such questions so embarrassing? All victims are not created equal. As a white male brought up in a bourgeois suburb of central Connecticut in the mid-1950s, my childhood and family traumas don't carry much weight, especially in relative terms. The disempowerments all around me are much greater than my own. But does this inherently make me part of the problem rather than part of the solution? Of course not. We are powerless to change the facts of our history. What we *can* change is its legacy, its present emphasis, and its future direction.

The life one has built—the sum of past choices, constraints, triumphs, and mistakes—confronts one in the present as an externality. There is always tension between living within the confines of this received life and changing or transforming it. This is certainly not a resolvable problem; rather, it is one to be struggled with—a continuing war of position within oneself. Questions of efficacy, personal ability, pragmatic possibility, and paths unexplored are always present. But within this range of ambiguous and sometimes guilty possibilities, it is important not to disempower those eager to confront life's diversities and critique its inequalities, regardless of what racial or sexual or ethnic or class or national position they come from. It is useless to flagellate oneself for not being more of a victim. Paralysis or loss of nerve is not the answer. So, too, inescapable history does not disempower us from productive attempts in the present. These attempts are invariably contextual—they are bequeathed by one's good and bad past choices, training, temperament, age, opportunity, and, of course, relative disempowerment. Given this diversity, there is neither a litmus test nor a safe justification for any personal position. But neither is this an excuse for copping out or failing to work as hard and as progressively as one can. This presumes some grounding values. The goal, as I see it, is to appreciate diversity and critique inequality. These goals potentiate rather than preclude the dedication to objectivism as a tool of analysis. Ethnography is subversive because it provides the hard sharpening stone of empiricism through which our concepts are refined, our values engaged, and our unadmitted assumptions brought to light.

conclusions
and criticisms

Why are genealogies of the present important, and why are critically humanist sensibilities valuable? During a period of theoretical flux and radical questioning, it can be useful for a field such as cultural anthropology to examine its recent past and its larger trajectory. Current directions often proliferate as permutations on general themes. But in the push for individual distinction within established traditions and newer additions, the larger impetus of the field can get neglected. In current theoretical and ethnographic developments as well as received historical ones, the valorization of subjective diversity and the critique of inequality and disempowerment remain important for cultural anthropology. The complementary relationship between these basic strains has been herein configured as parts of a critically humanist perspective.

Critically humanist sensibilities project these twin foci both as goals and as points of orientation for appraising a range of recent approaches. These include various permutations upon postmodernism, practice theories, Foucauldian analysis, post-Marxist perspectives, and selected dimensions of cultural studies, gendered ethnography, post-positivist feminism, and multiculturalism. All of these developments are complexly intertwined, but there is heuristic value in considering them as mutually stimulating directions that resonate in different ways with basic groundings of contemporary cultural anthropology. Genealogical configurations acknowledge that ties between the present and the past—in this case, the present and past of cultural anthropology—are constructions rather than givens and that they are plural rather than singular. But they may house enduring suppositions.

Critically humanist sensibilities do not assume that the appreciation of cultural diversity or the exposure and critique of inequality progresses toward purer truth or higher virtue; the present story of cultural anthropology does not presume ever-ascending progress on a singular scale of improvement. The shapes of diversity and of disempowerment change over time, as does our perspective for viewing them. These complementary concerns provide ethical and pragmatic foundations rather than epistemological ones. Thus released, however, they provide a practical continuity of value and rigor in the ongoing spins of our disciplinary spiral. They embrace the need for objectivity even as they acknowledge the value of a perspectival relativity and relinquish the goal of ultimate truth. The point here is not that there are no defensible standards of greater and lesser objectivity, but rather that the world—and our perception of it—is both more diverse and more quickly changing than our ability to discern its complex causations. Because our point of reference is always the altered context of the emergent present, each current moment has its own unique position as well as its own unique world of current realities to view—to appreciate in their diversity and to critique in their inequality. This shiftiness of reference points and objects, so difficult from a pure scientific perspective, is also a rich opportunity to find new insights about new phenomena from newly constituted vantage points. The value of this endeavor is not abstract or absolute; it can remain both ethically and empirically grounded. This grounding makes cultural anthropology productive, enriching, and scholarly rather than cynical, depressive, or superficial.

None of this suggests compromise when it comes to ethnographic substance, academic rigor, or empirical commitment. A critically humanist perspective upholds painstaking documentation, careful analysis, critical debate, and trenchant understanding. But it also acknowledges that understandings are multiple and that the ultimate purpose and goal of learning cannot be justified on external or objectivist grounds. Value in cultural anthropology rests in the process itself—of vigorously exploring cultural diversity and critically evaluating inequality at each new point in time and space. Critically humanist sensibilities strive to be as objective as possible in their means even as they relinquish the holy grail of objectivism as an ultimate purpose. This makes cultural anthropology a "calling" in a Weberian sense—replete with all the internal contradictions and ultimate inexplicability of motive that this implies. But truth be told (and as Weber emphasized), suppositions of value that are ultimately nonrational underlie academic callings in general. Pure science is arguably no exception.

Directed reflexively, a critically humanist perspective encourages us to explore how our own intellectual genealogies have comprehended or failed to comprehend cultural diversity and inequality or domination. As such, focal debates within contemporary cultural anthropology are centrally engaged. Sometimes, however, these debates appear to be pulling the field apart. Competing approaches and cross-disciplinary influences can appear to proliferate in a sea of chaos. It is particularly at such times that it can be useful to emphasize larger trends of value through which current tendencies appear as distinct and important permutations. A critically humanist perspective identifies basic axes that orient genealogical engagements and give perspective on their individual strengths, weaknesses, and potentials for refinement. Though doomed to fail in any absolute sense, the attempt to identify and evaluate recent genealogies through a common perspective can have pedagogical utility. It provides students and scholars some basic and important reference points as they negotiate a maze of recent developments. It also gives us perspective on the relationship between short-term trends and longer trajectories in our field. Finally, it may provide a convenient target for criticism: a stimulus for better models and for more insightful views of cultural anthropology's recent developments and future directions.

Critical Summations

It is useful here to summarize how the major approaches considered in previous chapters relate to critically humanist goals. The issue is not so much whether a given perspective trumpets a topical concern with issues of cultural diversity, on the one hand, or advertises a critique of disempowerment, on the other. It is rather the analytic strength and empirical nuance of articulation between these strands that is at issue.

Postmodern views have greatly increased cultural anthropology's understanding and appreciation of subjective diversity. This diversity is no longer limited to the relativity of others' cultures. Indeed, postmodern perspectives are often strongest in exploring our own subjectivities; they expose diverse pitfalls and possibilities in our own representations. On the other hand, the postmodern impetus, especially in its purer forms, lacks both an empirical basis to expose inequality and an effective theory to critique it. Like its existential predecessors, postmodernism's self-absorption easily leads to asocial textualization and egotistical aestheticism. In and of themselves, postmodern irony and comic detachment lead to apathy rather than to documentation or critical theorization. They flirt with the excesses of a will to discursive power adopted for its own sake and underscore the need for grounding in empiricism, on the one hand, and ethics, on the other.

Cultural anthropology, however, is weathering such excesses. This is in part because a critique of inequality—however ungrounded, contradictory, or implicit—has continued to inform many of the rhetorical and reflexive experiments of cultural anthropology during the 1980s and early 1990s. This uneasy bedfellowship—between postmodern sensibilities and critiques of inequality—continues to expand. Thankfully, anthropology's postmodern legacy is increasingly that of critical theorists such as David Harvey rather than that of Jean Baudrillard.

These trends can be seen against interdisciplinary directions that can tempt us to go in the opposite direction. Initially, cultural studies and postcolonial studies were strongly grounded in critical theory from Gramscian and post-Marxist legacies and were mindful of ethnographic or historical detail—for instance, at the Birmingham Centre for Contemporary Cultural Studies in England, as influenced by Stuart Hall, and in Indian subaltern studies, as influenced by Ranajit Guha. By the early 1990s, however, cultural and postcolonial studies have been increasingly internationalized and Americanized. In the process, they have become susceptible to postmodern excesses if not themselves postmodernized. These more recent developments combine strong critical inclinations with hyperrelativized forms of representation that undercut their ability to document or refine their arguments in a socially and empirically meaningful way. These are the present weaknesses of cultural studies and postcolonial studies. In contrast, cultural anthropology has begun to substantialize its critiques of representation over this same period—both analytically, with increasing commitment to critical theory, and empirically, with commitment to ethnography.

Notwithstanding their contemporary difficulties, however, cultural studies and postcolonial studies remain highly important for cultural anthropology. They continue to cross-pollinate critical sensibilities across a wide range of humanities fields and open anthropology (as well as other fields) to fresh authorships from a variety of foreign, minority, and other subaltern perspectives. The task for critically humanist sensibilities in cultural anthropology is to actively encourage and reflexively absorb this probing of subjective diversity without thereby compromising our commitment to rigorous ethnography, sustained documentation, and sophisticated critical theory.

In contrast to postmodern elaborations, practice theories and Foucauldian perspectives confront inequality more directly. Domination and power are shown to inform our deepest presumptions of habit, on the one hand, and knowledge, on the other. Reciprocally, however, Bourdieu's work and the early and midcareer studies of Foucault have been relatively thin in their analysis of cultural and subjective diversity. In this respect, their work has been ripe for engagement by ethnography and its accompanying theory. This is illustrated in the current emphasis in the United States on the theoretical and empirical interface among culture-power-history. Failing such engagement with cultural and historical specifics, brilliant general theorizations about epistemic and symbolic power remain only loosely articulated to local and global complexities of inequality and domination. They also tend to neglect domination based on gendered, racial, religious, ethnic, or national inequality. Bourdieu's concepts of symbolic capital, habitus, doxa, hexis, and so on do provide a major and enduring contribution to the understanding of disempowerment and the relationship between subjective and economic forms of domination. But ethnographic studies underscore that practice is more complex than Bourdieu's theory allows; more than reflexes of domination or distinction, practice can also be a conduit for creativity, resistance, and change. Bourdieu's general theory of how dominance and subordination are internalized and perpetuated can be improved upon by confronting greater cultural and historical diversity, including most basically a greater consideration of gendered, racial, religious, ethnic, and national inequalities. The hopeful possibility is for more refined studies of practices, subjectivities, and structural tensions across a fuller range of contemporary and historic variation.

In partial contrast to Bourdieu, Foucault's work has little aspiration to tease apart the implications of inequality for social or material relations; he is concerned primarily with the operation of power at the epistemic level. Within this realm, diversity and its relationship to power are explored in Foucault's case studies of eccentric or extreme resistance at the epistemic margins and, in a more nuanced way, in his late studies of subjectivation and technologies of the self in Greek and Greco-Roman antiquity. In topical terms, Foucault almost never moves outside a Western historical compass. But his work has provided a springboard in cultural anthropology for the epistemic critique of Western imperialism and colonialism as well as the general will to knowledge in the human sciences. The part of Foucault's legacy that is less explored in cultural anthropology—and greatly in need of exploration—is how indigenous forms of knowledge have reached out with their own brands of power and subjectivation to engage those intruding from outside. The relationship of subjectivity to power can be productively documented and analyzed across a world of late modern variation, not excluding more refined consideration of Western genres of writing and representation. In all these respects, Foucauldian insights on epistemic power can be productively complemented in cultural anthropology by greater and more nuanced attention to cultural and historical detail.

In American cultural anthropology, considerations of epistemic power and those of practice are productively intertwining. Recent ethnographic insights complicate Foucault's notions of epistemic continuity and schism as well as Bourdieu's set-piece assumptions about symbolic and economic capital. Practice and knowledge are increasingly seen as highly variable fulcrums that connect existing patterns of domination with emergent properties of and potentials for agency. In the United States, a new generation of scholars are refracting and reflecting upon this relationship in important ways. As this salutary trend continues in cultural anthropology, it needs to deepen rather than slacken its commitment to ethnographic and historical rigor. This commitment is especially important as the legacies of practice and epistemic critique engage the more reflexive concerns of contemporary cultural and postcolonial studies. As mentioned earlier, the latter are often weak when it comes to systematically documenting cultural diversity, on the one hand, and substantively theorizing inequality, on the other. From a critically humanist vantage point, the hope is that a growing sensitivity to representational diversity will be informed by a growing depth of both ethnographic commitment and critical theory.

The respective contributions of Gramsci and Bakhtin are particularly helpful in this regard. Each is analytically sensitive to (and in his own way, rigorous about) the relationship between domination and subjective diversity. Gramsci's post-Marxism stresses cultural variability as both a historical condition and a tactic of positioning and resistance. Even as his critique of class domination provides the iron thread that runs through his political analyses, Gramsci's appreciation of cultural, historical, and linguistic specifics is theoretically important and nuanced. Gramsci remained limited in scope to a largely European purview. The point is not that he did or did not develop non-Western appreciations, but that variability in collective representation is key to Gramsci's conceptualization of counterhegemony and resistance. However, Gramsci continues to see cultural variation primarily through the lens of class domination or the struggle against it; he is less inclined to complement his critique with moments that appreciate subjective diversity in and of itself.

From a critically humanist vantage point, Bakhtin is a wonderful complement to Gramsci. Bakhtin's perspective is galvanized by his analysis of expressive diversity, including his emphasis on heteroglossia, pluralities of voicing and speech genres, and the cultural and historical distinctiveness of different chronotopes. Though presented primarily through European and Russian literary analyses, Bakhtin exhibits a nuanced sensitivity to subjective diversity on both individual and collective levels. Far from being aesthetically sealed, Bakhtin's larger theory casts subjective diversity as a creative and irrepressible centrifugal force— the resistance of dialogue against monologue and discursive suppression. This motivates Bakhtin's perspective with a critique of authoritarianism and domination that is linguistically concrete at the same time that it is socially and politically implicit. Creativity flowers through dialogue and interpersonal experience across and against autocracy; the communication that forms the basis for social being is also the human root for resilience and resistance in the face of domination. From a critically humanist perspective, the critique of inequality that is implicit in Bakhtin becomes explicit in Gramsci; conversely, the aestheticism of progressive diversity implicit in Gramsci comes to fruition in Bakhtin. Their strengths complement each other.

Predominant views of Gramsci and Bakhtin in fields such as cultural anthropology both reflect and exaggerate their differences. Gramsci has often been taken as the preeminent theorist of late modern Marxism, first by cultural studies and subaltern studies in the late 1970s and early 1980s, and then by many cultural anthropologists interested in culture and power in the late 1980s and early 1990s. Bakhtin, on the other hand, has been seen as most influential for the aesthetic or interpretive rather than the political-economic dimensions of anthropology; his work has become crucial for consideration of poetics, the ethnography of communication, and textual and intertextual analysis. As illustrated in chapter 6, the dialogic connection between Bakhtin and Gramsci reveals the value of articulating their perspectives. This is a productive way to help mediate the divide that still lingers in cultural anthropology between textual, interpretative, or literary concerns and the critical analysis of political economy.

The reciprocal relationship between Bakhtinian and Gramscian approaches also articulates with considerations of habitual practice and epistemic power. An attraction of this combination for the present moment in cultural anthropology is its open space (amid scintillating general insights) for concrete ethnographic engagement, analytic refinement, and theoretical innovation.

New incarnations of gender in early 1990s ethnography illustrate some of the ways in which cultural anthropologists are engaging these potentials and difficulties. A corpus of recent ethnographies are inflected by gender-related critiques; they combine nuanced appreciation of women's voices with strong and yet flexible consideration of gendered inequity. In the process, ethnographic sensitivities are linked to larger issues of subjectivity and representation and to other axes of domination, including class, age, ethnicity, race, nationality, and sexual orientation. In a sense, this work mediates between the classic concerns of female status in anthropology—which were considered especially in economic and symbolic terms during the 1970s and 1980s—and newer developments in postmodern feminism and queer theory. The latter perspectives open wider and more provocative theoretical views on sexuality and gender. But in contrast to these latter approaches, which come largely from humanities fields and consider texts in and of themselves, recent directions in gendered ethnography are enriched by the salutary commitment to carefully observe and document the lived experiences and expressions of common people. In the process, they are highly sensitive to alternative dimensions of power and domination that locally reinforce or cross-cut those of gender and sexuality. If there is a complement needed to current trends in gendered ethnography (which present only one movement among several, even within feminist anthropology), it is perhaps a greater linkage from locally gendered processes to larger political-economic developments. This connection can be encouraged by more explicit and explicitly critical theorization. A number of works on gender and power appear to be moving in this direction—for instance, in studies that articulate an understanding of gendered experience with consideration of domesticity versus wage labor and emerging patterns of consumption amid changing values of late modern acquisition.

Multicultural concerns provide ballast and grounding for the reflexive side of cultural anthropology and bring us back to our practices within the academy; the values of theories come home to roost. Multiculturalism harbors an undeniable tension; it both ameliorates stigmatizing differences through dialogue and exacerbates them through moments of essential resistance. The question is thus a pragmatic one: how to negotiate this opposition productively in specific cases to maximize both the larger critique of disempowerment and the larger appreciation of cultural and subjective diversity. This requires an ongoing war of position that struggles to critique and combat diverse forms of inequality even as it attempts to avoid essentialism and promote diversity. In a critically humanist perspective, the tension between these competing goals is a self-directed corollary of the relation between valorizing diversity and exposing inequity. In both instances, the conflict between alternatives cannot be simply resolved or transcended.

Within the academy, wars of position need to work against categories that reinforce stigmatizing difference. This does not mean refusing strategic polarizations so much as using them very selectively to promote rather than compromise alternative tactics that are less essentializing. It remains vital to critique and combat disempowerment, even as strategies that reinforce these divisions are also critiqued as problematic. The larger objective is to mediate a continuing respect for diversity with a war of position against the full range of inequalities. This goal is pursued in a contextually dependent manner that is responsive to particular circumstances and the tactics that prove most effective in the situation at hand. That we want the university to reflect the highest standards of academic sophistication and scholarship becomes a contradiction only when we view the struggle against disempowerment as mutually exclusive with larger processes of education, intellectual cultivation, and support.

LIKE DISCOURSE GENERALLY, FIELDS SUCH AS CULTURAL ANTHROPOLOGY house a dynamic tension between centripetal moments that assert coherence and centrifugal ones that break out in creative dispersement. This book charts but does not restrict or mute this dynamic; rather, it projects common themes that can be played off or counteracted by a range of voices. We need to encourage rather than dampen a fuller consideration of diverse authorships and interpretations. In the process, cultural anthropology can combine its more venerable ancestries with newer ones to gain purchase on contemporary circumstances and future possibilities. In a far-flung field such as cultural anthropology, there is always a problem of being too disciplined or, just as frequently, not disciplined enough. If the critically humanist perspective of this book appears as too limited or constraining, it is balanced by many trends in the field that are currently much less so.

Against the potentials for articulating moments of greater and lesser coherence in cultural anthropology are at least three dangers. The first, as discussed at the end of chapter 1, is a retreat into neoempiricism. Even as it has often provided an important counterbalance against theoretical excesses, the valorization of anthropology through empirical particularism poses its own difficulties. These difficulties do go away as the privileged units of academic meaning shift from culture traits or other units of objective data to the presentation of disempowered voices or personal experiences. In either case, particularism based on a presumably authentic unit of analysis begs larger and more explicit justification. The attempt to avoid or circumvent this justification leads to the second and third dangers, which are reciprocals of one another. One of these is the postmodern politics of refusal, which rarefies analysis and disconnects it needlessly from both ethnographic depiction and systematic analysis. The other is uncritical positivism, that is, a reliance on objectivist assumptions in the absence of a critical and historical understanding of the categories of knowledge upon which this objectivism is based.

As opposed to these excesses—and steering between them—critically humanist sensibilities attempt to maintain an ongoing balance between moments of objectivism and those of relativity, and between moments of empiricism and those of a larger theoretical and ethical justification.

As for directions, it seems clear that cultural anthropologists will continue to draw on permutations of cultural diversity—now expanded to a broader range of subjective diversities among others and among ourselves. So too we will expand our exposure and refine our critiques of inequalities through a range of critical theorizations of domination, power, and resistance. There may be less value in trying to forecast (much less direct) these strands than to use their relationship to point from the past with renewed commitment and clarity through the present. Critically humanist perspectives are perpetual works in progress—projects without guarantees. Combining a belief and a wish, it is probably unanswerable whether they or other assessments of intellectual direction can separate the external state of the art from the internal state of the heart.

Auto-critique as Epilogue
Beyond Cataclysm

I have realized from the inception of this work that it can attract many criticisms. It cultivates humanist sensibilities, albeit critically, to evaluate developments that are in significant measure antihumanist. It appears to criticize postmodern perspectives when they come in a purer white form, yet seems to tolerate them when they come in alternative colors or genders. It flags but does not grapple fully with the political and economic processes that can be central in the substantive analyses it calls for. The same could be argued, from a different perspective, for issues in public culture and related matters of aesthetics, language, or textual representation.

Reservations may also apply to my treatment of anthropology's theoretical history. Is the treatment anticanonical, or does it historicize the past only to solidify a new set of heroes or a new kind of canon? Is the claim to appreciate diversity itself undercut by a tendency to reify and essentialize theoretical approaches? Even as a heuristic device, the delineation of "isms"—much less large-scale trends in a thing called "cultural anthropology"—may be seen as suspect. And whether the plethora of citations and references refines or blurs the scope of the argument could be raised as an open question.

Finally, concerning ethics and politics, can there really be an organic connection between anthropology's past and the cultural contestations of the present? The inclusion of ethics may be timely, but what other ethical concerns are left out or collapsed by the focus on human diversity, on the one hand, and inequality or domination, on the other? Though the presentation asserts and illustrates the valorization of diversity and the critical exposure of inequality, it does less to circumscribe these categories or define their internal components. On the less academic and more practical side, is critical humanism committed to social and political action, or is this merely an *idea* of contestation in the absence of practice? Even if the intrinsic connection between cultural assertion and political process renders this last question moot, does this link support or undercut ethnography as cultural anthropology's base?

The typical answer to such queries is to claim that the work is intended more to raise questions than provide answers. Though true in part, such an answer would also be elusive. Using critically humanist sensibilities, this book does propose excesses to avoid and issues and values to emphasize in confronting ethics, theory, and ethnography in contemporary cultural anthropology. The long-standing goals of appreciating cultural diversity and exposing and critiquing inequality and domination are not presented here as a rigid system, but they do provide general parameters for orientation and guidance, including for students. Given the degree of ambivalence and self-questioning in cultural anthropology in recent years, there is arguably now a need for reasserting basic concerns and assessing their general relationship to theoretical innovations and ethnographic commitments. Larger orientations can be useful to think with when one becomes empirically entangled, theoretically confused, or ethically uncertain. These difficulties have become a significant problem for cultural anthropology.

A work that praises open contextuality and yet develops a "critically humanist perspective" may seem to work against itself. This tension is sharpened when a cry for more rigorous ethnography is embraced along with a concern with hybridity, dialogue, and wars of position. But the point is to pursue a perspective that is self-challenging without being self-destructive. Keeping alternate approaches or perspectives in dialogue— as complementary moments of analysis—can stimulate rather than debilitate an important diversity of theoretical and ethnographic engagements. The notion that we must choose between empirical substance and cutting-edge sensitivities is itself a false dichotomy that limits the growth and creativity of cultural anthropology.

Notwithstanding the received connotations of "humanism" per se, critically humanist sensibilities encourage reflexivity and epistemic criticisms. As a key moment of internal critique, interrogation of assumptions and biases is part of their core. Accordingly, critical humanism is not a totalizing approach or a master narrative. At the same time, its perspective does not eschew or avoid complementary notions that bracket relativity and make objectivist attributions, analytic assessments, and historical generalizations. As such, a critically humanist perspective emerges as a hybrid of modern and postmodern sensibilities. Of course, maybe this divide is unbridgeable and such a hybrid isn't possible. If so, this book is compromised. But on the other hand, maybe this antithesis, like so many others, is only a logical rather than a practical difficulty. Maybe its seeming impossibility will itself seem, in due course, to be an outmoded antinomy.

One purpose of this work has been to critically evaluate selected directions in anthropology's present without giving up the attempt to assert their larger direction. This goes against the grain of much current (anti)theorizing. But it will be enough if this work is shot down productively as a target—if it provides a sharpening stone or stimulus for better views and practices. We should not shy from moments of larger perspective and direction, even as we remain opposed to totalism or heroism. Theoretical genealogies cannot be put in perspective without some broader terms and portrayals. If one hopes to get a larger view, generalization comes with the territory.

Generalization is not intrinsically bad; it only becomes essentialist when it harbors a stigmatizing edge that is pernicious or excessive in its evaluations. The point is not to avoid generalizations but to use them heuristically—not to pretend that they mirror the complexity of underlying variations. This does not preclude refinement but rather begs for it by way of detailed, smaller-scale studies. As I tried to illustrate in several chapters, ethnographic, historical, and analytic nuance can increase as the scale of generality decreases. One way to lessen the distance between the general and the particular in the history of our own scholarship is to give specific citations in notes and references. Alluding to particular arguments without digressing or diluting one's main thrust has strengths as well as weaknesses, including a bibliography for readers who may not be familiar with details across diverse fields. In my view, this is preferable to the tendency—so frustrating and common—of alluding but vaguely to authors and approaches. Too often in academics, the taken-for-granted masks a habitus of discursive pretension. This is not a service to either our students or ourselves.

In terms of topical scope, it has been not possible—nor intended—to give equal attention to all the approaches mentioned. Given the constraints of my own training and time, many developments in cultural anthropology have been underplayed or only pointed at. Both the aesthetic and the political-economic articulations of my analysis could be extended. My purpose has been to identify core dynamics that have broad relevance in cultural anthropology rather than reviewing or charting the field's constituent parts.

Concerning my differing opinions about vanilla and other flavored versions of postmodernism, the point is a simple one: Not all refractions of the postmodern impetus are equally deserving of continuation or expansion. Postmodern feminism, postcolonial studies, black studies, and the multiculturalism of cultural studies all carry a political grounding and a concern with inequality that postmodernism in its purer forms has lacked. Many of these approaches imply a greater respect for diversity—their own as well as others—than was evident in postmodern precursors. At the same time, this does not reduce my hesitation about the textualism, rarefaction, and disconnection from documentation and lived experience that these perspectives can all be heir to, nor my reservation about their capacity to privilege some forms of inequality (such as race or sex) over others (such as class background) that may be equally important in both the academy and in fieldwork.

Issues that surround the relationship of ethics to personal practice are particularly complex. To the degree that theorizing and writing and speaking and teaching *are* practice—pedagogical practice—their ethics have an intrinsic practical edge. The university is itself a realm of practical action. It remains an influential place, and its politics both matter and engage the world outside itself. These connections are facilitated rather than blunted by providing pedagogical training that appreciatively documents cultural diversity and exposes the unfairness of diverse inequalities. Whether the movement from thought to action in teaching and research or academic politics is genuine or merely metaphoric will probably always remain an open question. But given this ongoing debate, it is better to move ahead practically in our everyday actions—regardless of how they are defined—than to get snagged on the semantics of what is an "authentic" versus a "spurious" connection between ideas and practice. The same is true, on a larger scale, concerning our sense of cultural diversity and inequality in general. This book presumes that these referents carry basic and widespread meaning in cultural anthropology. Given this, I have chosen to explore their relationship through a range of examples rather than building a conceptual edifice that circumscribes rigid definitions or subcategories of "diversity" and "inequality."

The ways that concepts become useful remind us again of fieldwork, which remains one of the most engaged ways to live with human diversity and confront inequity. For cultural anthropology, the lived experience of fieldwork remains the grounding point and the catalyst for teaching and theorizing. This book has tried to engage ethnographic specifics with a range of approaches that resonate with recent theoretical innovations and with critically humanist sensibilities. As I hope I have shown, these sensibilities resonate with older as well as newer genealogies of anthropology's past. In all likelihood, they will continue to prove relevant in the future.

Major questions always remain. Like culture, cultural anthropology is a conversation, more or less contested, between different views. Some of the best parts of this conversation come from its dialogue between moments that appreciate cultural diversity and those that critique inequality and domination. The present work is not a mandate so much as an encouragement and a target for criticism from such critical discourse. As one voice in a dialogue, it welcomes others.

notes

Chapter 1 Stories, Histories, and Theories

1. Contrast Ortner 1984; see a recent overview collection edited by Borofsky (1994). Earlier attempts to review the field include Diamond 1980; Voget 1975; Harris 1968; Tax 1964; Kroeber 1953; and Lowie 1937; cf. Stocking 1989b.
2. Concerning modernism and modernist anthropology, see Berman 1994; Manganaro 1990.
3. Direct wars included the U. S. invasion of Grenada and the British reconquest of the Falkland Islands. By contrast, high-casualty wars typically involved superpower backing but, in the aftermath of Vietnam, were careful not to take Western lives; warfare was facilitated between Third World peoples themselves.
4. See Marcus and Fischer 1986; Clifford and Marcus 1986; Clifford 1988; Rabinow 1985, 1986; cf. Geertz 1983; Fabian, 1983.
5. This emphasis may be contrasted to the more encyclopedic cast of anthropological influences collected in Voget's *History of Ethnology* (1975), which nonetheless retains a large photo of Boas as its frontispiece. Eggan's ancestry of "One Hundred Years of Ethnology and Social Anthropology" (1968) is somewhat intermediate between Voget and Lowie in emphasizing the schools of anthropology's institutional founders. As is the case for Lowie, Eggan mentions neither Marx nor Weber in his account.
6. Freud was particularly important in programs emphasizing psychological anthropology; see also previous note.
7. Concerning Herder's use of *Kultur*, see Young 1995a:ch. 2; Meyer 1963; Kroeber and Kluckhohn 1952; cf. Berlin 1976.
8. Williams traced this usage to the general influence of the so-called

Germano-Coleridgian school in England and its influence on the early work of John Stuart Mill. Though the word *culture* was not used in the plural, it was employed in a highly pluralizing sense that connoted relative value.

> Human nature had exhibited many of its noblest manifestations, not in Christian counties only, but in the ancient world, in Athens, Sparta, Rome; nay, even barbarians, as the Germans, or still more unmitigated savages, the wild Indians, and again the Chinese, the Egyptians, the Arabs, all had their own education, their own culture; a culture which whatever might be its tendency upon the whole, had been successful in some respect or other. Every form of polity, every condition of society, whatever else it had done, had formed its type of national character. (Mill 1962:132; quoted in Williams 1958:60)

As Williams puts it:

> The social idea of Culture, now introduced into English thinking, meant that an idea had been formulated which expressed value in terms independent of "civilization," and hence, in a period of radical change, in terms independent of the progress of society. (Williams 1958:63)

It is ironic that Mill's notions, like those of Victorian anthropology, later evolved into a totalizing notion of culture. As Stocking (1987:41) suggests, the "Germano-Coleridgian impulse" was ultimately "domesticated to the dominant English utilitarian tradition." Williams (1958:68–70) likewise contrasts the more holistic impetus of Coleridge to the totalizing rationalism that was prominent in Mill's later and more influential works.

9. See especially Herder 1966, 1968, 1969; Dilthey 1954, 1976; Berlin 1976; Barnard 1965; Makkreel 1975.

10. Indeed, the study of material culture and prehistory is preeminent in works such as Penniman's *A Hundred Years of Anthropology* (1952). In many of the scholarly institutes of eastern and southern Europe and Asia, "anthropology" is still considered in large part to be the study of physical and material human history.

11. See historical overviews in Kuper 1983; Stocking 1984; Kuklick 1991; Urry 1993; Goody 1995.

12. After World War II, Lévi-Strauss stayed in the United States as a French cultural attaché before returning to France (Leach 1970:xi).

13. For instance, see Penniman 1952; Brew 1968; Harris 1968; Bohannan and Glazer 1988; cf. Stocking 1987.

14. In contrast to Morgan's scheme, the band-tribe-chiefdom-state model was multilinear; it admitted individual paths of development that were diverse and historically specific.

15. Wolf, for instance, led teach-ins at Michigan and published papers such as

"Introduction to the National Teach-In" (1967), "American Intellectuals Against the Viet Nam War" (published in French in *Les Temps Modernes*, 1965), and devoted a chapter and the political context of his famous book *Peasant Wars of the Twentieth Century* to a historical analysis of the suppression of peasant uprisings in Vietnam. The book ends by declaring, "The peasantry confronts tragedy, but hope is on its side; doubly tragic are their adversaries who would deny that hope to both peasantry and to themselves. This also is America's dilemma in the world today: to act in aid of human hope or crush it, not only for the world's sake but for her own" (Wolf 1969:301–302).

16. See, for instance, Polanyi 1963, 1971; Thompson 1963, 1978; Williams 1977; Anderson 1976, 1984; Bloch 1975, 1983.

17. For instance, see Althusser and Balibar 1970; Rey 1973; Terray 1972; Godelier 1977; Meillassoux 1981.

18. For instance, see Wolf 1959, 1964, 1966, 1969, 1982.

19. See, for instance, Wolf 1959, 1969, 1982; Worsley 1968, 1984; Wallerstein 1979, 1980, 1989; see Schneider and Rapp 1995; cf. Braudel 1973.

20. Marx read Morgan's work, drew heavily upon his ideas in his last studies, and sent some of his own writings to Morgan in return—even though the American apparently never responded.

21. This growth, and its theoretical corollaries, pertains especially to American anthropology. British anthropology, by contrast, was subject to retrenchment and uncertainty during the 1970s (Kuper 1983:ch. 8). Many of the most promising British anthropologists came to the United States, either temporarily or permanently, during this period.

22. By 1994, Giddens's 1971 summary on Marx, Durkheim, and Weber had sold a remarkable 100,000 copies.

23. This was reflected in the interests of my doctoral committee members in social structural, materialist, symbolic, and Marxist approaches—as per Raymond Kelly, Roy Rappaport, Sherry Ortner, and Aram Yengoyan. Through Sherry Ortner, I was also strongly exposed to the initial American interest in Bourdieu, Giddens, and theories of practice.

24. For instance, see crtiques by Sangren 1988; Polier and Roseberry 1989; Birth 1990; cf. Spiro 1986.

25. See, for instance, journals such as *Critical Inquiry, Cultural Critique, Cultural Studies, New Formations, Social Text, Third Text, Diaspora, Identities, Diacritics, Transitions, Differences,* and *Representations,* as well as *Public Culture, Cultural Anthropology,* and more recently (some would argue) *American Anthropologist* itself.

26. See an effective critique of recent developments in the Annales school by Dosse (1994; cf. Nora 1989). Macrohistory trends in the Annales school are illustrated by the work of Braudel (1973), which strongly influenced Immanuel Wallerstein, world systems theory, and the large-scale approach to political economy developed by anthropologists such as Eric Wolf

(1982), the more critical theorizations of Peter Worsley (1984), and the structural history of Marshall Sahlins (1981, 1985). Microhistory and the "history of mentalities" is illustrated in the Annales school by authors such as Emmanuel Le Roy Ladurie (e.g., 1973, 1979, 1987) and in Italian history by the influential work of Carlo Ginzberg (e.g., 1980, 1989, 1993). For a concise overview of the Annales school, see especially Burke (1990).

27. Geertz has predicted that anthropology will no longer exist in fifty years or so (quoted in Handler 1991: 612). Sahlins's evaluation of cultural anthropology's current state (e.g., 1993a, 1993b) leads him to assess that the field is "in the twilight of its career" (1995:14). Wolf castigates the discipline's proliferations ("They Divide and Subdivide, and Call it Anthropology," 1980), and suggests that there is a "general retreatism in anthropology" (quoted in Friedman 1987:116). Though such discontents are not unmitigated, they reflect widely shared opinions.

Chapter 2 Critically Humanist Sensibilities

1. See Bourdieu 1988a, 1990c; cf. Kuper 1988; Stocking 1987.
2. This point was made by Stocking (1968:199).
3. Elias (1978) traces the divergence between French emphasis on "civilization" and Germanic emphasis on *Kultur* to national differences in the seventeenth and eighteenth centuries. French nationalism cohered aristocratic, bourgeois, and intellectual interests, whereas the lack of German political integration resonated with splintered opposition between aristocratic sensibilities, on the one hand, and intellectualist, bourgeois, and middle-class perspectives, on the other. The latter tended to regard upper-class styles as effete and removed from the experience of common life. These differences paralleled the Germanic emphasis on *Kultur* as a valued if not romanticized attribute of the common folk, in contrast to the French (and English) valorization of "civilization" or "society" as the epitome of rational cultivation and refinement. Meyer (1963) has provided an etymological account of *Kultur* in Germanic history; its larger intellectual parameters are sketched by Dumont (1994:chs. 1 and 2). The implications of *Kultur* for social theory are explored by Williams (1958) and considered in the contemporary theoretical context of hybridity and cultural difference by Young (1995a:ch. 2) and Pagden (1995).
4. Stocking (1992:97) later writes, "The political meaning of Boas' scientific life may be seen as a transvalued and dichotomized *Kulturkampf*: on the one hand, as a struggle to preserve the cultural conditions of the search for universal rational knowledge, and on the other, as a struggle to defend the validity of alternative cultural worlds."
5. See Williams 1958:ch. 3; Stocking 1987:36–41.

6. For the French humanistic context, see especially Todorov's (1993:383ff.) concluding analysis.

7. E.g., Bakhtin 1986b:110; see chapter 6 of this book.

8. See Stocking 1987; McGrane 1989; Hodgen 1964; Kuper 1988; Pagden 1986; cf. Fabian 1983, 1991.

9. Against this, overdetermination of key concepts at new stages of work can unduly reify them. Papering over broad notions with constituent concepts or categories can be deceptively simple and encourage premature deconstruction.

10. Each of these goals carries its own assumptions and problems, one of the greatest being whether its intended purpose is realistic or attainable. Anthropologists live within a world of larger structural constraints and powers; our limited abilities and training as professionals must be weighed against the unintended consequences that result when we attempt to engineer change. Good intentions do not ensure good results. However, this need not minimize the importance of pursuits that go beyond the purview of cultural anthropology as an academic field per se.

11. This disagreement pertains particularly to Durkheim's and Weber's relationship to the earlier work of Marx.

12. See Malinowski 1922; Geertz 1988; cf. Manganaro 1990.

Chapter 3 Pushing Anthropology Past the Posts

1. See influential works by Marcus and Fischer 1986, Clifford and Marcus 1986, Clifford 1988, and Taussig 1987, 1992.

2. See Bertens 1995; Dunning 1995; Docker 1994; Seidman 1994; cf. Berman 1994.

3. See Habermas 1981; cf. Bauman 1992, 1993.

4. Examples include Caton 1990; Comaroff and Comaroff 1991, 1992; Donham 1990; Hale 1994; Lomnitz-Adler 1992; Malkki 1995; Messick 1993; Ortner 1989; Povinelli 1993; Trouillot 1989, 1990; Verdery 1991; and Williams 1991, as well as many others

5. The contours of modernity are now generating a new round of interest; see A. Berman 1994; Bertens 1995; Touraine 1995; Miller 1994, 1995; cf. M. Berman 1982; Jameson 1991.

6. See Fiske 1987, 1989a, 1989b; Hebdige 1988; Bennett and Woollacott 1987; Urry 1990; Grossberg 1992; cf. Grossberg 1986; McRobbie 1991.

7. The connection between the American and the postmodern is not incidental. As Huyssen suggests, the European origin of many postmodern theorizations did not preclude their greater elaboration in the United States. Indeed, the term itself "accrued its emphatic connotations in the United States, not in Europe" (Huyssen 1986:190).

8. Among cultural anthropologists, Gramscian perceptions have been on the rise during the late 1980s and early 1990s. On occasion, the notion of

"culture" is itself replaced with the Gramscian notion of "hegemony" (e.g., Ortner 1990a; cf. Comaroff and Comaroff 1991:19–27). Gramscian sensitivities have informed important articles in journals such as *American Ethnologist*, which has provided a premier combination of ethnography and cultural theory in recent years. Important ethnographies have creatively applied Gramscian thought (e.g., Trouillot 1990; Hale 1994), and many others have drawn on it. As such, the current legacy of Gramsci in anthropology should not be collapsed into the trend to eschew substantive analysis in contemporary cultural studies.

9. Irigaray's flavor is captured in the book's opening, addressed to Nietzsche:

> And you had to lose sight of me so I could come back, toward you, with an other gaze.
>
> And, certainly, the most arduous thing has been to seal my lips, out of love. To close off this mouth that always sought to flow free.
>
> But, had I never held back, never would you have remembered that something exists which has a language other than your own. That, from her prison, someone was calling out to return to the air. That your words reasoned all the better because within them a voice was captive. Amplifying your speech with an endless resonance.
>
> I was your resonance.
>
> Drum. I was merely the drum in your own ear sending back to itself its own truth. (Irigaray 1991a:3)

10. Nietzsche claims that blacks are representatives of primitive man and are relatively impervious to pain (1969a:68). He suggests that Jewish priestly impotence and slave morality have insidiously crept into Western traditions and have presaged the despicable aspects of Christianity through "Jewish hatred—the profoundest and sublimest kind of hatred," which "has hitherto triumphed again and again over all other ideals, over all nobler ideals" (1969a:34f.). That Jewish *ressentiment* may be positively cultivated by Nietzsche in other passages does not alleviate his great disapproval of Jews. In many respects, Nietzsche's super-man evolutionism is worse than its late-nineteenth-century counterparts, critiqued in Kuper 1988 and meticulously documented in Stocking 1987. Cf. also Kuklick 1991 and McGrane 1989.

11. A crude index of this is evident in Hollingdale's broad sampler, *A Nietzsche Reader* (Nietzsche 1977); passages under the headings of "anti-nihilism," "will to power," and "superman" constitute forty-four pages with fifty-one sections, while those under "nihilism" comprise but eight pages of thirteen aphorisms.

12. See Weiner 1992, 1993; Mimica 1993; cf. Heidegger 1962, 1977a, 1977b, 1982. Major reanalyses of Heidegger outside anthropology include Hodge 1995; Rockmore 1995; Janicaud and Mattei 1995; Van Buren 1994; Kisiel and Van Buren 1994; Harries and Jamme 1994; Vogel 1994; Gadamer 1994; and Rosen 1993. Heidegger's ethics are a major focus in many of these works.

13. As a counter to the current resurgence of interest in Heidegger, Bourdieu

later published his study as a book, *The Political Ontology of Martin Heidegger* (1991b).

14. There is evidence that shifting siltation in areas where the pipe passes beneath the lower branches of the river system may expose the line to rupture by ships during the dry season, when rivers are low (Daniel Kennedy, pers. comm.).

15. The bill also makes it a criminal offense to give evidence challenging the constitutionality of the new law (*Post Courier* 1995a).

Chapter 4 Practices

1. See Bourdieu (1977, 1984, 1988a, 1990a, 1990b, 1990c, 1991a, 1993c; Bourdieu and Wacquant 1992); Giddens (1979a, 1981, 1984, 1985a, 1985b, 1987, 1989a, 1989b, 1990b, 1992, 1993, 1994, 1995); Ortner (1984, 1989, 1990a, 1990b; cf. 1973); and Sahlins (1981, 1983, 1985, 1990).

2. Ortner's reaction appears more tempered (e.g., Ortner 1991:164f.; Dirks, Eley, and Ortner 1994).

3. See Bryant and Jary 1991; Clark et. al. 1990; Held and Thompson 1989; cf. also Livesay 1989; Sewell 1993.

4. See Sahlins 1958, 1960, 1972, 1976, 1981, 1983, 1985, 1990, 1992, 1993b, 1995.

5. For a concise overview of the Annales school, see Burke 1990.

6. Ortner is now moving to the anthropology department at Columbia University.

7. In terms of relative chronology, 1972 was the year that Sahlins published *Stone Age Economics*, one year after Giddens's *Capitalism and Modern Social Theory*, and one year before Ortner's classic paper "Key Symbols."

8. Alexander (1995:199–202) highlights the changes between the French and English versions of *Outline of a Theory of Practice*. The former foregrounds Bourdieu's Kabyle ethnography and includes a stronger materialist cast, à la Althusser. By contrast, the English translation is written primarily as a theoretical treatise and pursues a stronger critique of both Marxist materialism and Lévi-Straussian structuralism.

9. An exception is Harker et al. 1990:8.

10. Bourdieu's major works on these topics are referenced in the bibliography.

11. Major books in English about Bourdieu's work include Calhoun et al. 1993; Harker et al. 1990; Jenkins 1992; and Robbins 1991. Major articles about Bourdieu from an anthropological perspective (in English) include Eickelman 1979; Foster 1986; Lamaison 1989; Marcus 1990 (cf. also Ortner 1984); and, from a sociological perspective, di Maggio 1979; Frow 1987; Garnham 1986; Garnham and Williams 1980; Gerhards and Anheier 1989; Honneth 1986; Honneth et al. 1986; and McCleary 1989.

12. Bourdieu is increasingly aware of this problem but tends to project it onto others:

I have never had much taste for "grand theory" and, when I read works which attempt to enter this category, I cannot keep myself from being irritated by their typically scholastic combination of false audacity and wisdom. (1992:249; translation by Knauft)

13. For instance, Bourdieu responded to criticism of his statistical usages in *Distinction* by complaining that audiences failed to appreciate his new numerical logic—a logic that he claims somehow transcended the objectivist strictures of mathematical probability. He writes, "Sometimes I feel like Manet who was criticized for not being 'capable' of understanding the laws of perspective!" (1984:22). In the absence of concrete evidence, such pretension to mathematical genius seems inflated.

14. Disciplinary divisions remain strong in French academia; French anthropology of the mid-1990s presents a distinct intellectual field typically opposed to critical French sociology. As became evident during a fellowship to the École des hautes études en sciences sociales in 1994, current foci of research interest in French anthropology include semi-complex and complex structures of kinship; material culture; myth and the sacred; subjectivity and Otherness; the relationship between French structuralism and psychoanalysis; and long-term and/or repeated ethnographic field research in remote world areas, especially in West Africa and Oceania. (See Héritier 1994; Godelier n.d. a, n.d. b; Godelier and Hassoun 1996; Lemonnier 1990, 1993; Balandier 1994; Descola 1994; Juillerat 1992, 1993; cf. Augé 1994.) Current directions in French anthropology are not well known in the United States. This is partly due to the time lag between French publications and English translations. But the ethnographic and theoretical focus of French anthropology often creates little demand from Anglo-American anthropologists for translation. It has been French critical theorists who are *not* anthropologists—Derrida, Lyotard, Foucault, de Certeau, Baudrillard, Lacan and others—who have had such a large impact in American cultural anthropology since the late 1970s. At least as of 1994, French *anthropologists* continued to be largely interested in more traditional ethnographic concerns. Many of them find it curious and amusing, if not retrograde, that American and English anthropologists accord such great importance—based on superficial understanding—to such a prickly group of 1970s French intellectuals from other fields who understand or sympathize little with anthropology's traditional concerns. For many French anthropologists, Lévi-Strauss remains the most towering intellectual figure. The task of extending and mediating structuralist perspectives—for instance, with material and psychoanalytic frameworks—remains highly compelling. It is thus important from an Anglo or American perspective not to confuse the distinctive legacy of French *anthropology* with that of other French fields.

Though some of the younger generation of American cultural anthropologists would find the current interests of French anthropology anomalous if not anachronistic, it would be shortsighted to underestimate the continuing *value* of this international difference, including for contemporary American perspectives on culture and representation. Many of the latter too easily minimize or castigate the importance of modernist theory. And in contrast to what many Americans might (mis)perceive, French anthropology maintains a rigorous and continuing dedication to ethnography in foreign lands. Despite lower levels of French research funding, this fieldwork impetus is in some respects stronger among French than American graduate students of anthropology.

15. De Certeau (1984:chs. 4, 5) stressed this point in an influential critique of Bourdieu.

16. The rigid and structured nature of practice for Bourdieu is epitomized in the English titling of his 1980 work *Le sens pratique* as *The Logic of Practice* (1990a).

17. Concerning hegemony as a key concept in contemporary anthropology, see Ortner 1990a, Comaroff and Comaroff 1991, 1992, and selected contributions to journals such as *American Ethnologist*. Notions of "imaginary" and "ethnoscape" are foregrounded in Appadurai 1990; Gupta and Ferguson 1992; and selected articles in *Cultural Anthropology* and *Public Culture*.

18. My own path of analysis here is likely influenced by my early exposure to practice theories from Ortner while a graduate student at the University of Michigan.

19. Different permutations on the culture-power-history nexus are foregrounded in anthropology-related graduate programs at the University of Michigan, the Johns Hopkins University, the City University of New York, Stanford University, the University of Chicago, various campuses of the University of California, and Washington University in St. Louis, among others. Though admitting of exceptions, many East Coast programs take a stronger political economy perspective on this triad, while many West Coast schools approach it with greater concern for reflexivity and representation. Midwest schools such as Michigan and Chicago tend to be intermediate in this regard.

20. See, for instance, Errington and Gewertz 1995; Foster 1995a, 1995b; Battaglia 1995; Polier 1994, n.d.; Robbins 1994, 1995.

21. See Keesing 1989, 1992; Jolly and Thomas 1992; Keesing and Tonkinson 1982; Foster 1995a; White and Lindstrom 1993; Feinberg and Zimmer-Tamakoshi 1995.

22. See Sullivan 1993; Kulick 1990; Kulick and Willson 1994; Gewertz and Errington 1991; Wardlow in press.

23. Insofar as global processes are compromised in their very realization, the local ramifications of this compromise dovetail with the diversification of culture even as the forces that connect this diversity generalize and inten-

sify (cf. Comaroff and Comaroff 1992:38; Friedman 1994; Sahlins 1985:143f.).

24. Indeed, it was startling to realize that in my own recent book on south coast New Guinea (Knauft 1993a), I was able to reference only two New Guinean authors—Billai Laba (1975a, 1975b) and Abraham Kuruwaip (1984)—out of 404 persons cited.

Chapter 5 Moments of Knowledge and Power

1. The *episteme* for Foucault is "the total set of relations that unite, at a given period, the discursive practices that give rise to epistemological figures, sciences, and possibly formalized systems. . . . The episteme is not a form of knowledge (*connaissance*) or type of rationality . . . ; it is the totality of relations that can be discovered . . . at the level of discursive regularities" (1980c:191).

2. Among many other works, see Marcus and Fischer 1986; Clifford and Marcus 1986; Clifford 1988; Taussig 1987; Rabinow 1985, 1986, cf. Rabinow 1977.

3. Rabinow's *Foucault Reader* (1984) is still the most widely used compendium of Foucault's readings in English, and *Michel Foucault* (Dreyfus and Rabinow 1983) has been a highly influential interpretation of Foucault's corpus.

4. A sample of recent volumes about Foucault might include Arac 1988; Barker 1993; Bernauer 1990; Burke 1992; Caputo and Yount 1993; Cook 1993; Eribon 1991; Macey 1993; Mahon 1992; May 1993; Miller 1993; Gutting 1994; Jones and Porter 1994; McNay 1994; Prado 1995; Visker 1995; Halperin 1995; and Simons 1995.

5. Austronesian-speaking groups such as Mekeo to the east lie outside this region. To the north, lowland but inland regions such as the Strickland-Bosavi area exhibit important cultural differences and are largely excluded from the present analysis (Knauft 1985b, 1993a:212).

6. See Alder 1922; Bevan 1890; Butcher 1964; Dupeyrat 1954; McFarlane 1888; Miller 1950; Pratt 1906; Strachan 1888. Savage imagery was often in the titles of monographs and scholarly travel accounts as well, including those by Beaver (1920), Haddon (1901–35), and Riley (1925).

7. Missionary accounts of native life along the New Guinea south coast include Butcher 1964; Chalmers 1887, 1895; Holmes 1924; McFarlane 1888; and Riley 1925; see Langmore 1989.

8. See Riley 1925:216; Chalmers 1903:109; Holmes 1924; cf. Langmore 1989:124ff.

9. See Hope 1979; Pratt 1906.

10. Even the capital harbor of Papua, Port Moresby, was not discovered until 1873 (Moresby 1876a; cf. Jukes 1847; D'Albertis 1880).

11. See Beaver 1920:40.

12. See Smith 1985; Bitterli 1989:ch. 7; Sahlins 1985; Borofsky and Howard 1989.

13. See Spencer and Gillen 1899; Durkheim 1912.

14. Early Melanesianists such as Haddon, Seligman, and the young Rivers asserted the slow evolution of precolonial Melanesia and attempted to reconstruct the diffusion of precolonial customs, beliefs, and material culture across the region. Missionaries, on the other hand, worked to advance Melanesians quickly through moral and social enlightenment. These were seen as two ends of a single continuum, and they were combined by missionary-ethnographers such as Robert Codrington (1891) and others.

15. Accounts by missionary and government officials that denounced the labor recruiters include Fison 1872–73; Miklouho-Maclay 1874, 1881; Moresby 1876b; Inglis 1872; Macdonald 1878; Markham 1873; Steel 1880; Palmer 1871; Paton 1907; Paton 1913. Traders were largely unlettered, and their rebuttals are less copious (Wawn 1893; Rannie 1912). Secondary accounts of the nineteenth-century Melanesian labor trade include Docker 1970; Corris 1968, 1973; Scarr 1967; Drost 1938; Dunbabin 1935; McKinnon 1975; see a recent reinterpretation, Shlomowitz 1993.

16. See Griffin et al. 1979:chs. 2, 3; Parnaby 1964:ch. 6; Morrell 1960:chs. 7, 9, 13; West 1968; Murray 1912.

17. See Knauft 1993a:ch. 2; McLaren 1923; Pratt 1906. In the eastern parts of Papua, gold was discovered, prospectors poured in, and exploitation followed (Nelson 1976). Farther to the west, in the Vogelkop or "Bird's Head" peninsula of Dutch New Guinea, slave-raiding and trade in firearms were endemic by the late nineteenth century (Miedema 1988; Strachan 1888:chs. 11–15; Miklouho-Maclay 1874). And in the Torres Strait to the south, the search for pearls and pearl shells led to "kidnapping and processes akin to kidnapping [that] went on long after the law forbade this sort of semi-slavery" (Bartlett 1954:89). But there is little indication that any of these developments intensified along the swampy bulk of the New Guinea south coast.

18. This tension was keenly felt by researchers such as F. E. Williams and Jan van Baal, who maintained both anthropological and official colonial commitments.

19. See especially Williams 1924, 1936, 1940; Landtman 1917, 1927; Wirz 1922–25, 1928; Baal 1966; Seligman 1910; Beaver 1920; Haddon 1901–35, 1920, 1923, 1924, 1927, 1928, 1936. See also Holmes 1924; Riley 1925; Chalmers 1895; cf. extensive bibliography in Knauft 1993a.

20. See Quiggin 1942; Urry 1973, 1982, 1984, 1993; cf. Stocking 1987.

21. Monographs by Dutch researchers include Baal 1966; Serpenti 1965; Boelaars 1981; Zegwaard and Boelaars 1955; cf. Eyde 1967; Zegwaard 1959.

22. F. E. Williams is a partial exception, but he espouses a highly ambivalent relationship to Malinowskian functionalism (e.g., 1936, 1940).

23. The view of ethnography as a survey of traits also informed less well-known Boasian and Germanic ethnography of north New Guinea and island Melanesia between about 1900 and the end of World War I, e.g., the work of A. B. Lewis, Thurnwald, Speiser, and others.

24. Lawrence Hammar has recently completed a thesis and important articles on postcolonial sexual practices and sexwork on Daru Island (see Hammar 1992, 1995, in press). Crawford's (1981) photographic study of the Gogodala is located on the margin of the south coast region presently under consideration.

25. E.g., Meggitt 1964; Meigs 1976; M. Strathern 1972; Brown and Buchbinder 1976. These works complemented the dominant ethnographic focus on highlands social organization, politics, and exchange.

26. For example, see Herdt 1981, 1982; Herdt and Poole 1982.

27. See Herdt 1981, 1982, 1984a, 1984b, 1987a, 1987b, 1991; Herdt and Stoller 1990.

28. South coast ethnographies dovetailed particularly with work done between the 1960s and the 1980s in the Strickland-Bosavi and Anga areas further inland.

29. See Feil 1987:ch. 7; Lindenbaum 1984, 1987; Schiefenhövel 1990; Herdt 1991:606; Lidz and Lidz 1989; cf. Whitehead 1986.

30. See Knauft 1990a, 1993a:ch. 3.

31. See Herdt 1984a, 1987a, 1987b, 1991, 1992; cf. Knauft 1987b, 1993a:app. A.

32. See Herdt and Stoller 1990; Herdt 1992; Herdt and Boxer 1993; Herdt 1994.

33. For example, see Nicholson 1990; Alcoff and Potter 1993; Flax 1993; Butler 1990, 1993a; Sedgwick 1990; Herdt 1994.

34. In the context of Melanesian homosexuality, see especially Knauft 1986, 1987b, 1993a; Herdt and Stoller 1990; Ernst 1991.

35. In the New Guinea context, see Hammar 1992, 1995, in press; Clark 1993, n.d.; Clark and Hughes 1995; Nihill 1994; Marksbury 1993; Jenkins 1994; Polier n.d.

36. Figurations of postcoloniality include Spivak 1990; Prakash 1992; Coronil 1992b; and Olaniyan 1992; recent collections and readers in postcolonial theory include Ashcroft et al. 1995; Williams and Chrisman 1994; and Chambers and Curti 1996; see also Ashcroft et al. 1989.

37. As emphasized by Deleuze, actual and institutionalized power (*pouvoir*) can be contrasted to power as the diffuse force of existence, capacity, or onto-logical intensity, i.e., *puissance* (see Massumi 1987:xvii; cf. Deleuze 1993).

38. See, specifically Stocking 1989a and de Zengotita 1989.

39. Elema were an exception in this regard (see Knauft 1993a:215f).

40. See Langmore 1989; Hope 1979; South Pacific Commission 1955.

41. Concerning south coast "cargo cults," see Maher 1961; Williams 1923b; Trenkenschuh 1982; cf. Worsley 1968; Knauft 1978; Schwartz 1962. A crit-

ical genealogy of cargo cults in the Western imaginary has been published by Lindstrom (1993; cf. 1990).

42. See Knauft 1993a:ch. 8; South Pacific Commission 1955; Baal 1966.

43. Such an argument has been put forward for "tribal warfare" generally by Ferguson and Whitehead (1992); see critique and analysis in the Melanesian context by Knauft (1990b, 1992, 1993b).

44. See, for instance, Hartsock 1990; Devreaux 1994.

45. The high frequency and extreme nature of Foucault's homosexual engagements, especially in the San Francisco leather-bar scene, are widely known and have been documented by his biographers (e.g. Macey 1993; Miller 1993; Eribon 1991). Though Foucault did not deny his sexual orientations, he tended to refuse questions about his personal life. He does refer to his sexual inclinations in a few passages in print, but most of these references are oblique and in minor publications. In short, Foucault's sexual proclivities were neither disclosed nor denied in his persona as a famous French intellectual.

46. See the strident critique of Foucault by Richard Mohr in *Gay Ideas* (1992:ch. 7), and a contrasting viewpoint in Edward Stein's *Forms of Desire* (1990).

47. Foucault also had published an abridged French translation of *My Secret Life*, a multivolume chronicle of a compulsive Victorian's sexual exploits (Macey 1993:356–7; cf. Butler 1993c).

48. In this respect, Foucault's final work also has strong and underappreciated resonance with critical genres of ethnopsychology and psychological anthropology. His view resonates particularly well with the emphasis of Lutz and Abu-Lughod (1990) on power in subjective practice. Ethnopsychology can be productively considered through the lens of power and action that underlies the use of pleasure and the care of the self.

49. Available information concerning Asmat homosexuality is compiled and analyzed in Knauft (1993a:228–37).

50. A similar point has been raised recently in discussions of domestic violence within gay and lesbian partnerships in the United States.

51. For instance, see Marksbury 1993; Carrier and Carrier 1989; Gewertz and Errington 1991.

52. See Clark 1993, cf. 1992; Nihill 1994; Jenkins 1994; Polier n.d.; on a national level, see Zimmer-Tamakoshi 1993a, 1993b.

53. Sobering reviews of the social and political problems facing Papua New Guinea have recently been authored by Jorgensen (1995), Wesley-Smith (1995), and Strathern (1993); see also Hart Nibbrig 1992; Goddard 1995.

54. The sadomasochistic dimensions of Foucault's life and work are documented in recent books on Foucault by David Macey (1993:chs. 14, 16) and James Miller (1993). Miller concludes that "Foucault's lifework, as I have come to understand it, is far more unconventional—and far more discomfiting—than some of his 'progressive' admirers seem ready to admit"

(1993:394). My own argument does not presume—as Foucault himself disavowed—that his "lifework" was a coherent unity.

Chapter 6 Gramsci and Bakhtin

1. The actual pattern of historical development would not have been a surprise to Marx himself, who believed toward the end of his life that Russia might prove the starting point of the revolution (McLellan 1975:67).
2. This last question became poignant as fascism and totalitarianism became preeminent in the 1920s and 1930s in Italy under Mussolini, from the late 1920s on in Russia under Stalin, and from the early 1930s in Hitler's Germany.
3. Gramsci and the early Bakhtin captured features of Marx's early writings without having been exposed to them. Marx's early Paris manuscripts were not first published until about 1930 (McLellan 1975:86). Gramsci was barred from access to such material while in prison. The basic features of Bakhtin's philosophy were developed prior to 1930, and there is no evidence that he was directly influenced by the writings of the early Marx.
4. Prominent biographies of Gramsci include Davidson 1977 and Fiori 1971.
5. Quoted in Hoare and Nowell-Smith [1971:lxxxvii].
6. Cited in Hoare and Nowell-Smith 1971:lxxxix.
7. Buttigieg 1992:38.
8. The quote was taken from Romain Rolland, one of young Gramsci's favorite authors (see Davidson 1977:101; Buttigieg 1992:12).
9. See Buttigieg 1992:3–4; Holub 1992:ch. 7.
10. Major works to which Bakhtin was likely either author or primary contributor include especially *Marxism and the Philosophy of Language* (first published in 1929) and *Freudianism: A Critical Sketch* (first published in 1927), both of which were published under the name of V. N. Volosinov, and *The Formal Method in Literary Study: A Critical Introduction to Sociological Poetics* (first published in 1928 under the name of P. N. Medvedev). The authorship of these texts has been a matter of debate, and the issues are complex, since Volosinov and Medvedev were both colleagues and supporters of Bakhtin, and both were dead by 1938. The bulk of textual and historical evidence and testimony of relatives suggests that the ideas in these works are distinctively Bakhtin's and that he wrote them, at least in large part. However, no one contests the dialogic nature of Bakhtin's personal interaction with his two colleagues. The case for non-Bakhtinian authorship is probably strongest for the opening sections of *Marxism and the Philosophy of Language*, which could well have been authored and written by Volosinov. A case for full authorship of this work by Volosinov has been made by Morson and Emerson (1990:ch. 3) and by Volosinov's translators (Matejka and Tutunik 1986). However, my own reading concurs with the dominant scholarly assessment, which is that Bakhtin is the primary author

of this work (see Todorov 1984:ch. 1; Holquist 1990; Clark and Holquist 1984:ch. 6; cf. Danow 1991). Notwithstanding this conclusion, it bears emphasis that Bakhtin delighted in the ambiguity of dialogic authorship, as opposed to the monologic closure of a single authorial stamp.

11. Recent debates over Bakhtin's authorship of these works (as discussed in the previous note) would likely have amused Bakhtin himself.

12. Other volumes of Gramsci's early writings, letters, and cultural writings were translated during the 1980s, but volume 1 of the complete critical English version of Gramsci's *Prison Notebooks*, edited by Joseph Buttigieg, was not finally published until 1992. *Further Selections from the Prison Notebooks*, edited by Derek Boothman, was published in 1995.

13. Bakhtin's volume on Dostoevsky's Poetics was reissued in Russian in 1963 and published in English translation a decade later; *Rabelais and His World* was first published in 1965 and translated into English in 1968. Both works were updated with cautious final caveats by Bakhtin himself.

14. *The Dialogic Imagination* was published in 1981, *Speech Genres and Other Late Essays* in 1986, and *Art and Answerability* in 1990. Bakhtin's important *Toward a Philosophy of the Act*, written between 1919 and 1921, was not printed in Russian until 1986; it was not published in English translation until 1993.

15. Paraphrased from Bakhtin 1981:358f.

16. See analysis developed by Booker and Juraga (1995:ch. 1).

17. Paraphrased from Docker 1994:171.

18. For instance, see Adamson 1980; Bellamy and Schecter 1993; Clark 1977; Femia 1987; Fontana 1993; Germino 1990; Gill 1993; Golding 1992; Morera 1990; and Mouffe 1979.

19. Compare Stallybrass and White 1986.

20. Todorov 1984:ix.

21. Forgacs and Nowell-Smith 1985:14.

22. Emerson 1984:xxx–xxxi.

23. Forgacs and Nowell-Smith 1985:10; phrases from the original passage have been omitted in quotation.

24. Gramsci 1971:351, 355.

25. Bakhtin 1993:56, 59, 13.

26. Gramsci 1971:352.

27. Bakhtin 1981:7; 1993:8, 12, 56, 60.

28. Bakhtin 1984:287.

29. Gramsci 1971:360.

30. Bakhtin 1990:144; 1986a:87.

31. Gramsci 1971:200.

32. Bakhtin 1978:158.

33. Gramsci 1971:337, 455.

34. Bakhtin 1978:15; 1990:264.

35. Gramsci 1971:178.

36. Bakhtin 1993:49.
37. Gramsci 1971:369.
38. Gramsci 1971:348–49, 325.
39. Bakhtin 1986a:91.
40. Gramsci 1985:205, 226.
41. Bakhtin 1981:84f.
42. Gramsci 1985:177.
43. Bakhtin 1986b:140.
44. Gramsci 1985:217.
45. Bakhtin 1968:3, 433.
46. Gramsci 1985:236.
47. Bakhtin 1968:474, 473.
48. Gramsci 1985:126.
49. Bakhtin 1968: 473, 34.
50. Gramsci 1971:348.
51. Gramsci 1985:125.
52. Bakhtin 1984:32.
53. Gramsci 1985:293.
54. Bakhtin, quoted in Docker 1994:170.
55. Gramsci 1985:293–94.
56. Bakhtin 1984:63.
57. Gramsci 1985:98.
58. Bakhtin 1986a:70, 23.
59. Gramsci 1985:99, 180–81.
60. Bakhtin 1981:263, 359, 358.
61. Gramsci 1985:181.
62. Bakhtin 1981:272.
63. Gramsci 1985:98.
64. Bakhtin 1986a:70.
65. Gramsci 1985:115.
66. Bakhtin 1986a:10, 13.
67. Bakhtin 1981:342.
68. Gramsci 1971:12.
69. Bakhtin 1981:342, 345f.
70. Gramsci 1971:333.
71. Bakhtin 1986a:88.
72. Gramsci 1971:333, 235, 234.
73. Bakhtin 1986b:xiii; 1993:14.
74. Gramsci 1971:330.
75. Bakhtin 1986b:110.
76. Gramsci 1994:30.
77. Bakhtin 1984:68.
78. Bakhtin 1984:68.
79. Gramsci 1971:337; 1994:255.

80. Bakhtin 1981:40.

81. Gramsci 1985:403.

82. Bakhtin 1993:52.

83. For instance, Landy (1994:91) notes the strong connection between Bakhtin's conception of heteroglossia and Gramsci's notion of common sense as composite, fragmentary, historically eclectic, and heterogeneous.

84. This view has long been established in works that consider spirit possession and millenarianism, including classic studies such as Lanternari's *Religions of the Oppressed* (1965), Worsley's *The Trumpet Shall Sound* (1968), Lewis's *Ecstatic Religion* (1989), and ethnographies such as Peter Fry's *Spirits of Protest* (1976), David Lan's *Guns and Rain* (1985), Jean Comaroff's *Body of Power, Spirit of Resistance* (1985), and Janice Boddy's *Wombs and Alien Spirits* (1989).

85. See, for example, Taussig 1987; Steedly 1993; Lavie 1990; Tsing 1993; cf. Brenneis and Myers 1991.

86. See Bakhtin 1986a:110.

87. In a sense, women are the ultimate audience of the spirit séance—its super-addressee.

88. The medium's own spirit is believed to be absent during the séance and does not take offense at the escapades of his spirit wife and her friends.

89. Though Gebusi women may go off alone to attract a lover, this is a nonbinding form of sexuality that carries no obligation for the man and high potential cost to the woman. Except when they are eminently marriageable, women fear this option and guard against it. Men justify nonconsensual sex by arguing that if the woman was not willing, she would not let herself be accosted while alone.

90. See Knauft 1985a:ch. 5, 1987a, 1991; cf. Kelly 1993.

91. Though material compensation has been quite developed in the New Guinea highlands and other areas of Melanesia, Gebusi have favored a person-for-person model of exchange (Knauft 1985b; cf. Strathern 1971, 1982; Godelier 1986). This direct exchange is reflected in Gebusi practices of sister-exchange marriage rather than marriage through bridewealth, and in exact reciprocity that demands the life of the sorcery suspect as recompense for the life of the sickness victim. Nominal colonial pacification reduced the rate of Gebusi violence somewhat, but not as much as might have been supposed. Because most killings are consensual and occur within the community, they have often been kept from the awareness of government officials.

92. The designation of "dividuality" in intersubjective personhood emerged first in the South Asian context (e.g., Marriott 1976; Daniel 1984).

93. Sweet potatoes are not frequently raised by Gebusi but are known to be desired by government workers.

94. These themes are now emerging in Papua New Guinea's media as well—for instance, in Albert Toro's film "Tukana—Who's to Blame" (see Sullivan 1993:539ff.).

95. This tension was effectively explored for Melanesia in the 1950s ethnography of Kenelm Burridge (1960, 1969).

96. Ellipses in this statement are not shown.

97. See, for instance, Smith 1994; Foster 1995; Errington and Gewertz 1995; Carrier and Carrier 1989; cf. Burridge 1960.

98. During her long absence from her husband, the female hero in Wahiaw's second narrative is neither subject to nor solicitous of sexual advances. Even at the end of the narrative, the implicit connection between herself and the patrol officer is left as a comradeship rather than a romance.

99. Patrol Officer Hoad (1962–1963) reported in 1962 that even large trees were still felled by stone axes in the area of Wahiaw's hamlet.

100. In late 1981, an advance exploration team for the Chevron Oil Corporation established a base camp north of Gebusi territory. The team conducted a seismic survey for oil reserves; for this purpose, they needed transects cut randomly across a rainforest area two days' walk north of Gebusi settlements. Much of the timber was cut with chainsaws by immigrant Southeast Asian laborers, but some—perhaps for public-relations reasons—was hand-cut by men hired from the local area. These included some Gebusi men (as well as Bedamini, Samo, and Kubor) who were willing to walk to the base camp and work for several weeks or months away from their villages. A few Gebusi men departed for this labor and were paid about twenty kina a week; most returned home either sick or homesick within a few weeks. Wahiaw's new séance genre developed about the same time that some of these men were returning to their Gebusi settlements. His spirit innovations do not refer to these events directly, but they do resonate with its context as well as with the working conditions of paid officials and their retinue at the Nomad patrol post more generally. I do not believe any of the Gebusi laborers in 1981 departed from or returned to Wahiaw's own settlement, but he knew of these developments from stories and hearsay. The actual economic impact of these developments was not particularly great, as the goods available for cash were few and the prices very high. In addition, the Chevron seismic team departed shortly thereafter, and the possibility of further work departed with them. Though similar explorations had been conducted about 1970 with no ultimate result, later in the 1980s a large oil well was finally drilled farther to the northeast. As in the present case, news of this project has traveled widely and has had significant cultural impact outside the area of immediate influence (e.g., Stürzenhoefecker 1994).

Chapter 7 Gender, Ethnography, and Critical Query

1. Selected 1990s ethnographies do problematize male gender, particularly in relation to sexuality. Even within the strictures spelled out later, Lancaster's *Life Is Hard* (1992) could be included within a corpus of recent gendered ethnographies. His ethnography foregrounds issues of gender and power

to effectively trace the workings of Nicaraguan *machismo* through political revolution, poverty, domestic violence, poignant life histories, social change, and the shame of the *cochòn* (homosexual recipient/insertee). The theoretical and topical importance of sexual diversity in cultural anthropology is also reflected in recent works by Herdt (1992, 1993); Parker and Gagnon (1995); Kulick and Willson (1995); Abelove (1993); Lewin (1993); and Weston (1993a); cf. earlier work by Newton (1972) and Rubin (1984). By contrast, ethnographies that document or theorize important ranges of *hetero*sexual diversity are still uncommon (but see Parker 1991).

2. A special issue of *Critique of Anthropology* (1993, vol. 13, no. 4) on "Women Writing Culture" contains a useful introduction to the current anthropological relevance of several of these authors (cf. more recently, Behar and Gordon 1995). Original works include Bohannan 1954; Briggs 1970; Deloria 1932, 1944, 1988; Hurston 1935, 1937; Reichard 1928; 1934; 1936; 1939; 1950. Other classic examples of "women writing culture" include Powdermaker 1966, Thomas 1959, and Wolf 1968; see also Shostak 1981.

3. The above list could also be expanded to include works such as Karen Brown's *Mama Lola* (1991), Judith Stacey's *Brave New Families* (1990), and Ellen Lewin's *Lesbian Mothers* (1993) [North America]; Mary Steedly's *Hanging Without a Rope* (1993) [Southeast Asia]; Margaret Trawick's *Notes on Love in a Tamil Family* (1990) [South Asia]; and Maria Lepowsky's *Fruits of the Motherland* (1993) [Melanesia], to name just a few.

4. This larger terrain was sketched by Sherry Ortner in her important article "Gender Hegemonies" (1990a).

5. For Kondo, the history and structure of Japanese "part-time" female work complements female experience crafted between gendered asymmetries of the work experience and those of domestic life. Tsing's work shows how marginality echoes across the shadows of gendered inequality in a particularly "out-of-the-way" place where family planning, government administration, and female spirit possession reflect both the hegemonies and the ineffectualities of state epistemic and political power. Polier shows how Christianity and neocolonialism in Papua New Guinea weave across indigenous patriarchy to both complicate and enrich theoretical understandings of religion, political economy, and resistance. For Lavie, the historical structure of Israeli occupation sets the political stage upon which Mzeina allegories of resistance and Lavie's own lyricism are cast. Scheper-Hughes's work on Brazilian women predicates a heavy critique of state, religious, and biomedical structures. Kratz's monograph frames the experience of female initiation within strictures of patriarchy and eldership, on the one hand, and ethnic stigma, on the other.

6. See overviews in Fraser and Bartky 1992; Spivak 1981.

7. See, for instance, Benhabib et al. 1995; Morton 1993; Martin 1994; Mohr 1992; Grewal and Kaplan 1994; hooks 1994; Butler 1993b; Braidotti 1994; Fuss 1991; Abelove et al. 1993.

8. Though beyond the scope of this discussion, analogous trends appear in postcolonial studies, diasporic studies, and cultural studies generally.

9. The term *postfeminist* needs to be used carefully (see Rapp 1988). In a critical and usually academic sense, the concept can denote the widening of feminist sensitivities to a range of female positionings and disempowerments that cannot be lumped under a singular or universal category of "female gender" or "womanhood." Postfeminism in this sense is not a denial, repudiation, or reversal of the historical importance of feminism, even as it attempts to go beyond these contributions. *The meaning of the term is commonly reversed, however, in casual conversation.* This latter sense of post-feminism echoes with reactionary perspectives, such as Elizabeth Fox-Genovese's desultory diatribe, *Feminism is* Not *the Story of My Life* (1996).

10. See, diversely, Herdt 1992, 1993; Blackwood 1986; Grewal and Kaplan 1994; Mohanty 1991a, 1991b; hooks 1981; Spivak 1994; Minh-ha 1990, 1991. Concerning "third sex/third gender," see especially Herdt 1994.

Chapter 8 Multicultural Speaking

1. See Horton 1993:2.

2. The sociocultural construction of whiteness has been examined by Frankenberg (1993), hooks (1992b), and McLaren (1994), among others. Concerning the social construction of race more generally, see especially Winant (1994) and Goldberg (1990); cf. also Williams (1989) and Gilroy (1987).

3. This point has been underscored by the Chicago Cultural Studies Group (1992); cf. also Turner (1993).

4. Within the black intellectual community, see recent criticisms by Adolf Reed (in press) and Leon Wieseltier (1995) against Cornel West, and by Brackette Williams (1994) against bell hooks.

5. Another important discussion of critical multiculturalism was published by the Chicago Cultural Studies Group (1992); cf., more generally, Goldberg (1994) and Kanpol and McLaren (1995).

6. See Giroux 1992; Laclau and Mouffe 1985; Mouffe 1992, 1993; Laclau 1990, 1994; Kanpol and McLaren 1995; Rosaldo 1989, 1992; Trend 1996.

7. It can be useful to return to Gramsci to see what is given up in this formulation—what is lost by minimizing the moment of essential opposition based on identity. For Gramsci, this opposition is based on class essentialism: Class forms the ultimate axis of stigmatized division and of failure or triumph in contests of power. As Laclau and Mouffe (1985:69) note, for Gramsci, "Political struggle is still a zero-sum game among classes. This is the inner essentialist core which continues to be present in Gramsci's thought, setting a limit to the deconstructive logic of hegemony."

The best possible outcome of this division for Gramsci is political revolution: overthrowing the state political apparatus by force to empower working-class interests. As part of this process, Gramsci leaves the door of authoritarian leadership ajar, especially within the Communist Party. Notwithstanding Gramsci's understanding of Mussolini's fascism and his resonance with Marx's critique of Louis Bonaparte, he clearly believed that the Communist Party elite were privileged to seize authority during crucial revolutionary periods. As clearly spelled out in his Machiavellian essay "The Modern Prince," Gramsci was sympathetic to Leninist principles. Particularly in a late modern era, however, the ability to generate fundamental structural change in Western societies through such means seems minimal; the "system" is so pervasive and virtual as to be refractory to frontal assault (Taussig 1992; Foucault 1980c). Under such conditions, apocalyptic confrontation seems as misguided as it is impractical. The disappointing and sometimes horrific results of political revolutions in the twentieth century—including some that started out with highly progressive hopes—underscore these problems. It is quite understandable that leftist intellectuals have now largely given up on grand revolutionary projects. As suggested by Mercer (1994:259), "Today the word 'revolution' sounds vaguely embarrassing when it comes out of the mouths of people on the Left: it only sounds as if it means what it says when uttered in the mouths of the radicalized Right."

8. These issues are magnified in a period of budget cutbacks. Even in their absence, steps to increase the support of one group can unwittingly penalize another; for instance, see Debra Blum's (1995) "Competing Equities: Some Fear that Steps to Help Female Athletes May Curb Opportunities for Blacks."

9. Sixty years ago, Gregory Bateson (1936) elucidated the general structure of such relationships in his discussion of complementary and symmetric schizmogenesis.

10. See, for example, Carby 1987; Collins 1990; Dyson 1995; Gates 1986, 1991, 1992; Gilroy 1987, 1993, 1994; hooks 1981, 1990, 1992a, 1994; Mercer 1994; Wallace 1990; and West 1989, 1993a, 1993b.

references

Abelove, Henry, Michele A. Barale, and David M. Halperin (eds.)
1993   *The Lesbian and Gay Studies Reader*. New York: Routledge.

Abu-Lughod, Lila
1986   *Veiled Sentiments: Honor and Poetry in a Bedouin Society*. Berkeley: University of California Press.
1988   Can There be a Feminist Ethnography? *Women and Performance* 5:7–27.
1990a The Romance of Resistance: Tracing Transformations of Power Through Bedouin Women. *American Ethnologist* 17:41–55.
1990b Shifting Politics in Bedouin Love Poetry. In *Language and the Politics of Emotion*, edited by Catherine Lutz and Lila Abu-Lughod, pp. 24–45. New York: Cambridge University Press.
1991   Writing Against Culture. In *Recapturing Anthropology: Working in the Present*, edited by Richard Fox, pp. 137–62. Santa Fe, NM: School of American Research Press.
1993   *Writing Women's Worlds: Bedouin Stories*. Berkeley: University of California Press.

Adamson, Walter L.
1980   *Hegemony and Revolution: A Study of Antonio Gramsci's Political and Cultural Theory*. Berkeley: University of California Press.

Adorno, Theodor W.
1973   *Negative Dialectics*. New York: Seabury.
1982   *Against Epistemology—A Metacritique: Studies in Husserl and the Phenomenological Antinomies*. Cambridge, MA: MIT Press.
1986   *Aesthetic Theory*. London: Routledge and Kegan Paul.
1991   *The Culture Industry: Selected Essays on Mass Culture*, edited and introduced by J. M. Bernstein. New York: Routledge.
1993   *Hegel: Three Studies*. Cambridge, MA: MIT Press.
1994   *Adorno: The Stars Down to Earth and Other Essays on the Irrational in Culture*, edited and introduced by Stephen Cook. New York: Routledge.

Ahearn, Laura (organizer)
   1995   "Agency." Session of papers presented at the annual meetings of the
          American Anthropological Association, Washington, D. C.
Alcoff, Linda
   1988   Cultural Feminism Versus Post-Structuralism: The Identity Crisis in
          Feminist Theory. *Signs* 13:405–36.
   1991   The Problem of Speaking for Others. *Critical Inquiry* 20:5–32.
Alcoff, Linda, and Elizabeth Potter (eds.)
   1993   *Feminist Epistemologies*. New York: Routledge.
Alder, William F.
   1922   *The Isle of Vanishing Men: A Narrative of Adventure in Cannibal-land*. New
          York: Century Co.
Alexander, Jeffrey C.
   1995   *Fin de Siècle Social Theory: Relativism, Reduction, and the Problem of Reason*.
          London: Verso.
Althusser, Louis
   1969   *For Marx*. New York: Pantheon [Original 1965].
Althusser, Louis and Etienne Balibar
   1970   *Reading Capital*. London: New Left Books [Original, 1968].
Anderson, Benedict
   1983   *Imagined Communities: Reflections on the Origin and Spread of Nationalism*.
          London: Verso.
Anderson, Perry
   1976   *Considerations on Western Marxism*. London: New Left Books.
   1984   *In the Tracks of Historical Materialism*. Chicago: University of Chicago Press.
Anzaldúa, Gloria
   1987   *Borderlands/La Frontera: The New Mestiza*. San Francisco: Spinsters/Aunt
          Lute.
Appadurai, Arjun
   1986   Theory in Anthropology: Center and Periphery. *Comparative Studies in
          Society and History* 28:356–61.
   1988   Introduction: Place and Voice in Anthropological Theory. *Cultural
          Anthropology* 3:16–20.
   1990   Disjuncture and Difference in the Global Cultural Economy. *Public Culture*
          2:1–24.
   1993   Patriotism and its Futures. *Public Culture* 5:411–29.
Appiah, Kwame Anthony
   1991   Is the Post- in Postmodernism the Post- in Postcolonial? *Critical Inquiry*
          17:336–57.
   1992   *In My Father's House: Africa in the Philosophy of Culture*. New York: Oxford
          University Press.
Apter, Terri and Elizabeth Garnsey
   1994   Enacting Inequality: Structure, Agency, and Gender. *Women's Studies
          International Forum* 17:19–31.
Arac, Jonathan (ed.)
   1988   *After Foucault: Humanistic Knowledge, Postmodern Challenges*. New
          Brunswick, NJ: Rutgers University Press.

Arendt, Hannah
1963   *On Revolution.* New York: Viking.
1978   *The Life of the Mind.* New York: Harcourt, Brace, and Jovanovich.
1979   *The Origins of Totalitarianism.* San Diego: Harcourt, Brace, and Jovanovich.
Aronowitz, Stanley
1994   The Situtation of the Left in the United States. *Socialist Review* 23:5–79.
Asad, Talal (ed.)
1973   *Anthropology and the Colonial Encounter.* New York: Humanities Press.
Ashcroft, Bill, Gareth Griffiths, and Helen Tiffin
1989   *The Empire Writes Back: Theory and Practice in Post-Colonial Literatures.*
        London: Routledge.
1995   (Eds.) *The Post-Colonial Studies Reader.* New York: Routledge.
Augé, Marc
1994   *Le sens des autres: Actualité de l'anthropologie.* Paris: Fayard.
Austrailian Council for Overseas Aid
1995   Trouble at Freeport. Report of April 5. Canberra.
Ayres, R. Drummond, Jr.
1995   Conservatives Forge New Strategy to Challenge Affirmative Action. *New
        York Times,* February 16, pp. A1, A11.
Baal, Jan van
1966   *Dema: Description and Analysis of Marind-Anim Culture (South New Guinea).*
        The Hague: Martinus Nijhoff.
Bakhtin, Mikhail M.
1968   *Rabelais and His World.* Cambridge, MA: MIT Press [Original pub., 1965].
1976   *Freudianism: A Marxist Critique.* [V. N. Volosinov/M. Bakhtin.] New York:
        Academic. [Original, 1927].
1978   *The Formal Method in Literary Scholarship: A Critical Introduction to
        Sociological Poetics.* [P. N. Medvedev/M. Bakhtin.] Baltimore, MD: Johns
        Hopkins University Press [Original, 1928].
1981   *The Dialogic Imagination.* Austin, TX: University of Texas Press.
1984   *Problems of Dostoevsky's Poetics.* Minneapolis: University of Minnesota Press
        [Original, 1929].
1986a   *Marxism and the Philosophy of Language.* [V. N. Volosinov.] Cambridge, MA:
        Harvard University Press. [Original, 1929].
1986b   *Speech Genres and Other Late Essays.* Austin, TX: University of Texas Press.
1990   *Art and Answerability: Early Philosophical Essays.* Austin, TX: University of
        Texas Press.
1993   *Toward a Philosophy of the Act.* Austin, TX: University of Texas Press
        [Original ms., 1919–21].
Balandier, Georges
1994   *Le Dedale: Pour en finir avec le XXe siècle.* Paris: Fayard.
Baldwin, James
1953   *Go Tell it on the Mountain.* New York: Knopf.
1955   *Notes of a Native Son.* Boston: Beacon
1962   *Another Country.* New York: Dial.
1963   *The Fire Next Time.* New York: Dial.

Barker, Philip
  1993   *Michel Foucault: Subversions of the Subject.* Hempstead, UK: Harvester
          Wheatsheaf.
Barnard, Frederick M.
  1965   *Herder's Social and Political Thought: From Enlightenment to Nationalism.*
          Oxford: Clarendon.
Barth, Fredrik
  1981   *Process and Form in Social Life: Selected Essays of Fredrik Barth,* vol. 1.
          London: Routledge and Kegan Paul.
  1994   A Personal View of Present Tasks and Priorities in Cultural and Social
          Anthropology. In *Assessing Cultural Anthropology,* edited by Robert
          Borofsky, pp. 349–61. New York: McGraw-Hill.
Bartlett, Norman
  1954   *The Pearl Seekers.* New York: Coward-McCann.
Bateson, Gregory
  1936   *Naven: A Survey of the Problems Suggested by a Composite Picture of the
          Culture of a New Guinea Tribe Drawn from Three Points of View.* Cambridge:
          Cambridge University Press. 2nd ed., Stanford: Stanford University Press,
          1958.
  1972   *Steps to an Ecology of Mind: Collected Essays in Anthropology, Psychiatry,
          Evolution, and Epistemology.* San Francisco: Chandler.
  1983   *Mind and Nature: A Necessary Unity.* New York: Bantam.
Battaglia, Debbora
  1995   On Practical Nostalgia: Self-Prospecting Among Urban Trobrianders. In
          Rhetorics of Self-Making, edited by Debbora Battaglia, pp. 77–96. Berkeley:
          University of California Press.
Baudrillard, Jean
  1968   *Le Système des objets.* Paris: Denoel-Gonthier.
  1970   *La Société de consommation.* Paris: Gallimard.
  1975   *The Mirror of Production.* St. Louis: Telos Press [Original, 1973].
  1981   *Notes for a Critique of the Political Economy of the Sign.* St. Louis: Telos
          [Original, 1972].
  1983a   *In the Shadow of the Silent Majorities.* New York: Semiotext(e).
  1983b   *Simulations.* New York: Semiotext(e).
  1983c   What Are You Doing After the Orgy? *Artforum,* October, pp. 42–46.
  1985   *La Gauche divine.* Paris: Grasset.
  1987   *Forget Foucault.* New York: Semiotext(e) [Original, 1977].
  1988a   *America.* London: Verso [Original, 1986].
  1988b   *The Ecstasy of Communication.* New York: Semiotext(e) [Original, 1987].
  1988c   *Jean Baudrillard: Selected Writings,* edited by Mark Poster. Stanford:
          Stanford University Press.
  1990a   *Cool Memories.* London: Verso [Original, 1987].
  1990b   *Seduction.* London: Macmillan [Original, 1979].
  1992   *Baudrillard Live,* edited by Mike Gane. London: Routledge.
  1993a   *The Transparency of Evil: Essays on Extreme Phenomena.* London: Verso
          [Original, 1990].
  1993b   *Symbolic Exchange and Death.* London: Sage [Original, 1976].
  1994a   *Simulacra and Simulation.* Ann Arbor: University of Michigan Press.

1994b   *The Illusion of the End.* Stanford: Stanford University Press.
1995a   *Le Crime parfait.* Paris: Galilée.
1995b   *The Gulf War Did Not Take Place.* Bloomington: Indiana University Press.
Bauman, Zygmunt
1988   Is There a Postmodern Sociology? *Theory, Culture, and Society* 5:217–37.
1992   *Intimations of Postmodernity.* London: Routledge.
1993   *Postmodern Ethics.* Oxford: Basil Blackwell.
Beaver, Wilfred N.
1920   *Unexplored New Guinea: A Record of the Travels, Adventures, and Experiences of a Resident Magistrate Amongst the Head-hunting Savages and Cannibals of the Unexplored Interior of New Guinea.* London: Seeley, Service and Co.
Behar, Ruth
1993a   *Translated Woman: Crossing the Border with Esperanza's Story.* Boston: Beacon.
1993b   Introduction: Women Writing Culture: Another Telling of the Story of American Anthropology. *Critique of Anthropology* 13:307–25.
Behar, Ruth and Deborah A. Gordon (eds.)
1995   *Women Writing Culture.* Berkeley: University of California Press.
Bell, Daniel
1978   *The Cultural Contradictions of Capitalism.* New York: Basic Books.
Bellamy, Richard and David Schecter
1993   *Gramsci and the Italian State.* Manchester: Manchester University Press.
Benedict, Ruth
1934   *Patterns of Culture.* Boston: Houghton Mifflin.
1946   *The Chrysanthemum and the Sword: Patterns of Japanese Culture.* Boston: Houghton Mifflin.
Benhabib, Seyla
1992   *Situating the Self: Gender, Community, and Postmodernism in Contemporary Ethics.* New York: Routledge.
Benhabib, Seyla, Judith Butler, Drucilla Cornell, and Nancy Fraser
1995   *Feminist Contentions: A Philosophical Exchange.* New York: Routledge.
Benjamin, Walter
1969   *Illuminations*, edited and introduced by Hannah Arendt. New York: Schocken.
1978   *Reflections: Essays, Aphorisms, Autobiographical Writings*, edited and introduced by Peter Demetz. New York: Harcourt, Brace, and Jovanovich.
1989   *The Dialectics of Seeing: Walter Benjamin and the Arcades Project.* Cambridge, MA: MIT Press.
Bennett, Judith A.
1994   Forestry, Public Land, and the Colonial Legacy in Solomon Islands. *Contemporary Pacific* 7:243–75.
Bennett, Tony, G. Martin, C. Mercer, and J. Woollacott (eds.)
1981   *Popular Television and Film.* London: BFI.
Bennett, Tony and Janet Woollacott
1987   *Bond and Beyond: The Political Career of a Popular Hero.* London: Macmillan.
Bercovitch, Eytan
1994   The Agent in the Gift: Hidden Exchange in Inner New Guinea. *Cultural Anthropology* 9:498–536.

Berger, Peter L. and Thomas Luckmann
 1967   *The Social Construction of Reality: A Treatise in the Sociology of Knowledge.*
        Garden City, NY: Anchor.
Berkowitz, Peter
 1995   *Nietzsche: The Ethics of an Immoralist.* Cambridge, MA: Harvard University
        Press.
Berlin, Isaiah
 1976   *Vico and Herder: Two Studies in the History of Ideas.* New York: Viking.
Berman, Art
 1994   *Preface to Modernism.* Urbana: University of Illinois Press.
Berman, Marshall
 1982   *All that Is Solid Melts into Air: The Experience of Modernity.* New York:
        Simon and Schuster.
Bernasconi, Robert
 1993   *Heidegger in Question: The Art of Existing.* Atlantic Highlands, NJ:
        Humanities Press.
Bernauer, James W.
 1990   *Michel Foucault's Force of Flight: Toward an Ethics for Thought.* Atlantic
        Highlands, NJ: Humanities Press.
Bertens, Hans
 1995   *The Idea of the Postmodern: A History.* London: Routledge.
Bevan, Theodore F.
 1890   *Toil, Travel, and Discovery in British New Guinea.* London: Kegan Paul,
        Trench, Trubner and Co.
Bhabha, Homi K.
 1990   (Ed.) *Nation and Narration.* London: Routledge.
 1992   Postcolonial Authority and Postmodern Guilt. In *Cultural Studies*, edited
        by Lawrence Grossberg, Cary Nelson, and Paula Treichler, pp. 56–80.
        New York: Routledge.
 1994   *The Location of Culture.* London: Routledge.
Bird, John, Barry Curtis, Tim Putnam, George Robertson, and Lisa Tickner
 1993   *Mapping the Futures: Local Cultures, Global Change.* London: Routledge.
Birth, Kevin K.
 1990   Reading and the Righting of Writing Ethnographies. *American Ethnologist*
        17:549–57.
Bitterli, Urs
 1989   *Cultures in Conflict: Encounters Between European and Non-European Cultures,
        1492–1800.* Stanford: Stanford University Press.
Blackwood, Evelyn (ed.)
 1986   *Anthropology and Homosexual Behavior.* New York: Haworth.
Blitz, Mark
 1981   *Heidegger's* Being and Time *and the Possibility of Political Philosophy.* Ithaca,
        NY: Cornell University Press.
Bloch, Maurice
 1975   (Ed.) *Marxist Analysis and Social Anthropology.* London: Malaby.
 1983   *Marxism and Anthropology: The History of Relationship.* Oxford: Clarendon.
Blum, Debra E.
 1995   Competing Equities?: Some Fear that Steps to Help Female Athletes May

Curb Opportunities for Blacks. *The Chronicle of Higher Education*, 41(37):A37–38 (May 26).

Boas, Franz
1888   *The Central Eskimo*. Report of the Bureau of Ethnology, 1884–1885, pp. 399–669. Washington, DC: Smithsonian Institution.
1897   *The Social Organization and Secret Societies of the Kwakiutl Indians*. Report of the U. S. National Museum, 1895. Washington, DC: Government Printing Office.
1911   *The Mind of Primitive Man*. New York: Macmillan
1928   *Anthropology and Modern Life*. New York: Norton.
1940   *Race, Language and Culture*. New York: Free Press.
1966   *Kwakiutl Ethnography*, edited by Helen Codere. Chicago: University of Chicago Press.
1974   *A Franz Boas Reader*, edited by George Stocking, Jr. Chicago: University of Chicago Press.

Boddy, Janice
1989   *Wombs and Alien Spirits: Women, Men, and the Zar Cult in Northern Sudan*. Madison: University of Wisconsin Press.

Boelaars, J. H. M. C.
1981   *Head-Hunters About Themselves: An Ethnographic Report from Irian Jaya, Indonesia*. The Hague: Martinus Nijhoff.

Bohannan, Laura [nom de plume: Elenore Smith Bowen]
1954   *Return to Laughter*. New York: Harper Brothers.

Bohannan, Paul and Mark Glazer (eds.)
1988   *High Points in Anthropology*, 2nd ed. New York: Knopf.

Booker, M. Keith and Dubravka Juraga
1995   *Bakhtin, Stalin, and Modern Russian Fiction*. Westport, CT: Greenwood Press.

Boon, James A.
1990   *Affinities and Extremes: Crisscrossing the Bittersweet Ethnology of East Indies History, Hindu-Balinese Culture, and Indo-European Allure*. Chicago: University of Chicago Press.

Bordo, Susan
1992   Postmodern Subjects, Postmodern Bodies. *Feminist Studies* 18:159–75.
1993   *Unbearable Weight: Feminism, Western Culture, and the Body*. Berkeley: University of California Press.

Borofsky, Robert (ed.)
1994   *Assessing Cultural Anthropology*. New York: McGraw-Hill.

Borofsky, Robert and Alan Howard
1989   The Early Contact Period. In *Developments in Polynesian Ethnology*, edited by Alan Howard and Robert Borofsky, pp. 241–75. Honolulu: University of Hawaii Press.

Boserup, Ester
1970   *Woman's Role in Economic Development*. New York: St. Martin's.

Bourdieu, Pierre
1962   *The Algerians*. Boston: Beacon [Original, 1958].
1976   Marital Strategies as Strategies of Social Reproduction. In *Family and*

Society: Selections from the Annales, edited by R. Forster and O. Ranum. Baltimore, MD: Johns Hopkins University Press [Original, 1972].

1977   *Outline of a Theory of Practice*. Translated by Richard Nice. Cambridge: Cambridge University Press [Original, 1972].

1979   *Algeria 1960: The Disenchantment of the World, the Sense of Honour, the Kabyle House or the World Reversed*. Cambridge: Cambridge University Press [Original, 1977].

1984   *Distinction: A Social Critique of the Judgement of Taste*. Cambridge, MA: Harvard University Press [Original, 1979].

1988a *Homo Academicus*. Translated by P. Collier. Stanford: Stanford University Press [Original, 1984].

1988b Flaubert's Point of View. *Critical Inquiry* 14:539–62.

1989   *La Noblesse d'état*. Paris: Les Editions de Minuit.

1990a *The Logic of Practice*. Translated by Richard Nice. Stanford: Stanford University Press [Original, 1980].

1990b The Scholastic Point of View. *Cultural Anthropology* 5:380–91.

1990c *In Other Words: Essays Towards a Reflexive Sociology*. Translated by Matthew Adamson. Stanford: Stanford University Press [Original, 1987].

1991a *Language and Symbolic Power: The Economy of Linguistic Exchange*. Edited by John B. Thompson; translated by Gino Raymond and Matthew Adamson. Cambridge, MA: Harvard University Press [Original, 1982].

1991b *The Political Ontology of Martin Heidegger*. Stanford: Stanford University Press [Original, 1988].

1991c Towards a Sociology of Photography. *Visual Anthropology Review* 7:129–33.

1992   *Les Regles de l'art*. Paris: Editions de Seuil.

1993a (Ed.) *La Misère du monde*. Paris: Editions de Seuil.

1993b *The Field of Cultural Production: Essays on Art and Literature*, edited and introduced by Randal Johnson. New York: Columbia University Press.

1993c *Sociology in Question*. London: Sage.

Bourdieu, Pierre (with L. Boltanski, R. Castel, J.-C. Chamboredon, and D. Schnapper)

1990   *Photography: A Middle-brow Art*. Cambridge: Polity Press [Original, 1965].

Bourdieu, Pierre and A. Darbel (with D. Schnapper)

1991   *The Love of Art: European Art Museums and Their Public*. Cambridge: Polity Press [Original, 1969].

Bourdieu, Pierre and Jean-Claude Passeron

1977   *Reproduction in Education, Society, and Culture*. London: Sage [Original, 1970].

1979   *The Inheritors: French Students and Their Relations to Culture*. Chicago: University of Chicago Press [Original, 1964].

Bourdieu, Pierre and Loïc J. D. Wacquant

1992   *An Invitation to Reflexive Sociology*. Chicago: University of Chicago Press.

Bourgois, Philippe

1989   *Ethnicity at Work: Divided Labor on a Central American Banana Plantation*. Baltimore: Johns Hopkins University Press.

1995a From Jibaro to Crack Dealer: Confronting the Restructuring of Capitalism in El Barrio. In *Articulating Hidden Histories: Exploring the Influence of Eric R. Wolf*, edited by Jane Schneider and Rayna Rapp, pp. 125–41. Berkeley: University of California Press.

1995b   *In Search of Respect: Selling Crack in Spanish Harlem*. New York: Cambridge University Press.

Bourque, Susan C. and Kay B. Warren
1981   *Women of the Andes: Patriarchy and Social Change in Two Peruvian Towns.* Ann Arbor: University of Michigan Press.

Braidotti, Rosi
1991   *Patterns of Dissonance: A Study of Women in Contemporary Philosophy.* New York: Routledge.
1994   *Nomadic Subjects: Embodiment and Sexual Difference in Contemporary Feminist Theory.* New York: Columbia University Press.

Braudel, Fernand
1973   *The Mediterranean and the Mediterranean World in the Age of Philip II.* 2 vols. New York: Harper and Row [Original, 1949].

Brenneis, Donald and Fred R. Myers (eds.)
1991   *Dangerous Words: Language and Politics in the Pacific.* Prospect Heights, IL: Waveland.

Brew, J. O. (ed.)
1968   *One Hundred Years of Anthropology.* Cambridge, MA: Harvard University Press.

Briggs, Jean L.
1970   *Never in Anger: Portrait of an Eskimo Family.* Cambridge, MA: Harvard University Press.

Brown, Karen McCarthy
1991   *Mama Lola: A Vodou Priestess in Brooklyn.* Berkeley: University of California Press.

Brown, Paula, and Georgeda Buchbinder (eds.)
1976   *Man and Woman in the New Guinea Highlands.* Washington, DC: American Anthropological Association (special publication no. 8).

Bryant, Christopher G. A. and David Jary (eds.)
1991   *Giddens' Theory of Structuration: A Critical Appreciation.* London: Routledge.

Bryce, Robert
1995   Aid Canceled for Gold Project in Indonesia. *New York Times*, November 2. (International Business Section.)

Buber, Martin
1970   *I and Thou.* New York: Scribner.
1984   *Martin Buber: A Centenary Volume.* New York: Ktav.
1992   *On Intersubjectivity and Cultural Creativity.* Chicago: University of Chicago Press.

Burke, Peter
1990   *The French Historical Revolution: the Annales School, 1929–89.* Stanford: Stanford University Press.
1992   *Critical Essays on Michel Foucault.* Aldershot, UK: Scolar Press.

Burnett, John
1995   Radio report. Morning Edition, National Public Radio. Report broadcast on December 14.

Burridge, Kenelm O. L.
1960   *Mambu: A Melanesian Millennium.* London: Methuen.
1969   *Tangu Traditions: A Study of the Way of Life, Mythology, and Developing Experience of a New Guinea People.* Oxford: Clarendon.

Butcher, Benjamin T.
1964   *My Friends, the New Guinea Headhunters*. Garden City, NY: Doubleday.
Butler, Judith
1987   *Subjects of Desire: Hegelian Reflections in Twentieth-Century France*. New York: Columbia University Press.
1990   *Gender Trouble: Feminism and the Subversion of Identity*. New York: Routledge.
1993a   *Bodies that Matter: On the Discursive Limits of "Sex."* New York: Routledge.
1993b   Critically Queer. *GLQ: A Journal of Lesbian and Gay Studies* 1:17–32.
1993c   Sexual Inversions. In *Foucault and the Critique of Institutions*, edited by John Caputo and Mark Yount, pp. 81–98. University Park, PA: Pennsylvania State University Press.
1994   Contingent Foundations: Feminism and the Question of "Postmodernism." In *The Postmodern Turn: New Perspectives on Social Theory*, edited by Steven Seidman, pp. 153–70. Cambridge: Cambridge University Press.
Buttigieg, Joseph A.
1992   Introduction to *Antonio Gramsci: Prison Notebooks*, vol. 1. Edited by Joseph A. Buttigieg. New York: Columbia University Press.
Caley-Webster, H.
1898   *Through New Guinea and the Cannibal Countries*. London: T. Fisher Unwin.
Calhoun, Craig, Edward LiPuma, and Mishe Postone (eds.)
1993   *Bourdieu: Critical Perspectives*. Chicago: University of Chicago Press.
Cantrell, Eileen M.
n.d.   Gebusi Gender Relations. Ph. D. dissertation in process. Department of Anthropology, University of Michigan, Ann Arbor.
Caputo, John D., and Mark Yount (eds.)
1993   *Foucault and the Critique of Institutions*. University Park, PA: Pennsylvania State University Press.
Carby, Hazel V.
1987   *Reconstructing Womanhood: The Emergence of the Afro-American Woman Novelist*. New York: Oxford University Press.
Carrier, James
1992   Occidentalism: The World Turned Upside-Down. *American Ethnologist* 19:195–212.
1995   (Ed.) *Occidentalism: Images of the West*. Oxford: Oxford University Press.
Carrier, James G. and Achsah H. Carrier
1989   *Wage, Trade, and Exchange in Melanesia: A Manus Society in the Modern State*. Berkeley: University of California Press.
Cassirer, Ernst
1955–57 *The Philosophy of Symbolic Forms*. 3 vols. New Haven, CT: Yale University Press.
Caton, Steven C.
1990   *"Peaks of Yemen I Summon": Poetry as Cultural Practice in a North Yemeni Tribe*. Berkeley: University of California Press.
Centre for Contemporary Cultural Studies (CCCS)
1982   *The Empire Strikes Back: Race and Racism in 1970s Britain*. London: Hutchinson.

Chabram-Dernersesian, Angie
  1992   I Throw Punches for My Race, but I Don't Want to Be a Man: Writing
          Us—Chica-nos (Girl, Us)/Chicanas—into the Movement Script. In
          Cultural Studies, edited by Lawrence Grossberg, Cary Nelson, and Paula
          Treichler, pp. 81–95. New York: Routledge.
Chakrabarty, Dipesh
  1992   Postcoloniality and the Artifice of History: Who Speaks for "Indian"
          Pasts? *Representations*, no. 37:1–26.
Chalmers, James
  1887   *Pioneering in New Guinea*. London: Religious Tract Society.
  1895   *Pioneer Life and Work in New Guinea, 1877–1894*. London: Religious Tract
          Society.
  1903   Notes on the Bugilai, British New Guinea. *Journal of the Royal
          Anthropological Institute of Great Britain and Ireland* 33:108–10.
Chambers, Iain and Lidia Curti (eds.)
  1996   *The Post-Colonial Question: Common Skies, Divided Horizons*. London:
          Routledge.
Chaney, David
  1994   *The Cultural Turn: Scene-setting Essays on Contemporary Social History*.
          London: Routledge.
Chatterjee, Partha
  1993   *The Nation and its Fragments: Colonial and Post-colonial Histories*. Princeton,
          NJ: Princeton University Press.
Chatterjee, Pratap and Kalinga Seneviratne
  1996   Indonesia: Irian Jaya Hostage Crisis Continues. Interpress Third World
          News Agency, January 25. APC Network: <ipsrom@gn.apc.org>
Chicago Cultural Studies Group
  1992   Critical Multiculturalism. *Critical Inquiry* 18:530–55.
Cixous, Hélène
  1994   *The Hélène Cixous Reader*. New York: Routledge.
Clark, Jeffrey
  1992   Madness and Colonization: The Embodiment of Power in Pangia. *Oceania*
          63:15–26.
  1993   Gold, Sex, and Pollution: Male Illness and Mythology at Mt. Kare.
          American Ethnologist 20:742–57.
  n.d.   Desire in the Time of AIDS: Huli Sexuality and the State. (Unpublished
          ms.)
Clark, Jeffrey, and Jenny Hughes
  1995   A History of Sexuality and Gender in Tari. In *Papuan Borderlands: Huli,
          Duna, and Ipili Perspectives on the Papua New Guinea Highlands*, edited by
          Aletta Biersack, pp. 315–40. Ann Arbor: University of Michigan Press.
Clark, John, Celia Modgil, and Sohan Modgil (eds.)
  1990   *Anthony Giddens: Consensus and Controversy*. London: Falmer.
Clark, Katerina and Michael Holquist
  1984   *Mikhail Bakhtin*. Cambridge, MA: Harvard University Press.
Clark, Martin
  1977   *Antonio Gramsci and the Revolution that Failed*. New Haven: Yale University
          Press.

Clifford, James
  1988   *The Predicament of Culture: Twentieth-Century Ethnography, Literature, and Art*. Cambridge, MA: Harvard University Press.
Clifford, James and George E. Marcus (eds.)
  1986   *Writing Culture: The Poetics and Politics of Ethnography*. Berkeley: University of California Press.
Codrington, Robert H.
  1891   *The Melanesians: Studies in Their Anthropology and Folklore*. Oxford: Clarendon.
Cole, Sally and Lynne Phillips (eds.)
  1995   *Ethnographic Feminisms: Essays in Anthropology*. Ottawa: Carleton University Press.
Collier, Jane F. and Sylvia J. Yanagisako
  1987   *Gender and Kinship: Essays Toward a Unified Analysis*. Stanford: Stanford University Press.
Collins, Patricia Hill
  1990   *Black Feminist Thought: Knowledge, Consciousness, and the Politics of Empowerment*. Boston: Unwin Hyman.
  1993   Black Feminist Thought in the Matrix of Domination. In *Social Theory*, edited by Charles Lemert, pp. 615–26. Boulder, CO: Westview.
Comaroff, Jean
  1985   *Body of Power, Spirit of Resistance: The Culture and History of a South African People*. Chicago: University of Chicago Press.
Comaroff, Jean and John Comaroff
  1991   *Of Revelation and Revolution: Christianity and Consciousness in South Africa*, vol. 1. Chicago: University of Chicago Press.
  1993   (Eds.) *Modernity and its Malcontents: Ritual and Power in Postcolonial Africa*. Chicago: University of Chicago Press.
Comaroff, John and Jean Comaroff
  1992   *Ethnography and the Historical Imagination*. Boulder, CO: Westview Press.
Comte, Auguste
  1853   *The Positive Philosophy of Auguste Comte*. 2 vols. London: J. Chapman.
Connell, John and John Lea
  1994   Cities of Parts, Cities Apart? Changing Places in Modern Melanesia. *Contemporary Pacific* 6:257–309.
Cook, Deborah
  1993   *The Subject Finds a Voice: Foucault's Turn Toward Subjectivity*. New York: P. Lang.
Coombe, Rosemary J.
  1991   Encountering the Postmodern: New Directions in Cultural Anthropology. *Canadian Review of Sociology and Anthropology* 28:188–205.
Coronil, Fernando
  1992a Beyond Occidentalism: Towards Post-Imperial Geohistorical Categories. (Unpublished ms.)
  1992b Can Postcoloniality Be Decolonized?: Imperial Banality and Postcolonial Power. *Public Culture* 5:89–108.
Corris, Peter
  1968   "Blackbirding" in New Guinea Waters. *Journal of Pacific History* 3:85–105.

1973   *Passage, Port, and Plantation: A History of Solomon Islands Labour Migration,*
        1870–1914. Carlton, Australia: Melbourne University Press.
Crawford, Anthony L.
1981   *Aida: Life and Ceremony of the Gogodala.* Bathurst, Australia: National
        Cultural Council of Papua New Guinea/Robert Brown and Associates.
D'Albertis, Luigi M.
1880   *New Guinea: What I Did, What I Saw.* 2 vols. London: Sampson, Marston,
        Searle and Rivington.
Daniel, E. Valentine
1984   *Fluid Signs: Being a Person the Tamil Way.* Berkeley: University of
        California Press.
Danow, David K.
1991   *The Thought of Mikhail Bakhtin: From Word to Culture.* New York: St.
        Martin's Press.
Davidson, Alistair
1977   *Antonio Gramsci: Towards an Intellectual Biography.* Atlantic Highlands, NJ:
        Humanities Press.
Davies, Carole Boyce
1994   *Black Women, Writing, and Identity: Migrations of the Subject.* London:
        Routledge.
de Certeau, Michel
1984   *The Practice of Everyday Life.* Berkeley: University of California Press.
1988   *The Writing of History.* Translated by Tom Conley. New York: Columbia
        University Press [Original, 1975].
de Lauretis, Teresa
1984   *Alice Doesn't: Feminism, Semiotics, Cinema.* Bloomington: Indiana University
        Press.
1987   *Technologies of Gender: Essays on Theory, Film, and Fiction.* Bloomington:
        Indiana University Press.
1994   *The Practice of Love: Lesbian Sexuality and Perverse Desire.* Bloomington:
        Indiana University Press.
de Man, Paul
1979   *Allegories of Reading: Figural Langauage in Rousseau, Nietzsche, Rilke, and*
        Proust. New Haven, CT: Yale University Press.
1983   *Blindness and Insight: Essays in the Rhetoric of Contemporary Criticism,* 2nd.
        ed. Minneapolis: University of Minnesota Press.
1984   *The Rhetoric of Romanticism.* New York: Columbia University Press.
de Zengotita, Thomas
1989   Speakers of Being: Romantic Refusion and Cultural Anthropology.
        In *Romantic Motives: Essays on Anthropological Sensibility,* edited by
        George Stocking, Jr., pp. 74–123. Madison: University of Wisconsin
        Press.
Deleuze, Gilles
1983   *Nietzsche and Philosophy.* New York: Columbia University Press.
1988   *Foucault.* Minneapolis: University of Minnesota Press.
1993   *The Deleuze Reader,* edited by Constantin V. Boundas. New York:
        Columbia University Press.

Deleuze, Gilles, and Félix Guattari
 1987   *A Thousand Plateaus: Capitalism and Schizophrenia.* Minneapolis: University of Minnesota Press.
Deloria, Ella
 1932   *Dakota Texts.* New York: Stechert.
 1944   *Speaking of Indians.* Vermillion, SD: State Publishing.
 1988   *Waterlily.* Lincoln: University of Nebraska Press.
Derrida, Jacques
 1976   *Of Grammatology.* Baltimore: Johns Hopkins University Press [Original, 1967].
 1977   *Writing and Difference.* London: Routledge and Kegan Paul [Original, 1967].
Descola, Philippe
 1994   *In the Society of Nature: A Native Ecology in Amazonia.* Cambridge: Cambridge University Press.
Devreaux, Monique
 1994   Feminism and Empowerment: A Critical Reading of Foucault. *Feminist Studies* 20:223–45.
di Leonardo, Micaela
 1991   (Ed.) *Gender at the Crossroads of Knowledge: Feminist Anthropology in the Postmodern Era.* Berkeley: University of California Press.
 1994   White Ethnicities, Identity Politics, and Baby Bear's Chair. *Social Text* 41:165–91.
di Maggio, P.
 1979   On Pierre Bourdieu. *American Journal of Sociology* 84:1460–74.
Diamond, Stanley (ed.)
 1980   *Anthropology: Ancestors and Heirs.* The Hague: Mouton.
Dilthey, Wilhelm
 1883   *Einleitung in die Geisteswissenschaften.* Leipzig: Duncker and Humbolt.
 1954   *The Essence of Philosophy.* Chapel Hill: University of North Carolina Press [Original, 1907].
 1976   *W. Dilthey: Selected Writings*, edited by H. Rickhman. Cambridge: Cambridge University Press.
Dirks, Nicholas B.
 1987   *The Hollow Crown.* Cambridge: Cambridge University Press.
Dirks, Nicholas B., Geoff Eley, and Sherry B. Ortner
 1994   Introduction to *Culture/Power/History*, edited by Nicholas B. Dirks, Geoff Eley, and Sherry B. Ortner, pp. 3–45. Princeton, NJ: Princeton University Press.
Dirlik, Arif
 1994   The Postcolonial Aura: Third World Criticism in the Age of Global Capitalism. *Critical Inquiry* 20:328–56.
Djebar, Assia
 1993   *Fantasia: An Algerian Cavalcade.* Portsmouth, NH: Heinemann.
Docker, Edward W.
 1970   *The Blackbirders: The Recruiting of South Seas Labour for Queensland, 1893–1907.* Sydney: Angus and Robertson.

Docker, John
1994   *Postmodernism and Popular Culture: A Cultural History.* Cambridge: Cambridge University Press.
Dominguez, Virginia R.
1992   Invoking Culture: The Messy Side of "Cultural Politics." *South Atlantic Quarterly* 91(1):19–42.
1994   A Taste for "the Other": Intellectual Complicity in Racializing Practices. *Current Anthropology* 35:333–48.
Donham, Donald L.
1990   *History, Power, Ideology: Central Issues in Marxism and Anthropology.* Cambridge: Cambridge University Press.
1993   A Note on Space in the Ethiopian Revolution. *Africa* 63: 583–90.
Dosse, François
1994   *New History in France: The Triumph of the Annales.* Urbana: University of Illinois Press [Original 1987].
Dreyfus, Hubert L. and Paul Rabinow
1983   *Michel Foucault: Beyond Structuralism and Hermeneutics,* 2nd ed. Chicago: University of Chicago Press.
Drost, E.
1938   *Forced Labor in the South Pacific, 1850–1914.* Iowa City: Iowa State University Press.
DuBois, W. E. B.
1903   *The Souls of Black Folk.* Reprint. New York: Bantam, 1989.
1993   Double-Consciousness and the Veil. In *Social Theory: The Multicultural and Classic Readings,* edited by Charles Lemert, pp. 177–82.
Dumont, Louis
1970   *Homo Hierarchicus: The Caste System and Its Implications.* Chicago: University of Chicago Press.
1994   *German Ideology: From France to Germany and Back.* Chicago: University of Chicago Press.
Dunbabin, Thomas
1935   *Slavers of the South Seas.* Sydney: Angus and Robertson.
Dunning, William V.
1995   *The Roots of Postmodernism.* Englewood Cliffs, NJ: Prentice-Hall.
Dupeyrat, Andrew
1954   *Savage Papua: A Missionary Among Cannibals.* New York: Dutton.
Durkheim, Emile
1964   *The Division of Labor in Society.* New York: Free Press [Original, 1893].
1965   *The Elementary Forms of the Religious Life.* New York: Free Press [Original, 1912].
1966a *The Rules of Sociological Method.* New York: Free Press [Original, 1895].
1966b *Suicide.* New York: Free Press [Original, 1897].
Durkheim, Emile and Marcel Mauss
1963   *Primitive Classification.* Chicago: University of Chicago Press [Original, 1903].
During, Simon
1993   *The Cultural Studies Reader.* London: Routledge.

Dyson, Michael E.
  1993   *Reflecting Black: African American Cultural Criticism.* Minneapolis:
         University of Minnesota Press.
  1994   Essentialism and the Complexities of Racial Identity. In *Multiculturalism: A
         Critical Reader*, edited by David Theo Goldberg, pp. 218–29. Oxford: Basil
         Blackwell.
  1995   Contesting Racial America: From Identity Politics Toward Post-
         Multiculturalism. In *Higher Education Under Fire*, edited by Michael
         Bérubé and Cary Nelson, pp. 336–52. New York: Routledge.
Eduards, Maud L.
  1994   Women's Agency and Collective Action. *Women's Studies International
         Forum* 17:181–86.
Eggan, Fred
  1968   One Hundred Years of Ethnology and Social Anthropology. In *One
         Hundred Years of Anthropology*, edited by J. O. Brew, pp. 116–49.
         Cambridge, MA: Harvard University Press.
Eickelman, D. F.
  1979   The Political Economy of Meaning. *American Ethnologist* 6:386–93.
Elias, Norbert
  1978   *The History of Manners: The Civilizing Process*, vol. 1. New York: Pantheon.
Emerson, Caryl
  1984   Preface to Mikhail Bakhtin, *Problems of Dostoevsky's Poetics*, pp. xxix–xliii.
         Minneapolis: University of Minnesota Press.
Engels, Friedrich
  1972   *The Origin of the Family, Private Property, and the State.* London: Lawrence
         and Wishart [Original, 1884].
Enloe, Cynthia
  1990   *Bananas, Beaches, and Bases: Making Feminist Sense of International Politics.*
         Berkeley: University of California Press.
Eribon, Didier
  1991   *Michel Foucault.* Cambridge, MA: Harvard University Press.
Ernst, Thomas M.
  1991   Onabasulu Male Homosexuality: Cosmology, Affect, and Prescribed Male
         Homosexual Activity Among the Onabasulu of the Great Papuan Plateau.
         Oceania 62:1–11.
  1992   Appendix 3: Interim Report: Incorporated Land Groups, Fasu Area. In *Social
         Mapping and Incorporated Land Groups Report* [for Chevron Niugini Pty. Ltd.],
         by Thomas M. Ernst and John Burton. National Capital District, Papua
         New Guinea: Unisearch PNG Pty. Ltd., University P. O. Box 320.
Ernst, Thomas M. and John Burton
  1992   *Social Mapping and Incorporated Land Groups Report* [for Chevron Niugini
         Pty. Ltd.]. National Capital District, Papua New Guinea: Unisearch PNG
         Pty. Ltd., University P. O. Box 320.
Errington, Frederick K. and Deborah B. Gewertz
  1995   *Articulating Change in the "Last Unknown."* Boulder, CO: Westview.
Evans-Pritchard, E. E.
  1937   *Witchcraft, Oracles, and Magic Among the Azande.* Oxford: Oxford
         University Press.

1940   *The Nuer*. Oxford: Oxford University Press.
1951   *Kinship and Marriage Among the Nuer*. Oxford: Oxford University Press.
Eyde, David B.
1967   Cultural Correlates of Warfare Among the Asmat of South-West New Guinea. Ph. D. dissertation, Department of Anthropology, Yale University.
Fabian, Johannes
1983   *Time and the Other: How Anthropology Makes its Object*. New York: Columbia University Press.
1991   *Time and the Work of Anthropology: Critical Essays, 1971–1991*. Chur, Switzerland: Harwood.
Fanon, Frantz
1968   *The Wretched of the Earth*. Harmondsworth, UK: Penguin [Original, 1961].
1991   *Black Skin, White Masks*. New York: Grove Weidenfeld [Original, 1952].
Fardon, Richard (ed.)
1990   *Localizing Strategies: Regional Traditions of Ethnographic Writing*. Washington, DC: Smithsonian Institution Press.
Farias, Victor
1989   *Heidegger and Nazism*. Philadelphia: Temple University Press [Original, 1987].
Featherstone, Mike
1991   *Consumer Culture and Postmodernism*. London: Sage.
Featherstone, Mike, Scott Lash, and Roland Robertson (eds.)
1995   *Global Modernities*. London: Sage.
Feher, Michel
1990   Carmelo Bene and Michel Foucault: Nominalism, Body, and Subjectivity. Paper presented at the annual meetings of the American Ethnological Society, Atlanta, GA.
Feil, Daryl K.
1987   *The Evolution of Highland Papua New Guinea Societies*. Cambridge: Cambridge University Press.
Feinberg, Richard and Laura Zimmer-Tamakoshi (eds.)
1995   *The Politics of Culture in the Pacific Islands. Ethnology*, vol. 34, no. 3.
Femia, Joseph
1987   *Gramsci's Political Thought: Hegemony, Consciousness, and the Revolutionary Process*. Oxford: Clarendon.
Ferguson, R. Brian and Neil L. Whitehead (eds.)
1992   *War in the Tribal Zone: Expanding States and Indigenous Warfare*. Santa Fe, NM: School of American Research Press.
Feuerbach, Ludwig
1843   Vorläufige Thesen zur Reformation der Philosophie. In *Ankedota zur neuesten deutschen Philosophie und Publizistik*, vol. 2. Zürich: Winterthur.
Fife, Wayne
1995   Models for Masculinity in Colonial and Post-Colonial Papua New Guinea. *Contemporary Pacific* 7:277–302.
Filer, Colin
1990   The Bougainville Rebellion, the Mining Industry, and the Process of Social Disintegration in Papua New Guinea. *Canberra Anthropology* 13(1):1–39.

Fiori, Guiseppe
  1971   *Antonio Gramsci: Life of a Revolutionary*. New York: E. P. Dutton.
Fischer, Michael M. J. and Mehdi Abedi
  1990   *Debating Muslims: Cultural Dialogues in Postmodernity and Tradition*.
          Madison: University of Wisconsin Press.
Fiske, John
  1987   *Television Culture*. London: Routledge.
  1989a   *Reading the Popular*. Boston: Unwin Hyman.
  1989b   *Understanding Popular Culture*. Boston: Unwin Hyman.
Fison, Lorimar
1872–73 The South Seas Labour Traffic. *London Daily Telegraph*. [Series of nine
          articles from December 21, 1872, to March 15, 1873, under the nom de
          plume "Outis."]
Flax, Jane
  1990   *Thinking Fragments: Psychoanalysis, Feminism, and Postmodernism in the
          Contemporary West*. Berkeley: University of California Press.
  1993   *Disputed Subjects: Essays on Psychoanalysis, Politics, and Philosophy*. New York:
          Routledge.
Fontana, Benedetto
  1993   *Hegemony and Power: On the Relation Between Gramsci and Machiavelli*.
          Minneapolis: University of Minnesota Press.
Forgacs, David and Geoffrey Nowell-Smith
  1985   Introduction to *Antonio Gramsci: Selections from Cultural Writings*.
          Cambridge, MA: Harvard University Press.
Fortes, Meyer
  1945   *The Dynamics of Clanship Among the Tallensi*. London: Oxford University
          Press.
  1949   *The Web of Kinship Among the Tallensi*. London: Oxford University Press.
  1953   The Structure of Unilineal Descent Groups. *American Anthropologist*
          55:17–41.
  1971   The Developmental Cycle in Domestic Groups. In *Kinship: Selected
          Readings*, edited by Jack Goody, pp. 85–98. New York: Penguin Books.
Foster, Robert J.
  1991   Making National Cultures in the Global Ecumene. *Annual Reviews in
          Anthropology* 20:235–60.
  1995a   *Social Reproduction and History in Melanesia: Mortuary Ritual, Gift Exchange,
          and Custom in the Tanga Islands*. Cambridge: Cambridge University Press.
  1995b   (Ed.) *Nation Making: Emergent Identities in Postcolonial Melanesia*. Ann
          Arbor: University of Michigan Press.
Foster, Stephen W.
  1986   Reading Pierre Bourdieu. *Cultural Anthropology* 1:103–10.
Foucault, Michel
  1965   *Madness and Civilization: A History of Insanity in the Age of Reason*. New
          York: Times Mirror.
  1970   *The Order of Things: An Archaeology of the Human Sciences*. New York:
          Vintage.
  1972   *The Archaeology of Knowledge and the Discourse on Language*. New York:
          Pantheon.

1973   *The Birth of the Clinic: An Archaeology of Medical Perception.* New York: Pantheon.

1975   *I, Pierre Rivière, Having Slaughtered My Mother, My Sister, and My Brother ... A Case of Parricide in the 19th Century.* New York: Pantheon.

1979   *Discipline and Punish: The Birth of the Prison.* New York: Vintage.

1980a   *The History of Sexuality, Volume 1: An Introduction.* New York: Vintage.

1980b   *Herculine Barbin, Being the Recently Discovered Memoirs of a Nineteenth-Century Hermaphrodite.* New York: Colophon.

1980c   *Power/Knowledge: Selected Interviews and Other Writings, 1972–1977*, edited by Colin Gordon. New York: Pantheon.

1983   The Subject and Power. In *Michel Foucault: Beyond Structuralism and Hermeneutics*, 2nd ed., by Hubert L. Dreyfus and Paul Rabinow, pp. 208–26. Chicago: University of Chicago Press.

1984   *The Foucault Reader*, edited by Paul Rabinow. New York: Pantheon.

1985   *The Use of Pleasure (Volume 2 of the History of Sexuality).* New York: Vintage.

1986   *The Care of the Self (Volume 3 of the History of Sexuality).* New York: Vintage.

1988   Technologies of the Self. In *Technologies of the Self: A Seminar with Michel Foucault*, edited by Luther H. Martin, Huck Butman, and Patrick H. Hutton, pp. 16–49. Amherst: University of Massachusetts Press.

Fox, Richard G.

1985   *Lions of the Punjab: Culture in the Making.* Berkeley: University of California Press.

1991   (Ed.) *Recapturing Anthropology: Working in the Present.* Santa Fe, NM: School of American Research Press.

Fox-Genovese, Elizabeth

1996   *Feminism is Not the Story of My Life: How Today's Feminist Elite has Lost Touch with the Real Concerns of Women.* New York: Nan A. Talese.

Frankenberg, Ruth

1993   *White Women, Race Matters: The Social Construction of Whiteness.* Minneapolis: University of Minnesota Press.

Franklin, Sarah, C. Lury, and J. Stacey (eds.)

1991   *Off-Centre: Feminism and Cultural Studies.* London: HarperCollins.

Fraser, Nancy

1989   *Unruly Practices: Power, Discourse and Gender in Contemporary Social Theory.* Minneapolis: University of Minnesota Press.

Fraser, Nancy and Sandra Lee Bartky (eds.)

1992   *Revaluing French Feminism: Critical Essays on Difference, Agency, and Culture.* Bloomington: Indiana University Press.

Freeman, Carla S.

1993   Designing Women: Corporate Discipline and Barbados's Off-Shore Pink-Collar Sector. *Cultural Anthropology* 8:169–86.

Freud, Sigmund

1900   *The Interpretation of Dreams.* Reprint. New York: Macmillan, 1913.

1913   *Totem and Taboo.* Reprint. New York: Moffat and Yard, 1918.

1920   *Beyond the Pleasure Principle.* Reprint. London: Hogarth, 1950.

1930   *Civilization and its Discontents.* Reprint. London: Hogarth, 1957.

1935   *A General Introduction to Psychoanalysis.* New York: Liveright.

1963   *Character and Culture.* New York: Macmillan.

Freundlieb, Dieter
  1994   Foucault's Theory of Discourse and Human Agency. In *Reassessing Foucault: Power, Medicine and the Body*, edited by Colin Jones and Roy Porter, pp. 152–80. London: Routledge.
Friedl, Ernestine
  1975   *Women and Men: An Anthropologist's View*. New York: Holt, Rinehart, and Winston.
Friedman, Jonathan
  1974   Marxism, Structuralism and Vulgar Materialism. *Man* 9:444–469.
  1987   An Interview with Eric Wolf. *Current Anthropology* 28: 107–18.
  1994   *Cultural Identity and Global Process*. Thousand Oaks, CA: Sage.
Frow, J.
  1987   Accounting for Tastes: Some Problems in Bourdieu's Sociology of Culture. *Cultural Studies* 1:59–73.
Fry, Peter
  1976   *Spirits of Protest: Spirit Mediums and the Articulation of Consensus Among the Zezuru of Southern Rhodesia (Zimbabwe)*. Cambridge: Cambridge University Press.
Fuss, Diana
  1989   *Essentially Speaking: Feminism, Nature, and Difference*. New York: Routledge.
  1991   *Inside/Out: Lesbian Theories, Gay Theories*. New York: Routledge.
  1995   *Identification Papers*. New York: Routledge.
Gadamer, Hans-Georg
  1976   *Philosophical Hermeneutics*. Berkeley: University of California Press.
  1989   *Truth and Method* (rev. ed.). New York: Crossroads.
  1994   *Heidegger's Ways*. Albany: State University of New York Press.
Gal, Susan
  1995   Language and the Arts of Resistance. *Cultural Anthropology* 10:407–24.
Gardiner, Judith K. (ed.)
  1995   *Provoking Agents: Gender and Agency in Theory and Practice*. Urbana: University of Illinois Press.
Garnham, N.
  1986   An Extended Review of Bourdieu's *Distinction*. *Sociological Review* 34:423–33.
Garnham, N. and R. Williams
  1980   Pierre Bourdieu and the Sociology of Culture: An Introduction. *Media, Culture, and Society* 2:209–23.
Garrett, Jemima
  1992   A New Island Oil Bonanza? *Pacific Islands Monthly* (September), p. 23.
Gates, Henry Louis Jr.
  1986   (Ed.) *"Race," Writing, and Difference*. Chicago: University of Chicago Press.
  1991   Goodbye, Columbus? Notes on the Culture of Criticism. *American Literary History* 3:711–27.
  1992   *Loose Canons: Notes on the Culture Wars*. New York: Oxford.
Geertz, Clifford
  1960   *The Religion of Java*. Chicago: University of Chicago Press.
  1963   *Peddlers and Princes: Social Development and Economic Change in Two Indonesian Towns*. Chicago: University of Chicago Press.

1968 *Islam Observed: Religious Development in Morocco and Indonesia.* Chicago: University of Chicago Press.

1973 *The Interpretation of Cultures.* New York: Basic Books.

1980 *Negara: The Theater State in Nineteenth-Century Bali.* Princeton, NJ: Princeton University Press.

1983 *Local Knowledge: Further Essays in Interpretive Anthropology.* New York: Basic Books.

1988 *Works and Lives: The Anthropologist as Author.* Stanford: Stanford University Press.

1995 *After the Fact: Two Countries, Four Decades, One Anthropologist.* Cambridge, MA: Harvard University Press.

Gerhards, J. and H. K. Anheier

1989 The Literary Field: An Empirical Investigation of Bourdieu's Sociology of Art. *International Sociology* 4:131–46.

Germino, Dante

1990 *Antonio Gramsci: Architect of a New Politics.* Baton Rouge: Louisiana State University Press.

Gewertz, Deborah B. and Frederick Errington

1991 *Twisted Histories, Altered Contexts: Representing the Chambri in a World System.* Cambridge: Cambridge University Press.

Ghani, Ashraf

1987 A Conversation with Eric Wolf. *American Ethnologist* 14:346–66.

Giddens, Anthony

1971 *Capitalism and Modern Society Theory: An Analysis of the Writings of Marx, Durkheim, and Weber.* Cambridge: Cambridge University Press.

1972a (Ed., trans., and intro.) *Emile Durkheim: Selected Writings.* Cambridge: Cambridge University Press.

1972b *Politics and Sociology in the Thought of Max Weber.* London: Macmillan.

1973 *The Class Structure of the Advanced Societies.* London: Hutchinson.

1977 *New Rules of Sociological Method.* New York: Basic Books.

1979a *Central Problems in Modern Social Theory: Action, Structure, and Contradiction in Social Analysis.* Berkeley: University of California Press.

1979b *Emile Durkheim.* New York: Viking.

1981 *Power, Property, and the State.* (A Contemporary Critique of Historical Materialism, vol. 1.) Berkeley: University of California Press.

1984 *The Constitution of Society: Outline of the Theory of Structuration.* Berkeley: University of California Press.

1985a Time, Space, and Regionalization. In *Social Relations and Spatial Structures,* edited by Derek Gregory and John Urry, pp. 265–95. New York: St. Martin's.

1985b *The Nation-State and Violence.* (A Contemporary Critique of Historical Materialism, vol. 2). Berkeley: University of California Press.

1987 *Social Theory and Modern Sociology.* Berkeley: University of California Press.

1989a *Sociology.* Cambridge: Polity.

1989b Response to My Critics. In *Anthony Giddens and His Critics,* edited by D. Held and J. Thompson, pp. 249–301. Cambridge: Cambridge University Press.

1990a *The Consequences of Modernity.* Cambridge: Polity.

1990b   Structuration Theory and Sociological Analysis. In *Anthony Giddens: Consensus and Controversy*, edited by John Clark, Celia Modgil, and Sohan Modgil, pp. 297–315. London: Falmer.

1991   *Modernity and Self-Identity: Self and Society in the Late Modern Age*. Stanford: Stanford University Press.

1992   *The Transformation of Intimacy: Sexuality, Love, and Eroticism in Modern Societies*. Stanford: Stanford University Press.

1993   *The Giddens Reader*, ed. by Philip Cassel. Stanford: Stanford University Press.

1994a   Living in a Post-Traditional Society. In *Reflexive Modernization: Politics, Tradition, and Aesthetics*, by Ulrich Beck, Anthony Giddens, and Scott Lash, pp. 56–109. Stanford: Stanford University Press.

1994b   *Beyond Left and Right: The Future of Radical Politics*. Stanford: Stanford University Press.

1995   *Politics, Sociology, and Social Theory: Encounters with Classical and Contemporary Social Thought*. Stanford: Stanford University Press.

Gietzelt, Dale
1988   The Indonesianization of West Papua. *Oceania* 59:201–21.

Gill, Stephen (ed.)
1993   *Gramsci, Historical Materialism, and International Relations*. Cambridge: Cambridge University Press.

Gilmore, David D.
1990   *Manhood in the Making: Cultural Concepts of Masculinity*. New Haven, CT: Yale University Press.

Gilroy, Paul
1987   *There Ain't No Black in the Union Jack: The Cultural Politics of Race and Nation*. London: Hutchinson.

1993   *The Black Atlantic: Modernity and Double Consciousness*. Cambridge, MA: Harvard University Press.

1994   "After the Love Has Gone": Bio-politics and Etho-poetics in the Black Public Sphere. *Public Culture* 7:49–76.

Ginsburg, Faye D. and Rayna Rapp (eds.)
1995   *Conceiving the New World Order: The Global Politics of Reproduction*. Berkeley: University of California Press.

Ginzberg, Carlo
1980   *The Cheese and the Worms: The Cosmos of a Sixteenth-Century Miller*. New York: Penguin [Original, 1976].

1989   *Clues, Myths, and the Historical Method*. Baltimore: Johns Hopkins University Press.

1993   Microhistory: Two or Three Things that I Know About It. *Critical Inquiry* 20:10–35.

Giroux, Henry A.
1992   *Border Crossings: Cultural Workers and the Politics of Education*. New York: Routledge.

Gluckman, Max
1956   *Custom and Conflict in Africa*. Glencoe, IL: Free Press.

Goddard, Michael
1995   The Rascal Road: Crime, Prestige, and Development in Papua New Guinea. *Contemporary Pacific* 7:55–80.

Godelier, Maurice
1977　(Ed.) *Perspectives in Marxist Anthropology*. Cambridge: Cambridge University Press.
1986　*The Making of Great Men: Male Domination and Power Among the New Guinea Baruya*. Cambridge: Cambridge University Press.
n.d.a　Inceste, parenté, pouvoirs. Unpublished manuscript.
n.d.b.　L'Anthropologie Sociale: Est-elle indissolublement lieé à l'occident, sa terre natale? Unpublished ms.
Godelier, Maurice and Jacques Hassoun (eds.)
1996　*Meutre du père/Sacrifice de sexualité*. Arcanes: Strasbourg.
Goffman, Erving
1959　*The Presentation of Self in Everyday Life*. Garden City, NY: Doubleday.
1963a　*Stigma: Notes on the Management of Spoiled Identity*. Englewood Cliffs, NJ: Prentice-Hall.
1963b　*Behavior in Public Places: Notes on the Social Organization of Gatherings*. New York: Free Press.
1967　*Interaction Ritual: Essays on Face-to-Face Behavior*. Garden City, NY: Anchor.
1974　*Frame Analysis: An Essay on the Organization of Experience*. New York: Harper and Row.
1981　*Forms of Talk*. Philadelphia: University of Pennsylvania Press.
Goldberg, David Theo (ed.)
1990　*Anatomy of Racism*. Minneapolis: University of Minnesota Press.
1994　*Multiculturalism: A Critical Reader*. Oxford: Basil Blackwell.
Goldenweiser, Alex A.
1922　*Early Civilization: An Introduction to Anthropology*. New York: Knopf.
1933　*History, Psychology, and Culture*. New York: Knopf.
1937　*Anthropology: An Introduction to Primitive Culture*. New York: Appleton.
Golding, Sue
1992　*Gramsci's Democratic Theory*. Toronto: University of Toronto Press.
Goldschmidt, Walter
1959　*Man's Way: A Preface to the Understanding of Human Society*. New York: Holt, Rinehart, and Winston.
1966　*Comparative Functionalism*. Berkeley: University of California Press.
Goody, Jack
1995　*The Expansive Moment: Anthropology in Britain and Africa, 1918–1970*. Cambridge: Cambridge University Press.
Gordon, Deborah
1988　Writing Culture, Writing Feminism: The Poetics and Politics of Experimental Ethnography. *Inscriptions* 3/4:7–24.
Gramsci, Antonio
1971　*Selections from the Prison Notebooks of Antonio Gramsci*, edited by Quintin Hoare and Geoffrey Nowell-Smith. London: Lawrence and Wishart.
1978　*Selections from the Political Writings*, edited by Quintin Hoare. London: Lawrence and Wishart.
1985　*Antonio Gramsci: Selections from Cultural Writings*, edited by David Forgacs and Geoffrey Nowell-Smith. Cambridge, MA: Harvard University Press.
1992　*Antonio Gramsci: Prison Notebooks*, vol. 1. Edited and introduced by Joseph A. Buttigieg. New York: Columbia University Press.

1994   *Pre-Prison Writings*, edited by Richard Bellamy, translated by Virginia Cox. Cambridge: Cambridge University Press.

1995   *Further Selections from the Prison Notebooks*. Edited by Derek Boothman. Minneapolis: University of Minnesota Press.

Grene, Marjorie

1968   Martin Heidegger. *Encyclopedia of Philosophy* 3:459–65.

Grewal, Inderpal and Caren Kaplan (eds.)

1994   *Scattered Hegemonies*. Minneapolis: University of Minnesota Press.

Griffin, James, Hank Nelson, and Stewart Firth

1979   *Papua New Guinea: A Political History*. Richmond, Victoria (Australia): Heinemann Educational Australia.

Grossberg, Lawrence

1986   On Postmodernism and Articulation: An Interview with Stuart Hall. *Journal of Communication Inquiry* 10:45–61.

1992   *We Gotta Get Out of This Place: Popular Conservatism and Postmodern Culture*. New York: Routledge.

Grossberg, Lawrence, Cary Nelson, and Paula A. Treichler (eds.)

1992   *Cultural Studies*. New York: Routledge.

Guha, Ranajit

1988a   On Some Aspects of the Historiography of Colonial India. In *Selected Subaltern Studies*, edited by Ranajit Guha and Gayatri C. Spivak, pp. 37–44. New York: Oxford University Press.

1988b   The Prose of Counter-insurgency. In *Selected Subaltern Studies*, edited by Ranajit Guha and Gayatri C. Spivak, pp. 45–86. New York: Oxford University Press.

1989   Dominance Without Hegemony and its Historiography. In *Subaltern Studies VI*, edited by Ranajit Guha, pp. 210–309. Delhi: Oxford University Press.

1992   Discipline and Mobilize. In *Subaltern Studies VII*, edited by Partha Chatterjeee and Gyanendra Pandey, pp. 69–120. Delhi: Oxford University Press.

Gupta, Akhil and James Ferguson

1992   Beyond "Culture": Space, Identity, and the Politics of Difference. *Cultural Anthropology* 7:6–23.

Gutting, Gary (ed.)

1994   *The Cambridge Companion to Foucault*. Cambridge: Cambridge University Press.

Habermas, Jürgen

1981   Modernity Versus Postmodernity. *New German Critique* 22 (winter):3–14.

1984   *The Theory of Communicative Action*. Boston: Beacon.

1987   *The Philosophical Discourse of Modernity: Twelve Lectures*. Cambridge, MA: MIT Press.

Haddon, Alfred C.

1901–35   (Ed.) *Reports of the Cambridge Anthropological Expedition to Torres Strait*. Cambridge: Cambridge University Press.

1918   The Agiba Cult of the Kerewa Culture. *Man* 18: 177–83(No. 99).

1920   The Migrations of Cultures in British New Guinea. *Journal of the Royal Anthropological Institute of Great Britain and Ireland* 50:234–80.

1923   Stuffed Human Heads from New Guinea. *Man* 23: 36–39(No.20).

1924 Introduction to *In Primitive New Guinea*, by John H. Holmes, pp. i-xii. New York: G. P. Putnam's Sons.

1927 Introduction to *The Kiwai Papuans of British New Guinea*, by Gunnar Landtman, pp. ix–xx. London: Macmillan. Reprint. New York: Johnson Reprint Co., 1970.

1928 Introduction to *Rossel Island: An Ethnological Study*, by Wallace E. Armstrong. Cambridge: Cambridge University Press.

1936 Introduction to *Papuans of the Trans-Fly*, by F. E. Williams, pp. xxiii–xxxiv. Oxford: Clarendon.

Hale, Charles R.

1994 *Resistance and Contradiction: Miskitu Indians and the Nicaraguan State, 1894–1987*. Stanford: Stanford University Press.

Hall, Stuart

1986a Gramsci's Relevance for the Study of Race and Ethnicity. *Journal of Communication Inquiry* 10:5–27.

1986b The Problem of Ideology—Marxism Without Guarantees. *Journal of Communication Inquiry* 10:28–44.

1986c On Postmodernism and Articulation: An Interview with Stuart Hall. *Journal of Communication Inquiry* 10:45–60.

1988 *The Hard Road to Renewal: Thatcherism and the Crisis on the Left*. London: Verso.

1992 Cultural Studies and Its Theoretical Legacies. In *Cultural Studies*, edited by Lawrence Grossberg, Cary Nelson, and Paula Treichler, pp. 277–94. New York: Routledge.

1996 When was 'The Post-Colonial'? Thinking at the Limit. In *The Post-Colonial Question: Common Skies, Divided Horizons*. Edited by Iain Chambers and Lidia Curti, pp. 242–60. London: Routledge.

Hall, Stuart, C. Critcher, T. Jefferson, J. Clarke, and B. Roberts

1978 *Policing the Crisis: Mugging, the State, and Law and Order*. London: Macmillan.

Hall, Stuart, D. Hobson, A. Lowe, and P. Willis (eds.)

1980 *Culture, Media, Language: Working Papers in Cultural Studies, 1972–79*. London: Hutchinson.

Hall, Stuart and M. Jacques (eds.)

1983 *The Politics of Thatcherism*. London: Lawrence and Wishart.

Hall, Stuart and T. Jefferson (eds.)

1976 *Resistance Through Rituals*. London: Hutchinson.

Halperin, David M.

1995 *Saint Foucault: Towards a Gay Hagiography*. New York: Oxford.

Hammar, Lawrence

1992 Sexual Transactions on Daru: With Some Observations on the Ethnographic Enterprise. *Research in Melanesia* 16:21–54.

1995 Crisis in the South Fly: The Problem with Sex and the Sex Industry on Daru Island, Western Province, Papua New Guinea. Ph. D. dissertation, Department of Anthropology, Graduate Center, City University of New York.

in press Bad Canoes and *Bafalo*: The Political Economy of Sex on Daru Island, Western Province, Papua New Guinea. *Genders* 23.

Handler, Richard
  1991   An Interview with Clifford Geertz. *Cultural Anthropology* 32:603–13.
Hannerz, Ulf
  1990   Cosmopolitans and Locals in World Culture. *Theory, Culture, and Society* 7:237–52.
Haraway, Donna
  1989   *Primate Visions: Gender, Race and Nature in the World of Modern Science.* New York: Routledge.
  1990   *Simians, Cyborgs, and Women: The Reinvention of Nature.* London: Free Association Books.
Hardt, Michael
  1993   *Gilles Deleuze: An Apprenticeship in Philosophy.* Minneapolis: University of Minnesota Press.
Harker, Richard, Cheleen Mahar, and Chris Wilkes (eds.)
  1990   *An Introduction to the Work of Pierre Bourdieu: The Practice of Theory.* London: Macmillan.
Harries, Karsten and Christoph Jamme
  1994   *Martin Heidegger: Politics, Art, and Technology.* New York: Holmes and Meier.
Harris, David
  1992   *From Class Struggle to the Politics of Pleasure: The Effects of Gramscianism on Cultural Studies.* London: Routledge.
Harris, Marvin
  1968   *The Rise of Anthropological Theory.* New York: Thomas Crowell.
  1979   *Cultural Materialism: The Struggle for a Science of Culture.* New York: Vintage.
Hart Nibbrig, Nand E.
  1992   Rascals in Paradise: Urban Gangs in Papua New Guinea. *Pacific Studies* 15(3):115–34.
Hartsock, Nancy
  1983   *Money, Sex, and Power: Towards a Feminist Historical Materialism.* New York: Longman.
  1990   Foucault on Power: A Theory for Women? In *Feminism/Postmodernism*, edited by Linda Nicholson, pp. 157–75. New York: Routledge.
Harvey, David
  1982   *Limits to Capital.* Oxford: Basil Blackwell.
  1990   *The Condition of Postmodernity: An Enquiry into the Origins of Culture Change.* Cambridge: Basil Blackwell.
  1993a   From Space to Place and Back Again: Reflections on the Condition of Postmodernity. In *Mapping the Futures: Local Cultures, Global Change*, edited by J. Bird, B. Curtis, T. Putnam, G. Robertson, and L. Tickner, pp. 3–29. London: Routledge.
  1993b   Class Relations, Social Justice and the Politics of Difference. In *Place and Politics of Identity*, edited by Michael Keith and Steve Pile, pp. 41–66. London: Routledge.
Hau'ofa Epeli
  1975   Anthropology and Pacific Islanders. *Oceania* 45:283–89.
  1994   Our Sea of Islands. *Contemporary Pacific* 6:148–61.

Hebdige, Dick
  1979   *Subcultures: The Meaning of Style.* London: Methuen.
  1988   *Hiding in the Light: On Images and Things.* London: Routledge.
Heelas, Paul, Scott Lash, and Paul Morris (eds.)
  1996   *Detraditionalization: Critical Reflections on Authority and Identity.* Oxford:
          Basil Blackwell.
Hegel, Georg W.
  1830   *Encyclopaedia of the Philosophical Sciences.* Reprint. London: Oxford
          University Press, 1971.
Heidegger, Martin
  1962   *Being and Time.* London: SCM.
  1977a   *The Question Concerning Technology and Other Essays.* New York: Harper and
          Row.
  1977b   *Martin Heidegger: Basic Writings.* New York: Harper and Row.
  1982   *The Basic Problems of Phenomenology.* Bloomington: Indiana University
          Press.
  1991   *Nietzsche.* San Francisco: Harper.
Held, David and John B. Thompson (eds.)
  1989   *Social Theory of Modern Societies: Anthony Giddens and His Critics.*
          Cambridge: Cambridge University Press.
Herder, Johann Gottfried von
  1966   Essay on the Origin of Language. In *On the Origin of Languages,* by Jean-
          Jacques Rousseau and Johann Gottfried Herder. New York: Ungar.
  1968   *Reflections on the Philosophy of the History of Mankind,* edited by Frank E.
          Munueul. Chicago: University of Chicago Press.
  1969   *J.G. Herder on Social and Political Culture,* edited by Frederick M. Barnard.
          Cambridge University Press.
Herdt, Gilbert H.
  1981   *Guardians of the Flutes: Idioms of Masculinity.* New York: McGraw-Hill.
  1982   Fetish and Fantasy in Sambia Initiation. In *Rituals of Manhood: Male
          Initiation in Papua New Guinea,* edited by Gilbert H. Herdt, pp. 44–98.
          Berkeley: University of California Press.
  1984a   Ritualized Homosexual Behavior in the Male Cults of Melanesia,
          1862–1983: An Introduction. In *Ritualized Homosexuality in Melanesia,*
          edited by Gilbert H. Herdt, pp. 1–81. Berkeley: University of California
          Press.
  1984b   Semen Transactions in Sambia Culture. In *Ritualized Homosexuality in
          Melanesia,* edited by Gilbert H. Herdt, pp. 167–210. Berkeley: University
          of California Press.
  1987a   *The Sambia: Ritual and Gender in New Guinea.* New York: Holt, Rinehart,
          and Winston.
  1987b   Homosexuality. In *The Encyclopedia of Religion* 6:445–52, edited by Mircea
          Eliade. New York: Macmillan.
  1991   Representations of Homosexuality: An Essay on Cultural Ontology and
          Historical Comparison, parts I and II. *Journal of the History of Sexuality*
          1:481–504, 603–32.
  1992   (Ed.) *Gay Culture in America: Essays from the Field.* Boston: Beacon
  1993   Retrospective on Ritualized Homosexuality in Melanesia: Introduction to

the New Edition. In *Ritualized Homosexuality in Melanesia*, 2nd ed. Berkeley: University of California Press.

1994   (Ed.) *Third Sex, Third Gender: Beyond Sexual Dimorphism in Culture and History*. New York: Zone Books.

Herdt, Gilbert H. and Andrew Boxer
1993   *Children of Horizons: How Gay and Lesbian Teens Are Leading a New Way Out of the Closet*. Boston: Beacon.

Herdt, Gilbert H. and John F. P. Poole
1982   "Sexual Antagonism": The History of a Concept in New Guinea Anthropology. *Social Analysis* 12:3–28.

Herdt, Gilbert H. and Robert J. Stoller
1990   *Intimate Communications: Erotics and the Study of Culture*. New York: Columbia University Press.

Heritier, François
1994   *Les Deux soeurs et leur mère: l'Anthropologie de l'inceste*. Paris: Odile Jacob.

Herodotus
1987   *The History*. Translated by David Grene. Chicago: University of Chicago Press.

1992   *The Histories: New Translation, Selections, Backgrounds, Commentaries*, edited by Walter Blanco and Jennifer T. Roberts. New York: Norton.

Herskovits, Melville J.
1938   *Acculturation: The Study of Culture Contact*. Locust Valley, NY: J. J. Augustin.

1948   *Man and His Works: The Science of Cultural Anthropology*. New York: Knopf.

1952   *Economic Anthropology*. New York: Knopf.

1953   *Franz Boas: The Science of Man in the Making*. New York: Scribner.

Hewitt, Nancy A.
1992   Compounding Differences. *Feminist Studies* 18:313–26.

Hides, Jack
1936   *Papuan Wonderland*. Sydney: Angus and Robertson.

Hoad, Richard A.
1962–63 Patrol Report No. 1. Nomad Sub-District Office, Western Province, Territory of Papua New Guinea.

Hoare, Quintin and Geoffrey Nowell-Smith
1971   Introduction. In *Selections from the Prison Notebooks of Antonio Gramsci*. Edited by Quintin Hoare and Geoffrey Nowell-Smith, pp. xvii–xcvi. London: Lawrence and Wishart.

Hobsbawm, Eric J.
1959   *Primitive Rebels: Studies in Archaic Forms of Social Movement in the Nineteenth and Twentieth Centuries*. Manchester: Manchester University Press.

1965   (Ed.) *Pre-capitalist Economic Formations*, by Karl Marx. New York: International Publishers.

Hodge, Joanna
1995   *Heidegger and Ethics*. London: Routledge.

Hodgen, Margaret T.
1964   *Early Anthropology in the Sixteenth and Seventeenth Centuries*. Philadelphia: University of Pennsylvania Press.

Hoggart, Richard
1957 *The Uses of Literacy: Aspects of Working-Class Life with Special Reference to Publications and Entertainments.* London: Chatto and Windus.
1970 *Speaking to Each Other: Essays.* 2 vols. New York: Oxford University Press.
Hollinger, David A.
1995 *Postethnic America: Beyond Multiculturalism.* New York: Basic Books.
Holmes, John H.
1924 *In Primitive New Guinea.* London: Seeley Service.
Holquist, Michael
1990 *Dialogism: Bakhtin and His World.* London: Routledge.
Holub, Renate
1992 *Antonio Gramsci: Beyond Marxism and Postmodernism.* London: Routledge.
Honneth, Axel
1986 The Fragmented World of Symbolic Forms: Reflections on Pierre Bourdieu's Sociology of Culture. *Theory, Culture, and Society* 3:55–66.
Honneth, Axel, Hermann Kocyba, and Bernd Schwibs
1986 The Struggle for Symbolic Order: An Interview with Pierre Bourdieu. *Theory, Culture and Society* 3:35–51.
hooks, bell
1981 *Ain't I a Woman: Black Women and Feminism.* Boston: South End.
1990 *Yearning: Race, Gender, and Cultural Politics.* Boston: South End.
1992a *Black Looks: Race and Representation.* Boston: South End.
1992b Representing Whiteness in the Black Imagination. In *Cultural Studies*, edited by Lawrence Grossberg, Cary Nelson, and Paula Treichler, pp. 338–46. New York: Routledge.
1994 *Teaching to Transgress: Education as the Practice of Freedom.* New York: Routledge.
Hope, Penelope
1979 *Long Ago Is Far Away: Accounts of the Early Exploration and Settlement of the Papuan Gulf Area.* Canberra: Australian National University Press.
Horkheimer, Max
1972 *Critical Theory: Selected Essays.* New York: Herder and Herder.
1993 *Between Philosophy and Social Science: Selected Early Writings.* Cambridge, MA: MIT Press.
Horkheimer, Max and Theodor W. Adorno
1972 *Dialectic of Enlightenment.* New York: Continuum.
Horton, John
1993 Liberalism, Multiculturalism, and Toleration. In *Liberalism, Multiculturalism, and Toleration*, edited by John Horton, pp. 1–17. London: Macmillan.
Hurston, Zora Neale
1935 *Mules and Men.* Reprint. New York: Harper, 1990.
1937 *Their Eyes Were Watching God: A Novel.* Philadelphia: J. B. Lippincott.
Husserl, Edmund
1982 *General Introduction to a Pure Phenomenology.* Boston: Kluwer Academic.
1989 *Studies in the Phenomenology of Constitution.* Boston: Kluwer Academic.
1991 *On the Phenomenology of Consciousness of Internal Time.* Boston: Kluwer Academic.

Hutcheon, Linda
  1989   *The Politics of Postmodernism*. London: Routledge.
Huyssen, Andreas
  1986   *After the Great Divide: Modernism, Mass Culture, Postmodernism*. Blooming-
          ton: Indiana University Press.
Hyndman, David
  1994   *Ancestral Rain Forests and the Mountain of Gold: Indigenous Peoples and
          Mining in New Guinea*. Boulder, CO: Westview Press.
Iamo, Warilea
  1992   The Stigma of New Guinea: Reflections on Anthropology and
          Anthropologists. In *Confronting the Margaret Mead Legacy: Scholarship,
          Empire, and the South Pacific*, edited by Lenora Foerstel and Angela
          Gilliam, pp. 75–99. Philadelphia: Temple University Press.
Inglis, John (ed.)
  1872   *The Slave Trade in the New Hebrides*. Edinburgh: Edmonson and Douglas.
Inhorn, Marcia C.
  1994   *Quest for Conception: Gender, Infertility, and Egyptian Medical Traditions*.
          Philadelphia: University of Pennsylvania Press.
Irigaray, Luce
  1985   *Speculum of the Other Woman*. Ithaca, NY: Cornell University Press.
  1991a   *The Marine Lover of Friedrich Nietzsche*. New York: Columbia University
          Press.
  1991b   *The Irigaray Reader*. Cambridge, MA: Basil Blackwell.
  1993a   *Sexes and Genealogies*. New York: Columbia University Press.
  1993b   *An Ethics of Sexual Difference*. Ithaca, NY: Cornell University Press.
Jacoby, Russell
  1995   Marginal Returns: The Trouble with Post-colonial Theory. *Lingua Franca*,
          Sept./Oct.:30–37.
Jakobson, Roman
  1987   *Language in Literature*, edited by Krystyna Pomorska and Stephen Rudy.
          Cambridge, MA: Belknap.
  1990   *On Language*, edited by Linda R. Waugh and Monique Monville-Burston.
          Cambridge, MA: Harvard University Press.
Jakobson, Roman and Linda R. Waugh
  1987   *The Sound Shape of Language*, 2nd. ed. New York: Mouton de Gruyter.
Jameson, Frederic
  1991   *Postmodernism, or the Cultural Logic of Late Capitalism*. Durham, NC: Duke
          University Press.
Janicaud, Dominique and Jean-François Mattei
  1995   *Heidegger from Metaphysics to Thought*. Albany: State University of New
          York Press.
Jenkins, Carol
  1994   *National Study of Sexual and Reproductive Knowledge and Behavior in Papua
          New Guinea*. Papua New Guinea Institute of Medical Research
          Monograph 10. Goroka, Papua New Guinea.
Jenkins, Richard
  1992   *Pierre Bourdieu*. London: Routledge.

Jolly, Margaret and Nicholas Thomas (eds.)
1992   The Politics of Tradition. Special issue, *Oceania* 62(4):241–354.
Jones, Colin and Roy Porter (eds.)
1994   *Reassessing Foucault: Power, Medicine, and the Body*. London:
        Routledge.
Jorgensen, Dan
1995   [Overview of recent developments in Papua New Guinea.] *Northeast
        Wantok System Newsletter (N.E.W.S.)*, Namba 22, parts 1–6. Internet:
        dwj@julian.uwo.ca.edu.
Juillerat, Bernard
1992   (Ed.) *Shooting the Sun: Ritual and Meaning in West Sepik*. Washington, DC:
        Smithsonian Institution Press.
1993   *La Revocation des Tambaran: Les Banaro et Richard Thurnwald revisités*. Paris:
        CNRS.
Jukes, J. Beete
1847   *Narrative of the Surveying Voyage of the H.M.S. Fly, Commanded by Captain
        F. P. Blackwood*. 2 vols. London: n.p.
Kanpol, Barry and Peter McLaren (eds.)
1995   *Critical Multiculturalism: Uncommon Voices in a Common Struggle*. Westport,
        CT: Bergin and Garvey.
Kaufmann, Walter
1974   *Nietzsche: Philosopher, Psychologist, Antichrist*. 4th ed. Princeton, NJ:
        Princeton University Press.
Keesing, Roger M.
1989   Creating the Past: Custom and Identity in the Contemporary Pacific.
        Contemporary Pacific 1:19–42.
1992   *Custom and Confrontation: The Kwaio Struggle for Cultural Autonomy*.
        Chicago: University of Chicago Press.
Keesing, Robert M. and Robert Tonkinson (eds.)
1982   Reinventing Traditional Culture: The Politics of Kastom in Island
        Melanesia. Special issue, *Mankind* 13:297–399.
Keith, Michael and Steve Pile (eds.)
1993   *Place and the Politics of Identity*. London: Routledge.
Kellner, Douglas
1989   *Jean Baudrillard: From Marxism to Postmodernism and Beyond*. Stanford:
        Stanford University Press.
1992   *The Persian Gulf TV War*. Boulder, CO: Westview Press.
Kelly, Raymond C.
1977   *Etoro Social Structure: A Study in Structural Contradiction*. Ann Arbor:
        University of Michigan Press.
1985   *The Nuer Conquest: The Structure and Development of an Expansionist System*.
        Ann Arbor: University of Michigan Press.
1993   *Constructing Inequality: The Fabrication of a Hierarchy of Virtue Among the
        Etoro*. Ann Arbor: University of Michigan Press.
Khaldūn, Ibn
1374–77 *The Muqaddimah (An Introduction to History)*. 3 vols. Princeton, NJ:
        Princeton University Press, 1967.

Kirsch, Stuart
  1993   Resisting the Mine: Pollution as Environmental "Sorcery." Paper
          presented at the annual meetings of the American Anthropological
          Association, Washington, DC.
  1995   Indigenous Response to Environmental Impact along the Ok Tedi. Papua
          New Guinea Law Reform Commission Monograph No. 6. Port Moresby.
Kisiel, Theodore J. and John Van Buren (eds.)
  1994   *Reading Heidegger from the Start: Essays in His Earliest Thought*. Albany:
          State University of New York Press.
Knauft, Bruce M.
  1978   Cargo Cults and Relational Separation. *Behavior Science Research* 13:185–240.
  1985a   *Good Company and Violence: Sorcery and Social Action in a Lowland New
          Guinea Society*. Berkeley: University of California Press.
  1985b   Ritual Form and Permutation in New Guinea: Implications of Symbolic
          Process for Sociopolitical Evolution. *American Ethnologist* 12:321–40.
  1986   Text and Social Practice: Narrative "Longing" and Bisexuality Among the
          Gebusi of New Guinea. *Ethos* 14:252–81.
  1987a   Reconsidering Violence in Simple Human Societies: Homicide Among the
          Gebusi of New Guinea. *Current Anthropology* 28:457–500.
  1987b   Homosexuality in Melanesia. *The Journal of Psychoanalytic Anthropology*
          10:155–91.
  1989a   Bodily Images in Melanesia: Cultural Substances and Natural Metaphors.
          In *Fragments for a History of the Human Body, Part Three*, edited by Michel
          Feher, Ramona Nadaff, and Nadia Tazi, pp. 198–279. New York: Urzone.
  1989b   Imagery, Pronouncement, and the Aesthetics of Reception in Gebusi
          Spirit Mediumship. In *The Religious Imagination in New Guinea*, edited by
          Gilbert H. Herdt and Michele Stephen, pp. 67–98. New Brunswick, NJ:
          Rutgers University Press.
  1990a   The Question of Homosexuality Among the Kiwai of South New Guinea.
          Journal of Pacific History 25:188–210.
  1990b   Melanesian Warfare: A Theoretical History. *Oceania* 60:250–311.
  1991   Violence and Sociality in Human Evolution. *Current Anthropology*
          32:391–428.
  1992   Warfare, Western Intrusion, and Ecology in Melanesia. *Man* (n.s.)
          27:399–401.
  1993a   *South Coast New Guinea Cultures: History, Comparison, Dialectic*. Cambridge:
          Cambridge University Press.
  1993b   Inducements to Conflict. *Science* 260 (May 21):1184–86.
  1993c   Monument of Miscast Error: Obeyesekere Versus Sahlins and Captain
          Cook. *Social Analysis* 34:34–42.
  1995a   Beyond Classic Scribes and Others' Dia-Tribes: Ethnography and History
          Along the New Guinea South Coast. *Pacific Studies* 18(4):176–91.
  1995b   Post-Melanesian Studies? Paper presented at the annual meetings of the
          American Anthropological Association, Washington, DC.
  1995c   Agency in Cultural Anthropology in the mid-90s: A Commentary.
          Presented at the annual meetings of the American Anthropological
          Association, Washington, DC.

Kondo, Dorinne K.
1990   *Crafting Selves: Power, Gender, and Discourses of Identity in a Japanese Workplace*. Chicago: University of Chicago Press.

Krader, Lawrence
1972   *The Ethnological Notebooks of Karl Marx*. Assen: Van Gorcum.

Kratz, Corinne A.
1994   *Affecting Performance: Meaning, Movement, and Experience in Okiek Women's Initiation*. Washington, DC: Smithsonian Institution Press.

Kristeva, Julia
1987   *The Kristeva Reader*. New York: Columbia University Press.

Kroeber, Alfred L.
1939   *Cultural and Natural Areas of Native North America*. University of California Publications in American Archaeology and Ethnology, vol. 38.
1944   *Configurations of Culture Growth*. Berkeley: University of California Press.
1948   *Anthropology*. New York: Harcourt Brace.
1952   *The Nature of Culture*. Chicago: University of Chicago Press.
1953   (Ed.) *Anthropology Today: An Encyclopedic Inventory*. Chicago: University of Chicago Press.
1957   *Style and Civilizations*. Ithaca, NY: Cornell University Press.

Kroeber, Alfred L. and Clyde Kluckhohn
1952   *Culture: A Critical Review of Concepts and Definitions*. Papers of the Peabody Museum of American Archaeology and Ethnology, vol. 47. Cambridge, MA: Harvard University.

Kroker, Arthur, Marilouise Kroker, and David Cook (eds.)
1989   *Panic Encyclopedia: The Definitive Guide to the Postmodern Scene*. New York: St. Martin's.

Kuklick, Henrika
1991   *The Savage Within: The Social History of British Anthropology, 1885–1945*. Cambridge: Cambridge University Press.

Kulick, Don
1990   Christianity, Cargo, and Ideas of Self: Patterns of Literacy in a Papua New Guinea Village. *Man* (n.s.) 25:286–304.
1992   *Language Shift and Cultural Reproduction: Socialization, Self, and Syncretism in a Papua New Guinean Village*. Cambridge: Cambridge University Press.
1993   Heroes from Hell: Representations of "Rascals" in Papua New Guinea Village. *Anthropology Today* 9:9–14.

Kulick, Don and Margaret Willson
1994   Rambo's Wife Saves the Day: Subjugating the Gaze and Subverting the Narrative in a Papua New Guinean Swamp. *Visual Anthropology Review* 10:1–13.
1995   (Eds.) *Taboo: Sex and Erotic Subjectivity in Anthropological Fieldwork*. New York: Routledge.

Kuper, Adam
1983   *Anthropology and Anthropologists: The Modern British School*. London: Routledge and Kegan Paul.
1988   *The Invention of Primitive Society: Transformations of an Illusion*. London: Routledge.

1994   Culture, Identity, and the Project of a Cosmopolitan Anthropology. *Man* 29:537–54.

Kuruwaip, Abraham
1984   The Asmat Bis Pole: Its Background and Meaning. In *An Asmat Sketch Book #4*, edited by Frank Trenkenschuh, pp. 11–30. Hastings, NE: Crosier Missions.

Kutubu Plan
1989   *Kutubu Petroleum Development Project Environmental Plan*. Report 10: Socioeconomic Impact Study. Melbourne, Australia: Shedden Agribusiness.

Kyakas, Alome and Polly Wiessner
1992   *From Inside the Women's House: Enga Women's Lives and Traditions*. Buranda, Queensland, Australia: Robert Brown.

Laba, Billai
1975a   Waidoro—A Papuan Village in an Era of Change. Part One: The Village and its Neighbours. *South Pacific Bulletin (Official Journal of the South Pacific Commission)* 25(3):31–37.
1975b   Waidoro—A Papuan Village in an Era of Change. Part Two: The Village Today. *South Pacific Bulletin (Official Journal of the South Pacific Commission)* 25(4):15–23.

Laclau, Ernesto
1990   *New Reflections on the Revolution of Our Time*. London: Verso.
1994   (Ed.) *The Making of Political Identities*. London: Verso.

Laclau, Ernesto and Chantal Mouffe
1985   *Hegemony and Socialist Strategy: Towards a Radical Democratic Politics*. London: Verso.

Lacan, Jacques
1977   *Ecrits: A Selection*. New York: Norton.

Lamaison, Pierre
1989   From Rules to Strategies: An Interview with Pierre Bourdieu. *Cultural Anthropology* 1:110–20.

Lambek Michael
1993   *Knowledge and Practice in Mayotte: Local Discourses of Islam, Sorcery, and Spirit Possession*. Toronto: University of Toronto Press.

Lan, David
1985   *Guns and Rain: Guerrillas and Spirit Mediums in Zimbabwe*. Berkeley: University of California Press.

Lancaster, Roger
1992   *Life Is Hard: Machismo, Danger, and the Intimacy of Power in Nicaragua*. Berkeley: University of California Press.
n.d.   *The Queer Body*. Berkeley: University of California Press.

Landtman, Gunnar
1917   *The Folk-Tales of the Kiwai Papuans*. Helsinki: Finnish Society of Literature.
1927   *The Kiwai Papuans of British New Guinea*. London: Macmillan.

Landy, Marcia
1994   *Film, Politics, and Gramsci*. Minneapolis: University of Minnesota Press.

Langmore, Diane
1974   *Tamate—A King: James Chalmers in New Guinea, 1877–1901*. Melbourne: Melbourne University Press.

1989   *Missionary Lives: Papua, 1874–1914*. Honolulu: University of Hawaii Press.
Lanternari, Vittorio
1965   *Religions of the Oppressed: A Study of Modern Messianic Cults*. New York: New American Library.
Lash, Scott and Jonathan Friedman (eds.)
1992   *Modernity and Identity*. Oxford: Basil Blackwell.
Lash, Scott and John Urry
1987   *The End of Organised Capitalism*. Oxford: Basil Blackwell.
1994   *Economies of Signs and Space*. London: Sage.
Lattas, Andrew (ed.)
1992   Alienating Mirrors: Christianity, Cargo Cults, and Colonialism in Melanesia. Special issue, *Ocenia* 63(1): 1–93.
Lavie, Smadar
1990   *The Poetics of Military Occupation: Mzeina Allegories of Bedouin Identity Under Israeli and Egyptian Rule*. Berkeley: University of California Press.
Lavie, Smadar and Ted Swedenburg
1996   Between and Among the Boundaries of Culture: Bridging Text and Lived Experience in the Third Timespace. *Cultural Studies* 10:154–79.
Lawrence, Peter
1964   *Road Belong Cargo: A Study of the Cargo Cult in Southern Madang District, New Guinea*. New York: Humanities Press.
Le Roy Ladurie, Emmanuel
1973   *The Peasants of Languedoc*. Urbana: University of Illinois Press [Original, 1966].
1979   *Montaillou: The Promised Land of Error*. New York: Vintage [Original, 1978].
1987   *The French Peasantry, 1450–1660*. Translated by Alan Sheridan. Aldershot, England: Scolar.
Leach, Edmund
1970   *Claude Lévi-Strauss*, revised ed. Harmondsworth, UK: Penguin.
Leacock, Eleanor
1981   *Myths of Male Dominance: Collected Articles on Women Cross-Culturally*. New York: Monthly Review Press.
Lemert, Charles (ed.)
1993   *Social Theory: The Multicultural and Classic Readings*. Boulder, CO: Westview.
Lemonnier, Pierre
1990   Guerres et festins: Paix, échanges, et competition dans les Highlands de Nouvelle-Guinée. Paris: Maison de l'homme.
1993   (Ed.) Technological Choices: Transformation in Material Culture Since the Neolithic. London: Routledge.
Lepowsky, Maria
1993   *Fruit of the Motherland: Gender in an Egalitarian Society*. New York: Columbia University Press.
Lévi-Strauss, Claude
1964–71 *Mythologiques I–IV*. Paris: Plon.
1966   *The Savage Mind*. Chicago: University of Chicago Press [Original, 1962].
1967   *Structural Anthropology*. New York: Anchor [Original, 1958].

1969　*The Elementary Structures of Kinship*. Boston: Beacon [Original, 1949].

Lewin, Ellen

1993　*Lesbian Mothers: Accounts of Gender in American Culture*. Ithaca, NY: Cornell University Press.

Lewis, A. B.

1932　*Ethnology of Melanesia*. Chicago: Field Museum of Natural History. Reprint. Chicago: Field Museum of Natural History, 1945.

Lewis, Ioan M.

1989　*Ecstatic Religion: A Study of Shamanism and Spirit Possession*, 2nd ed. London: Routledge.

Lidz, Theodore and Ruth W. Lidz

1989　*Oedipus in the Stone Age: A Psychoanalytic Study of Masculinization in Papua New Guinea*. Madison, CT: International Universities Press.

Lindenbaum, Shirley

1984　Variations on a Sociosexual Theme in Melanesia. In *Ritualized Homosexuality in Melanesia*, edited by Gilbert H. Herdt, pp. 337–61. Berkeley: University of California Press.

1987　The Mystification of Female Labors. In *Gender and Kinship: Essays Toward a Unified Analysis*, edited by Jane F. Collier and Sylvia J. Yanagisako, pp. 221–43. Stanford: Stanford University Press.

Lindstrom, Lamont

1990　*Knowledge and Power in a South Pacific Society*. Washington, DC: Smithsonian Institution Press.

1993　*Cargo Cult: Strange Stories of Desire from Melanesia and Beyond*. Honolulu: University of Hawaii Press.

Liria, Yauka Aluambo

1993　*Bougainville Campaign Diary*. Melbourne: Indra Publishing.

Livesay, Jeff

1989　Structuration Theory and the Unacknowledged Conditions of Action. *Theory, Culture, and Society* 6:263–292.

Lock, Margaret and Shirley Lindenbaum (eds.)

1993　*Knowledge, Power, and Practice: The Anthropology of Medicine and Everyday Life*. Berkeley: University of California Press.

Lomnitz-Adler, Claudio

1992　*Exits from the Labyrinth: Culture and Ideology in the Mexican National Space*. Berkeley: University of California Press.

Lorde, Audre

1984　*Sister Outsider: Essays and Speeches*. Trumansburg, NY: Crossing.

Lowie, Robert

1920　*Primitive Society*. New York: Boni and Liveright.

1927　*The Origin of the State*. New York: Harcourt, Brace.

1937　*The History of Ethnological Theory*. New York: Holt, Rinehart, and Winston.

Lukács, Georg

1923　*History and Class Consciousness: Studies in Marxist Dialectics*. Reprint. Cambridge, MA: MIT Press, 1971.

Lutz, Catherine

1990　The Erasure of Women's Writing in Sociocultural Anthropology. *American Ethnologist* 17:611–27.

1993　Social Contexts of Postmodern Cultural Analysis. In *Postmodern*

Contentions: Epochs, Politics, Space, edited by John Paul Jones III, Wolfgang Natter, and Theodore R. Schatzki, pp. 137–64. New York: Guilford.

1995   The Gender of Theory. In *Women Writing Culture,* edited by Ruth Behar and Deborah A. Gordon, pp. 249–66. Berkeley: University of California Press.

Lutz, Catherine, and Lila Abu-Lughod (eds.)

1990   *Language and the Politics of Emotion.* Cambridge: Cambridge University Press.

Luxemburg, Rosa

1963   *The Accumulation of Capital.* London: Routledge and Kegan Paul.

1971   *Selected Political Writings of Rosa Luxemburg,* edited and introduced by Dick Howard. New York: Monthly Review Press.

Lyotard, Jean-François

1984   *The Postmodern Condition: A Report on Knowledge.* Translated by Geoff Bennington and Brian Massumi. Minneapolis: University of Minnesota Press [Original, 1979].

1988   *The Differend: Phrases in Dispute.* Minneapolis: University of Minnesota Press.

Macdonald, D.

1878   *The Labour Traffic Versus Christianity in the South Sea Islands.* Melbourne: Hutchinson.

Macey, David

1993   *The Lives of Michel Foucault.* London: Hutchinson.

MacLeod, Arlene E.

1992   Hegemonic Relations and Gender Resistance: The New Veiling as Accommodating Protest in Cairo. *Signs* 17:533–57.

Maher, Robert F.

1961   *New Men of Papua: A Study in Culture Change.* Madison: University of Wisconsin Press.

Mahon, Michael

1992   *Foucault's Nietzschean Genealogy: Truth, Power, and the Subject.* Albany: State University of New York Press.

Makkreel, Rudolf A.

1975   *Dilthey: Philosopher of the Human Sciences.* Princeton, NJ: Princeton University Press.

Malinowski, Bronislaw

1922   *Argonauts of the Western Pacific.* New York: Dutton.

1926   *Crime and Custom in Savage Society.* London: Routledge and Kegan Paul.

1929   *The Sexual Lives of Savages in North-Western Melanesia.* London: Routledge and Sons.

1935   *Coral Gardens and Their Magic.* 2 vols. London: Allen and Unwin.

Malkki, Liisa H.

1995   *Purity and Exile: Violence, Memory, and National Cosmology among Hutu Refugees in Tanzania.* Chicago: University of Chicago Press.

Mandel, Ernest

1975   *Late Capitalism.* London: New Left Books.

Manganaro, Marc (ed.)

1990   *Modernist Anthropology: From Field Work to Text.* Princeton, NJ: Princeton University Press.

Mann, Patricia S.
1994   *Micro-Politics: Agency in a Postfeminist Era*. Minneapolis: University of Minnesota Press.

Marcus, George E.
1990   Some Quotes as Queries Pertaining to Bourdieu's Own Scholastic Point of View. *Cultural Anthropology* 5:392–95.
1995   Ethnography in/of the World System: The Emergence of Multi-Sited Ethnography. *Annual Review of Anthropology* 24:95–117.

Marcus, George E. and Michael M. J. Fischer
1986   *Anthropology as Cultural Critique: An Experimental Moment in the Human Sciences*. Chicago: University of Chicago Press.

Markham, Albert H.
1873   *The Cruise of the "Rosario" amongst the New Hebrides and Santa Cruz Islands, Exposing the Recent Atrocities with the Kidnapping of Natives of the South Seas*. 2nd ed. London: S. Low and Co.

Marksbury, Richard A. (ed.)
1993   *The Business of Marriage: Transformations in Oceanic Matrimony*. Pittsburgh: University of Pittsburgh Press.

Marriott, McKim
1976   Hindu Transactions: Diversity Without Dualism. In *Transaction and Meaning: Directions in the Anthropology of Exchange and Symbolic Behavior*, edited by Bruce Kapferer. Philadelphia: Institute for the Study of Human Issues.

Martin, Biddy
1994   Sexualities Without Gender and Other Queer Utopias. *Diacritics* 24:104–21.

Martin, Emily
1987   *The Woman in the Body: A Cultural Analysis of Reproduction*. Boston: Beacon.

Marx, Karl
1963   *Karl Marx: Early Writings* ["On the Jewish Question," "Contribution to the Critique of Hegel's Philosophy of Right," and "Economic and Philosophical Manuscripts"], edited by T. B. Bottomore. New York: McGraw-Hill [Original, 1844].
1964   *Marx and Engels on Religion*. New York: Schocken.
1965   *Pre-capitalist Economic Formations*. New York: International Publishers.
1970   *A Contribution to the Critique of Political Economy*. Moscow: Progress Publishers [Original, 1859].
1971   *The Grundrisse*. Edited by David McLellan. New York: Harper [Original, 1857–58].
1972a   The Eighteenth Brumaire of Louis Bonaparte. In *The Marx-Engels Reader*, edited by Robert C. Tucker. New York: Norton [Original, 1852]
1972b   *Capital* 3 vols. New York: International Publishers [Original, 1867–94].
1972c   *The Marx-Engels Reader*, edited by Robert C. Tucker. New York: Norton.

Marx, Karl and Frederick Engels
1968   *The Communist Manifesto*. Peking: Foreign Languages Press [Original, 1848].

Massumi, Brian
1987   Notes on Deleuze and Guattari's A Thousand Plateaus. In *A Thousand Plateaus: Capitalism and Schizophrenia*, by Gilles Deleuze and Félix Guattari. Minneapolis: University of Minnesota Press.

Matejka, Ladislaw and I. R. Tutunik
1986   Introduction to *Marxism and the Philosophy of Language*, by V. N. Volosinov [M. M. Bakhtin]. Cambridge: Cambridge University Press.

Mauss, Marcel
1950   *Sociologie et anthropologie*. Paris: Presses universitaires de Paris.
1967   *The Gift*. New York: Norton [Original, 1925].

May, R. J. (ed.)
1986   *Between Two Nations: The Indonesia–Papua New Guinea Border and West Papua Nationalism*. Bathurst, NSW, Australia: Robert Brown.

May, R. J. and Matthew Spriggs (eds.)
1991   *The Bougainville Crisis*. Bathurst, NSW, Australia: Crawford House.

May, Todd
1993   *Between Genealogy and Epistemology: Psychology, Politics, and Knowledge in the Thought of Michel Foucault*. University Park, PA: Pennsylvania State University Press.

Mbembe, Achille
1992   The Banality of Power and the Aesthetics of Vulgarity in the Postcolony. *Public Culture* 4:1–31.

Mbembe, Achille and Janet Roitman
1995   Figures of the Subject in Times of Crisis. *Public Culture* 7:323–52.

McCleary, Dick
1989   Extended review of Bourdieu's *Choses Dites*. *The Sociological Review* 37:373–83.

McClintock, Anne
1992   The Angel of Progress: Pitfalls of the Term "Post-colonialism." *Social Text* 31/32:84–98.

McCoy, Charles
1992   Good Intentions: Chevron Tries to Show It Can Protect Jungle While Pumping Oil, But Papua New Guinea Tribes Grow Restless Over Pact for Pipeline and a Road. *Wall Street Journal*, June 9, p. 1.

McFarlane, Samuel
1888   *Among the Cannibals of New Guinea, Being the Story of the New Guinea Mission of the London Missionary Society*. Philadelphia: Presbyterian Board of Publication.

McGrane, Bernard
1989   *Beyond Anthropology: Society and the Other*. New York: Columbia University Press.

McKinnon, J. M.
1975   Tomahawks, Turtles, and Traders. *Oceania* 45:290–307.

McLaren, Jack
1923   *My Odyssey*. London: Ernest Benn.

McLaren, Peter
1994   White Terror and Oppositional Agency: Towards a Critical Multiculturalism. In *Multiculturalism: A Critical Reader*, edited by David Theo Goldberg, pp. 45–74. Oxford: Basil Blackwell.

McLellan, David
1975   *Karl Marx*. Harmondsworth, UK: Penguin.

McNay, Lois
1993   *Foucault and Feminism: Power, Gender, and the Self*. Boston: Northeastern University Press.

1994   *Foucault: A Critical Introduction.* New York: Continuum.

McRobbie, Angela
1991   Moving Cultural Studies On: Post-Modernism and Beyond. *Magazine of Cultural Studies* 4:18–22.

Mead, Margaret
1928   *Coming of Age in Samoa.* New York: William Morrow.
1930   *Growing Up in New Guinea.* New York: Blue Ribbon.
1935   *Sex and Temperament in Three Primitive Societies.* New York: Morrow.

Medvedev, P. N. [M. M. Bakhtin]
1978   *The Formal Method in Literary Scholarship: A Critical Introduction to Sociological Poetics.* Baltimore: Johns Hopkins University Press [Original, 1928].

Meggitt, Mervyn J.
1964   Male-Female Relationships in the Highlands of Australian New Guinea. *American Anthropologist* 66:204–24.

Meigs, Anna S.
1976   Male Pregnancy and the Reduction of Sexual Opposition in the New Guinea Highlands. *Ethnology* 9:393–407.

Meillassoux, Claude
1981   *Maidens, Meal, and Money: Capitalism and the Domestic Community.* Cambridge: Cambridge University Press.

Mercer, Kobena
1994   *Welcome to the Jungle: New Positions in Black Cultural Studies.* New York: Routledge.

Messick, Brinkley
1993   *The Calligraphic State: Textual Domination and History in a Muslim Society.* Berkeley: University of California Press.

Meyer, Alfred G.
1963   Appendix A: Historical Notes on Ideological Aspects of the Concept of Culture in Germany and Russia. In *Culture: A Critical Review of Concepts and Definitions,* by Alfred L. Kroeber and Clyde Kluckhohn, pp. 403–13. New York: Vintage.

Miedema, Jelle
1988   Anthropology, Demography and History: Shortage of Women, Intertribal Marriage Relations, and Slave Trading in the Bird's Head of New Guinea. *Bijdragen tot de Taal-, Land- en Volkenkunde* 144:494–509.

Mies, Maria
1986   *Patriarchy and Accumulation on a World Scale: Women in the International Division of Labor.* London: Zed.
1988   *Women: The Last Colony.* London: Zed.

Miklouho-Maclay, Nikolai
1874   On the Political and Social Position of the Papuans of the Papua Kowiai Coast on the Southwestern Shore of New Guinea. In *Travels to New Guinea: Diaries, Letters, Documents,* edited by D. Tumarkin, translated by S. Mikhailov, pp. 439–44. Reprint. Moscow: Progress, 1982.
1881   Notes in *Re* Kidnapping and Slavery in the Western Pacific. In *Travels to New Guinea: Diaries, Letters, Documents,* edited by D. Tumarkin, translated by S. Mikhailov, pp. 461–71. Reprint. Moscow: Progress, 1982.

Mill, John Stuart
1872   *A System of Logic,* 8th ed. London.

1961   *Auguste Comte and Positivism*. Ann Arbor, MI [Original, 1865].

1962   *John Stuart Mill on Bentham and Coleridge*, edited by F. R. Leavis. New York [Original, 1838].

Miller, Charles

1950   *Cannibal Caravan*. London: Methuen.

Miller, Daniel

1994   *Modernity, An Ethnographic Approach: Dualism and Mass Consumption in Trinidad*. Oxford: Berg.

1995   (Ed.) *Worlds Apart: Modernity Through the Prism of the Local*. London: Routledge.

Miller, James

1993   *The Passion of Michel Foucault*. New York: Simon and Schuster.

Mimica, Jadran

1993   The Foi and Heidegger: Western Philosophical Poetics and a New Guinea Life-World. *TAJA (The Australian Journal of Anthropology)* 4:79–95.

Minh-ha, Trinh T.

1990   *Woman, Native, Other: Writing Postcoloniality and Feminism*. Bloomington: Indiana University Press.

1991   *When the Moon Waxes Red: Representation, Gender, and Cultural Politics*. New York: Routledge.

Mohanty, Chandra T.

1991a   Introduction: Cartographies of Struggle: Third World Women and the Politics of Feminism. In *Third World Women and the Politics of Feminism*, edited by Chandra T. Mohanty, pp. 1–47. Bloomington: Indiana University Press.

1991b   Under Western Eyes: Feminist Scholarship and Colonial Discourses. In *Third World Women and the Politics of Feminism*, edited by Chandra T. Mohanty, pp. 51–80. Bloomington: Indiana University Press.

Mohr, Richard D.

1992   *Gay Ideas: Outing and Other Controversies*. Boston: Beacon.

Monbiot, George

1989   *Poisoned Arrows: An Investigative Journey Through Indonesia*. London: Michael Joseph.

Moore, Henrietta L.

1988   *Feminism and Anthropology*. Minneapolis: University of Minnesota Press.

1994a   *A Passion for Difference: Essays in Anthropology and Gender*. Bloomington: Indiana University Press.

1994b   "Divided We Stand": Sex, Gender, and Sexual Difference. *Feminist Review* 47:78–95.

Morauta, Louise

1979   Indigenous Anthropology in Papua New Guinea. *Current Anthropology* 20: 561–76.

Morera, Esteve

1990   *Gramsci's Historicism*. London: Routledge.

Moresby, Captain John

1876a   *Discoveries and Surveys in New Guinea and the D'Entrecasteaux Islands*. London: John Murray.

1876b   Our Duty to New Guinea and Polynesia. In *Discoveries and Surveys in New Guinea and the D'Entrecasteaux Islands*, pp. 295–305. London: John Murray.

Morgan, Lewis Henry
  1870   *Systems of Consanguinity and Affinity of the Human Family*. Washington, DC:
         Smithsonian Institution.
  1877   *Ancient Society*. Gloucester, MA: Peter Smith, 1974.
Morgen, Sandra (ed.)
  1989   *Gender and Anthropology: Critical Reviews for Research and Teaching*.
         Washington, D. C.: American Anthropological Association.
Morrell, W. P.
  1960   *Britain in the Pacific Islands*. Oxford: Clarendon.
Morris, Meaghan
  1988   *The Pirate's Fiancée: Feminism, Reading, Postmodernism*. London: Verso.
Morson, Gary S. and Caryl Emerson
  1990   *Mikhail Bakhtin: Creation of a Prosaics*. Stanford: Stanford University Press.
Morton, Donald
  1993   The Politics of Queer Theory in the (Post)Modern Moment. *Genders*
         17:121–50.
Mouffe, Chantal
  1979   (Ed.) *Gramsci and Marxist Theory*. London: Routledge.
  1992   (Ed.) *Dimensions of Radical Democracy: Pluralism, Citizenship, Community*.
         London: Verso.
  1993   *The Return of the Political*. London: Verso.
Mukhopadhyay, Carol C. and Patricia J. Higgins
  1988   Anthropological Studies of Women's Status Revisited: 1977–1987. *Annual
         Review of Anthropology* 17:461–95.
Murdock, George Peter
  1949   *Social Structure*. New York: Free Press.
Murphy, Robert F.
  1971   *The Dialectics of Social Life: Alarms and Excursions in Anthropological Theory*.
         New York: Basic Books.
Murray, J. Hubert P.
  1912   *Papua or British New Guinea*. London: T. Fisher Unwin.
Narayan, Kirin
  1993   How Native is a "Native" Anthropologist? *American Anthropologist*
         95:671–86.
Nash, June and Helen I. Safa (eds.)
  1976   *Sex and Class in Latin America*. New York: Praeger.
Nelson, Cary, Paula A. Treichler, and Lawrence Grossberg
  1992   Cultural Studies: An Introduction. In *Cultural Studies*, edited by L. Gross-
         berg, C. Nelson, and P. Treichler, pp. 1–22. New York: Routledge.
Nelson, Hank
  1976   *Black, White, and Gold: Goldmining in Papua New Guinea, 1878–1930*.
         Canberra: Australian National University Press.
Newton, Esther
  1972   *Mother Camp: Female Impersonators in America*. Engelwood Cliffs, NJ:
         Prentice-Hall.
Nicholson, Linda J.
  1990   (Ed.) *Feminism/Postmodernism*. New York: Routledge.
  1995   Introduction to *Feminist Contentions: A Philosophical Exchange*, by Seyla
         Benhabib et al., pp. 1–16. New York: Routledge.

Nietschmann, Bernard
   1987   The Third World War. *Cultural Survival Quarterly* 11(3):1–16.
Nietzsche, Friedrich
   1968a   *The Birth of Tragedy.* In *Basic Writings of Nietzsche.* Translated and edited by
            Walter Kaufmann. New York: Modern Library.
   1968b   *Beyond Good and Evil.* In *Basic Writings of Nietzsche.* Translated and edited
            by Walter Kaufmann. New York: Modern Library.
   1968c   *Twilight of the Idols* and *The Antichrist.* Baltimore: Penguin.
   1969a   *On the Genealogy of Morals.* Translated by Walter Kaufmann and R. J.
            Hollingdale. New York: Vintage.
   1969b   *Ecce Homo.* Translated by Walter Kaufmann. New York: Vintage.
   1974   *The Gay Science.* Translated by Walter Kaufmann. New York: Random House.
   1977   *A Nietzsche Reader.* Selected and translated with an introduction by R. J.
            Hollingdale. Harmondsworth, England: Penguin.
Nihill, Michael
   1994   New Women and Wild Men: "Development," Changing Sexual Practice,
            and Gender in Highland Papua New Guinea. *Cambridge Anthropology*
            17:48–72.
Nora, Pierre
   1984–92   *Les Lieux de mémoire,* 3 vols. Paris: Gallimard.
   1989   Between Memory and History: *Les Lieux de mémoire. Representations*
            26:7–25.
Norris, Christopher
   1993   *Uncritical Theory: Postmodernism, Intellectuals, and the Gulf War.* London:
            Routledge.
Olaniyan, Tejumola
   1992   Narrativizing Postcoloniality: Responsibilities. *Public Culture* 5:47–56.
Oliver, Kelly
   1995   *Womanizing Nietzsche: Philosophy's Relation to the "Feminine."* New York:
            Routledge.
Ong, Aihwa
   1987   *Spirits of Resistance and Capitalist Discipline: Factory Women in Malaysia.*
            Albany: State University of New York Press.
   1988   Colonialism and Modernity: Feminist Re-presentations of Women in
            Non-Western Societies. *Inscriptions* 3/4:79–93.
   1991a   The Gender and Labor Politics of Postmodernity. *Annual Review of
            Anthropology* 20:279–309.
   1991b   Flexible Citizenship Among Chinese in Diaspora. *Positions* 1:745–78.
Oppel, Frances
   1993   "Speaking of Immemorial Waters": Irigaray with Nietzsche. In *Nietzsche,
            Feminism, and Political Theory,* edited by Paul Patton, pp. 88–109. London:
            Routledge.
Ortner, Sherry B.
   1973   On Key Symbols. *American Anthropologist* 75:1338–46.
   1974   Is Female to Male as Nature Is to Culture? In *Woman, Culture, and Society,*
            edited by Michelle Z. Rosaldo and Louise Lamphere, pp. 67–87. Stanford:
            Stanford University Press.
   1984   Theory in Anthropology Since the Sixties. *Comparative Studies in Society
            and History* 26:126–66.

1989   *High Religion: A Cultural and Political History of Sherpa Buddhism*. Princeton,
        NJ: Princeton University Press.
1990a   Gender Hegemonies. *Cultural Critique* 14:35–80.
1990b   Patterns of History: Cultural Schemas in the Founding of Sherpa
        Religious Institutions. In *Culture Through Time: Anthropological Approaches*,
        edited by Emiko Ohnuki-Tierney, pp. 57–93. Stanford: Stanford
        University Press.
1991   Reading America: Preliminary Notes on Class and Culture. In *Recapturing
        Anthropology: Working in the Present*, edited by Richard G. Fox, pp. 163–89.
        Santa Fe, NM: School of American Research Press.
1993   On Cultural Studies. Paper presented at the annual meetings of the
        American Anthropological Association, Washington, DC.
1995a   Resistance and the Problem of Ethnographic Refusal. *Comparative Studies
        in Society and History* 37:173–93.
1995b   Ethnography among the Newark: The Class of '58 of Weequahic High
        School. In *Naturalizing Power: Essays in Feminist Cultural Analysis*, edited by
        Sylvia Yanagisako and Carol Delaney, pp. 257–73. New York: Routledge.

Ortner, Sherry B. and Harriet Whitehead (eds.)
1981   *Sexual Meanings: The Cultural Construction of Gender and Sexuality*.
        Cambridge: Cambridge University Press.

Pagden, Anthony
1986   *The Fall of Natural Man: The American Indian and the Origins of Comparative
        Ethnology*. Cambridge: Cambridge University Press.
1995   The Effacement of Difference: Colonialism and the Origins of
        Nationalism in Diderot and Herder. In *After Colonialism: Imperial Histories
        and Postcolonial Displacements*, edited by Gyan Prakash, pp. 129–52.
        Princeton, NJ: Princeton University Press.

Palmer, George
1871   *Kidnapping in the South Seas: Being a Narrative of a Three Months' Cruise of
        H. M. Ship "Rosario."* Edinburgh: n.p.

Palmer, Richard E.
1969   *Hermeneutics: Interpretation Theory in Schleiermacher, Dilthey, Heidegger, and
        Gadamer*. Evanston, IL: Northwestern University Press.

Parker, Richard G.
1991   *Bodies, Pleasures, and Passions: Sexual Culture in Contemporary Brazil*. Boston:
        Beacon.

Parker, Richard G. and John H. Gagnon (eds.)
1995   *Conceiving Sexuality: Approaches to Sex in a Postmodern World*. New York:
        Routledge.

Parnaby, Owen W.
1964   *Britain and the Labor Trade in the Southwest Pacific*. Durham, NC: Duke
        University Press.

Parsons, Talcott
1937   *The Structure of Social Action*. New York: McGraw-Hill.
1951   *The Social System*. Glencoe, IL: Free Press.
1960   *Structure and Process in Modern Societies*. Glencoe, IL: Free Press.
1966   *Societies: Comparative and Evolutionary Perspectives*. Englewood Cliffs, NJ:
        Prentice-Hall.

Paton, John G.
1907   *John G. Paton, Missionary to the New Hebrides: An Autobiography*. Chicago: Fleming H. Revell.
Paton, Rank H. L.
1913   *Slavery Under the British Flag*. Melbourne: Brown Prior.
Patton, Paul (ed.)
1993   *Nietzsche, Feminism, and Political Theory*. London: Routledge.
PIM = *Pacific Islands Monthly*
1991   PNG Gas Project Obstructed. March, p. 36.
1994a   Now Where Did that Mineral Boom Go? March, pp. 27–29.
1994b   In the Red. October, pp. 7–9.
1994c   The Rise and Fall of the Kina. November, pp. 24–25.
1994d   Boost for PNG Oil Industry. February, p. 12.
1994e   Liquid Gas Next on the List. September, pp. 43–47.
1994f   Yet Another Claim. June, p. 25.
1994g   Another Bougainville? June, p. 17.
1994h   The Tree Trap: Solomons Government Caught up in Vicious Logging Circle. March.
Penniman, T. K.
1952   *A Hundred Years of Anthropology*. 2nd ed. London: Duckworth.
Polanyi, Karl
1963   *The Great Transformation*. Boston: Beacon.
1971   *Primitive, Archaic, and Modern Economies: Essays of Karl Polanyi*. Boston: Beacon.
Polier, Nicole
1994   A View from the "Cyanide Room": Politics and Culture in a Mining Township in Papua New Guinea. *Identities* 1:63–84.
n.d.   Stella's Stori: Colonialism, Christianity, and Confrontation in the Life of a Papua New Guinean Migrant Woman. [under review.]
Polier, Nicole and William Roseberry
1989   Tristes Tropes: Postmodern Anthropologists Encounter the Other and Discover Themselves. *Economy and Society* 18:245–64.
Pool, Robert
1991   Postmodern Ethnography? *Critique of Anthropology* 11:309–31.
Popper, Sir Karl
1945   *The Open Society and Its Enemies*. 2 vols. London: Routledge and Kegan Paul.
1957   *The Poverty of Historicism*. London: Routledge and Kegan Paul.
1959   *The Logic of Scientific Discovery*. London: Hutchinson.
Post Courier (Port Moresby daily newspaper, Papua New Guinea)
1995a   Australian Judges Slam PNG-BHP Legislation. September 15, p. 5.
1995b   PNG Hangs Out on Log Code Move. September 15, p. 3.
Poster, Mark
1975   Introduction to *The Mirror of Production*. By Jean Baudrillard, pp. 1–15. St. Louis: Telos.
1990   *The Mode of Information: Postmodernism and Social Context*. Chicago: University of Chicago Press.
Povinelli, Elizabeth A.
1991   Organizing Women: Rhetoric, Economy, and Politics in Process among

Australian Aborigines. In *Gender at the Crossroads of Knowledge: Feminist Anthropology in the Postmodern Era*, edited by Micaela di Leonardo, pp. 235–54. Berkeley: University of California Press.

1993　*Labor's Lot: The Power, History, and Culture of Aboriginal Action*. Chicago: University of Chicago Press.

1994　Sexual Savages/Sexual Sovereignty: Australian Colonial Texts and the Postcolonial Politics of Nationalism. *Diacritics* 24:122–50.

1995　Do Rocks Listen? The Cultural Politics of Apprehending Australian Aboriginal Labor. *American Anthropologist* 97:505–18.

n.d.　Those Most Miserable of Savages: (Ab)original Humanity and Postcolonial Governance. Unpublished manuscript.

Powdermaker, Hortense

1966　*Stranger and Friend: The Way of an Anthropologist*. New York: Norton.

Prado, C. G.

1995　*Starting with Foucault: An Introduction*. Boulder, CO: Westview.

Prakash, Gyan

1992　Postcolonial Criticism and Indian Historiography. *Social Text* 10(31/32):8–19.

1995　(Ed.) *After Colonialism: Imperial Histories and Postcolonial Displacements*. Princeton, NJ: Princeton University Press.

Pratt, A. E.

1906　*Two Years Among New Guinea Cannibals*. Philadelphia: J. B. Lippincott.

Press, Eyal

1995　Freeport: Corporate Predator. *The Nation*, July 31, pp. 125–30.

Probyn, Elspeth

1993　*Sexing the Self: Gendered Positions in Cultural Studies*. New York: Routledge.

Quiggin, A. Hingston

1942　*Haddon the Head Hunter: A Short Sketch of the Life of A. C. Haddon*. Cambridge: Cambridge University Press.

Rabinow, Paul

1977　*Reflections on Fieldwork in Morocco*. Berkeley: University of California Press.

1984　(Ed.) *The Foucault Reader*. New York: Pantheon.

1985　Discourse and Power: On the Limits of Ethnographic Texts. *Dialectical Anthropology* 10:1–12.

1986　Representations Are Social Facts: Modernity and Post-modernity in Anthropology. In *Writing Culture: The Poetics and Politics of Ethnography*, edited by James Clifford and George E. Marcus, pp. 234–61. Berkeley: University of California Press.

Radcliffe-Brown, A. R.

1948　*A Natural Science of Society*. New York: Free Press.

1952　*Structure and Function in Primitive Society*. London: Oxford University Press.

1958　*Method in Social Anthropology*. Chicago: University of Chicago Press.

Radin, Paul

1928　*The Winnebago Tribe*. Washington, DC: Government Printing Office.

1933　*The Method and Theory of Ethnography: An Essay in Criticism*. New York: McGraw-Hill.

1957a　*Primitive Man as Philosopher*. New York: Dover.

1957b　*Primitive Religion: Its Nature and Origin*. New York: Dover.

Raheja, Gloria and Ann Gold
1994   *Listen to the Heron's Words: Reimagining Gender and Kinship in North India.*
        Berkeley: University of California Press.
Ramazanoglu, Caroline
1993   *Up Against Foucault: Explorations of Some Tensions Between Foucault and
        Feminism.* New York: Routledge.
Rannie, Douglas
1912   *My Adventures Among South Sea Cannibals: An Account of the Experiences and
        Adventures of a Government Official Among the Natives of Oceania.* London:
        Seeley, Service and Co.
Ransome, Paul
1992   *Antonio Gramsci: A New Introduction.* New York: Harvester Wheatsheaf.
Rapp, Rayna
1988   Is the Legacy of Second Wave Feminism Postfeminism? *Socialist Review*
        18(1):31–37.
Rappaport, Roy A.
1968   *Pigs for the Ancestors.* New Haven, CT: Yale University Press.
1977   Maladaptation in Social Systems. In *Evolution of Social Systems*, edited by
        Jonathan Friedman and M. Rowlands. London: Duckworth.
1984   *Pigs for the Ancestors.* 2nd edition. New Haven, CT: Yale University Press.
Reed, Adolf, Jr.
in press From Willie Best to Cornel West: The Black "Public Intellectual." *Village
        Voice*, forthcoming.
Reichard, Gladys A.
1928   *Social Life of the Navajo Indians.* New York: Columbia University Press.
1934   *Spider Woman.* New York: Macmillan.
1936   *Navajo Shepherd and Weaver.* New York: J. J. Augustin.
1939   *Dezba, Woman of the Desert.* New York: J. J. Augustin.
1950   *Navajo Religion: A Study in Symbolism.* 2 vols. New York: Pantheon.
Reiter, Rayna Rapp (ed.)
1975   *Toward an Anthropology of Women.* New York: Monthly Review Press.
Rey, Pierre-Philippe
1973   *Les Alliances de classes: Sur l'articulation des modes de production.* Paris: F.
        Maspéro.
Ribeiro, Gustavo L.
1994   *Transnational Capitalism and Hydropolitics in Argentina.* Gainesville:
        University Press of Florida.
Rich, Adrienne
1989   *Time's Power: Poems 1985–1988.* New York: Norton.
Ricoeur, Paul
1984   *Time and Narrative.* Chicago: University of Chicago Press.
1991   *A Ricoeur Reader: Reflection and Imagination*, edited by Mario J. Valdes.
        Toronto: University of Toronto Press.
Riley, E. Baxter
1925   *Among Papuan Headhunters.* Philadelphia: J. B. Lippincott.
Robbins, Derek
1991   *The Work of Pierre Bourdieu: Recognizing Society.* Buckingham, UK: Open
        University Press.

Robbins, Joel
  1994   Christianity and Desire among the Urapmin of Papua New Guinea. Paper
         presented at the annual meetings of the American Anthropological
         Association, Atlanta, GA.
  1995   Dispossessing the Spirits: Christian Transformations of Desire and
         Ecology among the Urapmin of Papua New Guinea. *Ethnology* 34:211–24.
Robie, David
  1989   Bougainville One Year Later. *Pacific Islands Monthly*, November, pp. 10–18.
  1996   Customary Land Fight Over Oil Wealth. Gemini News Service, London,
         January 16. <journupng@pactok.peg.apc.org>.
Rockmore, Tom
  1995   *Heidegger and French Philosophy: Humanism, Antihumanism, and Being.*
         London: Routledge.
Rogers, Susan C.
  1975   Female Forms of Power and the Myth of Male Dominance. *American
         Ethnologist* 2:727–57.
Rorty, Richard
  1980   *Philosophy and the Mirror of Nature.* Princeton, NJ: Princeton University
         Press.
Rosaldo, Michelle Z. and Louise Lamphere (eds.)
  1974   *Women, Culture, and Society.* Stanford: Stanford University Press.
Rosaldo, Renato
  1989   *Culture and Truth: The Remaking of Social Analysis.* Boston: Beacon.
  1992   Cultural Citizenship. Talk presented at Stanford University, spring.
  1994   Whose Cultural Studies? *American Anthropologist* 96:524–29.
Rosen, Stanley
  1993   *The Question of Being: A Reversal of Heidegger.* New Haven, CT: Yale
         University Press.
Rosenthal, Michael
  1992   What was Postmodernim? *Socialist Review* 22:83–105.
Rouse, Roger
  1991   Mexican Migration and the Social Space of Postmodernism: *Diaspora*
         1:8–23.
  1995   Thinking Through Transnationalism: Notes on the Cultural Politics of
         Class Relations in the Contemporary United States. *Public Culture*
         7:353–402.
Rousseau, Jean-Jacques
  1938   *The Social Contract.* New York: Dutton [Original, 1762].
  1964   *The First and Second Discourses.* New York: St. Martin's [Original, 1751–55].
Rubin, Gayle
  1984   Thinking Sex: Notes for a Radical Theory of the Politics of Sexuality. In
         Pleasure and Danger: Exploring Female Sexuality, edited by Carol S. Vance.
         London: Routledge and Kegan Paul.
Sacks, Karen
  1979   *Sisters and Wives: The Past and Future of Sexual Equality.* Westport, CT:
         Greenwood.
Sahlins, Marshall D.
  1958   *Social Stratification in Polynesia.* Seattle: University of Washington Press.
  1960   (Ed.) *Evolution and Culture.* Ann Arbor: University of Michigan Press.

1972   *Stone Age Economics*. Chicago: Aldine.

1976   *Culture and Practical Reason*. Chicago: University of Chicago Press.

1981   *Historical Metaphors and Mythical Realities: Structure in the Early History of the Sandwich Islands Kingdom*. Ann Arbor: University of Michigan Press.

1983   Other Times, Other Customs: The Anthropology of History. *American Anthropologist* 85:517–44.

1985   *Islands of History*. Chicago: University of Chicago Press.

1990   The Return of the Event, Again; with Reflections on the Beginnings of the Great Fijian War of 1843 to 1855 Between the Kingdoms of Bau and Rewa. In *Clio in Oceania: Toward a Historical Anthropology*, edited by Aletta Biersack, pp. 37–99. Washington, DC: Smithsonian Institution Press.

1992   *Anahulu: The Anthropology of History in the Kingdom of Hawaii*, vol. 1: *Historical Ethnography*. Chicago: University of Chicago Press.

1993a   *Waiting for Foucault*. Cambridge: Prickly Pear Press.

1993b   Goodbye to *Tristes Tropes*: Ethnography in the Context of Modern World History. *Journal of Modern History* 65:1–25.

1995   *How Natives Think: About Captain Cook, for Example*. Chicago: University of Chicago Press.

Said, Edward W.

1978   *Orientalism*. New York: Pantheon.

1993   *Culture and Imperialism*. New York: Knopf.

Sanday, Peggy R.

1981   *Female Power and Male Dominance: On the Origins of Sexual Inequality*. Cambridge: Cambridge University Press.

Sangren, Steven P.

1988   Rhetoric and the Authority of Ethnography: "Postmodernism" and the Social Reproduction of Texts. *Current Anthropology* 29:405-35.

Sapir, Edward

1957   *Selected Writings of Edward Sapir*, edited by David G. Mandelbaum. Berkeley: University of California Press.

Sartre, Jean-Paul

1976   *Critique of Dialectical Reason*, vol. 1: *Theory of Practical Ensembles*. Translated by Alan Sheridan. London: Verso.

1991   *Critique of Dialectical Reason*, vol. 2 (unfinished): *The Intelligibility of History*. Translated by Quintin Hoare, edited by Arlette Elkaim-Sartre. London: Verso.

Sasako, Alfred

1991   Inside Bougainville: There is No Turning Back, Says Francis Ona, as Supplies Run Out and Doctors Watch Women and Children Die. *Pacific Islands Monthly*, February, pp. 19–21.

Saussure, Ferdinand de

1966   *Course in General Linguistics*, edited by Charles Bally and Albert Sechehaye. New York: McGraw-Hill.

Scarr, Deryck

1967   Recruits and Recruiters: A Portrait of the Pacific Islands Labour Trade. *Journal of Pacific History* 2:5–24.

Scheper-Hughes, Nancy

1992   *Death Without Weeping: The Violence of Everyday Life in Brazil*. Berkeley: University of California Press.

Schiefenhövel, Wulf
   1990   Ritualized Adult-Male/Adolescent-Male Sexual Behavior in Melanesia: An
           Anthropological and Ethological Perspective. In *Pedophilia: Biosocial
           Dimensions*, edited by Jay R. Feierman, pp. 394–421. New York: Springer-
           Verlag.
Schieffelin, Edward L.
   1976   *The Sorrow of the Lonely and the Burning of the Dancers*. New York: St.
           Martin's.
   1995   Attitudes Toward Logging on the "Great Papuan Plateau." ASAONET
           Bulletin Board, September 13. Internet: ASAONET@uicvm.uic.edu.
Schieffelin, Edward L. and Robert Crittenden
   1991   *Like People You See in a Dream: First Contact in Six Papuan Societies*.
           Stanford: Stanford University Press.
Schlegel, Alice (ed.)
   1977   *Sexual Stratification*. New York: Columbia University Press.
Schleiermacher, Friedrich
   1963   *The Christian Faith*. New York: Harper and Row.
   1977   *Hermeneutics: The Handwritten Manuscripts*. Missoula, MT: Scholar's Press.
Schlesinger, Arthur M., Jr.
   1994   Unity, Multiculturalism, and the American Creed: An Interview with
           Arthur M. Schlesinger, Jr. on National Public Radio. *Cultural Survival
           Quarterly* 18(2–3):87–88.
Schneebaum, Tobias
   1988   *Where the Spirits Dwell: An Odyssey in the New Guinea Jungle*. New York:
           Grove Weidenfeld.
   1990   *Embodied Spirits: Ritual Carvings of the Asmat*. Salem, MA: Peabody
           Museum of Salem.
Schneider, David M.
   1980   *American Kinship: A Cultural Account*, 2nd ed. Chicago: University of
           Chicago Press.
Schneider, Jane and Rayna Rapp (eds.)
   1995   *Articulating Hidden Histories: Exploring the Influence of Eric R. Wolf*.
           Berkeley: University of California Press.
Schwartz, Theodore
   1962   The Paliau Movement in the Admiralty Islands, 1946–1954. *Anthropological
           Papers of the American Museum of Natural History*, vol. 49, part 2, pp.
           211–421. New York: American Museum of Natural History.
Scott, James C.
   1985   *Weapons of the Weak: Everyday Forms of Peasant Resistance*. New Haven, CT:
           Yale University Press.
   1990   *Domination and the Arts of Resistance: Hidden Transcripts*. New Haven, CT:
           Yale University Press.
Scott, Joan
   1988   *Gender and the Politics of History*. New York: Columbia University Press.
Sedgwick, Eve K.
   1990   *Epistemology of the Closet*. Berkeley: University of California Press.
   1993a   *Tendencies*. Durham, NC: Duke University Press.

1993b Queer Performativity: Henry James' *The Art of the Novel. GLQ: A Journal of Lesbian and Gay Studies* 1:1–16.

1994 *Fat Art, Thin Art.* Durham, NC: Duke University Press.

Seidman, Steven (ed.)

1994 *The Postmodern Turn: New Perspectives on Social Theory.* Cambridge: Cambridge University Press.

Seligman[n], Charles G.

1910 *The Melanesians of British New Guinea.* Cambridge: Cambridge University Press.

Serpenti, Laurent M.

1965 *Cultivators in the Swamps.* Assen, The Netherlands: Van Gorcum.

1984 The Ritual Meaning of Homosexuality and Pedophilia Among the Kimam-Papuans of South Irian Jaya. In *Ritualized Homosexuality in Melanesia,* edited by Gilbert H. Herdt, pp. 292–336. Berkeley: University of California Press.

Service, Elman R.

1971a *Cultural Evolutionism: Theory in Practice.* New York: Holt, Rinehart, and Winston.

1971b *Primitive Social Organization: An Evolutionary Perspective.* 2nd ed. New York: Random House.

1975 *Origin of the State and Civilization: The Process of Cultural Evolution.* New York: Norton.

Sewell, William H., Jr.

1989 Toward a Theory of Structure: Duality, Agency, and Transformation. Comparative Study of Social Transformations working paper #29. University of Michigan, Ann Arbor.

1993 A Theory of Structure: Duality, Agency, and Transformation. *American Journal of Sociology* 98: 1–29.

Shari, Michael, Gary McWilliams, and Stan Crock

1995 Gold Rush in New Guinea. *Business Week,* November 20, pp. 66, 68.

Shlomowitz, Ralph

1993 Marx and the Queensland Labour Trade. *Journal de la Société des Océanistes* 96:11–17.

Shohat, Ella

1992 Notes on the "Post-colonial." *Social Text* 10(31/32):99–113.

Shohat, Ella and Robert Stam

1994 *Unthinking Eurocentrism: Multiculturalism and the Media.* London: Routledge.

Shore, Bradd

1996 *Culture in Mind: Cognition, Culture, and the Problem of Meaning.* New York: Oxford University Press.

Shostak, Marjorie

1981 *Nisa: The Life and Words of a !Kung Woman.* New York: Vintage.

Smith, Bernard

1985 *European Vision and the South Pacific.* New Haven, CT: Yale University Press.

Smith, Gregory

1996 *Nietzsche, Heidegger, and the Transition to Postmodernity.* Chicago: University of Chicago Press.

Smith, Michael French
　1994　*Hard Times on Kairiru Island: Poverty, Development, and Morality in a Papua New Guinea Village*. Honolulu: University of Hawaii Press.
Soja, Edward
　1989　*Postmodern Geographies*. London: Verso.
South Pacific Commission
　1955　Marind-anim Report: An Investigation into the Medical and Social Causes of Depopulation Amongst the Marind-anim. South Pacific Commission Population Study S-18. Typescript.
Speck, Frank G.
　1935　*Naskapi: Savage Hunters of the Labrador Peninsula*. Norman: University of Oklahoma Press.
　1985　*A Northern Algonquian Source Book: Papers*. Edited by Edward S. Rogers. New York: Garland.
Speck, Frank G. and Leonard Broom
　1951　*Cherokee Dance and Drama*. Berkeley: University of California Press.
Speiser, Felix
　1991　*Ethnology of Vanuatu: An Early Twentieth Century Study*. Bathurst, Australia: Crawford House.
Spencer, Sir Baldwin and Frances J. Gillen
　1899　*The Native Tribes of Central Australia*. Reprint. New York: Dover, 1968.
Spencer, Herbert
　1877–96　*The Principles of Sociology*. Chicago: University of Chicago Press, 1967.
Spier, Leslie
　1935　*The Prophet Dance of the Northwest and its Derivations: The Source of the Ghost Dance*. Menasha, WI: Banta.
Spiro, Melford E.
　1986　Cultural Relativism and the Future of Anthropology. *Cultural Anthropology* 1:259–86.
Spitulnik, Debra
　1993　Anthropology and Mass Media. *Annual Review of Anthropology* 22:293–315.
Spivak, Gayatri
　1981　French Feminism in International Frame. *Yale French Studies* 26:155–84.
　1987　*In Other Worlds: Essays in Cultural Politics*. New York: Methuen.
　1990　*The Post-Colonial Critic: Interviews, Strategies, Dialogues*, edited by Sarah Harasym. New York: Routledge.
　1994　Can the Subaltern Speak? In *Colonial Discourse and Post-Colonial Theory: A Reader*, edited by Patrick Williams and Laura Chrisman, pp. 66–111. New York: Columbia University Press.
Stacey, Judith
　1987　Sexism by a Subtler Name? Postindustrial Conditions and Post-feminist Consciousness in the Silicon Valley. *Socialist Review* 17(6):7–28.
　1988　Can There Be a Feminist Ethnography? *Women's Studies International Forum* 11:21–27.
　1990　*Brave New Families: Stories of Domestic Upheaval in Late Twentieth-Century America*. New York: Basic Books.
Stallybrass, Oliver and Allon White
　1986　*The Politics and Poetics of Transgression*. Ithaca, NY: Cornell University Press.

Stanton, Domna C. and Abigail J. Stewart (eds.)
1995   *Feminisms in the Academy*. Ann Arbor: University of Michigan Press.
Steedly, Mary M.
1993   *Hanging Without a Rope: Narrative Experience in Colonial and Postcolonial Karoland*. Princeton, NJ: Princeton University Press.
Steel, Robert
1880   *The New Hebrides and Christian Missions, with a Sketch of the Labour Trade*. London: Nisbet.
Stein, Edward (ed.)
1990   *Forms of Desire: Sexual Orientation and the Social Constructionist Controversy*. New York: Garland.
Steward, Julian
1938   *Basin-Plateau Aboriginal Sociopolitical Groups*. Bureau of American Ethnology Bulletin no. 120. Washington, DC: Bureau of American Ethnology.
1946–50 *Handbook of the South American Indians*. 6 vols. Washington, DC: Bureau of American Ethnology.
1955   *Theory of Culture Change*. Urbana: University of Illinois Press.
Stocking, George W., Jr.
1968   *Race, Culture, and Evolution: Essays in the History of Anthropology*. Chicago: University of Chicago Press.
1979   *Anthropology at Chicago: Tradition, Discipline, Department*. Chicago: University of Chicago Press.
1984   (Ed.) *Functionalism Historicized: Essays on British Social Anthropology*. Madison: University of Wisconsin Press.
1987   *Victorian Anthropology*. New York: Free Press.
1989a   (Ed.) *Romantic Motives: Essays on Anthropological Sensibility*. Madison: University of Wisconsin Press.
1989b   Paradigmatic Traditions in the History of Anthropology. In *Companions to the History of Modern Science*, edited by R. C. Olby et al. London: Routledge.
1992   *The Ethnographer's Magic and Other Essays in the History of Anthropology*. Madison: University of Wisconsin Press.
Stoler, Ann L.
1985   *Capitalism and Confrontation in Sumatra's Plantation Belt, 1870–1979*. New Haven, CT: Yale University Press.
1991   Carnal Knowledge and Imperial Power: Gender, Race, and Morality in Colonial Asia. In *Gender at the Crossroads of Knowledge: Feminist Anthropology in the Postmodern Era*, edited by Micaela di Leonardo, pp. 51–101. Berkeley: University of California Press.
1995   *Race and the Education of Desire: Foucault's* History of Sexuality *and the Colonial Order of Things*. Durham, NC: Duke University Press.
Strachan, Captain John
1888   *Explorations and Adventures in New Guinea*. London: Sampson Low, Marston, Searle, and Rivington.
Strathern, Andrew J.
1971   *Rope of Moka: Big Men and Ceremonial Exchange in Mount Hagen, New Guinea*. Cambridge: Cambridge University Press.
1982   Witchcraft, Greed, Cannibalism, and Death: Some Related Themes from

the New Guinea Highlands. In *Death and the Regeneration of Life*, edited by Maurice Bloch and Jonathan Parry, pp. 111–33. Cambridge: Cambridge University Press.

1984   *A Line of Power*. London: Tavistock.

1993   Violence and Political Change in Papua New Guinea. *Pacific Studies* 16(4):41–60.

Strathern, Marilyn

1972   *Women in Between: Female Roles in a Male World, Mount Hagen, New Guinea*. London: Seminar Press.

1987   An Awkward Relationship: The Case of Feminism and Anthropology. *Signs* 12:276–92.

1988   *The Gender of the Gift: Problems with Women and Problems with Society in Melanesia*. Berkeley: University of California Press.

1991   *Partial Connections*. Savage, MD: Rowman and Littlefield.

1992   *Reproducing the Future: Essays on Anthropology, Kinship, and the New Reproductive Technologies*. New York: Routledge.

1995   The Nice Things About Culture Is That Everyone Has It. In *Shifting Contexts: Transformations in Anthropological Knowledge*, edited by Marilyn Strathern, pp. 153–70. London: Routledge.

Stürzenhofecker, Gabriele

1994   Visions of a Landscape: Duna Premeditations on Ecological Change. *Canberra Anthropology* 17:27–47.

Suleri, Sara

1995   Woman Skin Deep: Feminism and the Postcolonial Condition. In *The Post-colonial Studies Reader*, edited by Bill Ashcroft, Gareth Griffiths, and Helen Tiffin, pp. 273–80. New York: Routledge.

Sullivan, Nancy

1993   Film and Television Production in Papua New Guinea: How Media Become the Message. *Public Culture* 5:533–55.

Taussig, Michael

1980   *The Devil and Commodity Fetishism in South America*. Chapel Hill, NC: University of North Carolina Press.

1987   *Shamanism, Colonialism, and the Wild Man: A Study in Terror and Healing*. Chicago: University of Chicago Press.

1992   *The Nervous System*. New York: Routledge.

1993   *Mimesis and Alterity*. New York: Routledge.

Tax, Sol

1964   (Ed.) *Horizons of Anthropology*. Chicago: Aldine.

Tedlock, Dennis and Bruce Mannheim (eds.)

1995   *The Dialogic Emergence of Culture*. Urbana: University of Illinois Press.

Terkel, Studs

1974   *Working*. New York: Avon.

Terray, Emmanuel

1972   *Marxism and "Primitive" Societies: Two Studies*. New York: Monthly Review Press.

Thomas, Elizabeth Marshall

1959   *The Harmless People*. New York: Knopf.

Thomas, Nicholas
    1994   *Colonialism's Culture: Anthropology, Travel, and Government.* Princeton, NJ: Princeton University Press.
Thompson, Edward P.
    1963   *The Making of the English Working Class.* London: Gollancz.
    1978   *The Poverty of Theory and Other Essays.* New York: Monthly Review Press.
Thurnwald, B. R.
    1916   Banaro Society: Social Organization and Kinship System of a Tribe in the Interior of New Guinea. *American Anthropological Association Memoirs* 3:253–391.
Todorov, Tzvetan
    1984   *Mikhail Bakhtin: The Dialogical Principle.* Minneapolis: University of Minnesota Press.
    1993   *On Human Diversity: Nationalism, Racism, and Exoticism in French Thought.* Cambridge, MA: Harvard University Press [Original, 1989].
Tong, Rosemarie
    1989   *Feminist Thought: A Comprehensive Introduction.* Boulder, CO: Westview.
Touraine, Alain
    1995   *Critique of Modernity.* Oxford: Basil Blackwell [Original, 1992].
Trawick, Margaret
    1990   *Notes on Love in a Tamil Family.* Berkeley: University of California Press.
Trend, David (ed.)
    1996   *Radical Democracy: Identity, Citizenship, and the State.* New York: Routledge.
Trenkenschuh, Father Frank A.
    1982   Cargo Cult in Asmat: Examples and Prospects. In *An Asmat Sketch Book #2*, edited by Frank A. Trenkenschuh, pp. 59–65. Hastings, NE: Crosier Missions.
Trouillot, Michel-Rolph
    1989   *Peasants and Capital: Dominica in the World Economy.* Baltimore, MD: Johns Hopkins University Press.
    1990   *Haiti: State Against Nation.* New York: Monthly Review Press.
    1991   Anthropology and the Savage Slot: The Poetics and Politics of Otherness. In *Recapturing Anthropology: Working in the Present*, edited by Richard G. Fox, pp. 17–44. Santa Fe, NM: School of American Research Press.
Tsing, Anna L.
    1993   *In the Realm of the Diamond Queen: Marginality in an Out-of-the-way Place.* Princeton, NJ: Princeton University Press.
    1994   From the Margins. *Cultural Anthropology* 9:279–97.
Turner, Terence
    1992   Defiant Images: The Kayapo Appropriation of Video. *Anthropology Today* 8(6):5–16.
    1993   Anthropology and Multiculturalism: What Is Anthropology that Multi-culturalists Should Be Mindful of It? *Cultural Anthropology* 8:411–29.
Turner, Victor W.
    1957   *Schism and Continuity in an African Society.* Manchester: Manchester University Press.
    1967   *The Forest of Symbols.* Ithaca, NY: Cornell University Press.

1972   *The Ritual Process*. Ithaca, NY: Cornell University Press.

1974   *Dramas, Fields, and Metaphors*. Ithaca, NY: Cornell University Press.

Tyler, Stephen

1990   *The Unspeakable: Discourse, Dialogue, and Rhetoric in the Postmodern World*. Madison: University of Wisconsin Press.

Tylor, Edward Burnett

1871   *Primitive Culture*. London: J. Murray.

Urry, James

1973   Notes and Queries on Anthropology and the Development of Field Methods in British Anthropology, 1870–1920. *Proceedings of the Royal Anthropological Institute for 1972*, pp. 45–57. London: William Clowes and Sons.

1982   From Zoology to Ethnology: A. C. Haddon's Conversion to Anthropology, 1890–1900. *Canberra Anthropology* 5:58–85.

1984   A History of Field Methods. In *Ethnographic Research: A Guide to General Conduct*, edited by Roy F. Ellen, pp. 35–61. London: Academic.

1993   *Before Social Anthropology: Essays on the History of British Anthropology*. Chur, Switzerland: Harwood Academic.

Urry, John

1990   *The Tourist Gaze: Leisure and Travel in Contemporary Societies*. London: Sage.

Van Buren, John

1994   *The Young Heidegger: Rumor of the Hidden King*. Bloomington: Indiana University Press.

Vaughn, Tom

1995   Feld Speaks on Freeport. *The Daily Texan*, December 7.

Vayda, Andrew

1960   *Maori Warfare*. Polynesian Society Maori Monographs, no. 2. Wellington: Polynesian Society.

Verdery, Katherine

1991   *National Ideology Under Socialism: Identity and Cultural Politics in Ceausescu's Romania*. Berkeley: University of California Press.

Vico, Giambattista

1984   *The New Science of Giambattista Vico*. Ithaca, NY: Cornell University Press.

Visker, Rudi

1995   *Michel Foucault: Genealogy as Critique*. London: Verso.

Visweswaran, Kamala

1988   Defining Feminist Ethnography. *Inscriptions* 3/4:29–44.

1994   *Fictions of Feminist Ethnography*. Minneapolis: University of Minnesota Press.

Vogel, Lawrence

1994   *The Fragile "We": Ethical Implications of Heidegger's Being and Time*. Evanston, IL: Northwestern University Press.

Voget, Fred W.

1975   *A History of Ethnology*. New York: Holt, Rinehart, and Winston.

Volosinov, V. N. [M. M. Bakhtin]

1976   *Freudianism: A Critical Sketch*. New York: Academic [Original, 1927].

1986   *Marxism and the Philosophy of Language*. Cambridge, MA: Harvard University Press [Original, 1929].

Wagner, Roy

1967   *The Curse of Souw*. Chicago: University of Chicago Press.

1972   *Habu*. Chicago: University of Chicago Press.
1975   *The Invention of Culture*. Chicago: University of Chicago Press.
Waiko, John D.
1992   *Tugata:* Culture, Identity, and Commitment. In *Confronting the Margaret Mead Legacy: Scholarship, Empire, and the South Pacific*, edited by Lenora Foerstel and Angela Gilliam, pp. 233–66. Philadelphia: Temple University Press.
Wallace, Michele
1990   *Invisibility Blues: From Pop to Theory*. London: Verso.
Wallerstein, Immanuel
1979   *The Capitalist World-Economy*. Cambridge: Cambridge University Press.
1980   *Mercantilism and the Consolidation of the European World Economy, 1600–1750*. New York: Academic.
1989   *The Second Great Era of Expansion of the Capitalist World Economy, 1730–1840s*. San Diego: Academic.
1991   *Geopolitics and Geoculture: Essays on the Changing World-System*. Cambridge: Cambridge University Press.
Wardlow, Holly
in press Bobby Teardrops: A Turkish Video in Papua New Guinea: *Reflections* on Cultural Studies, Feminism, and the Anthropology of Mass Media. *Visual Anthropology Review*, forthcoming.
Warren, Kay
1978   *The Symbolism of Subordination: Indian Identity in a Guatemalan Town*. Austin, TX: University of Texas Press.
Wawn, William T.
1893   *The South Sea Islanders and the Queensland Labour Trade*. London: Swan Sonnenschein and Co. Reprint. Edited by Peter Corris. Honolulu: University Press of Hawaii, 1973.
Weber, Max
1904–5 *The Protestant Ethic and the Spirit of Capitalism*. Reprint. New York: Scribner's, 1958.
1958   *From Max Weber: Essays in Sociology*, edited by H. N. Gerth and C. Wright Mills. New York: Oxford University Press.
1978a   *Economy and Society*, edited by Guenther Roth and Claus Wittich. Berkeley: University of California Press.
1978b   *Weber: Selections in Translation*, edited by W. G. Runciman and Eric Matthews Trent. Cambridge: Cambridge University Press.
Weiner, Annette B.
1976   *Women of Value, Men of Renown: New Perspectives in Trobriand Exchange*. Austin, TX: University of Texas Press.
1992a   *Inalienable Possessions: The Paradox of Keeping-While-Giving*. Berkeley: University of California Press.
1992b   Anthropology's Lessons for Cultural Diversity: The Discipline Can Help Refine Current Debates. *The Chronicle of Higher Education*, July 22, pp. B1–2.
Weiner, James F.
1991   Colonial Engagement in Third World Oil Extraction: Some Examples from Papua New Guinea. *World Energy Council Journal* (December), pp. 69–74.

1992   Anthropology Contra Heidegger Part I: Anthropology's Nihilism. *Critique of Anthropology* 12:75–90.

1993   Anthropology Contra Heidegger, Part II: The Limit of Relationship. *Critique of Anthropology* 13: 285–301.

Wesley-Smith, Terence

1992   (Ed.) A Legacy of Development: Three Years of Crisis in Bougainville. Special Issue. *Contemporary Pacific*, vol. 4, no. 2.

1995   Melanesia in Review—Issues and Events, 1994: Papua New Guinea. *The Contemporary Pacific* 7:364–74.

West, Cornel

1989   *The Ethical Dimensions of Marxist Thought.* New York: Monthly Review Press.

1993a   *Keeping Faith: Philosophy and Race in America.* New York: Routledge.

1993b   *Race Matters.* Boston: Beacon.

1993c   The New Cultural Politics of Difference. In *Social Theory: The Multicultural and Classic Readings*, edited by Charles Lemert, pp. 577–89. Boulder, CO: Westview.

West, Francis

1968   *Hubert Murray: The Australian Pro-consul.* Melbourne: Oxford University Press.

Weston, Kath

1991   *Families We Choose: Lesbians, Gays, Kinship.* New York: Columbia University Press.

1993a   Lesbian/Gay Studies in the House of Anthropology. *Annual Review of Anthropology* 22:339–67.

1993b   Do Clothes Make the Woman? Gender, Performance Theory, and Lesbian Eroticism. *Genders* 17:1–21.

White, Alan

1990   *Within Nietzsche's Labyrinth.* New York: Routledge.

White, Geoffrey M. and Lamont Lindstrom (eds.)

1993   *Custom Today. Anthropological Forum*, vol. 6. No. 4.

White, Leslie A.

1940   *Pioneers in American Anthropology: The Bandelier-Morgan Letters, 1873–1883.* Albuquerque: University of New Mexico Press.

1942   *The Pueblo of Santa Ana, New Mexico.* American Anthropological Association Memoir no. 60, vol. 44, no. 4, pt. 2.

1949   *The Science of Culture.* New York: Farrar, Straus, and Giroux.

1959   *The Evolution of Culture.* New York: McGraw-Hill.

Whitehead, Harriet

1986   The Varieties of Fertility Cultism in New Guinea: Parts I and II. *American Ethnologist* 13:80–99, 271–89.

Whitehouse, Harvey

1995   *Inside the Cult: Religious Innovation and Transmission in Papua New Guinea.* Oxford: Clarendon.

Wieseltier, Leon

1995   The Decline of the Black Intellectual. *The New Republic.*

Williams, Brackette F.
 1989 A Class Act: Anthropology and the Race to Nation Across Ethnic Terrain. *Annual Review of Anthropology* 18:401–444.
 1991 *Stains on My Name, War in My Veins: Guyana and the Politics of Cultural Struggle*. Durham, NC: Duke University Press.
 1994 In the Years of Yearning Openly: On bell hooks and the Value of Daily Yearnings. *Visual Anthropology Review* 10:142–53.
Williams, Francis E.
 1923a The Pairama Ceremony in the Purari Delta, Papua. *Journal of the Royal Anthropological Institute of Great Britain and Ireland* 59:379–97.
 1923b *The Vailala Madness and the Destruction of Native Ceremonies in the Gulf Division*. Territory of Papua, Anthropology Report no. 4. Port Moresby: Government Printer.
 1924 *The Natives of the Purari Delta*. Territory of Papua, Anthropology Report no. 5. Port Moresby: Government Printer.
 1936 *Papuans of the Trans-Fly*. Oxford: Clarendon.
 1940 *Drama of Orokolo: The Social and Ceremonial Life of the Elema*. Oxford: Clarendon.
Williams, Patrick and Laura Chrisman (eds.)
 1994 *Colonial Discourse and Post-colonial Theory: A Reader*. New York: Columbia University Press.
Williams, Raymond
 1958 *Culture and Society: 1780–1950*. New York: Columbia University Press.
 1973 *The Country and the City*. New York: Oxford University Press.
 1977 *Marxism and Literature*. New York: Oxford University Press.
Willis, Paul
 1977 *Learning to Labour: How Working-Class Kids Get Working-Class Jobs*. Westmead, UK: Saxon House.
 1990 *Common Culture: Symbolic Work and Play in the Everyday Cultures of the Young*. Boulder, CO: Westview.
Winant, Howard
 1994 *Racial Conditions: Politics, Theory, Comparisons*. Minneapolis: University of Minnesota Press.
Wirz, Paul
 1922–25 *Die Marind-anim von Holländisch-Süd-Neu-Guinea, I–IV*. 2 vols. Hamburg: Friederichsen.
 1928 *Dämonen und Wilde in Neuguinea*. Stuttgart: Strecker und Schroder.
Wittgenstein, Ludwig
 1980 *Culture and Value*. Chicago: University of Chicago Press.
 1993 *Philosophical Occasions, 1912–1951*, edited by James C. Lagge and Alfred Nordmann. Indianapolis: Hackett.
 1994 *The Wittgenstein Reader*, edited by Anthony Kenny. Oxford: Basil Blackwell.
Wittig, Monique
 1986 *Lesbian Body*. Boston: Beacon.
 1992 *The Straight Mind and Other Essays*. Boston: Beacon.

Wolf, Diane L.
  1992   *Factory Daughters: Gender, Household Dynamics, and Rural Industrialization in Java*. Berkeley: University of California Press.
Wolf, Eric R.
  1959   *Sons of the Shaking Earth*. Chicago: University of Chicago Press.
  1964   *Anthropology*. Englewood Cliffs, NJ: Prentice-Hall.
  1965   Intellectuals Americans contre la guerre du Vietnam. *Les Temps Modernes* 21(235):1093–1109.
  1966   *Peasants*. Englewood Cliffs, NJ: Prentice-Hall.
  1967   Introduction to the National Teach-In. In *Teach-Ins*, edited by L. Menashe and R. Radosh. New York: Praeger.
  1969   *Peasant Wars of the Twentieth Century*. New York: Harper and Row.
  1980   They Divide and Subdivide, and Call it Anthropology. *New York Times*, November 30, p. E9.
  1982   *Europe and the People Without History*. Berkeley: University of California Press.
Wolf, Margery
  1968   *The House of Lim: A Study of a Chinese Family Farm*. New York: Appleton Century Crofts.
  1992   *A Thrice-Told Tale: Feminism, Postmodernism, and Ethnographic Responsibility*. Stanford: Stanford University Press.
Wolin, Richard (ed.)
  1991   *The Heidegger Controversy: A Critical Reader*. New York: Columbia University Press.
Worsley, Peter
  1968   *The Trumpet Shall Sound: A Study of "Cargo" Cults in Melanesia*, 2nd ed. New York: Schocken.
  1984   *The Three Worlds: Culture and World Development*. Chicago: University of Chicago Press.
Yanagisako, Sylvia and Carol Delaney (eds.)
  1995   *Naturalizing Power: Essays in Feminist Cultural Analysis*. New York: Routledge.
Yengoyan, Aram A.
  1968   Demographic and Ecological Influences on Aboriginal Australian Marriage Sections. In *Man the Hunter*, edited by Richard B. Lee and Irven DeVore, pp. 185–99. New York: Aldine.
  1986   Theory in Anthropology: On the Demise of the Concept of Culture. *Comparative Studies in Society and History* 28:368–74.
Young, Michael W.
  1988   Malinowski Among the Magi: Editor's Introduction. In *Malinowski Among the Magi: "The Natives of Mailu,"* by Bronislaw Malinowski, edited by Michael W. Young, pp. 1–76. London: Routledge.
Young, Robert J. C.
  1995a   *Colonial Desire: Hybridity in Theory, Culture, and Race*. London: Routledge.
  1995b   Foucault on Race and Colonialism. *New Formations* 25:57-65.
Zegwaard, Gerard A.
  1959   Headhunting Practices of the Asmat of West New Guinea. *American Anthropologist* 61:1020–41.

Zegwaard, Gerard A., and J. H. M. C. Boelaars
  1955   De Sociale Structuur van de Asmat-Bevolking. *Adatrechbundel* 45:244–403.
Zimmer-Tamakoshi, Laura
  1993a   Nationalism and Sexuality in Papua New Guinea. *Pacific Studies*
          16(4):61–97.
  1993b   Bachelors, Spinsters, and *Pamuk Meris*. In *The Business of Marriage:
          Transformations in Oceanic Matrimony*, edited by Richard A. Marksbury, pp.
          83–104. Pittsburgh: University of Pittsburgh Press.

index